CONTEMPORARY HALAKHIC PROBLEMS

THE LIBRARY OF JEWISH LAW AND ETHICS
VOLUME IV
EDITED BY NORMAN LAMM

Jakob and Erna Michael professor of Jewish philosophy
Yeshiva University

CONTEMPORARY HALAKHIC PROBLEMS

by

J. DAVID BLEICH

KTAV PUBLISHING HOUSE, INC
YESHIVA UNIVERSITY PRESS
NEW YORK
1977

Library of Congress Cataloging in Publication Data
Bleich, J David.
Contemporary halakhic problems.
(The Library of Jewish law and ethics; v. 4)
Includes bibliographical references and index.
1. Jewish law—Addresses, essays, lectures. 2. Judaism—20th century—Addresses, essays, lectures. I. Title.
BM520.3.B5 296.1'8 77-3432
ISBN 0-87068-450-7

Manufactured in the United States of America

Dedicated

to the memory of

my revered father and teacher

מוהר״ר מנחם צבי ב״ר משה אהרן ז״ל

Contents

PART II

Editor's Foreword

One of the happier phenomena in the rapidly changing American Jewish scene is the new prominence accorded to the Halakhah, traditional Jewish law. Often dismissed by non-Orthodox religious leaders and ignored by many a Jewish scholar in the past, the Halakhah is now more and more recognized as central to the Jewish tradition. The degree of its centrality may well be a question of one's religious commitment and theological perspective, but it is now recognized as indisputable that no appreciation of Judaism can be achieved without it.

What the casual student of Judaism often fails to understand is the seriousness with which Halakhah is taken by a large number of contemporary Jews. Far from being an ancient system of law that is essentially of antiquarian interest, Halakhah is being consulted more and more by Jews who seek its guidance—and by scholars who suspect that implicit within its legal formulations and involved dialectic there lies a body of values and norms and concepts of the greatest significance for the understanding of Judaism.

Indeed, Halakhah never experienced a complete hiatus in its inner development, that is, in the constant application and reapplication of its principles to the challenges of a society and culture in constant flux. While it is unquestionably true that at times its expositors were more creative and at other times less bold and less imaginative, every period of history made its contribution to the growing richness of Halakhah in its various branches—especially its responsa literature (the Halakhah's "case law"), which in the modern period often appears in periodicals throughout the world.

The present volume by Rabbi David Bleich is testimony to the ongoing nature of the halakhic enterprise. The very scope of the questions and problems treated by contemporary halakhists, as summarized and evaluated in this latest work by Dr. Bleich, is vivid testimony to the catholicity of the Halakhah's concerns and the vitality of its responsiveness. One will not find here the monolith that common prejudice has so often ascribed to the Halakhah. Instead, a variety of opinions, a multiplicity of voices, debate, controversy and argumentation are as characteristic of the halakhic process today as they were in the past. Yet clearly, the Halakhah, today no less than in the past, is not considered by its adherents and its major expositors as a system of vague "guidelines," a body of opinions variegated enough to pick and choose at will, and amorphous enough to sustain any predetermined conclusion. The goal of the process is a precise mode of action, the method is juridically sound, the foundation is an implicit and unshakable religious conviction.

The author has endeavored to include as many opinions as he can on each controversial subject but, because of the nature of this work, has restricted himself to those authorities whose credentials as decisors of Halakhah are widely recognized by the community of those who are committed to and observe the Halakhah. To do otherwise would be impossible within the confines of a volume of this kind. He has reported honestly, and where he ventures his own opinion, he has done so authoritatively and with intellectual integrity. Of course, he does not insist that his is the last word on the subject. But he has not allowed temerity, disguised as humility, to paralyze his critical judgment. For this too we are in his debt.

Contemporary Halakhic Problems is a most welcome addition to Ktav's *Library of Jewish Law and Ethics.*

NORMAN LAMM
Editor

Preface

The bulk of the material presented in this book originally appeared in the columns of *Tradition* over the course of the past number of years, and has been expanded and amplified for presentation in its present form. Portions of this work served as the subject matter of a seminar in medical ethics and Halakhah conducted on behalf of the students of the Albert Einstein College of Medicine and of courses in contemporary halakhic problems at Stern College for Women.

The present volume has been divided into two sections. Part I is composed of chapters each of which contains a series of relatively brief discussions of related issues in a given area. The material presented in this section is to a large extent, although by no means exclusively, drawn from current periodical halakhic literature. Each of the chapters in Part II is devoted to an extensive analysis of a single halakhic topic and focuses upon a far more wide-ranging array of sources.

I am indebted to Rabbi Walter Wurzburger, editor of *Tradition,* both for permission to reprint material which appeared in that journal and for his indulgent understanding over the years. It has been my position that in matters of Halakhah style and readability must give way to accuracy and precision. As a result, I bear sole responsibility for any lapses, whether of content or of style.

I also wish to express my thanks to the Memorial Foundation for Jewish Culture for a grant to defray expenses incurred in preparation of this manuscript; to my brother-in-law, Rabbi Mordecai Ochs, for his insightful assistance in reading the manuscript; and to Rabbi Norman Lamm, for his encouragement and valued aid in bringing this work to publication.

Le-talmidai yoter mi-kullam—to my students above all others I am indebted for their incisive and relentless questioning, which led to a sharpening and honing of the halakhic dialectic.

Introduction: The Methodology of Halakhah

Judaism is unique in its teaching that study is not merely a means but an end, and not merely an end among ends, but the highest and noblest of human aspirations. Study of Torah for its own sake is a sacramental act, the greatest of all *mizvot*. Throughout the generations Torah scholars were willing to live in poverty and deprivation in order to devote themselves to study. Every Jew, regardless of the degree of erudition he had attained, devoted a portion of his time to Torah learning. Those capable of doing so plumbed the depths of the Talmud. Others perused the Mishnah or studied the weekly Torah portion together with the commentary of Rashi. Even the unlettered recited psalms on a regular daily basis. To the Jew, Torah study has always been more than a ritual act; it has always been a religious experience.

The Jew has always perceived God speaking to him through the leaves of the Gemara, from the paragraphs of the *Shulḥan Arukh* and the words of the verses of the Bible. The Sages long ago taught, *"kudsha berikh hu ve-oraita ḥad,"* God and the Torah are one; the Torah is the manifestation of divine wisdom. God reveals Himself to anyone who immerses himself in the depths of Torah; the intensity of the revelation is directly proportionate to the depth of penetration and perceptive understanding. To the scholar, a novel, illuminating insight affords a more convincing demonstration of the Divine Presence than a multitude of philosophic arguments. It is a form of divine confrontation which must be experienced in order to be understood. Yet it is a relationship which every Jew may experience, at least *be-ze'er anpin,* in minuscule form, through Torah study.

Judaism is fundamentally a religion of law, a law which governs every facet of the human condition. The Torah contains not merely a set of laws but also canons of interpretation as well as principles according to which possible internal conflicts may be resolved. Maimonides records the doctrine that the Torah will not be altered, either in its entirety or in part, as one of the Thirteen Principles of Faith. The divine nature of Torah renders it immutable and hence not subject to amendment or modification.

Although the Torah itself is immutable, the Sages teach that the interpretation of its many laws and regulations is entirely within the province of human intellect. Torah is divine but *"lo ba-shamayim hi*—it is not in the heavens" (Deut. 30:12); it is to be interpreted and applied by man. A remarkable corollary to the principle of the immutability of the Torah is the principle that, following the revelation at Sinai, no further heavenly clarification of doubt or resolution of ambiguity is possible. Clarification and elucidation are themselves forms of change. Since there can be no new revelation, a prophet who claims the ability to resolve disputed legal points by virtue of his prophetic power stands convicted by his own mouth of being a false prophet.

Once revealed, the Torah does not remain in the heavenly domain. Man is charged with interpretation of the text, resolution of doubts, and application of the provisions of its laws to novel situations. The Gemara, *Baba Meẓi'a* 59b, presents a vivid illustration of the principle *lo ba-shamayim hi* in a narrative concerning a dispute between R. Eliezer and the Sages regarding a point of ritual law. R. Eliezer refused to be overridden by the view of the majority and went to great lengths in invoking heavenly signs in support of his own position. R. Eliezer had sufficient power to change the course of nature, to work miracles, and even to summon a heavenly voice in support of his position, but the Sages, quite correctly, failed to be impressed. Interpretation of Halakhah has been entrusted to the human intellect and, accordingly, human intellect must proceed in its own dispassionate way, uninfluenced and unprejudiced by supernatural phenomena. Even more dramatic is the narrative recorded in *Baba Meẓi'a* 86a. Here we are told of a controversy between the Heavenly Academy and God Himself with regard to a case of possible ritual defilement. The Almighty is cited as ruling that there was no cause for ritual defilement, while the Heavenly Academy ruled that there was. The Gemara records that the matter was left for final adjudication by Rabba bar Nachmani, "who is singular [in his proficiency] in such matters." Certainly God did not need to be instructed in His Law by mortal man. The Gemara teaches that the Law was designed to be understood, interpreted and transmitted by man. Accordingly, man's understanding of

Torah must prevail. Man's interpretation is not only inherent in the content of revelation but is the one which God Himself wills to prevail.

Moreover, Jewish teaching recognizes that two conflicting conclusions may, at times, be derived from identical sources by different scholars. Which is correct? Both are correct! "These and those are the words of the living God," declare the Sages (*Gittin* 6b). If two conflicting conclusions may be derived from the same corpus of law, then both must be inherent therein. In the realm of theory both are correct, both are Torah. Of course, in matters of practice, in terms of *psak halakhah,* of definitive halakhic ruling, there must be a means of deciding between the conflicting views, else legal anarchy would result. To this end Halakhah, as a legal system, includes canons of *psak,* canons of judicial determination. While these may produce decisions which are of absolute binding authority, this does not imply that the view which is set aside is thereby rejected as a nullity. On the contrary, insofar as the study and pursuit of Torah is concerned, such a view is of undiminished importance. No one has ever suggested that it is not necessary to recite *birkhat ha-Torah,* the blessing pronounced prior to engaging in Torah study, before studying the words of *Bet Shammai* on the grounds that the normative decision is in accordance with *Bet Hillel.* In the eyes of God both are of equal validity. Definitive *psak halakhah* is a matter of practical necessity, but not a reflection upon transcendental validity.

The foregoing should not in any sense generate the impression that subjective considerations or volitional inclinations may ever be allowed consciously to influence scholarly opinion. Torah study requires, first and foremost, intellectual honesty. *Bet Hillel* did not purposively adopt a policy of permissiveness and *Bet Shammai* a policy of stringency; *Bet Hillel* did not set out to be easygoing and *Bet Shammai* to be hard and unbudging. Each reported sincerely held convictions, conclusions reached in as detached and dispassionate a manner as is humanly possible. It is a travesty of the halakhic process to begin with a preconceived conclusion and then attempt to justify it by means of halakhic dialectic. Neither Hillel nor Shammai nor any of their spiritual heirs engaged in sophistry in order to justify previously held viewpoints. The dialectic of halakhic reasoning has always been conducted in the spirit of "*yikov ha-din et ha-har*—let the law bore through the mountain." The law must be determined on its own merit and let the chips fall where they may.

"These and those are the words of the living God" is a dictum applicable only when fundamental prerequisites have been met. The corpus of Halakhah must be mastered in its entirety and accepted in its entirety as the content of divine revelation. Canons of interpretation, which are themselves an integral part of the Torah itself, must be applied in an objective manner. Then and only then are the resultant conclusions the "words of the living God." Then and only then may it be assumed that, from the time of the giving of the Torah, it was destined that these conclusions be reached. It is conceivable that two different individuals of equal intelligence and erudition, both possessed of equal sincerity and objectivity, may reach antithetical conclusions. Since the Torah was given by God and disparate human intellects were created by God, the inference is virtually inescapable: it was part of the divine scheme that both conclusions be reached. Since both conclusions are derived from accepted premises and both are defended by cogent halakhic argumentation, it follows that both are legitimate expressions of Halakhah and hence both are of equal validity. Of insights attained in this manner the Sages taught, "Even that which a conscientious student will one day teach in the presence of his master was already told to Moses at Sinai" (Palestinian Talmud, *Pe'ah* 2:4).

Of course the development of correctly formulated decisions governing matters of practice is of singular importance. The methodology by which some opinions are accepted and others excluded from application to practice constitutes a highly complex aspect of Halakhah. Halakhic decisions are not a matter of arbitrary choice. Decision-making is also bound by rules of procedure.

The verse "Judges and officers shall you make for yourself in all your gates" (Deut. 16:18) bestows autonomous authority upon the rabbinic judges in each locale. They are empowered to promulgate their views in the area subject to their jurisdiction. The local populace may, with complete confidence, accept the teaching of the local *bet din*. Thus, in the city in which R. Eliezer was the chief authority the populace chopped trees, built a fire, and boiled water on the Sabbath in preparation for a circumcision, while in a neighboring town such actions constituted a capital offense. R. Eliezer's opinion to the effect that Sabbath restrictions are suspended not only for circumcision itself but even for preparation of the necessary accouterments of this rite was authoritative in his jurisdiction. The contradictory opinion of his colleagues was binding in their jurisdictions. Only upon a decision of the supreme halakhic authority, the *Bet Din ha-Gadol,* sitting in Jerusalem, did a given view become binding upon all of Israel.[1]

A rabbinic authority may issue decisions in accordance with his own views when such views are not in conflict with a position already binding upon the community of Israel as a whole. He may rely upon his own opinion only if he has attained the requisite degree of Torah scholarship and erudition and if the conclusion is genuinely arrived at on the basis of his own study and analysis. It goes without saying that his decisions are authoritative only if his personal piety and religious probity are beyond question.

Frequently, however, the rabbinic decisor is lacking in comprehensive scholarship or has not formulated a strongly held opinion of his own. In such cases, he must decide in accordance with one of a number of views expressed by his predecessors or colleagues. The ability to formulate definitive *psak* is the product of highly specialized skills. It is in choosing between conflicting precedents and opinions that the consummate expertise of the decisor becomes apparent. The decisor may not arbitrarily seize upon an individual opinion or a solitary source to the negation of the weight of halakhic precedent or consensus. He most certainly may not be swayed by the consideration that the resultant decision be popular or expedient or simply by the fact that it appeals to his own personal predilection. He must carefully weigh and balance opinions and decisions, assigning weight not merely on the basis of sheer number but also on the relative stature of the scholars whose opinions are under consideration, and must at the same time assess the complexities and relative importance of any number of component factors.

In order to understand the manner in which halakhic rulings are formulated, it is necessary to focus attention upon the deductive process by means of which definitive rulings are derived from fundamental principles. If the resultant halakhic discussion is at times somewhat involved, it must be emphasized that only by means of the halakhic dialectic is it possible to appreciate the halakhic process as it is employed *le-hasik shematteta aliba de-hilkhata,* in reaching definitive conclusions on the basis of pertinent sources.

The present work was not undertaken without feelings of trepidation. Is it possible to synopsize and compress complex discussions without

1. For a discussion of other equally binding decisions, see R. Elchanan Wasserman, *Kuntres Divrei Soferim,* no. 2, appended to *Kovez Shi'urim,* II (Givatayim, 5720).

sacrifice of accuracy? Is it possible to present the dialectic of Halakhah in a foreign idiom without distortion? However, with the proliferation of both popular and scholarly works in the vernacular dealing with matters of Jewish theology and practice, many of which, unfortunately, abound in misrepresentations and are distressingly inaccurate, it becomes imperative that attempts be made accurately to enunciate the views of normative Judaism.

This work is not intended as an introductory volume to be perused by the totally uninitiated. The present volume is too complex and too detailed to fulfill that function. Neither is it intended to be encyclopedic in nature or even to be exhaustive in its treatment of any selected topic. Nor is it intended to serve as a practical halakhic guide, and, indeed, no attempt has been made to present definitive *psak halakhah*. This work is devoted to an analysis of Halakhah and halakhic reasoning rather than to the formulation of halakhic decision. As such, it is directed primarily to those who have at least some background in the study of rabbinic literature but lack the requisite skills or the leisure to assimilate and analyze the maze of responsa pertaining to the topics treated in this volume. It is intended as an invitation to the reader to join in the noblest of Jewish activities and the supremest of joys—the study of Torah.

Part I

"All grasping the sword" (Song of Songs 3:8). R. Meir says, all were sharpening the Halakhah as a sword so that if a specific case were to be put before them, Halakhah would not [find it necessary to] call to them.

BEMIDBAR RABBAH XI, 7

CHAPTER I

Israel

The Land of Israel is beloved unto Me above all else. . . . Behold the Land is beloved unto Me and Israel is beloved unto Me; I shall cause Israel who is beloved unto Me to enter the Land which is beloved unto Me.

BEMIDBAR RABBAH XXIII, 7

The Land of Israel exerts an almost mystical attraction upon the people of Israel in all their habitations. Jews are unique not only in having survived as a distinct people despite generations of exile, but also in having maintained a bond with a homeland which for so long was merely an historic memory. There is undoubtedly a causal connection between the fervent aspiration of the community of Israel to return to its land and the survival of Jewry despite intense sociopolitical assimilationist pressure. "Lift up a banner for the ingathering of our exiles and gather us together from the four corners of the earth" is not only a prayer, it is a thrice-daily reaffirmation of the centrality of the Land of Israel in the life of the people of Israel. It is a key to the survival of the Jew.

The first Jew who prayed for *aliyah* to Israel was one whose prayer was destined to be denied. Moses was not granted permission to enter the Holy Land. This, to him, was the severest of all punishments and he prayed with all his might that it be rescinded. Expressing astonishment at Moses' intense yearning to enter the promised land, the Sages queried, "Did [Moses] then need to eat of its fruit or to be satiated by its goodness?" Their reply is illuminating: "Said Moses, 'Israel was commanded many *mizvot* which cannot be fulfilled other than in *Erez Yisra'el;* I will enter the land so that the commandments will be fulfilled through me' " (*Sotah* 14a). For Moses, entry into the Land of Israel and the establishment of a Jewish commonwealth could have but one purpose: it afforded the opportunity to fulfill the divine commandments, particularly those "commandments which are contingent upon the Land" and can be fulfilled only in *Erez Yisra'el.* The Sages could not ascribe to Moses the vision of an independent homeland as the fulfillment of an ethnic purpose; to them nationalistic aspirations could be but a means, never an end. National independence, political self-sufficiency, and even settlement of the land are objects of longing primarily because they are seen as providing fertile soil for the fulfillment of *mizvot.*

Throughout the centuries the Jews have affirmed their love of *Erez Yisra'el* through the study of Torah lore and law pertaining to the fulfillment of *mizvot* uniquely associated with the Land of Israel. Settlement in the land might be but a fervent dream, but the "commandments associated with the Land" were a reality which could be perceived in the discussions of the Talmud and in the words of the *Shulhan Arukh.* The laws were to be mastered in anticipation of a return to the Land. Such study bore eloquent testimony not only to an unabated desire for redemption from exile, but also to an appreciation of the ultimate goal of *aliyah.*

The love and zeal which this subject has always evoked have become even more manifest in recent years. Rabbinic scholars occupied themselves with such matters during the course of centuries even though their investigations and disputations were almost entirely theoretical. With the birth of the State of Israel these questions became topical and of immediate applicability. Quite naturally, in recent years questions pertaining to the "commandments contingent upon the Land" have become, to an even greater degree, a focal point of Torah scholarship both in Israel and in the Diaspora.

"And you shall inhabit the land and dwell therein" (Num. 33:53) is not simply a prognostication or blessing; it is a *mizvah,* a commandment constituting a religious obligation. As is the case with regard to all precepts, its ramifications and parameters require careful elucidation. Indeed, the very first question to be raised is whether or not settlement of the Land of Israel constitutes a binding imperative upon a people exiled from their land. The settlement of the Land of Israel is one *mizvah* among many. There are situations in which residence in Israel conflicts with other obligations or desiderata. As will be shown, the issues raised in such situations have been the subject of extensive halakhic discussion.

The establishment of an independent Jewish commonwealth understandably brings with it a host of questions regarding the prerogatives of the state. Not the least of these is the question of the authority of the state to wage war and the circumstances in which military action is justified. The interests of the state may at times conflict with the rights of its citizens and impinge upon their liberties. A halakhic adjudication of such conflicts is possible only upon a careful delineation of the extent and limits of the sovereign power of the state.

Settlement in Israel

The Six-Day War and the accompanying liberation of the Holy Places have brought in their wake renewed interest in settlement in Israel, and have resulted in a vast increase in the number of individuals, particularly among observant Jews, committed to *aliyah*. The exigencies of the present political situation in Israel are in themselves sufficient cause for us to welcome and foster any such *aliyah*. But aside from questions of immediate practical need, Jews have always viewed residence in the Holy Land as a unique privilege. To live in Israel is clearly a religious ideal. The establishment of a Jewish commonwealth following the crossing of the Jordan by our ancestors constituted the fulfillment of a biblical commandment. But does this commandment retain its binding force throughout the epoch following the destruction of the Temple and subsequent exile?

In a paper contributed to the 5729 issue of *Torah She-be-ʻal Peh,* Rabbi Ovadiah Yosef analyzes the various halakhic views with regard to the commandment concerning dwelling in *Ereẓ Yisra'el* and the applicability of this *miẓvah* in our own day. Rabbi Yosef, Sephardic Chief Rabbi of Israel, is the author of *Teshuvot Yabiʻa Omer,* a voluminous work exhibiting encyclopedic mastery of rabbinic scholarship. The various positions regarding this question are outlined by Rabbi Yosef as follows:

1. Chief among the authorities who maintain that the commandment to reside in Israel remains in force throughout the period of the dispersion is Nachmanides. In his commentary on the verse "And you shall inherit the land and dwell therein" (Num. 33:53), Nachmanides states that the passage is to be understood as a positive commandment to dwell in the Land of Israel while at the same time enjoining Jewry from establishing a national settlement outside of Israel. This view is reiterated by Nachmanides in his glosses appended to Maimonides' *Sefer ha-Miẓvot.* In the latter work Maimonides enumerates each of the commandments,

both positive and negative, which in their totality comprise the corpus of the 613 precepts of Judaism. Nachmanides remonstrates that Rambam, in cataloguing the various precepts, did not include the commandment concerning dwelling in the Land of Israel.

Further evidence that residence in Israel constitutes fulfillment of a *mizvah* in our own day as well may be gleaned from various halakhic provisions which are apparently predicated upon this rationale. Examples cited by Rabbi Yosef include permission to allow a gentile to draw up a bill of sale on the Sabbath on behalf of a Jew acquiring property in *Erez Yisra'el* from a non-Jew (*Gittin* 8b) and the obligation of one renting a dwelling in the Land of Israel to affix a *mezuzah* immediately upon taking up residence rather than thirty days thereafter as in the Diaspora (*Menahot* 44a). R. Joseph Karo in *Bet Yosef, Yoreh De'ah* 286, explains that in the Diaspora a new residence is not considered to be a permanent dwelling place prior to the thirtieth day, whereas in Israel a new home is immediately deemed to be a permanent domicile because the act of residing therein constitutes the fulfillment of a *mizvah* and hence acquires the characteristic of permanence.

2. R. Isaac de Leon, the author of *Megillat Ester,* an early commentary on Maimonides' *Sefer ha-Mizvot,* maintains that Rambam omitted the commandment to dwell in the Land of Israel in cataloguing the 613 precepts of Judaism because he was of the opinion that the obligation to dwell in Israel lapsed with the dispersion of Israel following the destruction of the Temple. *Megillat Ester* points out that the Gemara, *Ketubot* 111a, interprets the verse "I cause you to swear, O daughters of Jerusalem . . . that ye awaken not nor stir up love until it please" (Song of Songs 2:7) as an admonition not to rebel against the conquerors of Israel or to seize the land by force.

Rabbi Yosef rejects this analysis of Maimonides' position because (a) Maimonides includes in his enumeration of the 613 commandments precepts such as the rebuilding of the Temple, which in Maimonides' own opinion are not operative prior to the Messianic era, and (b) none of the numerous statements contained in talmudic and midrashic works supporting the view that settlement in Israel is a positive commandment in any way intimates that this commandment may be binding only in certain epochs. Of particular note is the statement in *Bereshit Rabbah* LXXVI, 2 explaining the reason for Jacob's fear that he might be vanquished in battle by Esau. Jacob's foreboding was based on the fact that Esau had acquired greater merit by virtue of having dwelt in *Erez Yis-*

ra'el uninterruptedly throughout the years spent by Jacob in the house of Laban.

3. Rashbam, *Baba Batra* 91a, states that while dwelling in Israel is not a commandment *per se,* the statement contained in the Gemara that it is forbidden to leave *Erez Yisra'el* other than in times of famine is based upon the consideration that living in the Land of Israel is a preparatory step to the fulfillment of commandments (*hekhsher mizvah*), there being numerous commandments which can be fulfilled only in Israel.

4. *Tosafot, Ketubot* 110b, records the opinion of Rabbenu Chaim Kohen, who maintains that in our time it is not obligatory to dwell in Israel because of the difficulties in observing the many commandments specifically associated with the Land of Israel. Rabbi Yosef points out that the authorship of this statement has been disputed and in all likelihood the comment attributed to R. Chaim Kohen was an addition appended at a much later date.[1] Furthermore, the recorded comment does not deny that dwelling in Israel *does* constitute fulfillment of a *mizvah;* it merely notes that, under certain conditions, other halakhic considerations may vitiate against fulfillment of this commandment. Such considerations were predicated upon economic and agricultural realities prevalent in days gone by but which, fortunately, are now considerably changed.

5. Rabbi Moses Feinstein, *Iggrot Mosheh, Even ha-Ezer,* I, no. 102, distinguishes between two distinct categories of positive commandments. There are precepts whose performance is mandatory, e.g., circumcision, the donning of phylacteries, etc., and others which are not mandated as obligatory responsibilities but nevertheless, when indeed performed, constitute the fulfillment of a commandment. Rabbi Feinstein maintains that even according to Nachmanides residence in *Erez Yisra'el* is not obligatory because this commandment is not a mandatory one. According to this interpretation, Nachmanides' position is that the act of dwelling in Israel constitutes the voluntary fulfillment of a commandment rather than the discharge of an obligation. Dissenting sharply, Rabbi Yosef asserts that the commandment constitutes a mandatory obligation, and that even in our own day there exists "a definite obligation upon all who

1. See *Teshuvot Maharit,* II, no. 28. This view is sharply disputed by R. Ya'akov of Lissa in a previously unpublished letter which appears in R. Yosef Sheinberger's *Amud Esh* (Jerusalem, 5714), pp. 105–109. This authority contends that even according to *Maharit* the statement is to be attributed to one of the Tosafists.

fear the word of God and His commandments to ascend to the Land of Israel."[1a]

Settlement in Israel in Face of Danger

Writing in the 5730 issue of *Torah She-be-'al Peh,* Rabbi Aaron Soloveitchik, *Rosh Yeshivah* of Yeshivat Brisk in Chicago, analyzes an interesting question related to the *mizvah* of settlement in Israel.

Halakhah stipulates that either husband or wife may insist upon the acquiescence of the other in establishing residence in Israel. However, the *Shulḥan Arukh* (*Even ha-Ezer* 75:5) cites an opinion to the effect that either partner may properly insist upon migration to Israel only if there is no danger attendant upon the move. If, however, the journey involves an element of danger, neither partner can force the other to take up residence in Israel. The ruling is both obvious and problematic. It is virtually axiomatic that an obligation with regard to the performance of any commandment is suspended in the face of accompanying danger. It should therefore be obvious that there is no room for coercion with regard to residence in Israel in time of danger. Yet the phraseology employed by the *Shulḥan Arukh* would indicate that although neither partner may coerce the other, either one may himself or herself seek to establish residence in Israel despite the attendant hazards. This apparently contradicts the general principle that one may not place oneself in danger in order to fulfill a commandment. An even greater difficulty is presented by the *Shitah Mekubezet, Ketubot* 110b, who declares that while neither partner is empowered to coerce the other to emigrate from the Diaspora to Israel in face of danger, nevertheless, either one may lawfully prevent the other from leaving Israel even if continued residence in the Holy Land is fraught with danger.

Rabbi Soloveitchik resolves these issues by noting that Ramban derives the obligation to establish residence in Israel from the verse "And

1a. This appears to be the opinion of *Hafla'ah, Ketubot* 110b, as well. R. Ya'akov of Lissa, *loc. cit.*, similarly appears to agree with this understanding of Nachmanides but adds ". . . we conduct ourselves in accordance with Maimonides who does not enumerate *aliyah* in our time as a positive commandment." Earlier he states, ". . . it is our tradition that in our time there is no obligation to ascend [to *Erez Yisra'el*]. See also letter of Chafetz Chaim published by R. Menachem Gerlitz, *Mara de-Ar'a Yisra'el,* (Jerusalem, 5734), II, 27-29 and *Kovez Mikhtavim* (B'nei Brak, 5735), pp. 19–21.

you shall inherit the land and you shall dwell therein" (Num. 33:53). This verse, of course, deals primarily with the commandment to wage war against the inhabitants of Canaan in order to establish a Jewish homeland. In every war there is naturally an element of physical danger; yet the commandment to wage war is binding despite such danger. Hence, obligatory wars constitute an exception to the general principle that fulfillment of precepts is suspended in face of danger.

The commandment "And you shall inherit the land," according to Ramban, has two facets: an obligation on the part of the community of Israel to conquer the land, and a personal obligation devolving upon each individual to "inherit" the land by means of settlement. The *Shulḥan Arukh* is of the opinion that while the first obligation is binding even in face of danger, the second is not mandatory when such danger is present. Yet even the second aspect of this commandment is not entirely suspended in time of peril. Although such performance is not mandatory, neither is it forbidden. This commandment *may* be fulfilled in face of danger even by an individual; it is mandatory in face of danger only with regard to the community. The permissibility of individual settlement in face of danger may be deduced from the mandatory communal obligation. Even in communal exercise of the obligation to engage in war, the fulfillment (*kiyum*) of the commandment is individual, i.e., each person performs the *miẓvah* of "inheriting the land" in contributing to the communal endeavor. Hence it may be inferred that settlement in Israel by an individual constitutes a permissible voluntary fulfillment of this commandment even when accompanied by an element of danger.

There is a further ramification of this problem not discussed by Rabbi Soloveitchik. May *aliyah* be forced upon a reluctant spouse despite attendant hazards in a situation in which continued residence in the Diaspora is also fraught with danger and risk? The irony of our contemporary situation is that one could well argue that residence virtually anywhere in the world today—in the Western Hemisphere no less than in the Middle East—is accompanied by an element of danger. All the more reason for believing Jews, *ma'aminim b'nei ma'aminim,* to turn their steps to Zion.

Aliyah Against Parental Objections

An increasing number of young men and women are joining the tide of immigrants leaving their native countries in order to settle in Israel. Quite frequently parents are unhappy at the prospect of their adolescent son or daughter living at such a great distance from the parental home. Are children permitted to emigrate to Israel despite their parents' objections, or does fulfilling the commandment to honor one's parents take precedence over the *mizvah* of dwelling in the Land of Israel? The question is reviewed in *Or ha-Mizraḥ* by Rabbis Judah Gershuni and Israel Schepansky in the Nisan 5731 issue, and by Rabbi Israel Hess of Rananah, Israel, in the Tishri 5732 edition.[2]

An important discussion of the entire matter is found in *Sha'arei Zedek* (*Mishpetei ha-Arez* 11:5), a halakhic compendium devoted exclusively to the laws pertaining to the Holy Land. The codifier of this work is R. Abraham Danzig, author of the widely used *Ḥayyei Adam* and *Ḥokhmat Adam*. R. Danzig cites an incident recorded in *Kiddushin* 31b relating that Rav Ami, with the sanction of Rav Yochanan, left the Holy Land for the purpose of meeting his mother. This narrative would indicate that the fulfillment of the precept regarding dwelling in the Land of Israel does not supersede one's duty to honor a father or mother. Nevertheless, R. Danzig refrains from issuing a final decision, noting that apparently another consideration is involved with regard to this complex matter. There is a general principle that honor is due parents only if according such honor does not conflict with the performance of religious precepts. Children are obligated to honor parents, but parents and children alike are obliged to honor God. Hence, the honor due to parents is subordinate to the honor due the Almighty, which finds expression in observance of His commandments.

Rabbi Schepansky observes that a much earlier authority, R. Meir of Rothenberg, *Teshuvot Maharam ben Barukh* (Berlin, 5651), no. 79, addressing himself to precisely the same question, states unequivocally that settlement in the Land of Israel constitutes fulfillment of a divine precept and hence the honor of God takes precedence over the honor due to one's parents.

The identical question is posed by *Teshuvot Mabit,* I, no. 139. This authority declares that the parents, no less than the child, are bound to pay honor to God, and adds that the parents "can also emigrate with him

---

2. An earlier treatment of this topic by R. Shaul Israeli and R. Schepansky appeared in *Shanah be-Shanah,* 5725. See also, R. Shaul Israeli, *Amud ha-Yemini* (Tel Aviv, 5726), no. 22, reprinted in *Ḥovat ha-Aliyah le-Erez Yisra'el,* ed. Yochanan Freid (Jerusalem, 5732). The latter publication also contains responsa on this subject authored by R. Zevi Friedman and R. Chaim David Halevy.

and both precepts will be fulfilled." Rabbi Hess cites the concurring opinion of *Maharik,* no. 166, and of *Hafla'ah,* R. Pinchas ha-Levi Hurwitz. In his biblical commentary, *Panim Yafot* (*Lekh Lekha*), the latter authority observes that Naomi's sons incurred the punishment of an early death (Ruth 1:2–5) precisely because they departed from the Land of Israel in order to pay honor to their father. Rabbi Gershuni cites a similar ruling, which is incorporated by R. Israel of Sokolov in his *Pe'at ha-Shulḥan, Hilkhot Ereẓ Yisra'el* 2:21, without mention of earlier sources.

R. Danzig, to whom the earlier responsa dealing with this subject were apparently unavailable, quotes an intriguing midrashic comment on the verse "Go you from your land and from your birthplace and from your father's house" (Gen. 12:1). Noting the seemingly redundant inclusion of the word "you—*lekha,*" the Midrash declares that this word was added for a specific purpose. "Our father Abraham was afraid and said, 'I will go and through me the Divine Name will be profaned; [people] will say he left a father and went away in his old age.' The Holy One, Blessed be He, said to him, 'Go *you;* you I exempt from the precept of honoring father and mother, but another I do not exempt from honoring father and mother.'" The exemption granted to Abraham, R. Danzig notes, was for the express purpose of dwelling in the Holy Land. Since this dispensation was granted solely to Abraham, it would appear that others must give priority to honoring parents over fulfillment of the commandment concerning settlement in Israel. Rabbi Schepansky, emphasizing the contrary rulings of the earlier authorities previously cited, observes that the evidence adduced from the midrashic comment is not conclusive. Abraham required special dispensation because, at the time of his departure from his parental home, settlement in the Holy Land did not yet constitute the fulfillment of a *miẓvah.* The Holy Land was not yet his possession and had not as yet become the "Land of Israel." Only with the granting of the Land of Canaan to Abraham as the homeland of the Jewish people did settlement in Israel constitute fulfillment of one of the commandments of the Torah.[2a] In all subsequent periods, Rabbi Schepansky argues, honor due to one's parents may not be permitted to inter-

---

2a. More fundamentally, it is doubtful that fulfillment of this commandment was at all a possibility prior to the sanctification of the Land of Israel in the time of Joshua. Thus *Tosafot, Gittin* 2a, maintains that areas not resettled by those who ascended from Babylonia are endowed with no sanctity whatsoever and hence one who dwells in such territories does not thereby fulfill a *miẓvah.* Cf. below, p. 318, n. 50, and p. 321, n. 56; cf. also *Ḥidushei Rabbenu ha-Graz Soloveitchik al ha-Torah, Lekh Lekha,* sec. 5.

fere with settlement in Israel, in the same manner that the obligation to honor one's parents may not be permitted to deter one in the performance of other precepts.

An interesting ramification of this issue involves a possible distinction between sons and daughters with regard to the question at hand. Since the objection to honor one's parents is set aside only for the sake of the fulfillment of another commandment, the discussion centers around the question of whether women are also bound by the commandment to dwell in Israel. Rabbi Schepansky cites the comment of Rabbenu Nissim, *Ketubot* 110b, *Teshuvot Rashbash,* no. 2, and *Maharit,* II, no. 28, who state explicitly that no distinction exists between males and females with regard to performance of this *mizvah.* However, he notes parenthetically, a dissenting opinion of *Teshuvot Rashbaz,* I, no. 21 and III, no. 198, to the effect that the commandment of dwelling in Israel consists not simply of living in the country but of establishing sovereignty and acquiring territory. *Rashbaz* views these tasks as being male prerogatives and rules that women are exempt from this commandment.

While there may be some difference of opinion with regard to settlement in Israel against parental objections, the case of students who wish to study Torah in Israel is entirely different. It is clear that parental disapproval need not stand in the way of children who desire to further their Torah studies in Israel or, indeed, in any other country. Since the *mizvah* of Torah study takes precedence over honoring one's parents, the student is free to study wherever he feels his efforts will lead to enhanced proficiency. The Gemara, *Megillah* 16b, tells us that Jacob was punished for being remiss in fulfilling the commandment of honoring one's parents throughout the years he spent in the home of Laban. He was not punished for the period he spent in the academy of Ever in the interim between leaving his father's home and arriving at the house of Laban. *Shulḥan Arukh, Yoreh De'ah* 230:25, emphasizes that parental directives may be disregarded with regard to a locale for Torah study even if such instructions are born of a well-grounded concern for the safety and well-being of the son.

Pitḥei Teshuvah adds that the same provision applies to the choice of a synagogue for prayer. Regardless of parental wishes in the matter, a child may elect to worship in whichever synagogue he feels he will be able to pray with the greatest measure of fervor. Rabbi Schepansky observes that, by the same token, the desire to pray at the Holy Places warrants disregard of parental objections to settlement in Israel.

Although *Shulḥan Arukh* declares that the intention to further Torah studies is in itself sufficient justification for ignoring parental preferences with regard to places of domicile, Rabbi Schepansky questions whether this is true only of male children, or whether a young woman's desire to study at a Torah institution also supersedes her duty to honor her parents. Here, too, the discussion centers around the nature of the obligations of women with regard to Torah study. However, in light of Rabbi Schepansky's previous comments, the desire to pray at the Holy Places is itself sufficient reason for disregarding the wishes of one's parents—a consideration which certainly applies to women as well as to men. Furthermore, the question of the technical nature of women's obligations with regard to Torah study may well be irrelevant to the question under discussion. Torah education serves to instill spiritual values in addition to imparting academic knowledge. Women are enjoined to strive for piety and devotion no less than men. A young woman who feels that study in Israel will enhance her commitment to Judaism and its precepts may allow these considerations to be the deciding factor.

It goes without saying that even when parental counsel does not carry with it a halakhic imperative, the considered judgment and mature advice of parents, who are deeply concerned for the welfare of their children, should not be disregarded lightly.

War and the State of Israel

In the relatively few years of its existence, the State of Israel has experienced four major armed conflicts: the War of Independence of 1948, the Sinai campaign of 1956, the Six-Day War of 1967 and the Yom Kippur War of 1973. Although very little has appeared in print, with the noteworthy exception of the writings of Rabbi Joel Teitelbaum, the "*Rebbe*" of Satmar, the halakhic sanction for these wars has been challenged in some rabbinic circles.[3] The venerable Rabbi Shlomoh Yosef Zevin, general editor of the *Encyclopedia Talmudit,* addresses himself to this emotion-laden topic in a scholarly, objective manner and endeavors to show that definite halakhic sanction does in fact exist for each of these wars. The basic issues with which Rabbi Zevin grapples are at the core of the theological controversy concerning the establishment

3. See R. Norman Lamm, "The Ideology of the Neturei Karta," *Tradition,* Fall 1971.

of the state. Rabbi Zevin's views are contained in an article appearing in the 5731 *Torah She-be-'al Peh* annual.

The prime argument cited in objection to the War of Independence, and indeed to the very establishment of the state itself, is based upon a literal understanding of the Talmud, *Ketubot* 111a. In an aggadic statement, the Talmud declares that prior to the exile and dispersal of the remnant of Israel, God caused the Jews to swear two solemn oaths: (1) not to endeavor to retake the Land of Israel by force, and (2) not to rebel against the nations of the world. Rabbi Zevin maintains that these talmudic oaths are not binding under circumstances such as the ones which surrounded the rebirth of the Jewish state. In support of this view he marshals evidence from a variety of sources. *Avnei Nezer, Yoreh De'ah,* II, 454:56, notes that there is no report in any of the classic writings regarding an actual assemblage for the purpose of accepting these oaths, as is to be found, for example, in the narrative concerning the oaths by which Moses bound the community of Israel prior to the crossing of the Jordan. The oaths administered before the exile are understood by *Avnei Nezer* as having been sworn by yet unborn souls prior to their descent into the terrestrial world. Such oaths, he argues, have no binding force in Halakhah. Similarly, the Maharal of Prague in his *Commentary on the Aggada, Ketubot* 111a, and in chapter 25 of his *Neẓaḥ Yisra'el,* interprets these oaths as being in the nature of a decree or punishment rather than as injunctions incumbent upon Jews in the Diaspora. There is obviously no transgression involved in attempting to mitigate the effects of an evil decree. A third authority, R. Meir Simchah of Dvinsk, author of the *Or Sameaḥ,* accepts the premise that these oaths do apply in a literal sense. However, he expresses the opinion that following the promulgation of the Balfour Declaration, establishment of a Jewish homeland in Palestine no longer constitutes a violation of the oath concerning rebellion against the nations of the world. The text of *Or Sameaḥ*'s statement on this important issue is reprinted by Z. A. Rabiner, *Toledot R. Meir Simḥah* (Tel Aviv, 5727), p. 164. Rabbi Zevin adds that this argument assumes even greater cogency subsequent to the United Nations resolution sanctioning the establishment of a Jewish state.

There is yet another line of reasoning on the basis of which Rabbi Zevin denies the binding nature of these oaths at the present juncture of Jewish history. He advances a forceful argument which, particularly in the present post-Holocaust era, must find a sympathetic echo in the heart of Jews who have witnessed an unprecedented erosion of all feelings of humanity among the nations of the world which permitted the horrendous oppression and torture of the Jewish people. The Talmud, *loc. cit.,* records that the two oaths sworn by the people of Israel were accompanied by a third oath which devolves upon the nations of the world; namely, that they shall not oppress Jews inordinately. According to Rabbi Zevin and others who have advanced the same argument, these three oaths, taken together, form the equivalent of a contractual relationship. Jews are bound by their oaths only as long as the gentile nations abide by theirs. Persecution of the Jews by the nations of the world in violation of this third oath releases the Jewish people from all further obligation to fulfill the terms of their agreement.[4]

Objections to the Sinai campaign and the Six-Day War are founded upon completely different considerations. According to Halakhah, the declaration of an offensive war requires the affirmative act of both the Sanhedrin and the king (*Sanhedrin* 2a and 20b), but in our day we possess neither Sanhedrin nor monarch. R. Abraham Isaac Kook, *Mishpat Kohen,* no. 144, sec. 15, has argued that the latter requirement is not a literal one because declaration of war is not a royal prerogative.[5] The king, in performing this function, merely serves as the agent of the nation. In the absence of a monarchy, authority for the declaration of war is vested in the established state authority. This contention is borne out by the words of Ramban in his addendum to Maimonides' *Sefer ha-Mizvot,* no. 17. Discussing the declaration of war, Ramban states that this is the prerogative of "the king, the judge, or whosoever exercises authority over the people." In contrast, the second requirement, namely, concurrence of the Sanhedrin, is crucial. Accordingly, Rabbi Zevin concludes that there is no possible halakhic authority for the waging of an offensive war in our time.

---

4. See also R. Aaron Soloveitchik and R. Meir Blumenfeld, *Shanah be-Shanah,* 5734. For additional sources regarding the applicability of these oaths, see R. Menachem M. Kasher, *Milḥemet Yom ha-Kippurim* (Jerusalem, 5734), pp. 63–83; and R. Shmuel ha-Kohen Weingarten, *Hishbati Etkhem* (Jerusalem, 5736). R. Chaim Vital, *Ez Ḥayyim* (Jerusalem, 5723), p. 3, quotes *Beraita de-Rabbi Yishma'el, Pirkei Heikhalot,* which declares that the oath remained in effect only for a period of one thousand years; see also *Zohar, Parshat Va-Yeira,* p. 117a.

5. This position is endorsed by R. Eliezer Waldenberg, *Hilkhot Medinah,* I, no. 3, chap. 5, and *Ziz Eli'ezer,* X, no. 1, chap. 3, sec. 14, who maintains that this is the opinion of R. Ya'akov Emden, *Mor u-Kezi'ah* 306. See also R. Benjamin Rabinowitz-Teumim, *Moriah,* Tevet 5735.

However, Rabbi Zevin asserts that these objections do not affect the halakhic status of the armed conflicts in which modern Israel was involved. A defensive war does not require the sanction of either the king or the Sanhedrin. These requirements apply only to wars of aggression carried out for purposes of exacting tribute, of territorial aggrandizement or of enhancing national prestige. Rabbi Zevin concludes that no objections can be raised against any of Israel's wars since they were all defensive in nature. Although Rabbi Zevin's article appeared before the events of October 1973, the conclusions he reaches apply with equal logic to Israel's most recent war as well.

These questions are also discussed by Rabbi Judah Gershuni, whose contribution dealing with this topic appears in the same issue of *Torah She-be-'al Peh* and in the Tevet 5731 edition of *Or ha-Mizraḥ*. Rabbi Gershuni asserts that the acquiescence of the Sanhedrin for the declaration of a war of offense may be dispensed with in our day. Quoting *Meshekh Ḥokhmah, Parshat Bo,* Rabbi Gershuni argues that only in the absence of a general desire on the part of the nation to engage in war is the agreement of the Sanhedrin necessary. *Meshekh Ḥokhmah* contends that the sanctification of the New Moon, ordinarily a prerogative of the Sanhedrin, may be performed by the community as a whole in the absence of the Sanhedrin. Rabbi Gershuni avers that this provision may be extended to declarations of war as well. Hence, in Rabbi Gershuni's opinion, the approval of the Sanhedrin is necessary only when the populace is unwilling to engage in battle of its own accord.

Moreover, declaration of war by the king and the concurrence of the Sanhedrin is not required with regard to obligatory wars such as the conquest of *Ereẓ Yisra'el.* Although some authorities disagree, Ramban is of the opinion that the commandment "And you shall inherit the land and dwell therein" (Num. 33:53) is binding in all generations. In his commentary on the above passage, Ramban clearly states that this *miẓvah* includes the commandment to conquer the Land of Israel.

Rabbi Gershuni, however, notes that another condition must be satisfied even with regard to obligatory wars. Both Ramban, in the previously cited gloss to the *Sefer ha-Miẓvot,* and Maimonides, *Sefer ha-Miẓvot, shoresh* 14, declare that even obligatory wars require consultation and guidance of the *urim ve-tumim.* Rabbi Gershuni argues that since this prerequisite cannot be fulfilled at the present time, war for the sake of conquering the territory of the Land of Israel cannot be sanctioned even according to Ramban.

There is, however, one category of warfare which does not require guidance of the *urim ve-tumim:* viz., the war against Amalek. It is usually assumed that because population shifts have occurred and ancient peoples are no longer ethnically identifiable, this *mizvah* cannot be fulfilled. Rambam, *Hilkhot Melakhim* 5:4–5, states that the commandment to eradicate the seven Canaanite peoples has lapsed because of precisely these considerations but fails to make a similar statement with regard to the people of Amalek. Rabbi Gershuni quotes an unpublished comment attributed to R. Chaim Soloveitchik of Brisk in resolution of this difficulty. R. Chaim is purported to have declared that the commandment to destroy Amalek extends not merely to genealogical descendants of that ancient people but encompasses all who embrace the ideology of Amalek and seek to annihilate the Jewish nation.[6] Hence, the "war of God against Amalek" continues "from generation to generation" against the professed enemies of Israel, and in our day is directed against those Arab nations which seek to eradicate the people of Israel. Since the battle against Amalek is in the nature of a continuous and ongoing war, it does not require the sanction of the *urim ve-tumim.*

Another version of what appears to be an identical attempt to resolve this difficulty is cited by Rabbi Joseph B. Soloveitchik in the name of his father, the late Rabbi Moshe Soloveitchik, in a footnote to his "*Kol Dodi Dofek,*" *Ha-Dat ve-ha-Medinah,* ed. M. Rottenberg (Tel Aviv, 5724), pp. 192–93.[7] Rabbi Soloveitchik argues that the commandment with regard to Amalek is really a twofold one: (1) an obligation devolving upon each individual Jew to destroy the genealogical descendants of Amalek; (2) a communal obligation to defend the Jewish people against any enemy threatening its destruction. These differing obligations are indeed recorded as separate commandments. The commandment recorded in Deuteronomy 25:19, "you shall erase the memory of Amalek," is addressed to all individual Jews and refers only to genealogical descendants of Amalek. Exodus 17:16, which speaks of "the war of God against Amalek," is addressed to the community as a whole and lends sanction to a preemptive war undertaken in the face of impending danger.

---

6. Of interest are the comments of Maharal of Prague, R. Judah Loew, *Or Ḥadash* (Jerusalem, 5720), p. 54a, who remarks that all enemies of Israel throughout the generations of their dispersion are, in point of fact, geneological descendants of Amalek.

7. This article is also included in *Torah u-Melukhah,* ed. S. Federbush (Jerusalem, 5721) and forms the second part of *Mosad ha-Rav Kook*'s edition of Rabbi Soloveitchik's *Ish ha-Emunah* (Jerusalem, 5735).

Since the latter type of warfare, although categorized as a war against "Amalek," must be waged against any would-be aggressor, Rambam eliminates mention of the fact that the genealogical descendants of Amalek are no longer identifiable. This thesis leads to a conclusion contradictory to that of Rabbi Gershuni. While Rabbi Gershuni's explanation would lend sanction to a war of aggression against professed enemies, according to this analysis only preemptive or defensive wars may be undertaken even against the avowed foes of the people of Israel.

Hijack Victims

The weeks preceding the High Holy Day period of the autumn of 1970 were a time of high tension for the Jewish community throughout the world. Members of an Arab terrorist movement succeeded in hijacking several jet airliners and in diverting them to a landing-strip in Jordan. Passengers and crew members were seized as hostages for the release of a large number of guerillas then held captive by Israel and several European governments.

During these harrowing weeks the State of Israel remained steadfast in its resolve not to free any imprisoned terrorists in exchange for these hostages. This decision was based upon two factors: (1) Acceding to the demands of the terrorists would establish a dangerous precedent and could at any time lead to further hijackings as a means of securing hostages in order to strengthen any future demands set forth by the guerillas. (2) Although release of the captured guerillas might save the lives of the hostages, the released terrorists would once more be free to return to their nefarious activities, thereby endangering the lives of Israeli citizens. The validity of these considerations as justification for a course of action which permitted continued danger to the lives of the hostages is examined by Rabbi Judah Gershuni in the Nisan 5731 edition of *Ha-Darom*. Related to this problem is the more general question of the propriety of paying ransom in order to secure the release of hostages.

The Mishnah, *Gittin* 45a, declares that captives are not to be ransomed if the sum demanded is "greater than their value"—a term which the vast majority of commentators understand as meaning a sum equal to that which the captive would command if he were to be sold as a slave. This limit is placed upon the amount which may be paid as ransom because of concern lest the abductors succeed in extorting exorbitant sums and potential captors thus be encouraged to kidnap additional victims. *Tosafot, Gittin* 58b, contends that this limitation does not apply if the captive's life is in danger. This exception, however, is not cited by either Rambam or *Shulḥan Arukh*. It may therefore be assumed that the latter authorities view the prescribed maximum as being applicable even in cases of actual danger to the victim. Latter-day authorities are divided with regard to a definitive decision on this matter; numerous responsa on the subject are cited by *Pitḥei Teshuvah, Yoreh De'ah* 252:4.

Tosafot, Gittin 54a, enumerates two other exceptions to the general rule that excessive ransom may not be paid. *Tosafot* maintains that restrictions upon the amount of ransom do not apply if the victim is a scholar of renown. Furthermore, such limitations are not imposed subsequent to the destruction of the Temple. For, *Tosafot* claims, during the period of the exile, the enemies of the people of Israel require no encouragement in their desire to victimize Jews. Hence, payment of an excessive ransom will not significantly intensify their motivation. The second exception formulated by *Tosafot* is not incorporated in *Shulḥan Arukh*'s codification of the relevant laws.

The 1970 hijackings, involving, as they did, the requested release of celebrated terrorists, pose an entirely different question. Is it obligatory or even permissible to endanger one person, or a group of people, in order to save the life of another? Release of known terrorists, who would then be enabled to return to their malevolent pursuits, should give rise to, at the very minimum, a *safek*, or reasonable fear, that the freeing of such terrorists will lead to their resumption of guerilla activities and ultimately result in loss of life. *Bet Yosef, Ḥoshen Mishpat* 426, is of the opinion that one is obligated to expose himself to possible danger in order to rescue another person from certain danger. Rabbi Gershuni, however, adduces numerous authorities who disagree and maintain that one is not obliged to expose himself to the possibility of danger in order to save another person's life. Certainly, argues Rabbi Gershuni, when both dangers are merely potential ones, the danger to the victim also being indefinite in nature, no overt action is mandated.

Rabbi Gershuni advances yet another argument in defense of the stance adopted by the Israeli government. It is his thesis that just as an individual is obliged to sacrifice his life on behalf of his country in time of war, so is he also duty-bound to assist in the preservation of law and order even at the risk of his own life. Rabbi Gershuni quotes R. Ya'akov Emden's explanation of the motive which prompted the tribe of Benjamin to enter into battle against the rest of Israel. Judges 19:25–29 describes how some members of the tribe of Benjamin subjected a concubine to repeated sexual assaults which ultimately resulted in her death. Subsequently the tribe of Benjamin resorted to warfare in order to preserve the perpetrators of this heinous deed from summary execution by members of the other tribes of Israel. In his *Migdal Oz,* R. Ya'akov Emden explains that it was the prerogative of each tribe to judge its own members and the tribe of Benjamin was therefore justified in resorting to violence in defense of this right. Surrender of this prerogative would have constituted capitulation to a measure of anarchy. Rabbi Gershuni views this analysis as establishing an obligation to risk one's life in order to preserve law and order. Since release of the terrorists would have undermined law and order in Israel, the government, in Rabbi Gershuni's opinion, was justified in refusing to release captured terrorists, despite the fact that the lives of innocent people were endangered thereby. These considerations are quite apart from the argument that it is within the sovereign power of a state to promulgate laws and issue edicts in order to protect the welfare and safety of its inhabitants, even though some individuals may be adversely affected.

Extradition

The avowed intention of the founders of the State of Israel was to provide a homeland for any Jew who sought to return to the land of his fathers. Following the Holocaust, the fledgling state opened its doors and became a haven of refuge to countless victims of oppression. This policy was formalized in the Law of Return, which grants any Jew the privileges of domicile and citizenship as vested legal rights. The law, however, contains a clause specifically denying these rights to individuals having prior criminal records. In the twenty-eight years of Israel's existence, relatively few would-be immigrants have been excluded on these grounds. Recently, however, this provision was invoked in denying permanent residence to Meyer Lanšky. The attendant publicity has generated much discussion of the moral and halakhic justification of this restrictive clause in the Law of Return.

This question, and the parallel question of extradition of persons facing criminal charges in their countries of origin, is examined by Rabbi Judah Gershuni in an article appearing in the Tevet 5732 issue of *Or ha-Mizraḥ* and reprinted in volume XIV (5732) of *Torah She-be-'al Peh.*

Rabbi Gershuni asserts that, with the exception of idolaters and apostates, every Jew has an inalienable right to reside in Israel. Ran, *Nedarim* 28a, offering one explanation of the halakhic obligation on the part of a Jew to obey the civil law of his country of residence, explains that in the Diaspora the land is the personal possession of the monarch, who has the option of making obedience to his edicts a condition of continued residence upon his property. However, continues Ran, the situation with regard to the Land of Israel is different, "for with regard to the land of Israel all the people of Israel are partners." Therefore, concludes Rabbi Gershuni, the Israeli government lacks the right to expel or to deny admission to any Jew desirous of living in Israel.

Extradition for purposes of criminal prosecution poses a different problem. Rambam, *Yesodei ha-Torah* 5:5, rules that a Jew cannot be turned over to a non-Jew for assassination or execution unless the individual whose custody is demanded is guilty of a capital crime. A demand of this nature must be rejected even if non-compliance poses a threat of death to the entire community. *Taz, Yoreh De'ah* 157:8, rules that a Jew dare not be turned over to a non-Jew even if the person whose custody is demanded is not in danger of being put to death but will be punished in some other manner. *Taz,* however, does permit the denunciation of malefactors, such as forgers, whose nefarious activities constitute a danger to the entire Jewish community. In times gone by it was not at all uncommon for the entire community to be punished for the misdeeds of a single individual. When this was the case, the transgressor had the status of a "pursuer" who placed the loves of others in jeopardy, and hence it was permissible to take any steps necessary in order to eliminate the danger. Where this consideration does not apply, Halakhah demands that the evildoer be tried and punished by a Jewish court. Therefore, concludes Rabbi Gershuni, rather than permit the extradition of criminals to other countries, Israel is bound to grant them asylum. At the same time Israeli courts must assume jurisdiction and bring the criminal to justice. If the latter responsibility is not shirked, the danger of Israel becoming a haven for undesirable elements is minimized.[8]

Guard Duty on the Temple Mount

The Six-Day War and the liberation of the Holy Places has brought to the foreground a host of halakhic questions which for long periods

8. See also Rabbi B. Rabinowitz-Teumim, *No'am* (5724), VII.

in Jewish history had been of merely theoretical interest. Although the Temple Mount is now in Jewish hands, it is nevertheless forbidden to enter the Temple site proper because of the fact that virtually all persons have become ritually impure, and pending restoration of the sacrificial order we lack the ashes of the red heifer which are required for performance of the purification ritual. Rambam, *Hilkhot Bet ha-Beḥirah* 6:15–16, rules that the intrinsic sanctity of the Temple site is unaffected by the destruction of the Temple itself. Rabad, in a gloss appended to the text of the Rambam, declares that with the destruction of the Temple, the sanctity of the area where the Temple once stood has indeed been abrogated, and therefore a person who enters that holy site no longer incurs the statutory punishment. *Magen Avraham* (*Oraḥ Ḥayyim* 561:62), *Bi'ur ha-Gra* (*Yoreh De'ah* 331:6), and *Mishneh Berurah* (*Oraḥ Ḥayyim* 561:5) all follow Rambam in ruling that entry onto the Temple Mount is forbidden.

Many latter-day authorities contend that entry onto the Temple Mount is forbidden even according to Rabad, and argue that his comments were intended merely to establish the absence of the punishment of *karet*—"cutting off"—a form of death at the hands of Heaven, but that the negative prohibition against such entry remains fully in effect. As evidence they point to the fact that elsewhere Rabad fails to disagree with Rambam's codification of certain laws which are predicated upon the assumption that the sanctity of the Temple site has not lapsed. In particular, Rambam declares that the laws pertaining to "fear of the Temple," which ban certain forms of unseemly conduct, remain binding even subsequent to the destruction and Rabad fails to disagree.

The apparent incongruity in Rabad's position is explained by the late Rabbi Kook in his *Mishpat Kohen,* no. 96. Throughout the period in which the Temple stood, the Temple site was possessed of two distinct forms of sanctity: sanctity by virtue of the fact that it was the "encampment" of the Shekhinah, and a second sanctity associated with the "walls" of the Temple structure. Rabbi Bezalel Zolti, *Torah She-be-'al Peh* (5728), X, draws essentially the same distinction and asserts that historically these two different sanctifications occurred at two distinct times: the Temple structure was sanctified by King Solomon, whereas the site was sanctified as the "encampment" of the Shekhinah by King David many years before the Temple was actually built. Punishment of *karet* is prescribed for defilement of the Temple itself, i.e., the physical structure, as indicated in Numbers 19:20, "That person shall be cut off from the midst of the community for he has defiled the Temple of God." The second prohibition, carrying with it a lesser punishment, reads "And they shall not defile their encampment in the midst whereof I dwell" (Num. 5:3). The latter reference makes no mention of the sanctity of the "walls" but refers to the sanctity of the "encampment." Rabad's position, then, is that the sanctity of the "walls" lapsed with the destruction of the Temple, whereas the sanctity of the "encampment" continues and is in no way abrogated by the destruction of the Temple walls. Consequently, even according to Rabad, the prohibition "They shall not defile their encampment," forbidding a person who has become ritually impure to enter the Temple Mount, remains in force even in our day.

The necessity of posting guards in the Temple area poses grave questions for observant soldiers assigned to such duty. Rabbi Shiloh Rafael discusses the ramifications of this problem in an article appearing in the Sivan–Tammuz 5732 issue of *Moriah.* In Rabbi Rafael's opinion, the security reasons which prompt the assignment of patrols in the area constitute *pikuaḥ nefesh*—a danger to life sufficiently serious to warrant transgression of prohibitions against entry onto the Temple Mount. Nevertheless, even in face of danger, infractions of Halakhah must be limited to that which is of absolute necessity. With regard to the posting of guards, the question to be clarified is how the transgression can be minimized insofar as possible.

The Temple Mount is divided into diverse areas, each having different regulations with regard to the entry of ritually unclean persons. One who has become defiled through contact with a corpse is barred only from the site of the Temple proper but not from the surrounding areas of the Temple Mount. Those who have become ritually unclean through certain other forms of defilement are banned from the surrounding areas as well. However, purification in the latter instances may be accomplished simply by means of immersion in a ritualarium. Accordingly, Rabbi Rafael advises that a soldier assigned to guard duty on the Temple Mount immerse himself in a ritualarium prior to assuming his post. Since the immersion is biblically ordained, only a ritualarium satisfying the requirements for the immersion of a *niddah* may be utilized. The regulations with regard to cutting of the nails, removal of foreign substances, prior cleansing, etc., are identical with those governing the immersion of a *niddah.* Citing R. Zadok ha-Kohen of Lublin, *Teshuvot Tiferet Ẓevi,* no. 27, sec. 11, Rabbi Rafael rules that a blessing must be recited following the immersion.

Since the precise boundaries of the various sections within the Temple

Mount cannot be determined with precision, Rabbi Rafael advises the soldiers to stand as close as possible to the walls surrounding the Temple area. (According to *Tosafot, Shevu'ot* 14b, even during the Babylonian period, Jews visiting the Land of Israel were not aware of the precise site of the Temple proper. Its exact location was apparently known only to local residents who were thoroughly familiar with the environs. Our knowledge of the Temple area is presumably no more accurate than that of Babylonian Jews during the talmudic period.)

Soldiers quite often have on their persons objects which are not essential for security purposes. This gives rise to an additional problem with regard to the introduction into the Temple area of clothes or utensils which are ritually unclean. The Gemara, *Eruvin* 104b, records that it is forbidden to bring any defiled object into the Temple. However, *Avnei Nezer, Yoreh De'ah,* no. 452, sec. 3 and *Arukh ha-Shulḥan he-Atid, Kodshim,* I, 37:16, declare that the prohibition against bringing unclean objects into the Temple applies only to the innermost areas and to the "courtyard," but not to the outermost reaches of the Temple Mount.

In contradistinction, the injunction "And you shall reverence My sanctuary" (Lev. 19:30) applies to the entire area of the Temple Mount. The Gemara, *Yevamot* 6a, and Rambam, *Bet ha-Beḥirah* 7:1–10, define this commandment as enjoining reverential behavior and deportment and, accordingly, specifically forbid an individual to enter the Temple Mount while bearing a staff, wearing shoes, carrying a purse, or with dust upon his feet. Noting that efficient performance of their duties requires the guards to be properly shod, Rabbi Rafael permits the wearing of shoes by soldiers on the grounds that failure to patrol the area properly would present an imminent danger.

This latter point is challenged by Rabbi Chanoch Zundel Grossberg in the Nisan 5733 issue of *Ha-Ma'ayan.* Apparently, Rabbi Rafael assumes that the prohibition against wearing shoes on the Temple Mount includes not only leather shoes but also shoes made of other materials as well. *Minḥat Ḥinukh,* no. 254, sec. 2, writes that it is "perhaps" permissible to wear shoes of materials other than leather when entering the Temple Mount. A later authority, R. Yechiel Michal Tucatzinsky, *Ir ha-Kodesh ve-ha-Mikdash,* IV, 27–28, states explicitly that shoes of such materials are permissible. Rabbi Grossberg finds clear evidence for this distinction on the basis of *Yevamot* 102b. He, therefore, concludes that the halakhah regarding the wearing of shoes on the Temple Mount parallels the regulation governing the wearing of shoes on the

Day of Atonement, and that in both instances a "shoe," by definition, is prohibited only if made of leather. Since leather shoes are not essential to the performance of their duties, Rabbi Grossberg advises that soldiers stationed on the Temple Mount be instructed to wear sneakers or the like.[9]

It is, of course, forbidden to eat, drink, spit, or sleep in the Temple area. Levity and frivolous conduct are also proscribed. *Arukh ha-Shulḥan he-Atid, Kodshim,* I, 14:5, declares that all forms of conversation are forbidden. Rabbi Rafael rules that smoking is also not permissible. Soldiers on guard duty are not exempt from the injunction concerning reverence for the Temple; accordingly, these proscribed activities are forbidden to them as well. Even while performing such duty they are to be mindful of the holiness of the place on which they stand.

Imprisonment or Death for Convicted Terrorists

Despite the carnage and loss of life which it has suffered as a result of terrorist activity, the State of Israel has refrained from imposing the death penalty upon convicted terrorists. In yet another in an intriguing series of articles dealing with the halakhic ramifications of policies adopted by the Israeli government, Rabbi Judah Gershuni, *Or ha-Mizraḥ,* Tevet 5733, seeks to clarify whether this policy is compatible with Halakhah or whether it is a violation of Jewish law.

It is obligatory upon the *Bet Din* to sit in judgment upon Jews accused of infractions of the law and to impose the death penalty upon those convicted of a capital crime (Rambam, *Sefer ha-Miẓvot, Aseh,* nos. 226–229; *Sefer ha-Ḥinukh,* nos. 47, 50, 261 and 555). In our day, in the absence of a Sanhedrin, this obligation cannot be fulfilled. The point which is obscure is whether or not a similar obligation exists with regard to the punishment of non-Jews as well. If such an obligation does in fact exist, it may be fulfilled in our day as well since a Sanhedrin is not required for the sentencing of a non-Jew.

Rambam, *Hilkhot Melakhim* 9:14, numbers the imposition of the death penalty for violation of the provisions of the Noachide Code among the seven commandments incumbent upon the "sons of Noah." In explaining the biblical narrative concerning the carnage of the inhabitants of the city of Shechem, Rambam declares that the people of

9. See also R. Shiloh Rafael, *Ha-Ma'ayan,* Tammuz 5733.

Shechem incurred the death penalty as a result of their culpability in not meting out punishment to Shechem for his transgression of the Noachide Code. Nevertheless, points out Rabbi Gershuni, Rambam's discussion is limited to the obligation of non-Jews with regard to the punishment of their fellow men but does not indicate that a Jew is under obligation to bring a non-Jew to justice. (Although *Tosafot, Avodah Zarah* 64b, indicates that once a death penalty has been pronounced, all persons, including Jews, are under an obligation to carry out the sentence.)

Rabbi Gershuni cites another ruling of Rambam which indicates that a Jew is obligated to impose the death penalty upon a non-Jewish transgressor. Rambam, *Hilkhot Milah* 1:6, declares that a gentile slave who refuses to accept the seven Noachide commandments is to be put to death. Rabbi Gershuni points out that according to this ruling the slave is, in effect, being executed for transgressing these laws and concludes that, according to Rambam, Jewish courts are indeed obligated to impose the death penalty upon non-Jewish transgressors.

Rabad disagrees with Rambam regarding the above case and states that the slave is to be sold to a non-Jew but is not to be executed. Rabbi Joseph Rosen, in his commentary on the Rambam, *Ẓafnat Pa'aneaḥ*, explains Rabad's position in the following manner: with the lapse of the Sanhedrin and the abrogation of capital punishment among Jews, Jews can no longer impose capital punishment upon non-Jews, even though the latter remain obligated to do so in administering their own system of law. Moreover, Ramban, in his commentary on Genesis 34:13, disagrees with Rambam and states that there is no statutory obligation requiring non-Jews to impose punishment upon transgressors. Imposition of capital punishment, he maintains, is discretionary under the Noachide Code. The injunction, "Thou shall not stand in fear of a man," *does* forbid a member of the *Bet Din* to refuse to sit in judgment; however this admonition applies only to instances when the defendant is a Jew. Since in Ramban's opinion a non-Jew, if he so desires, may decline to sit in judgment, it follows, according to this view, that Jewish courts have the same prerogative.

Whether or not Israeli courts are under an obligation to impose the death penalty for transgressions which are capital crimes under the Noachide Code is thus a subject of dispute among the authorities. According to both Ramban and Rabad, the Israeli courts are under no obligation to do so, and hence are at liberty to impose a prison sentence upon terrorists in lieu of capital punishment. Rabbi Gershuni concludes that the current Israeli practice is in consonance with halakhic norms.

Sale of Israeli Real Estate to Non-Jews

"And in the seventh year shall be a sabbath of solemn rest for the land. . . . you shall not sow your field, nor prune your vineyard" (Lev. 25:4). The commandment concerning the sabbatical year—*shmittah*—prescribes that land in *Ereẓ Yisra'el* be allowed to lie fallow every seventh year. According to rabbinic exegesis, not only is it forbidden to till the soil, it is also forbidden to sell produce which grows of its own accord. "And the sabbath-produce of the land shall be for food for you . . ." (Lev. 25:6). The Torah grants permission for the produce which grows of its own accord to be used "for food, but not for merchandise" (*Bekhorot* 12b). The year 5733 was a *shmittah* year, and quite appropriately the fifteenth annual *Torah She-be-'al Peh* colloquium held in Jerusalem under the auspices of *Mosad ha-Rav Kook* was devoted to matters pertaining to the sabbatical year. A number of the papers presented at this gathering, all of which were subsequently published in the *Torah She-be-'al Peh* annual, dealt with the practice of selling farms and orchards to a non-Jew in order to circumvent the prohibition against tilling the land and the restriction against commercial dealings involving the produce of the sabbatical year.

The problem of *shmittah* came to the fore as a matter of pressing concern in modern times a little less than a century ago, when the newly established *yishuv* in *Ereẓ Yisra'el* faced its first sabbatical year in 5649. Since that time a vast literature has emerged centering primarily upon the efficacy of the sale of land to a non-Jew as a means of lawfully circumventing the strictures of *shmittah*. Those who permit this procedure base themselves on the premise that laws governing the sabbatical year do not apply to territory in the possession of non-Jews. This premise is itself the subject of considerable controversy.

Granting *argumento* that the sale of land to a non-Jew constitutes a method of obviating the need for observance of the *shmittah* laws, a second, equally weighty problem arises: Is it permissible to transfer title to land within the boundaries of *Erez Yisra'el* to a gentile? Indeed, R. Naftali Zevi Yehudah Berlin, in a treatise entitled "*Kuntres Dvar ha-Shmittah*" (published in *Teshuvot Meshiv Davar,* II, following responsum no. 56) writes, "This is like one who runs from a wolf and is come upon by a lion! If you desire to escape the prohibition of working the land in the seventh year in our day, which according to the majority of authorities is a rabbinic transgression, you are caught in the prohibition of selling land to a gentile, which is a biblical transgression according to all." *Ḥazon Ish, Shevi'it* 24:4, invokes the talmudic principle, "There can be no proxy for transgression," and argues that not only is such sale forbidden, but if an agent or proxy is used in effecting the sale of land to a non-Jew, the sale is invalid. It is a principle of talmudic jurisprudence that an agent cannot be appointed for the performance of an act involving a transgression. If the sale of land in Israel to a non-Jew constitutes a transgression, such a sale cannot be effected by means of an agent. In practice, the Chief Rabbinate acts as the agent for most landowners who seek to effect such sales. Since *Ḥazon Ish* maintains that sale to a non-Jew is forbidden, he deems such sales to be null and void when executed through a proxy and hence of no possible effect in mitigating restrictions concerning the sabbatical year. The Chief Rabbinate, of course, views sale of land to a non-Jew as a permissible procedure and hence efficacious.

The considerations upon which this dispute is based are discussed in a number of contributions which appear in *Torah She-be-'al Peh.* The permissibility of selling land in *Ereẓ Yisra'el* to a non-Jew is discussed by Rabbi Ovadiah Yosef in the course of a detailed analysis of the general question of the sale of land to a non-Jew as a means of avoiding the onus of *shmittah* observance and by Rabbi Shmuel Tanchum Rubenstein in his treatment of the same topic. A third article, by Rabbi Eliyahu Bakshi-Duran, is devoted exclusively to the specific question of whether or not it is permissible to sell land in *Ereẓ Yisra'el* to a non-Jew. Also included in this volume is a responsum on the same subject authored by the late Rabbi Mordecai Zevi Tannenbaum.

The Mishnah, *Avodah Zarah* 19b, expressly forbids the sale of real estate in Israel to non-Jews. The Gemara explains that this prohibition is derived from the biblical injunction *"lo teḥanem,"* (Deut. 7:2), which, according to rabbinic exegesis, is to be understood as meaning "You shall not grant them permanent encampment (*ḥaniyah*)." Rambam, *Hilkhot Avodah Zarah* 10:4, amplifies this statement with the explanation, "For if they will not own land, their inhabitance will be temporary." Ramban, in his commentary on the Bible, Leviticus 25:23, finds that conveyance of land to a non-Jew involves yet another transgression. Scripture provides that all fields revert to their original owners in the jubilee year, and explicitly commands, "and the land shall not be sold in perpetuity." Ramban understands this verse as banning the sale of land to a non-Jew since the latter would retain permanent possession and not return the land to its original owner in the jubilee year. The verse concludes with the explanation "for the land is Mine," indicating that in actuality the land is the possession of God and that it is only by virtue of His largesse that man is permitted to dwell in, and derive enjoyment from, his terrestrial habitat. Accordingly, this passage gives expression to the divine will that Israel be the homeland of the Jewish people and that they not be displaced by foreign land-owners. According to Ramban, the purchase of land in Israel from a non-Jew constitutes a fulfillment of the commandment "You shall give a redemption unto the land" (Lev. 25:24). Rabbi Bakshi-Duran argues that, according to Ramban, there is yet another source militating against the sale of dwellings or fields in Israel to a non-Jew. According to Ramban, the verse "And you shall inherit the land and dwell therein" (Deut. 11:31) is not simply a prophetic prognostication or a divine promise but constitutes a positive commandment. Ramban comments, "We have been commanded to inhabit the land which God gave to our forefathers, Abraham, Isaac, and Jacob, that we not allow it to remain in the possession of any other nation or allow it to be desolate." Rabbi Bakshi-Duran understands the second clause in Ramban's comment as referring not to the establishment of political sovereignty but to actual ownership of territory. Thus any act which results in a non-Jew acquiring title to any portion of the land of Israel constitutes a violation of the commandment concerning settlement of *Ereẓ Yisra'el*.

Yet, over the years, a number of rabbinic authorities have sanctioned the sale of real estate to non-Jews, at least in certain limited circumstances. *Mizbeaḥ Adamah*, an important nineteenth-century Sephardic source, reports that noted rabbinic authorities had themselves done so in the past and cites several by name. Indeed, earlier scholars were perplexed by the narrative in I Kings 9:11 which reports that King Solomon bestowed twenty cities in the Galilee upon Hiram, king of Tyre, in appreciation of the latter's assistance in providing materials needed for use in the construction of the Temple. There is no record of Solomon having been censured for this action.[10] *Mizbeaḥ Adamah* explains that the prohibition against the sale of real estate to a non-Jew is applicable

10. See, however, the commentary of Abarbanel on I Kings 9:10.

only to idol worshippers but not to other gentiles. Indeed, idolaters are specifically denied the right of domicile in the Land of Israel lest they cause the Jewish populace to become enmeshed in pagan practices. "They shall not dwell in your land lest they cause you to sin against Me, for you will serve their gods" (Exod. 23:33). Many authorities (with the notable exception of Rambam, *Hilkhot Avodah Zarah* 10:6) rule that since specific reference is made to idolatrous influences, only pagans are excluded from the right of domicile. *Mizbeaḥ Adamah* views the prohibition against the sale of property as being simply an extension of the prohibition against domicile in the land of Israel, and hence similarly limited in its application solely to idolaters.[11] In accordance with the above distinction, *Mizbeaḥ Adamah* rules that there is no restriction against the sale of real estate to Moslems, who profess a monotheistic belief. This thesis also serves to explain Solomon's gift to Hiram. Since Hiram was not an idol worshipper, there existed no halakhic obstacle to the transfer of land to him by King Solomon. Rabbi Yosef notes that, quite obviously, this line of reasoning is cogent only with regard to the prohibition of *lo teḥanem,* but fails to satisfy objections which might be raised on the basis of Ramban's position that the sale of land to a non-Jew also entails transgression of the commandment "And the land shall not be sold in perpetuity." He notes that there is, however, the possibility that Solomon expressly stipulated as a condition of his gift to Hiram that the cities were to revert to their original owners upon the advent of the jubilee year. Rabbi Yosef opines that consideration of Ramban's position would not preclude sale of land "in our day" since observance of the jubilee year lapsed with the destruction of the Temple. This contention may, however, be challenged, since even under contemporary conditions, all lands which are sold are subject to reversion to their original owners in the messianic era, which is to be accompanied by reinstitution of the observance of the jubilee year.

Teshuvot Yeshu'ot Malko, Yoreh De'ah, no. 55, advances a number of other considerations which serve to render the sale of land during the *shmittah* year a permissible procedure. One argument advanced by this authority is that there is no restriction against such sale when it is nego-

---

11. This prohibition is also cited by R. Abraham I. Kook, *Mishpat Kohen,* nos. 58, 61, and 63, and by R. Zevi Pesach Frank, *Kerem Ẓion,* III, no. 13, as well as by R. Eliyahu Klatzkin, *Teshuvot Imrei Shefer,* no. 92, but is rejected by R. Ya'akov David Wilofsky (see *Mishpat Kohen,* no. 61), R. Naftali Zevi Yehudah Berlin, *Kuntres Dvar ha-Shmittah* and *Ḥazon Ish, Shevi'it* 24:3.

tiated primarily for the benefit of the seller. Since the sale of land for the period of the sabbatical year is entered into primarily for the purpose of strengthening the economic viability of the Jewish settlements in Israel, such transfer of property, in the opinion of *Yeshu'ot Malko,* does not fall within the parameters of this biblical prohibition. Similarly, he argues that property may be sold if it is the seller's intention to repurchase the land after its agricultural potential has been enhanced by the purchaser. Since routine chores, such as weeding and pruning, may not be performed during *shmittah,* the future agricultural yield of such lands is sharply reduced. Sale to a non-Jew, which enables these operations to be performed, serves to enhance the agricultural value of the property, Rabbi M. Rubin, *Shemen ha-Ma'or, Yoreh De'ah,* no. 4, adds that the ultimate purpose underlying the prohibition (viz., the prevention of "permanent" residence by non-Jews, which is a concommitant of the acquisition of real estate) would in this case be thwarted by a ban on the sale of land for the period of the sabbatical year. The economic hardships resulting from failure to obviate the difficulties associated with observance of *shmittah* through sale to a non-Jew would undoubtedly result in the abandonment of Jewish agricultural settlement and in a diminution of the Jewish populace. The net result would be greater "permanence" of the non-Jewish population. This point is also made by Rabbi Eliyahu David Rabinowitz-Teumim in a letter appended to Rabbi Kook's *Shabbat ha-Areẓ,* p. 128.

Yeshu'ot Malko further argues that only sales which result in the property remaining in the possession of the purchaser in perpetuity are forbidden. Sales in which the property reverts to the seller at a future date do not constitute a bestowal of "permanence" upon the dwelling of a non-Jew. In accordance with this line of reasoning *Yeshu'ot Malko* rules that an explicit stipulation should be made at the time of sale to the effect that the land will be resold by the purchaser after the expiration of the sabbatical year.

While he does not himself accept the argument, Rabbi Kook (*Shabbat ha-Areẓ,* introd., chap. 10, and *Minḥat Kohen,* no. 68) cites a contention advanced by Rabbi Zalman Shach to the effect that there is no restriction against selling land to a non-Jew who already owns real estate in Israel. The reasoning underlying this position is that since the purchaser already owns property, he has already acquired "permanence." Since a state of "permanence" is not newly bestowed upon the purchaser through the acquisition of additional parcels of land, the sale of real estate to such an individual is not forbidden.

The disagreement with regard to the permissibility of the sale of real estate to a non-Jew who already owns property in the Land of Israel is contingent upon an analysis of the nature of the prohibition *lo teḥanem*. On the basis of a contribution by Rabbi Bezalel Zolti to an earlier volume of *Torah She-be-'al Peh* (XI, 5729), it may be demonstrated that there exists a significant difference of opinion with regard to the technical nature of this prohibition. Some authorities deem the sale of land to be forbidden under all conditions because, in their opinion, the concept of granting "permanence" is simply the underlying rationale of a prohibition which, by definition, encompasses any transfer of title. Hence, according to these authorities, *any* sale of property to a non-Jew is forbidden, regardless of the effect such sale may or may not have upon the permanence of dwelling achieved by the purchaser as a result of consummation of the sale. Other authorities deem the essence of the prohibition to be the bestowal of "permanence" of dwelling rather than the sale itself, and hence they sanction sale for a stipulated period of time, exchange of parcels of real estate or even sale to a non-Jew who already owns property in Israel.

CHAPTER II

Sabbath and Festivals

The laws of the Sabbath are as mountains which hang by a hair; the verses are few, but the laws are many.

ḤAGIGAH 10a

The Hebrew term *kedushah,* usually translated as "sanctity" or "holiness," has as its root-meaning the connotation of separateness. That which is holy is separated from both the profane and the mundane. God is the epitome of *kedushah* because He is wholly transcendent and totally separated from the material universe.

Individuals may be sanctified by virture of a role or function which sets them apart from their fellow men. Such sanctification results from the renunciation of commonplace, mundane activities and the pursuit of matters of the spirit. Geographical sites may acquire sanctity by virtue of being removed from prosaic use and consecrated to sublime activity.

The sanctification of person and place is not unique to Judaism. Other creeds also profess the sanctity of persons and places. Judaism is unique in its teaching of a novel concept involving the sanctity of time. For Jews, the Sabbath is not simply a day of rest; it is not merely a day in which worldly cares are set aside. It is a day on which the Jew emulates the Deity.

The Mekhilta, *Parashat Ki Tissa* 1:5, teaches that one who observes the Sabbath testifies, by his very conduct, to the divine creation of the universe, while one who profanes the Sabbath denies the doctrine of creation. This is not simply an instance of midrashic hyperbole. Many scholars have pointed out that God and man are partners in the unfolding process of creation. During the six days of creation God created not only the kernel of wheat but also caused the wheat stalk to emerge from the ground fully grown. However, the wheat was not yet ready for human consumption. It had to be harvested, threshed, ground into flour, kneaded into dough, and baked in an oven. Yet God—Whose very name, *Shaddai,* our Sages tell us, means "I am He Who said to the world, 'Enough!' "—refused to allow these processes to unfold of their own accord. God created man and to him was given the task of completing the design of creation.

Man is bidden to emulate God in the task of creation. God created the universe during a period of six days and rested on the seventh; so, too, man is commanded to spend but six days in the completion of the human component in the creative process and to rest on the seventh. On the seventh day God's transcendence of the universe was complete; He abstained even from acts of creation. On the seventh day, man, too, is commanded to separate himself from the works of human creation, to withdraw from the world he has created for himself. In doing so man captures a measure of the transcendence and sanctity of the divine.

By its very nature, Sabbath observance bears witness to man's partnership with God in the process of creation and to man's trust in his divine partner. Preservation of the Sabbath has always required a high degree of faith. Throughout the ages, Jews suffered untold hardship and privation in order to keep the Sabbath holy. Their selfless devotion to the sanctity of the Sabbath gave eloquent testimony to the sovereignty of the Creator. The Mekhilta, *Parashat Ki Tissa* 1:11, points out that those *mizvot* which require sacrifice are never lost. The Sabbath is specifically enumerated as a commandment which requires considerable sacrifice but which, precisely for this reason, has never been lost to us.

The term "work," as applied to activities restricted on the Sabbath, has a highly technical meaning. It is not to be equated with labor or physical exertion. As has been shown by R. Abraham Samuel Sofer, R. Samson Raphael Hirsch and others, the activities banned on the Sabbath are those in which man completes the work of creation, those in which he takes the raw materials of the created universe and transforms them into finished products, implements or foodstuffs which he can enjoy. In refraining from creative activity man emulates the Creator, who desisted from further creation on the Sabbath day.

Halakhically, "work" is defined as any of the procedures employed in the fashioning and erection of the Tabernacle in the wilderness. Exodus 35:1–3, which reiterates the prohibition against "work" on the Sabbath, forms a preamble to the directives governing the specifications for the construction of the Tabernacle and its utensils. The Sages comment that the juxtaposition of these scriptural sections teaches that Sabbath regulations are not suspended for the purpose of constructing the Tabernacle. "Work" which is forbidden on the Sabbath is then defined as the activities involved in the construction of the Tabernacle. These activities, thirty-nine broad categories in number, ranging from planting to baking, from shearing to tearing for purposes of sewing, from trapping animals to cutting their hides, as well as numerous derivatives, were enumerated, defined, and transmitted to Moses as part of the Oral Law. To this list were added rabbinic enactments prohibiting other activities. These rabbinic decrees were variously designed as "a bridge around the Law" or as a means of promoting the Sabbath spirit.

Sale of Commercial Enterprises to Sabbath Violators

In one of the Halakhah-briefs published in the Tishri 5730 issue of *Ha-Darom,* Rabbi Nachum L. Rabinovitch, the principal of Jews' College in London, discusses a question which arises frequently in connection with commercial undertakings. The proprietor of an insurance firm found the volume of business too burdensome to handle personally, and therefore wished to sell his agency to a larger firm and accept employment as an insurance salesman with the purchasing company. The contemplated sale would involve transfer of the existing business to a Jewish firm whose business activities are openly conducted on the Sabbath.

The question poses two halakhic issues: (1) Is it permitted to sell or transfer a business undertaking with the knowledge that the purchaser will henceforth conduct the firm's commercial activities on the Sabbath? (2) Is the insurance agent, now to be employed by a Sabbath-violating firm, permitted to profit from the desecration of the Sabbath entailed by clerical work performed on his behalf and on behalf of his clients?

The second problem is readily resolved by Rabbi Rabinovitch by reference to a responsum of R. David Hoffmann, *Melamed le-Ho'il, Oraḥ Ḥayyim,* no. 40. R. Hoffmann states simply that the agent's profit in the form of a commission is paid solely for his efforts as a broker, and any activities on the part of those employing his services are in actuality conducted for their own convenience and benefit and not on behalf of the broker.

The first issue, the basic question regarding the transfer of a commercial enterprise to Sabbath violators, is more involved and is a recurrent one in modern responsa literature. The earliest discussion of the subject appears to be that of the *Melamed le-Ho'il, Oraḥ Ḥayyim,* no. 34. The issue centers around the question of whether such action involves a transgression of the biblical injunction "Thou shalt not place a stumbling block before the blind" or of the rabbinic prohibition against "abetting evildoers." R. Hoffmann quotes R. Jacob Ettlinger, *Binyan Ẓion,* no. 15, to the effect that these categories apply only in cases where (1) transgression would be impossible without the aid of another person, (2) a request is made for aid with specific reference to a transgression, or (3) despite the absence of the above conditions, the aid rendered is nevertheless utilized for purposes of transgression. R. Hoffmann rules that, in the case at hand, the first two factors are totally absent, and since the aid rendered is not proximate to the transgression, there is no halakhic impediment to the sale. He cautions, however, that if the purchaser will henceforth conduct the affairs of the firm on the Sabbath, the firm's name should be changed. Responding to a similar query in an article published in three parts in the Iyar, Sivan and Tammuz issues of *Ha-Pardes* 5713, the late Rabbi Yechiel Ya'akov Weinberg reaches an identical conclusion. A précis of this responsum appears in *Seridei Esh,* II, no. 19.

In this connection it should also be noted that Rabbi Moses Feinstein, *Iggrot Mosheh, Oraḥ Ḥayyim,* I, no. 67, addresses himself to the more limited question of selling a list of customers to a Sabbath violator. Despite the fact that the sales contacts can be made equally well on weekdays without desecration of the Sabbath, and hence there is no reason why this business should necessarily be transacted on the Sabbath, Rabbi Feinstein recommends that the sale be made to a Sabbath observer if this involves but a small loss. If the potential loss is great or if no other purchaser is to be found, Rabbi Feinstein regards the sale as being permissible.

Rabbi Rabinovitch treats the entire problem *de nouveau* and marshals evidence from various primary sources in sanctioning the proposed sale of the insurance firm in question to Sabbath violators. At the same time he emphasizes that all clients should be informed of the transfer and of the change in status of the former owner from proprietor to that of an employee of the new firm.

Sabbath Elevators

Automatic elevators designed for use on *Shabbat* were first introduced in the late 1950s. Such elevators are operated by means of a time-switch, which is set in advance so that no manual work is required on the Sabbath. The earliest halakhic discussion of the permissibility of the use of such elevators on the Sabbath is contained in an article by Rabbi Samuel Hubner, *Ha-Darom,* Nisan 5724. A further discussion, which raises a number of new points, appears in a contribution to the Iyar 5729 issue of *Moriah.*[1] Rabbi E. Kugel, the coordinator of the Halakhah Department of the Institute for Science and Halakhah, reports on the research in this area carried out by members of this pioneering institute. Chief among the problems attendant upon Sabbath use of automatic elevators is the increased flow of electric current due to the added weight of passengers and the increased sparking which may occur with each stop of the elevator. A technical exposition of the factors responsible for these phenomena and the principles governing the operation of the automatic apparatus is detailed in the first bulletin of the institute, published in February, 1967.

Rabbi Kugel asserts that it is forbidden to cause an increase in the consumption of electric current because the generation of additional current causes enhanced conduction and results in raising the temperature of various mechanisms employed in the generation of electricity to the level of "cooking." Production of the current in itself may perhaps be forbidden as being encompassed by the rabbinic prohibition against creating new entities (*molid*).[2]

The question pondered by Rabbi Kugel is whether the passive activity of simply standing inside the elevator car, thereby permitting one's weight to cause additional flow of current, constitutes an "action" within the province of Sabbath regulations. The Gemara, *Baba Kamma* 10b, indicates that individuals seated upon a couch who fail to remove themselves when additional weight is placed upon the piece of furniture on which they are seated incur financial liability for any resultant damages. Since the original act of seating themselves on the couch caused no dam-

1. For further discussion of some problems attendant upon use of elevators on *Shabbat* see also R. Yitzchak Schmelkes, *Bet Yiẓḥak, Yoreh De'ah,* II, *Mafteḥot,* no. 31; R. Eliezer Deutsch, *Pri ha-Sadeh,* IV, nos. 39 and 72; R. Ya'akov Breish, *Ḥelkat Ya'akov,* III, no. 137; R. Yitzchak Ya'akov Weisz, *Minḥat Yiẓḥak,* III, 60 and IV, no. 25; R. Solomon Braun, *She'arim ha-Meẓuyanim be-Halaklah,* II, 74:5; and R. Samuel Hubner, *Ha-Darom,* Tishri 5733.

2. See also R. Moses Feinstein, *Iggrot Mosheh, Oraḥ Ḥayyim,* III, no. 55. Cf., however, R. Yosef Eliyahu Henkin, *Edut le-Yisra'el,* p. 121, and R. Ovadiah Yosef, *Yabi'a Omer, I, Oraḥ Ḥayyim,* no. 19, sec. 18.

age, the inference to be drawn is that one's mere presence and the effects caused by sheer weight are considered as "actions."

The question as to whether sparks are to be deemed a form of "fire," or whether their transitory and ephemeral nature precludes their inclusion in this category, is the subject of long-standing dispute. Rabbi Kugel cites a long list of authorities who consider the production of sparks to be a biblical offense. The more permissive view expressed by some authorities is predicated upon the comments of the *Pri Megadim, Oraḥ Ḥayyim* 502:1. In a lengthy exposition and analysis of the views expressed by the *Pri Megadim,* Rabbi Kugel endeavors to show that these leniencies are based upon an erroneous interpretation resulting in a misunderstanding of the *Pri Megadim's* position regarding this question. Accordingly, Rabbi Kugel argues, the *Pri Megadim* concurs in the opinion that the causing of sparks is biblically forbidden and thus all subsequent lenient rulings in this matter are based upon an error of interpretation.

Of particular interest is an item in the second bulletin of the Institute for Science and Halakhah, dated 1969, reporting that scientific research by members of the institute has resolved the theoretical difficulties which stood in the way of the development of sparkless relays and that a prototype of this device is now being developed. This project is specifically designed to overcome the halakhic questions surrounding the use of automatic elevators on the Sabbath.

Erev Pesaḥ Which Occurs on Shabbat

The vagaries of the lunar calendar are such that *Erev Pesaḥ* coincides with *Shabbat* infrequently but with a peculiar pattern. There are intervals of as long as twenty years during which *Erev Pesaḥ* does not occur on *Shabbat,* which are followed by the occurrence of *Erev Pesaḥ* on *Shabbat* two or, more usually, three times within a relatively short span of time, followed by a rather long interval in which *Erev Pesaḥ* fails to coincide with *Shabbat*. Thus, although *Erev Pesaḥ* did not occur on *Shabbat* between 1954 and 1974, *Erev Pesaḥ* will again coincide with *Shabbat* in both 1977 and 1981.

The occurrence of *Erev Pesaḥ* on *Shabbat* gives rise to various complications with regard to the eating of *ḥameẓ* (leaven) and its disposal, the proper method with regard to fulfilling the *miẓvah* of the Sabbath repasts, etc.

There are a number of booklets and compendia designed to deal specifically with the laws of *Erev Pesaḥ* which occurs on *Shabbat*. Of greatest significance is *Ḥok le-Yisra'el,* authored by the late Rabbi Israel Veltz, formerly *Rosh Bet Din* of Budapest. A section devoted to this topic is included in the fourth edition of Rabbi Moshe Sternbuch's commentary on the Passover *Haggadah, Mo'adim u-Zemanim* (Jerusalem, 5734), and was also published as a separate pamphlet. Another useful work is the recently published *Erev Pesaḥ she-Ḥal be-Shabbat* (B'nei Brak, 5734), authored by Rabbi Zevi Cohen. English, Hebrew, and Yiddish versions of a booklet on this topic by Rabbi Simcha Weissman utilize a question and answer format for the presentation of these laws and regulations. A booklet by this writer discussing this subject was published under the aegis of the *Bet Din* of the Rabbinical Alliance of America.

Housewives, quite naturally, would prefer not to have *ḥamez* in their kitchens and dining rooms so close to the *Yom Tov*. The need for having available both *ḥamez* and Passover foods and utensils makes an already trying period even more difficult. In addition to making household chores more complex, simultaneous preparation of both *ḥamez* and Passover meals leads to concern over possible intermingling of utensils and food.

Shulḥan Arukh, Oraḥ Ḥayyim 444:4–6 states clearly that *ḥamez* may be eaten on *Erev Pesaḥ* which occurs on *Shabbat* provided that it is consumed during the period in which *ḥamez* may yet be eaten, i.e., before four hours of the day have elapsed. The "hour" for this purpose is not sixty minutes but is one-twelfth of the daylight hours. In order to determine the precise time for the eating of *ḥamez,* the length of the day between sunrise and sunset or, according to some authorities, between the appearance of the "morning star" and the emergence of stars at night, must be ascertained. This period is divided by twelve in order to determine the length of a single "hour" and then multiplied by four in order to determine how long after sunrise *ḥamez* may be eaten. *Ḥamez* which remains after the meal is completed cannot be burned on *Shabbat*. Small amounts of *ḥamez* which are left over may be given as a gift to a non-Jew, who may do with the *ḥamez* as he wishes (although it is forbidden specifically to instruct the non-Jew to remove the *ḥamez* from the premises), or may be covered with a pot or other utensil and nullified by means of the formula for *bittul* and burned after the Holy Day. *Mishneh Berurah* 444:21 also permits disposal of left-over *ḥamez* in the bathroom.

However, because of the difficulties attendant upon preparing for Passover under these circumstances, it has been suggested that when *Erev*

Pesaḥ occurs on *Shabbat,* either ordinary *maẓah* or egg *maẓah* be used for the Friday evening and *Shabbat* morning meals. This would eliminate the problem of the disposal of left-over *ḥameẓ* and would also preclude the possibility of inadvertent mixture of foods and utensils. Although these proposals would greatly facilitate matters, each of them presents halakhic problems which merit detailed review.

I. *Maẓah on Erev Pesaḥ*

The question of whether or not it is permissible to eat ordinary Passover *maẓah* on this *Shabbat* is discussed by the late Rabbi Moshe Rosen in an article which appeared in the Nisan 5714 issue of *Ha-Pardes* and was subsequently reprinted in a somewhat different form in his collected responsa, *Nezer ha-Kodesh,* no. 52.

Rabbi Rosen rules against the use of *maẓah.* He asserts that scrupulous avoidance of *ḥameẓ* on the day preceding Passover is tantamount to adding an additional day to that festival and constitutes a violation of the injunction, "You shall not add to the word which I command you" (Deut. 4:2). It would appear that the opposite conclusion might be deduced from *Rosh Hashanah* 28b and *Eruvin* 96a which indicate that sitting in a *sukkah* following the conclusion of the festival does not constitute a violation of this prohibition unless the individual has explicit intenton (*kavanah*) of fulfilling the commandment of dwelling in the *sukkah.* Rabbi Rosen, however, argues that we may not conclude that lack of such intention with regard to eating *maẓah* is sufficient to obviate the transgression of "Thou shalt not add." It is forbidden to sit in the *sukkah* after the holiday only if there is specific intent to fulfill a commandment, because there is nothing in the act itself which indicates that it is being done for the purpose of a *miẓvah;* the eating of *maẓah* at both Sabbath meals coupled with scrupulous avoidance of *ḥameẓ,* argues Rabbi Rosen, is in itself an indication that one is observing that day as one of the days of Passover. Employing a similar rationale, an early authority, *Mordekhai,* rules that although one must eat in the *sukkah* on *Shemini Aẓeret,* one may not sleep in the *sukkah* on that day. *Mordekhai* maintains that while partaking of food in a boothlike structure is not out of the ordinary, it is unusual for a person to sleep in a *sukkah* other than on *Sukkot.* By sleeping in a *sukkah* the individual "appears to be adding" to the biblical requirement.

An opposing point of view is expressed by Rabbi Moses Feinstein, *Iggrot Mosheh, Oraḥ Ḥayyim,* I, no. 155. Taking sharp issue with this conclusion, he points out that *Ba'al ha-Ma'or,* in his commentary to *Pesaḥim* 49a, and *Maggid Mishneh, Hilkhot Ḥameẓ u-Maẓah* 3:3, both rule that in the situation in question it is permissible to eat regular *maẓah* before noon. Rabbi Feinstein concludes that the transgression "Thou shalt not add" is not applicable unless there is specific intention of fulfilling the *miẓvah* of eating *maẓah.*

Nevertheless, Rabbi Feinstein, in practice, rules against the eating of ordinary *maẓah* for other reasons. The Gemara indicates that it is forbidden to partake of *maẓah* on *Erev Pesaḥ,* likening the person who does so "to one who cohabits with his betrothed in the home of his father-in-law." In order to assure that the *maẓah* eaten on the eve of Passover be eaten with relish, the Sages enacted a prohibition against eating *maẓah* on *Erev Pesaḥ.* This pleasure would be considerably diminished had the taste of *maẓah* been sampled earlier in the day. Some authorities, as earlier noted, are of the opinion that this prohibition is effective only from noon onward. Rabbi Feinstein, however, demonstrates that in terms of definitive halakhah, the prohibition against eating *maẓah* on *Erev Pesaḥ* goes into effect at daybreak rather than at noon. He also cites and affirms the view of *Magen Avraham* 471:6, who maintains that *maẓah* is forbidden not only on the day before *Pesaḥ* but the entire preceding evening as well. Hence, in the opinion of Rabbi Feinstein, ordinary *maẓah* should be used neither for the *Shabbat* morning meal nor for the meal on Friday evening.[3]

II. *Egg Maẓah on Erev Pesaḥ*

Rabbi Feinstein does, however, permit the use of egg *maẓah* on Friday evening and early in the day on the Sabbath morning. Citing *Bet Yosef, Oraḥ Ḥayyim* 444, Rabbi Feinstein indicates that the use of egg *maẓah* is the optimum method of avoiding all difficulties. Even though egg *maẓah* is usually deemed to be in the category of cake rather than bread, when it is used for the *Shabbat* meals one must wash, pronounce the blessing for bread, and recite the grace after meals. Egg *maẓah,* declares Rabbi Feinstein, acquires the status of bread by virtue of being used in place of bread for the Sabbath meal.[4]

3. Cf. *Le-Torah ve-Hora'ah,* no. 3 (Winter 5734), p. 21.

4. Cf. *Sha'arei Teshuvah, Oraḥ Ḥayyim,* 168:9 and R. Feinstein's novel interpretation of the authorities cited. See also *Sha'arei Teshuvah, Oraḥ Ḥayyim* 639:2; *Teshuvot ha-Ridbaz,* I, no. 489; R. S. Hubner, *Ha-Darom,* Nisan 5734; and R. M. Feinstein, *Le-Torah ve-Hora'ah,* no. 3, p. 7.

Rabbi Feinstein cautions that when egg *maẓah* is used for the morning meal, this repast must be completed early in the day before the time during which *ḥameẓ* may be consumed has elapsed. He points out that such procedure is necessary because Rema, *Oraḥ Ḥayyim* 462:4, records that use of egg *maẓah* is to be restricted to the sick and the elderly who are incapable of chewing ordinary *maẓah*. All others are not permitted to partake of egg *maẓah* during *Pesaḥ* or on *Erev Pesaḥ* after the fourth hour (Rema, *Oraḥ Ḥayyim* 444:1). The requirement that egg *maẓah* be eaten early in the day necessitates that the *Shabbat* services be held at an early hour in order to afford sufficient time for the Sabbath meal to be completed before the time has elapsed during which *ḥameẓ* may be eaten. Not cited by Rabbi Feinstein is the divergent opinion of *Arukh ha-Shulḥan* 444:5, who offers a different interpretation of Rema 444:1 and permits the use of egg *maẓah* later in the day as well.[5]

In opposition to this view, Rabbi Rosen objects to any use of egg *maẓah* on *Erev Pesaḥ*. Halakhah stipulates that only such *maẓah* which may be used for the fulfillment of the *miẓvah* of eating *maẓah* on Passover eve may not be eaten on *Erev Pesaḥ;* those who permit the eating of egg *maẓah* on *Erev Pesaḥ* do so because they maintain that egg *maẓah* cannot be used for the fulfillment of the *miẓvah* on Passover eve. Rabbi Rosen cites the opinion recorded in the Palestinian Talmud, *Pesaḥim* 2:4, which maintain that *maẓah* kneaded with liquids other than water may also be utilized on Passover eve. Furthermore, Rambam, *Hilkhot Ḥameẓ u-Maẓah* 6:5, rules that only *maẓah* kneaded with wine, oil or milk may not be used on Passover eve. *Maẓah* kneaded with eggs or fruit juice may, in Rambam's opinion, be used for fulfillment of the *miẓvah* of eating *maẓah* on the first night of Passover. Rabbi Rosen, therefore, rules that in accordance with these opinions, it would be forbidden to eat egg *maẓah* on *Erev Pesaḥ*.

III. *Mukẓah*

Another interesting point with regard to the laws of *Erev Pesaḥ* which occurs on *Shabbat* was raised by the late Rabbi Jacob Meskin in an article which appeared in the Nisan 5710 issue of *Ha-Pardes*. Food which may

---

5. *See also Shulḥan Arukh ha-Rav, Oraḥ Ḥayyim* 444:2-3; *Noda bi-Yehudah,* I, *Oraḥ Ḥayyim,* no. 21; and R. Moshe Binyamin Tomashoff, *Avnei Shoham,* III, no. 11. It should be noted that R. Feinstein's interpretation of Rema is consistent with the opinion of R. Akiva Eger as contained in a gloss on R. Ya'akov Emden's *Derekh ha-Ḥayyim* published in *Siddur Oẓar Yisra'el,* II, 958.

not be eaten on *Shabbat* is deemed *mukẓah* and may not be carried or moved from place to place on the Sabbath. Thus, after the fourth hour of *Erev Pesaḥ* which occurs on *Shabbat, ḥameẓ* is to be considered *mukẓah.* The *ḥameẓ* must be covered by a utensil or other covering and may not be moved. *Pri Megadim, Eshel Avraham* 444:1, declares that since *maẓah* may not be eaten on *Erev Pesaḥ,* the *maẓah* must be deemed to be *mukẓah* on *Shabbat* and may not be moved. Rabbi Meskin cites this authority and in accordance with this decision rules that Passover *maẓah* should not be touched on *Shabbat* which coincides with *Erev Pesaḥ.* This decision is apparently contrary to that of *Ḥazon Ish, Iggrot Ḥazon Ish,* I, no. 188, who advised that a well-wrapped *maẓah* be placed near the *ḥallah* for purposes of *leḥem mishneh.*[6]

Sale of Ḥameẓ by Tourists

The seven-hour time difference between the Eastern seaboard and Israel (which is reduced to six hours when daylight saving time is in effect) poses a problem with regard to the sale of *ḥameẓ* by the constantly increasing number of American Jews who seek to spend the Passover holiday in the Holy Land. Due to the time difference, both the commencement of the festival and the prohibition with regard to the retention of proprietary interest in *ḥameẓ* on the day preceding the festival occur many hours earlier than in the tourists' cities of origin.

A tourist finding himself in Israel, but whose possessions are in the United States, is confronted by a halakhic problem with regard to the disposal of his *ḥameẓ*. Is the prohibition with regard to the ownership of *ḥameẓ* a prohibition entirely contingent upon the locale in which the proprietor finds himself, i.e., the individual is forbidden to own *ḥameẓ* regardless of where such *ḥameẓ* may be during the period of time which he observes as *Pesaḥ,* or is the prohibition predicated upon the location of the *ḥameẓ,* banning the possession of *ḥameẓ* (regardless of where its owner may find himself) throughout the period of time during which *Pesaḥ* is observed in the locale in which the *ḥameẓ* is found? For the tourist finding himself in Israel, it is *Pesaḥ* a full seven hours before it becomes *Pesaḥ* in America, where his *ḥameẓ* is stored. If he is forbidden to own any *ḥameẓ,* regardless of its location, during the period that he observes as

6. See also R. Sternbuch, *Erev Peraḥ she-Ḥal be-Shabbat,* p. 5, note 5; R. Veltz, *Ḥok le-Yisra'el,* pp. 126–28; and R. Cohen, *Erev Pesaḥ she-Ḥal be-Shabbat,* pp. 44–45.

Pesaḥ, then it is incumbent upon him to dispose of his *ḥameẓ* in America a full seven hours prior to the time at which Jews in America are obligated to dispose of their *ḥameẓ*. A detailed analysis of this topic is to be found in Rabbi Moses Sternbuch's *Mo'adim u-Zemanim,* III, no. 269, sec. 4.[6a] Various opinions with regard to this question are quoted by *She'arim he-Meẓuyanim be-Halakhah* 113:1. Rabbinic authorities usually advise that care must be taken on both counts; no *ḥameẓ* should be owned by a Jew during the period which he observes as *Pesaḥ* (regardless of where the *ḥameẓ* may be found) and no *ḥameẓ* should be owned by a Jew during the period observed as *Pesaḥ* in the locale in which the *ḥameẓ* is stored.

In the normal course of events, a rabbi is authorized by his congregants to serve as an agent for the sale of *ḥameẓ* to a non-Jew. The rabbi then customarily disposes of the *ḥameẓ* on the day preceding *Pesaḥ* shortly before the hour at which ownership is forbidden. *Ḥameẓ* cannot be sold after the hour at which ownership is forbidden has passed. Thus the sale of *ḥameẓ* conducted by his local rabbi in the usual manner does not fulfill the needs of the tourist who spends *Pesaḥ* in Israel. In order to resolve the problem, the local rabbi may draw up a special bill of sale on behalf of his congregants in Israel and execute the transfer of their *ḥameẓ* at least seven hours prior to the specified time of sale in this country.

Alternatively, the tourist may choose to avail himself of the services of an Israeli rabbi for the sale of *ḥameẓ*. Since the specified time of sale in Israel is at the earlier hour, this course obviates the need for a special bill of sale. However, the latter solution poses a problem with regard to the repurchase of *ḥameẓ* at the conclusion of the festival. If it is the case that the prohibition is contingent upon the location of the *ḥameẓ* rather than upon the place in which the owner finds himself, then the tourist is not permitted to regain title to his *ḥameẓ* until after *Pesaḥ* has drawn to a close in America, seven hours after the conclusion of the festival in Israel. Furthermore, since in Israel the final day of the holiday is not observed, conclusion of *Pesaḥ* occurs more than a day earlier than in America. Customarily, the rabbi repurchases the *ḥameẓ* immediately following the conclusion of the holiday. May an American tourist avail himself of the services of an Israeli rabbi who will repurchase the *ḥameẓ* at a time prior to the hour at which the tourist is permitted to regain possession of the *ḥameẓ* which is located in America?

6a. See also *Ḥesed le-Avraham, Oraḥ Ḥayyim,* no. 35; R. Yitzchak Liebes, *No'am* (5729), XII; and R. Yeshayahu Epstein, *No'am* (5732), XV.

Rabbi Ephraim Yolles discusses this question in the Shevat-Adar 5733 issue of *Ha-Ma'or* and concludes that this practice is permissible. In the first place, Rabbi Yolles declares, one may assume that the Israeli rabbi stipulates that repossession of the *ḥameẓ* of his American clients should not become effective until after the conclusion of the festival in America. Moreover, citing *Taz, Oraḥ Ḥayyim* 448:6, Rabbi Yolles argues that such a stipulation, even if not expressly made, is a self-understood condition of the transaction. Secondly, the forms usually employed for the appointment of a rabbi as an agent for the sale of *ḥameẓ* do not expressly authorize him to repurchase the *ḥameẓ*. In the absence of such authorization, repurchase by the rabbi is not valid on behalf of his client unless it is in the latter's interest and meets with his approval. Since in the case at hand such repurchase is clearly not in the interest of the American tourist, the repurchase is not valid on his behalf. Thus, Rabbi Yolles concludes, there is no halakhic objection to the sale of a tourist's *ḥameẓ* by an Israeli rabbi. However, Rabbi Moses Feinstein's opinion, as cited in *Le-Torah ve-Hora'ah,* no. 1 (Chanukhah, 5735), pp. 14–15, is that the Israeli rabbi should repurchase the *ḥameẓ* of the tourist only after the eighth day of *Pesaḥ* has ended in America.

Baby Formula on Passover

In general, Halakhah requires that even infants not be fed any form of *ḥameẓ* (leaven) during the period of the Passover holiday. Problems arise in rare cases with regard to babies whose pediatricians have prescribed a specific formula containing an admixture of *ḥameẓ* and for whom, for medical reasons, it is not possible to substitute another. In light of the Gemara's declaration, *Yevamot* 114a, that depriving an infant of milk may endanger his life, there is no question that under such circumstances the child may be given the prescribed formula. However, apart from the prohibition against partaking of *ḥameẓ,* the very possession of such foodstuffs during Passover is forbidden. This prohibition is, of course, also suspended when danger to human life is involved, but only if no alternative can be devised. Is it possible for the parents, upon whom devolves the prohibition against owning *ḥameẓ,* to obviate transgression of this prohibition as it applies to the supplies of formula?

Magen Avraham, Oraḥ Ḥayyim 450:9 and 343:3, indicates that a child who must be fed *ḥameẓ* should be taken to the residence of a non-Jew and there be fed by the non-Jew, using the latter's own food. In the event that the child is too ill to be moved, *Magen Avraham* rules that the gentile may feed the child in the home of the parents, provided the food used in feeding the infant belongs to the gentile. The difficulties involved in such arrangements are obvious. Despite the attendant inconvenience, Rabbi Meir Goldberger, writing in the Nisan 5731 issue of *Ha-Ma'or,* states that no other procedure is permissible unless no gentile willing to perform this service can be found and lack of such food will result in actual danger to the child.

In an article appearing in the Adar 5731 issue of *Ha-Pardes,* Dr. Baruch Ness offers an interesting suggestion. The prohibition against possession of *ḥameẓ* during Passover applies only to *ḥameẓ* over which one enjoys proprietary ownership. Dr. Ness points out that it is possible to transfer ownership of the formula in question to the infant, who is of course a minor, thereby rendering the prohibition inoperative as far as the parents are concerned. Actual transfer of ownership can be accomplished by having an individual present a handkerchief (*sudar*) or other article of clothing to the father on behalf of the child in the presence of witnesses in exchange for the formula which thereby becomes the property of the child. Alternatively, this person may acquire title on behalf of the child by placing the formula in a container and lifting the container in his hands (*hagbahah*). It is further advised that the formula be placed in a particular closet, ownership of which is also transferred to the child by the act of sealing off the closet on behalf of the child, thereby transferring proprietorship of both the closet and its contents to the infant. The act of sealing the closet must also be done by an agent on behalf of the child, thereby effecting transfer of ownership from the father to the child.

A Responsum from behind the Iron Curtain

One of the most remarkable phenomena of our time is the extent to which Russian Jewry has succeeded in preserving its sense of identity despite decades of physical persecution and spiritual oppression. Fully cognizant of the deep meaning of the observance of *miẓvot,* the Communist regime has persistently placed obstacle after obstacle in the path of its Jewish nationals seeking to discharge their religious obligations. However, Russian Jews, in large numbers and often at great self-sacrifice, refuse to succumb to oppressive measures designed to stifle all meaningful forms of religious expression. For reasons which are at once religious, psychological and symbolic, the baking of *maẓot* for use on Passover has been a focal point of this struggle. Seemingly oblivious to the protestations and censure of democratic peoples throughout the world, the Soviet regime perennially seeks to hamper the preparation and distribution of *mazot*.

Although the restrictions surrounding the provision of *mazot* have received widespread attention only in the past few years, such harrassment is not of recent vintage. In *Or ha-Mizraḥ,* Tammuz 5731, there appears a hitherto unpublished responsum which is of more than passing historical interest. The manuscript, dated 1929, was authored by Rabbi Moshe Terashansky, who at the time served as rabbi of Kremenchug, one of the most prominent Jewish communities in the Ukraine. Although written well over forty years ago, the responsum is a reflection of much of what transpires today. In this document, the writer openly and candidly refers to malevolent "adversaries" who sought to interfere with ritual slaughter and had attempted to close the local synagogue and, in particular, he inveighs against the vexing impediments encountered in the baking of *mazot*.

The specific problem which Rabbi Terashansky discusses is the unavailability of flour ground in accordance with halakhic requirements. Wheat which comes into contact with any moisture may become *ḥamez* and hence unfit for use on Passover. Accordingly, *Oraḥ Ḥayyim* 453:4 stipulates that supervision must be provided at least during the grinding process in order to assure that the kernals do not become wet. Apparently, when this responsum was written it had already become impossible to arrange for such supervision in the U.S.S.R. Rabbi Terashansky's advice was sought with regard to the suggestion that, in light of the difficult circumstances, it might be possible to permit the use of ordinary flour even though the milling process then employed utilized water in separating the kernel from the husk. "Rinsing" of wheat for this purpose is permitted by the Gemara because the minimal contact with moisture entailed by this process, when properly performed, does not cause leavening. At a later period in Jewish history the practice was forbidden by the Ge'onim because they feared that knowledge of the precise nature of this art had become lost. Lack of expertise in the proper performance of this operation may readily cause the wheat to become *ḥamez*. The tentative proposal that this stringency be waived because of "dire necessity" is couched in poignant tones of anguish which cannot fail to arouse the reader's sympathy.

Rabbi Terashanasky responds that the questioner has either been inadvertently misled or intentionally deceived with regard to the milling process actually in use. In point of fact, Rabbi Terashansky claims, the process in use at the time required soaking of the kernels for a matter of hours.

This procedure would definitely have rendered the wheat unfit for Passover use under any circumstances. Rabbi Terashanasky adds that in his own community he had permitted the use of ordinary flour which had been ground in the surrounding villages without rabbinic supervision. Whereas commercial mills in the large cities employed more advanced methods necessitating soaking of the kernels, the villagers utilized a primitive, dry stone mill which would not, in the normal course of events, cause the grain or flour to become moist.

Despite the pathos in this communication, which reverberates from across the years and from behind the iron barriers, there is an element in the exchange which is most heartening. The document stands as eloquent testimony to the indomitable spirit of Russian Jewry and as an assurance that, whatever the obstacles, there will always be Jews to ask, Jews to respond, Jews to observe—Jews to affirm, together with the Psalmist, "I shall not die, but I shall live and proclaim the works of the Lord." (Ps. 118:17).

Shaving on the Intermediate Days of Festivals

This topic has been exhaustively discussed in the responsa literature over a period of centuries. An article authored by Rabbi Aaron Pinchik containing a useful summary of some of the material appears in the Tishri 5729 issue of *Or ha-Mizraḥ,* the 5729 edition of *No'am* and the 5729 edition of *Shanah be-Shanah*. Both *No'am* and *Shanah be-Shanah* are publications of the Heichal Shlomo Institute, and Rabbi Pinchik serves as editor of the latter annual. The complexities of this question necessitate a somewhat fuller analysis of the sources.

The prohibition against cutting one's hair during the intermediate days of the festival is derived from *Mo'ed Katan* 13b. The Mishnah permits cutting of hair during the intermediate days only in certain enumerated instances in which proper grooming prior to the holiday was precluded by circumstances beyond one's control. The Gemara explains that under ordinary circumstances all persons are restricted with regard to hair-cutting lest they neglect to cut their hair prior to the holiday.

The formulation of this statement by the Gemara, "lest he enter into the festival with a neglected appearance," would seem to imply that the prohibition against cutting the hair is rabbinic in origin, the edict having been legislated in order to enhance the dignity of the holiday by assuring that hair would be properly cut prior to the commencement of the festival.

Tosafot, however, are of the opinion that cutting of the hair constitutes an infraction of the biblical prohibition against "work" on the intermediate days of a festival. This position is adopted by *Tosafot* despite the general principle that "work" is permitted if directly connected with the holiday needs. Since a neat appearance is a holiday need, it would stand to reason that cutting of the hair be included in the category of such permitted activities. Nevertheless, the explanatory phrase "lest he enter into the festival with a neglected appearance" is interpreted by *Tosafot* as an explanation of why cutting the hair is not a permitted form of labor. According to this explanation, cutting the hair during the course of the festival itself cannot be deemed a holiday need because the hair should properly be cut prior to the holiday in honor of the oncoming festival. Therefore, in the opinion of *Tosafot,* cutting the hair during the intermediate days of the festival is biblically forbidden.

One authority, Rabbenu Tam, cited in *Tur, Oraḥ Ḥayyim* 531, maintains that the prohibition against cutting the hair is operative only if the hair has not been cut on the eve of the festival. Rabbenu Tam reasons that since the basis of the ban against this activity is "lest he enter into the festival with a neglected appearance," it follows that one who has not been remiss in this respect is not under restraint with regard to cutting the hair again on the intermediate days. Since Rabbenu Tam permits cutting the hair under these circumstances, it would appear that he does not consider this activity to be a form of "work" and hence deems the prohibition to be of rabbinic origin. *Tur* raises an objection against Rabbenu Tam's view on the basis of the previously cited Mishnah, *Mo'ed Katan* 13b, which specifically enumerates those exceptions where hair-cutting is permitted. According to Rabbenu Tam, there is yet another category of individuals permitted to cut their hair on the intermediate days of the festival—those who have already done so previously on the eve of the holiday. If so, queries *Tur,* why is this category not specifically included among those enumerated by the Mishnah? This question is particularly cogent since such an explanation is mentioned in a parallel case. Laundering is also forbidden on the intermediate days of the festival. In that case the Gemara, *Mo'ed Katan* 14a, specifically exempts an individual who has only one shirt because the garment, even if washed before the holiday, will again become soiled.

R. Ezekiel Landau, in his responsa, *Noda bi-Yehudah, Oraḥ Ḥayyim,* I, no. 13, endeavors to reinterpret Rabbenu Tam's position in a way which reconciles the latter's views with those of the authorities who allegedly dispute his position. Accepting the previously quoted explanation of *Tosafot,*

R. Landau explains that, according to Rabbenu Tam, hair-cutting constitutes forbidden "work" but, if not for rabbinic legislation, would be permissible by virtue of its necessity in fulfilling a holiday need. Rabbinic decree forbids what is otherwise permissible in order to promote cutting of hair prior to the festival "lest he enter into the festival with a neglected appearance." Once actually forbidden by the Sages, cutting of the hair can no longer be considered a holiday need and hence, in the final analysis, is included among the biblically forbidden categories of work. *Noda bi-Yehudah* adds that, according to Rabbenu Tam, if the hair has been cut immediately prior to the festival, there is no longer any need to cut the hair again during the festival because one who has indeed cut his hair prior to the festival does not require a second cutting within so short a period. For that individual, cutting of the hair cannot be deemed a holiday need. The result, *Noda bi-Yehudah* reasons, is that cutting of hair is prohibited to all individuals even according to Rabbenu Tam. Yet there is a crucial difference with regard to one who cut his hair prior to the holiday. If cutting the hair is prohibited only because of the "work" involved and not because of the superimposed rabbinic decree "lest he enter, etc.," the prohibition against cutting the hair will then be governed solely by the regulations applicable to work on the intermediate days. A poor laborer, lacking funds to buy provisions for the holiday, is permitted to perform such acts of "work" on the intermediate days of the festival. Hence it would be permissible to have a needy barber cut one's hair—but only if the hair has already been previously cut prior to the festival. If this was not done, the rabbinic edict "lest he enter into, etc.," becomes effective and cutting the hair is forbidden by rabbinic edict even in circumstances where "work" would otherwise be permitted. The explanation offered by *Noda bi-Yehudah* also resolves the previously mentioned difficulty raised by the *Tur*. Since, according to *Noda bi-Yehudah,* Rabbenu Tam intended to permit the cutting of hair for one who has already done so on the eve of the festival only through the employment of a needy barber, this category could not be included among those listed in the Mishnah because the ones so listed are not restricted in this manner. *Noda bi-Yehudah* maintains that there is complete unanimity of opinion between Rabbenu Tam and other authorities regarding the permissibility of hair-cutting and shaving by a needy barber if the client has also engaged in these preparations prior to the holiday.

R. Landau's lenient ruling with regard to shaving apparently gained wide acceptance in his own city of Prague. In volume II, *Oraḥ Ḥayyim,* no. 101, *Noda bi-Yehudah* reports that he caused the Jewish barbers of his city to take a solemn oath not to shave their clients with a razor, as this is prohibited by Leviticus 21:5. However, during the festivals many Jews, finding the Jewish barber shops closed, were wont surreptitiously to patronize gentile barbers. Of course these barbers did utilize razors as shaving implements. As documented in this responsum and in the one previous, no. 100, it was this breach in observance of Jewish law which *Noda bi-Yehudah* sought to repair by permitting Jewish barbers (at least those who were poor) to keep their establishments open during the intermediate days of the festival.

Noda bi-Yehudah's reputation was such that this innovating decision had far-reaching repercussions. R. Saul Loewenstamm of Amsterdam, to whom responsum 101 of volume II was addressed, speaks of *Noda bi-Yehudah* as the "wonder of the generation," and appeals to him to "repair the breach in the fence of the vineyard" by retracting this lenient ruling. Another interlocutor, to whom *Noda bi-Yehudah* replies in II, no. 99, bemoans the latter's decision, arguing that it is unwise to publicize this ruling, for "particularly in a wanton generation such as ours is it to be feared that sinners will stumble in many other areas if they see a leniency contrary to the *Shulḥan Arukh* and all later authorities." *Noda bi-Yehudah,* replies that his decision was originally rendered some "twelve or fifteen" years earlier and that at the time he concealed his true reasons and informed the individual who had consulted him regarding this matter that the considerations prompting a permissive ruling applied solely to the one case which had been brought to his attention. Interestingly, *Noda bi-Yehudah* adds that the motive which prompted this circumspect attitude was not trepidation with regard to halakhic innovation, but recognition of the fact that in other cities many persons had adopted the practice of shaving with razors. Apparently, the same people who usually shaved with a razor refrained from shaving on the intermediate days of the festival. Rabbi Landau, knowing that if they were to shave on the festival they would do so with razors, wished to preserve them from this transgression, at least during these holiday periods. *Noda bi-Yehudah* adds that in preparing his manuscripts for publication his original intention had been to suppress the responsum in question, but that in reconsidering the matter he became determined to publicize this decision. In a very intriguing comment *Noda bi-Yehudah* adds that the reasons prompting this decision must remain "concealed in my heart." Surprisingly, in his comments on this statement of *Noda bi-Yehudah,* Rabbi Pinchik does not refer to *Teshuvot Ḥatam Sofer, Oraḥ Ḥayyim,* no. 144. In this responsum Rabbi Moses Sofer declares, "I am a talebearer and will reveal the secret," and proceeds to show precisely what line of reasoning it was that prompted *Noda bi-Yehudah*'s decision, and at the same time *Ḥatam Sofer* indicates his own divergent view. Respecting *Noda bi-Yehudah*'s desire that the explanation remain *in pectore,* we will not enter into detailed discussion of this controversy.

Apart from this disagreement, *Ḥatam Sofer* takes issue with the main thesis of *Noda bi-Yehudah's* responsum. He quotes *Binyan Ari'el,* a commentary on *Mo'ed Katan* authored by R. Saul of Amsterdam, in disposing of the contention that shaving constitutes a forbidden form of "work." A similar prohibition against hair-cutting was placed on *kohanim* during their period of service in the Temple in order to prompt them to cut their hair prior to beginning their period of service. Rabbi Sofer argues that it would follow, on the basis of *Noda bi-Yehudah*'s reasoning, that a *kohen* who did cut his hair immediately prior to his period of service should not be restricted in any way during his period of service. Considerations based upon prohibited "work" are not applicable in light of the fact that there was no restriction againt "work" placed upon *kohanim* performing the Temple service. Yet no exception from this ban is recorded in the case of a *kohen* who cuts his hair prior to beginning his period of service.

Sedei Ḥemed, Ma'arekhet Ḥol ha-Mo'ed, cites sources which mention that at a subsequent date *Noda bi-Yehudah* retracted his lenient ruling. These claims are rejected as spurious by *Sedei Ḥemed* in light of the responsa printed in volume II of *Noda bi-Yehudah.* This volume was posthumously published by the author's son and it is unthinkable that the latter would have published as authoritative decisions and opinions which his father had retracted. *Sedei Ḥemed* does, however, cite a number of authorities in addition to *Ḥatam Sofer* who disagree with the lenient ruling of *Noda bi-Yehudah.*

The problem regarding shaving the beard during the intermediate days of a festival is somewhat modified in our day by the fact that virtually all men who shave do so each day. One objection raised by the *Tur* against the view of Rabbenu Tam, who permits cutting of the hair by one who has already done so before the festival, is based upon *Mo'ed Katan* 14a. The Gemara declares that hair-cutting cannot be permitted on the festival itself even if there existed valid reason for not having cut the hair prior to the festival, e.g., preoccupation with seeking a lost object. The explanation given is that as long as one's personal preoccupation is not public knowledge onlookers will not be aware of such reasons and will themselves become lax in observance of this law. The objection advanced by the *Tur* is that even if the person has indeed cut his hair on the eve of the festival, this would be unknown to onlookers seeing him with hair fully cut on the intermediate days. Hence cutting of the hair should always be forbidden according to the grounds advanced in the above-mentioned talmudic citation.

Rabbi Moses Feinstein, *Iggrot Mosheh, Oraḥ Ḥayyim,* I, no. 163, argues that in our times this objection does not apply since it is common knowledge that almost all men who do not sport beards shave daily and certainly shave on the eve of a festival. Therefore, in addition to the reasons advanced by *Noda bi-Yehudah,* there are yet other grounds upon which this practice may be permitted.

The other objection raised by the *Tur,* namely, that this exception to the general prohibition against cutting the hair on the intermediate days of a festival is not specifically mentioned in the Mishnah, is regarded by Rabbi Feinstein as presently inapplicable. A country or geographical area in which so large a number of people are habitually clean-shaven was unheard of in bygone days, and therefore there was no need to take such a situation into account. There remains, however, one possible objection. Both *Noda bi-Yehudah* and another source, *Naḥal Eshkol,* state that where shaving is not halakhically permitted such an act constitutes a form of "work" forbidden on the holiday. Although there would have been no reason for the Sages not to have permitted shaving in such circumstances as now prevail among most Jews, nevertheless this category did not present itself for their consideration, as can be inferred from the fact that no mention is made of an exception under conditions such as ours. If not specifically sanctioned, might not such acts be forbidden as a form of "work"? Rabbi Feinstein, disagreeing with these two authorities, argues that shaving constitutes one of the needs of the festival and cannot be banned as a form of "work." In a final observation, he adds that his practice is to permit shaving on the intermediate days of the festival only in cases of extreme need or great discomfort, but that no fault can be found with those who do so merely for purposes of a neat appearance.

Temporary Residents in Israel and Yom Tov Sheni

What was once a novel and infrequent problem is at present a matter which affects countless thousands of travelers at one time or another.

Today it is not at all rare for Jews from all corners of the globe to spend *Yom Tov* in Israel. Happily, it is also becoming increasingly common for students to devote a year to study in Israel. The magnetic attraction of Israel and of the Torah of *Ereẓ Yisra'el* is such that this year is often extended to two or three. Visitors to Israel find themselves faced by the question of observing the second day of the holiday while their Israeli hosts do not. A somewhat more complex question is posed by students spending a prolonged period of time in Israel. At what point, if at all, are they absolved from observance of *Yom Tov Sheni?* In the Nisan 5731 issue of *Or ha-Mizraḥ*, Rabbi Judah Gershuni examines this old, if newly relevant, question and while not presenting any innovative opinion, assembles the various halakhic views regarding this matter.

Although in terms of normative Halakhah tourists finding themselves in Israel over *Yom Tov* must observe the second day of the holiday as they do in their own homes, this practice is by no means universally agreed upon. Some of the divergent views which have been advanced are intriguing. One noted authority, R. Zevi Ashkenazi, *Ḥakham Ẓevi,* no. 167, declares that visitors to Israel are not required to observe the second day of the festivals and moreover, they are forbidden to do so. The argument for observance of the second day of *Yom Tov* in Israel is predicated upon the principle that a person away from home must continue to observe the more stringent practices of his place of domicile. However, observance of an extra day of *Yom Tov,* argues *Ḥakham Ẓevi,* involves a leniency no less than a stringency; observance of an additional day of *Yom Tov* is not permitted because it constitutes violation of the prohibition "Thou shalt not add thereto." On the basis of *Rosh Hashanah* 28b, numerous authorities conclude that, under certain conditions, sleeping in a *sukkah* on *Shemini Aẓeret* is an infraction of "Thou shalt not add to the word which I command you" (Deut. 4:2) and is a punishable offense.

In support of this view, Rabbi Yechiel Michal Tucatzinsky, *Sefer Ereẓ Yisra'el,* chap. 7, sec. 6, cites a further argument originally advanced by R. Shmuel Salant, the renowned nineteenth-century rabbinic personality who served as Chief Rabbi of Jerusalem for many decades. R. Shmuel Salant argued that, clearly, in days when the New Moon was proclaimed each month by the *Bet Din,* a visitor to Israel was exempt from observance of the second day of the festival. During that period anyone who was informed of the correct date had no need to observe the second day. The rabbinic decree accompanying the establishment of a fixed calendar was designed to preserve intact the situation which prevailed at that time with regard to *Yom Tov Sheni.* R. Shmuel Salant concludes that since in olden times visitors did not observe *Yom Tov Sheni* there is no reason for them to do so now.[7] There is some question with regard to whether R. Salant actually permitted tourists to perform acts normally forbidden on the second day of the festival or whether his ruling was limited to a directive that they recite weekday prayers rather than those of the Holy Day.

Normative Halakhah, however, follows the opinion of R. Joseph Karo, as recorded in his responsa collection, *Avkat Rokhel,* no. 26, and of *Pe'at ha-Shulḥan, Hilkhot Ereẓ Yisra'el* 2:15, who maintain that tourists are indeed obliged to observe the second day of *Yom Tov.* A further discussion of the basis of this final determination has been presented in *No'am* (5719), II, by Rabbi Yisraẹl Ze'ev Minzberg and Rabbi Nachum Shechter.

The problem with regard to students spending an extended period of time in Israel is somewhat more involved. Ordinarily, a person finding himself in Israel is deemed to be a resident of the Diaspora for purposes of *Yom Tov Sheni* unless he has no intention of returning to his original home. Similarly, a resident of Israel who leaves his homeland observes only one day of *Yom Tov* so long as he intends to return to Israel. R. Yechiel Michal Epstein, *Arukh ha-Shulḥan* 496:5, limits this period to one year. A person who does not plan to return to his home within a year is considered by *Arukh ha-Shulḥan* to be included in the category of those who have established residence in Israel. However, Rabbi Zevi Pesach Frank, *Har Ẓevi, Oraḥ Ḥayyim,* II, no. 78, notes that many Sephardic scholars disagree with *Arukh ha-Shulḥan* and rule that in light of the questionable nature of their status persons finding themselves in such a situation should adopt the stringencies of both Israel and the Diaspora, i.e., they are not permitted to perform actions forbidden on *Yom Tov* but must don *tefillin* and recite the weekday prayers.[8]

Sha'arei Teshuvah, Hilkhot Yom Tov 496:3, cites authorities who maintain that unmarried students, regardless of the length of their stay, should follow the practice of residents of Israel. Since they have no family responsibilities and no place of employment, their place of study is considered to be their abode. Other authorities not cited by Rabbi Gershuni,

---

7. See also Rabbi M. Lewittes, *Ha-Darom,* Nisan 5723.

8. See also *Iggrot Mosheh, Oraḥ Ḥayyim,* II, no. 101; R. Ovadiah Yosef, *Or Torah,* Iyar 5734, *Moriah,* Tevet 5735, and *Yabi'a Omer,* VI, *Oraḥ Ḥayyim,* no. 40.

among them *Pri Ḥadash, Oraḥ Ḥayyim* 468:4, and several commentaries on the *Levush, Oraḥ Ḥayyim* 496, declare that only those who plan to remain in Israel permanently may cease to observe *Yom Tov Sheni.*

Yom Tov Sheni

Abrogation of the second and last days of the various festivals was one of the earliest innovations of the German founders of the Reform movement. The primary contention advanced was that the observance of *Yom Tov Sheni* was an anachronism, having long since outlasted its original purpose. Historically, the institution of *Yom Tov Sheni* arose before holidays were observed on the basis of a permanently established calendar. The precise days on which festivals are to be observed depend upon the day proclaimed as *Rosh Ḥodesh.* Each month contains either twenty-nine or thirty days. In times gone by the *Bet Din* proclaimed the beginning of a new month on the basis of the testimony of witnesses who had actually sighted the new moon. The inauguration of a new month invariably took place on either the thirtieth or thirty-first day following the previous *Rosh Ḥodesh.* Thereafter messengers were dispatched to inform far-flung communities that a new month had begun. Communities too distant to be reached prior to the advent of the festival had no means of ascertaining whether the previous month was of twenty-nine or thirty days' duration. Thus they were always confronted by the possibility of an error of one day with regard to determination of the correct day of the month. Hence the observance of a second day was necessary in order to guarantee proper observance of the Holy Day. With the lapse of sanctification of the New Moon each month by an act of *Bet Din,* and the promulgation of a calendrical system by Hillel the Second, such errors can no longer occur. Since there is no longer any question with regard to the exact day of the month, runs the argument, there is no cogent reason for retaining the second day of *Yom Tov.* This contention was sharply rejected by nineteenth-century halakhic authorities, whose views were publicized in the periodical literature of the day. The halakhic ramifications of the issue are exhaustively discussed in *Teshuvot ha-Ge'onim,* no. 1, and by Rabbi Isaac Baer Bamberger, *Yad ha-Levi,* no. 99.[9]

---

9. See also *Meshekh Ḥokhmah, Parashat Bo* (Warsaw, 5644), pp. 47 f.; R. Ya'akov Ettlinger, *Shomer Zion ha-Ne'eman,* no. 177; *Iggrot Soferim,* ed. Solomon Schreiber (Vienna, Budapest, 5693), sec. 2, no. 63, pp. 63–64; and R. Aaron David Deutsch, *Goran David* (Paks, 5645), no. 41.

Since 1933 repeated proposals have been made within the Conservative movement in this country to drop the observance of the second days of festivals. Recently the Law Committee of the Rabbinical Assembly, rather than either affirm the sanctity of *Yom Tov Sheni* or abrogate its observance, adopted the curious position that the observance of the second and last days of festivals is to be optional at the discretion of local congregations. The various "responsa," both pro and con, considered by this body have been published in the Winter 1970 issue of *Conservative Judaism.* A review of this material would not ordinarily be presented in these pages, particularly since a recent article, "The Second Days" by Rabbi Norman Lamm, *Chavrusa,* June 1969, contains an excellent formulation of the Orthodox response to the Conservative position.

We should, however, take note of two salient points which emerge from the discussions included in this issue of *Conservative Judaism.* First, attention should be drawn to the intense opposition to this innovation expressed by some members of the Law Committee and other Conservative leaders. It is heartening to observe that this opposition displays a sensitivity to, and an understanding of, basic Jewish spiritual values. Thus, a Conservative spokesman, arguing for the continued observance of *Yom Tov Sheni,* emphasizes the importance of preserving the centuries-old unity of *Klal Yisra'el* and shows a deep appreciation of the concept of *galut* and spiritual exile and of our consequent need for "a permanent reminder of the spiritual superiority of *Ereẓ Yisra'el* in Jewish life" (p. 39). The same author incisively underscores the practical realities of Jewish religious life on this continent and asserts, "The formidable challenge we face is not to the second day of *Yom Tov,* but to the idea of holy days in general. In the struggle to maintain the second day we are fighting the battle of *Yom Tov* in the Diaspora" (p. 42).

Secondly, it is one matter to bemoan the strictures of Halakhah as being excessively demanding or to advocate concessions to the spirit of the times. It is quite another thing to hallow the compromise by clothing it in the garb of normative Halakhah and to crown the results with the extravagant declaration that "the second day is *halakhically indefensible*" (p. 32). It is this conceit which provokes one to recoil with the feeling of "*Ha-gam likhbosh et ha-malkah immi ba-bayit*—Will he even force the queen before me in the house!" The discussion, which is presented in the framework of halakhic dialectic, makes use of invalid reasoning in order to substantiate false conclusions based upon erroneous premises and in so doing it becomes a travesty of the very process it seeks to employ. One or two examples will suffice.

A brief paragraph on page 29 reads: "Actually the medieval Polish scholar, Moses Isserles, (sixteenth century) . . . pointed out that where the reason for an enactment (*gezeirah*) is no longer operative, the enactment itself is nullified. If this is true with a *gezeirah* it is even more so with a *minhag,* and *Yom Tov Sheni* is only a *minhag,* as Maimonides has made clear."

Actually, Rambam states exactly the opposite and does so with the utmost clarity. In *Hilkhot Kiddush ha-Ḥodesh* 5:5, Rambam unequivocally terms *Yom Tov Sheni* a rabbinic edict. In specific reference to the observance of the second day he states, "however, it is an edict of the Sages [*takkanat ḥakhamim*] that they observe the custom of their fathers which is in their hands.[10] In the section immediately following Rambam reiterates, "Hence the second day of *Yom Tov,* which we observe in the Diaspora in our day, is *mi-divrei soferim* who ordained this." Every student of Rambam is well aware of his usage of the term *divrei soferim* as a synonym for "rabbinic decree."

In support of the statement "where the reason for an enactment is no longer operative the enactment itself is nullified," the authors, in a footnote, give as their source *Shulḥan Arukh, Oraḥ Ḥayyim* 339:3. The citation as presented is misleading and incomplete. In the statement to which reference is made, the substantive reason given by Rema is based upon a totally different principle. The comment cited is carefully presented as "*yesh omrim*", a minority view listed only as a secondary consideration. Indeed, the preponderance of authoritative halakhic opinion is that rabbinic decrees remain in force until formally annulled by a *Bet Din* "greater in wisdom and number" even when the original considerations no longer apply. Furthermore, in instances—such as *Yom Tov Sheni*—where the enactment is for purposes of erecting "a fence around the Torah" in order to prevent transgression of a biblical prohibition, Rambam, *Hilkhot Mamrim* 2:3, declares that even if the original reasons are no longer valid the decree cannot be revoked even by a *Bet Din* "greater in wisdom and number."

The authors' error is further compounded by their conclusion that "if this is true with a *gezeirah* it is even more so with a *minhag* . . ." It

10. Similar unequivocal statements declaring *Yom Tov Sheni* to be an edict of the Sages are contained in the commentaries of *Shitah Mekubeẓet, Beiẓah* 4b and Ran, *Sukkah* 44b; see also the comments of the late *Brisker Rav, Ḥidushei Maran Riz ha-Levi* (Jerusalem, 5723), *Hilkhot Berakhot* 11:16.

remains for a Reform spokesman, whose observations are included in the same publication, to note, "the fact that the second day is 'only' a *minhag* does not invalidate its religious significance. It may even enhance it" (p. 53). Apparently neither the authors nor the critic are aware of the provision of *Yoreh De'ah* 214:2 that if a practice be accepted as a "fence" to prevent transgression of a biblical ordinance it is to be deemed a vow of a category which, as stated in *Yoreh De'ah* 228:28, cannot be annulled. Hence a mere *minhag* under such circumstances acquires the status of an irrevocable vow. The manifold errors in this short paragraph call to mind the popular joke concerning the mispelling of the two-letter Hebrew word *Noaḥ* with seven mistakes.

Elsewhere in the same paper we are informed: "the second day, unlike the first, has no *inherent* holiness, and our approach to it may take into consideration local needs, local custom and local sensitivity. This might almost lead to the inference that each congregation is talmudically entitled to deal with the second day of *Yom Tov* independently. . . ." (p. 27).

This remarkable conclusion is deduced from an incident recorded in *Pesaḥim* 51b. R. Safra, who, as *Tosafot* explains, lived in an area where only one day of *Yom Tov* was observed because it was accessible to messengers of the *Bet Din* was visiting in a locale which observed two days of *Yom Tov*. The Talmud establishes the principle that in such circumstances the visitor is obliged to observe two days in order to prevent quarrel and dissension. R. Safra asked a colleague whether he might work on the second day of *Yom Tov* in an uninhabited area where nobody could possibly witness his actions and hence there was no reason to fear that dissension might arise. The reply was in the affirmative. It is on the basis of this Gemara that we are told, "The obvious inference is that the second day, unlike the first, has no *inherent holiness*." That this conclusion is not at all "obvious" goes without saying. The fact that *Yom Tov Sheni* was ordained for the Diaspora, and not for the Land of Israel and its environs, certainly does not mean that "each congregation is talmudically entitled to deal with the second day of *Yom Tov* independently."

That a halakhic framework be utilized to camouflage reforms which obviously run counter to the basic principles of that Halakhah is lamentable. That inaccurate scholarship and specious reasoning be employed in those endeavors is an affront to intellectual integrity.

We, of course, are certain that *Yom Tov Sheni* will not be abrogated before the ingathering of the exiles. It is perhaps reassuring to note that even the Messiah will fail to be impressed by the pilpulism of Conservative "halakhists." A short note in the Tammuz 5729 issue of *Ha-Ma'or* draws the reader's attention to a statement in the commentary of the Radbaz on Rambam's *Hilkhot Nezirut* 4:11 to the effect that the Messiah himself, while in the *golah*, will observe *Yom Tov Sheni!*[11]

11. See also *Ḥatam Sofer, Beiẓah* 4b.

CHAPTER III

The Synagogue

Not only do you receive the Divine Presence in the synagogue but you depart therefrom laden with blessings.

DEVARIM RABBAH VII, 2.

It is popularly assumed that the synagogue emerged as a communal institution only subsequent to the destruction of the Temple. It is quite true that the synagogue is often referred to as a *mikdash me'at,* a miniature Temple, but such reference does not connote that the synagogue is merely a replica of, or a replacement for, the Temple which once stood in Jerusalem. Prayer does, indeed, serve as a substitute for the sacrificial order—"Let our lips compensate for bullocks" (Hos. 14:3)—and the formal order of prayer followed today is patterned after the sacrificial ritual. However, prayer constitutes a *mizvah* in and of itself, regardless of whether or not sacrifices are concomitantly offered in the Temple.

Prayer, fundamentally, is an expression of man's dependence upon God; communal prayer is an acknowledgment of the dependence of society as well as of the dependence of the individual. Both individually and collectively, men have expressed themselves in prayer to God since time immemorial. One may readily assume that even in antiquity people gathered together in specially designated places for purposes of communal prayer. Sacrificial offerings certainly did not obviate the necessity for prayer. In fact, the Mishnah, in several instances (*Yoma* VII:1 and *Sotah* VII:7–8), makes specific references to a synagogue which existed within the confines of the Temple itself. Priests and Levites who participated in the Temple ritual, as well as Israelites who brought offerings, had need of a synagogue in which to offer prayer and, accordingly, a synagogue was erected on the Temple Mount in order to accommodate their needs. The author of the Jerusalem Targum certainly viewed the synagogue as being ancient in origin. This Aramaic translation of the Bible, dating from the tannaitic period, speaks of the existence of synagogues as early as the time of Moses (Exod. 18:20 and I Chron. 16:39).

In their discussion of matters pertaining to the sanctity of the synagogue, rabbinic scholars view the laws and regulations pertaining to the Temple as the paradigm from which may be derived *halakhot* applicable to the "miniature Temple," i.e., the synagogue. Both are devoted to divine service: the Temple is consecrated to sacrificial service; the synagogue is dedicated to "service of the heart." Both the Temple and the synagogue derive their sanctity from the service for which they are utilized. Noteworthy is the opinion of *Mordekhai, Megillah* 28a, who equates the sanctity of the synagogue with that of the Temple and asserts that both are biblical in nature. It has been suggested that this is the position of Maimonides as well.[1] In his *Sefer ha-Mizvot,* negative precept 65, Maimonides states, "[We are commanded] not to destroy the Temple, synagogues, or houses of study . . . for it is stated, 'You shall surely destroy all the places wherein the nations . . . served their gods . . . you shall not do so unto the Lord, your God' (Deut. 12:2–4)." According to Maimonides, the Bible legislates against desecration of the synagogue. In doing so, the Bible itself ordains the sanctity of the synagogue.

In our own day, no less than in past generations, rabbinic authorities are zealous in their endeavors to preserve inviolate the sanctity of the synagogue. They recognize that the very edifice, as well as the rituals performed therein are imbued with holiness. Accordingly, every question pertaining to the synagogue is viewed with the utmost gravity. At stake is not simply a matter of ritual law but the preservation of a sanctity of the highest order.

Apartments over a Synagogue

Characteristic of the contemporary urban scene is the proliferation of high-rise apartment dwellings of skyscraper proportions. The scarcity of potential construction sites in metropolitan areas forces real estate de-

1. Rabbi David Ochs, in a responsum included in *The Sanctity of the Synagogue,* ed. Baruch Litvin (New York, 1959), pp. 179–80. See also R. Raphael Silber, *Marpe la-Nefesh,* I, no. 45. Cf., however, R. Chaim Halberstam, *Divrei Ḥayyim,* I, no. 3.

velopers to build the maximum number of stories on available lots. The exorbitant price of land, coupled with rising construction costs, presents a formidable financial obstacle to metropolitan residents seeking to erect new houses of worship and educational facilities. As one means of ameliorating the situation, it has been proposed that schools and houses of worship be constructed on the ground floor with apartment units on higher levels. Proceeds derived from the sale of air rights for development purposes serve to defray the construction costs of these communal institutions.

There are, however, a number of halakhic considerations which call into question the propriety of such an arrangement. The very erection of an edifice towering above the synagogue presents a problem since *Shulḥan Arukh, Oraḥ Ḥayyim* 150:2, records that a synagogue should be built upon the most elevated site in the city and that no dwelling should rise higher than the synagogue structure. Rema, however, notes that an exception may be made in case of need or in face of a government edict forbidding the preferred mode of construction.

The construction of apartment dwellings above the synagogue proper poses a more serious problem. *Oraḥ Ḥayyim* 151:12 rules that it is forbidden to sleep upon the roof of a synagogue and expresses doubt with regard to the propriety of utilizing the roof for secular purposes. *Mordekhai, Shabbat* 1:228, quoting Maharam of Rothenburg, asserts unequivocally that the roof of a synagogue is imbued with sanctity and should not be used for mundane pursuits, just as the roof of the Temple was sacred and could not be profaned by such use. There is also the well-known autobiographical comment of *Taz, Oraḥ Ḥayyim* 151:4, in which that authority recalls, "In my younger years I dwelt with my family in Cracow in my house of study, which was above the synagogue; I was greatly punished through the death of my children and I attributed it to this fact." These sources notwithstanding, the construction of dwellings above a synagogue is not uncommon. In an article published in the Tishri 5732 issue of *Ha-Darom,* Rabbi Samuel Hubner analyzes the various factors involved and cites the following authorities and their reasons for affirming this practice:[2]

1. Chida, *Ḥayyim Sha'al, Oraḥ Ḥayyim,* no. 56, draws a sharp distinction between a roof and an attic or upper story. Chida argues that early references to restrictions upon the use of the synagogue carefully employ

2. See also R. Yitzchak Ya'akov Weisz, *Minḥat Yiẓḥak,* II, no. 48, and III, no. 120.

the term "roof" rather than "attic." Unseemly use of an exposed roof of a synagogue in public view constitutes disrespectful behavior vis-à-vis the synagogue; the selfsame activity taking place in the privacy of a walled enclosure does not constitute unseemly conduct. This distinction is also drawn by *Mishneh Berurah, Bi'ur Halakhah* 151.

2. In the same discussion, Chida cites a responsum by Rambam, *Pe'er ha-Dor,* no. 74, in which the latter states that the prohibition against sleeping on a synagogue roof is limited to the section of the roof or attic directly above the Ark. According to Rambam, only that section is deemed to be imbued with a sanctity analagous to that of the Temple site. On the basis of this opinion, which is accepted as authoritative by *Mishneh Berurah* 151:40, apartments above a synagogue may be used for dwelling purposes provided care is taken not to place the beds directly above the Ark. Some scholars maintain that even this limitation applies solely to the story directly above the Ark but not to higher floors.

3. *Maharit, II, Yoreh De'ah,* no. 4, and *Ẓelaḥ, Pesaḥim* 86a, rule that the roof of a synagogue is sacred only if the roof opens directly into the synagogue. A roof lacking such an aperture does not acquire the sanctity of a synagogue and may therefore be used for secular purposes.

4. *Taz, Oraḥ Ḥayyim* 151:4, argues that apartments above a synagogue may be used for dwelling purposes provided that both the synagogue and the apartments are erected simultaneously. Under such circumstances the synagogue roof is originally intended to serve as the floor of the apartment rising above the synagogue and hence the roof never acquires the sanctity of the synagogue structure. Nevertheless, concludes *Taz,* the synagogue may not be demeaned by utilizing the upper stories for activities such as idol worship or storage of waste.

5. The Sages recognized that since Torah scholars "live" in the house of study, spending the major portion of their days and nights therein, the house of study is in effect their domicile. Hence, Rema, *Oraḥ Ḥayyim* 151:1, rules that it is permissible to sleep in a house of study. *Eshel Avraham, Oraḥ Ḥayyim* 151:12, concludes that since one may sleep in the house of study itself, *a fortiori* it is permissible to sleep upon the roof above it. Accordingly, there is no objection to the construction of apartment dwellings above the synagogue, provided that it is stipulated at the time of construction that the sanctity of the edifice be that of a house of study.

6. *Divrei Ḥayyim,* I, no. 3, rules that synagogue roofs have no intrinsic sanctity and may be used for secular purposes.

Rabbi Hubner concludes that the serious financial loss involved in rejecting the proposal for the use of air rights above the synagogue in order to construct apartment units constitutes a "grave need" and hence the lenient opinions may be followed.

Prayer from the Bimah

Traditional synagogue architecture provides for a table or stand situated in the center of the sanctuary to be used for the Reading of the Law and for a separate reader's stand located in the front of the synagogue for use by the reader. Recurrent acoustical problems have led many congregations to consider positioning the reader or cantor on the *bimah* in the center of the synagogue in order to increase audibility. Responsa dealing with the permissibility of this question are examined by Rabbi Moshe Dov Welner, the Chief Rabbi of Ashkelon, in the Ḥeshvan-Kislev and Tevet-Adar 5732 issues of *Moriah*.[3]

The principal objection to this innovation is based, not upon insistence that the reader station himself within a specific area of the sanctuary, but rather upon the fact that the table or stand from which the Torah is read is commonly placed upon a *bimah,* or platform, which rises above the surrounding floor. *Magen Avraham, Oraḥ Ḥayyim* 90:3, notes that in previous times synagogues were designed so that the reader's stand was placed at the lowest point in the sanctuary with the worshippers' pews rising on an incline behind the reader. This feature of synagogue architecture, still retained in some European-style edifices, declares *Magen Avraham,* is designed to give literal expression to the sentiments recorded by the Psalmist, "From the depths have I called upon You" (Ps. 130:1). It is this custom which is the source of the talmudic idiom which speaks of the reader as "*descending* before the reader's stand." (See, however, *Ma'adanei Yom Tov, Berakhot* 10:8.) The rationale advanced by *Magen Avraham* is clearly applicable to individual worshippers as well. Yet the custom of standing in a low spot while engaged in prayer is limited to the reader alone. The custom arose in this form, explains *Ketav Sofer, Oraḥ Ḥayyim,* no. 19, because it is impossible to station all worshippers in a low area. Height and depth are relative concepts; if all pews were to be lowered, the result would be

3. See also *Minḥat Yiẓḥak,* III, no. 8; and R. Moses Feinstein, *Iggrot Mosheh, Oraḥ Ḥayyim,* II, no. 28.

a level area. The reader was singled out and assigned the low position because he serves as the representative of the entire congregation.

Ketav Sofer draws a sharp distinction between stationing the reader in a depressed area, a practice which has largely fallen into disuse, and the innovative positioning of the reader upon an elevated structure. The Gemara, *Berakhot* 10b, declares: "One should not stand on a high spot and pray, but rather one should stand on a low spot and pray." *Ketav Sofer* asserts that praying on a low spot is merely a commendable practice preferable to engaging in prayer while standing on a level surface, but that praying from an elevated position is forbidden. Prayer "from the depths" is a manifestation of humility and, while not strictly required, is to be commended; prayer while in a posture of elevation is a sign of arrogance and as such is to be eschewed. "One should not stand on a high spot and pray" is to be understood as a normative prohibition, whereas "one should stand on a low spot and pray" is advocated as an act of piety.

Mikhtav Sofer, II, nos. 1 and 2, presents kabbalistic reasons for various aspects of synagogue design. According to his explanation, the reader's stand symbolizes the golden altar, which was located within the Holy of Holies in front of the Ark. The *kohen* performed his duties standing on the ground before the altar. Hence, in the synagogue, which is a "miniature Temple," the proper location for the reader's stand is in the front of the synagogue with the reader stationed no higher than floor level.

However, may synagogues beset by acoustical difficulties disregard these considerations? *Sukkah* 50b relates that Alexandria boasted a synagogue of unparalled proportions which accommodated myriads of people. In a synagogue of such tremendous size, it is quite understandable that the reader could not be heard. In an attempt to ameliorate this situation, there was constructed "a platform of wood in the center and the sexton of the assembly stood upon it with flags in his hands. When the time came to respond 'Amen,' he raised the flag and all the people answered 'Amen.'" The sole innovation seems to have been the placing of the sexton in a central, elevated location with flags to serve as signals. Although the reader's voice was not at all audible to vast numbers of worshippers, no attempt was made to rectify the situation by stationing the reader upon the raised *bimah* rather than in his traditional position at the front of the synagogue.

There is, however, one authority who does sanction this practice. Referring to the question of having the reader stand in an elevated location, *Avudraham* writes, "This custom is good, for otherwise they would not hear on account of the multitudes which assemble in the synagogue." Rabbi Welner notes that this permissive ruling applies only to situations in which it is otherwise impossible to hear the reader. It should also be noted that Rambam, *Hilkhot Tefilah* 5:7, declares that a raised platform, either enclosed by a railing or measuring four ells by four ells in area, is considered to be an independent and separate area and is not deemed to be a "high place."

Another factor enters into the resolution of this question in cases where the congregants seek to change the already established position of the reader from the front of the synagogue to the *bimah*. Rabbi Waldenberg, *Ẓiẓ Eli'ezer,* X, no. 22, contends that the principle governing this situation may be found in the Jerusalem Talmud, *Shabbat* 12:3, which records that the boards used in the walls surrounding the Tabernacle were not permitted to be transferred from one position to another. Even inanimate objects are endowed by Halakhah with rights and prerogatives with regard to their utilization in the performance of *miẓvot*. Therefore, argues Rabbi Waldenberg, once the reader has been stationed at the lectern in front of the synagogue, his position may not be shifted to the *bimah*.

Removal of Torah Scrolls

Communal services are usually held on a regular basis in synagogues which permanently house Torah scrolls. Hence on Sabbaths, Holy Days, Mondays and Thursdays, etc., when the reading of the Torah constitutes an integral part of the service, the Torah scroll is simply removed from the Ark and replaced after the reading is concluded. Ordinarily, there is no need to remove the scroll from the building, or even the room, in which it reposes permanently. However, situations do arise in which it is necessary or desirable to hold services elsewhere, e.g., in the house of a mourner or for the benefit of a sick person unable to attend services in the synagogue. May the Torah scroll be removed from its usual location and transported to a different site in order to accord those unable to worship in the synagogue the opportunity of participating in the reading of the Torah? This question is discussed by Rabbi Kasriel Tchursh, a member of Israel's Chief Rabbinate Council, in the 5734 issue of *Halikhot. Halikhot* is a periodical published by the Religious Council of the municipality of Tel Aviv and regularly features a department devoted to practical aspects of Jewish law.

The Torah scroll must be treated with the highest degree of dignity and respect. Thus, in general, the temporary removal of a Torah scroll is deemed to be incompatible with the honor demanded by its sacred character. *Shulḥan Arukh, Oraḥ Ḥayyim* 135:14, declares that it is not permissible to transport a Torah scroll to a prison for the benefit of Jewish inmates even on such solemn occasions as *Rosh Hashanah* and *Yom Kippur*. Rema modifies this ruling by stating that this restriction applies only to situations in which the scroll is to be transported merely for the brief period of the Torah reading and returned immediately thereafter. Rema states that there is no objection to the removal of the scroll if the Torah is transported "a day or two days" earlier. *Arukh ha-Shulḥan, Oraḥ Ḥayyim* 135:32, observes that Rema's modification has been somewhat narrowed in terms of custom and practice. Custom permits transportation of a Torah scroll only upon fulfillment of two conditions: (1) prior preparation of an ark, closet, or other suitable place in which the scroll may be housed; (2) utilization of the scroll for purposes of public reading at the new location on at least three occasions before its return.[4] It is in order to meet the latter requirement that it has become customary to conduct *minḥah* services on *Shabbat* afternoon in the house of a mourner for whose use a Torah scroll has been provided. In the normal course of events there are usually only two occasions during the period of mourning at which the Torah would be read in the home of the mourner, viz. Monday and Thursday mornings. Hence, even though the mourner is permitted to attend services in the synagogue on *Shabbat,* one service is conducted in the mourner's home in order to afford the opportunity of reading from the Torah scroll a third time.

Rabbi Avraham David Wahrman (*Rav* of Butshatch), *Eshel Avraham, Oraḥ Ḥayyim* 135:14, cites earlier authorities who permit the transportation of a Torah scroll even when these conditions are not satisfied, provided that the Torah scroll is accompanied by ten individuals, "for wherever there are ten, there rests the Divine Presence." This authority adds that the ten person must not merely accompany the Torah but must actually encircle the scroll. Rabbi Techorsh notes that it is customary to permit this procedure only when the scroll is transported to the synagogue courtyard or to another synagogue, but not to a private dwelling.

Mishneh Berurah, Bi'ur Halakhah, Oraḥ Ḥayyim 135:14, draws a sharp distinction between removal of the Torah scroll for the benefit of an individual worshipper and its removal on behalf of an entire *minyan*

4. Cf., however, R. Shabbetai Lifshitz, *Sha'arei Raḥamim* (commentary on R. Ephraim Zalman Margolies' *Sha'arei Ephraim*) 9:22.

unable to attend services elsewhere. *Mishneh Berurah* maintains that the restrictions codified by *Shulḥan Arukh* and Rema apply only to cases in which there are less than ten prison inmates (or other individuals) unable to attend synagogue services. While, of course, the Torah cannot be read other than in the presence of ten people, the *minyan* may be formed by co-opting other worshippers who agree to pray with the prisoners in order that the latter have a proper quorum for communal prayer and the reading of the Torah. *Mishneh Berurah* argues that the removal and transportation of the Torah scroll are not freely permitted in such cases only because the individual prisoners, since they themselves do not constitute a *minyan,* are not obligated to read the Torah even though it is meritorious for them to seek the formation of a *minyan* in order to do so. However, if the inmates are ten or more in number, there is a binding obligation upon them to engage in the reading of the Torah. This obligation, argues *Mishneh Berurah,* takes precedence over any other consideration. This distinction is, however, rejected by the prominent Sephardic codifier, *Kaf ha-Ḥayyim, Oraḥ Ḥayyim* 135:73.

Rema, *Oraḥ Ḥayyim* 135:14, expresses a further leniency and permits the transportation of a Torah scroll on behalf of a Torah scholar. Although the *Shulḥan Arukh* disagrees, Rema maintains that the removal of a Torah scroll on behalf of a scholar is in keeping with the honor due the Torah. *Eliyahu Rabbah* explains that Rema permits the procedure only if the scholar is also a prisoner or an invalid; otherwise, it would indeed be a sign of disrespect to bring the Torah to him instead of the scholar himself going to the synagogue. However, *Shemen ha-Ma'or,* and apparently also R. Elijah, Gaon of Vilna, understands Rema as permitting the transportation of a Torah scroll on behalf of a scholar under all circumstances. Rabbi Tchursh points out that in any event this would not be permissible for Sephardic Jews who follow the ruling of the *Shulḥan Arukh* since the latter disagrees with Rema's leniency with regard to scholars.

Thus, in terms of practice, Ashkenazic Jews may follow the rulings of the authorities who permit transportation of a Torah scroll on behalf of a scholar or on behalf of an assemblage of at least ten persons, whereas Oriental Jews, who regard the opinion of Sephardic scholars as definitive, may not rely upon these leniencies. Obviously, the Torah scroll should not be transported other than for purposes of public reading.[5]

5. See also R. Eliezer Waldenberg, *Ẓiẓ Eli'ezer,* XI, no. 16, and R. Moses Feinstein, *Iggrot Mosheh, Oraḥ Ḥayyim,* I, no. 34.

Yissokhor or Yissoskhor?

The Reading of the Torah on *Parashat Va-Yeẓei* is the occasion of perennial confusion and frequent conflict regarding the correct vocalization of the Hebrew name of Issachar. The sources underlying this question are collected and examined in a number of brief essays in the Israeli journal, *Ha-Ma'ayan*. It is accepted practice to vocalize this name as *Yissokhor* (*Yissakhar* according to Sephardic pronunciation) wherever it is found in Scripture, although the spelling of the word would indicate that it is to be enunciated *Yissoskhor* (*Yissaskhar* according to Sephardic usage). This is one of a fairly large number of instances where, according to Masoretic tradition, the vocalization (*kri*) differs from the written text (*ktiv*). Accordingly, our printed texts indicate no vowel sign in conjunction with the second *sin* of this word, nor, for that matter, do they place a dot over the left head of the letter to indicate a *sin* rather than a *shin*.

Despite the accepted reading of this name as *Yissokhor* throughout Scripture, there remains some controversy with regard to the first appearance of this word in Holy Writ in Genesis 30:18. Writing in the Tevet 5727 issue of *Ha-Ma'ayan*, Dr. Shlomoh Adler discusses the proper vocalization of this first occurrence of the name in the biblical narrative telling of the birth of Jacob's fifth son. Dr. Adler cites the authoritative *Minḥat Shai*, which indicates that the correct reading is *Yissokhor* in *all* occurrences of the name. Noting, however, that in this particular instance the reading of *Yissoskhor* also has its adherents, Dr. Adler seeks to find justification for this divergent practice as well. He quotes Rabbi Moses Sofer, who, in his commentary on Genesis, *Torat Mosheh*, states that in this case the double consonant is to be pronounced. Dr. Adler also reports that he remembers hearing this latter reading of the text in Genesis as a child in his native Germany.

In a reply published in the Tishri 5728 issue of the same publication, Professor Ephraim Yehudah Wiesenberg notes that these comments of *Torat Mosheh* are marked by an asterisk. In the preface of that work, the editor remarks that items marked in this manner were not penned by *Ḥatam Sofer* himself, but were the additions of students who purported to have recorded the novellae of their master. Professor Wiesenberg claims that, in this instance their report is almost certainly erroneous, and he marshals evidence from the body of *Torat Mosheh* itself indicating that the correct vocalization is *Yissokhor* even in the first occurrence of the name. However, Professor Wiesenberg does find a source for the *Yissoskhor* reading, tracing the custom to R. Joshua Heschel Babad, *Teshuvot Yehoshu'a,* no. 72. This opinion notwithstanding, Professor Wiesenberg shows that numerous authorities are explicit in rendering the pronunciation as *Yissokhor.* So, too, another respondent on this subject, Dr. Saul Esh, writing in the Nisan 5727 issue of *Ha-Ma'ayan,* cites the many proponents of the *Yissokhor* vocalization.[6]

Dr. Esh discusses a totally different, and virtually unknown, custom with regard to the reading of *Yissokhor,* a practice which he finds recorded in *Naḥalat Ya'akov*, a work devoted to various questions pertaining to the Reading of the Torah. According to this compendium, the name should be vocalized as *Yissoskhor* in all occurrences prior to Numbers 26:24 and as *Yissokhor* thereafter. Dr. Esh explains the rationale underlying this uncommon practice. He predicates the custom upon one of the numerous reasons for not pronouncing the second *sin* of this name. One opinion recorded in *Torah Shlemah* is that this letter was removed from the name of Issachar in order that it might be added to the name of one of his children. According to this explanation, the name *Yashuv*, occurring in Numbers 26:24, originally lacked a *shin.* The person denoted by the name *Yashuv* is one and the same as *Yov,* identified in Genesis 46:13 as a son of Issachar. According to some authorities, *Yov* was also the name of an object of pagan worship. Therefore, *Yov* requested that a *sin* be taken from his father's name and added to his name, rendering it *Yashuv*. This tradition, *Torah Shlemah* claims, is the basis for the practice in some places of vocalizing the double consonant in *Yissokhor* throughout Scripture until the point where the *sin* is recorded as part of the name *Yashuv* in Numbers 26:24; from this point on, the second *sin* is not vocalized. Both Dr. Esh and Professor Wiesenberg quote many scholars who reject this custom as being unauthoritative.

Rabbinic Contracts

It has become quite common for congregations to grant their rabbis tenure in the form of a life contract. In the Iyar-Sivan 5730 issue of *Ha-Ma'or,* Rabbi Shneur Zusha Reiss questions the halakhic foundations of this practice and, in the process, discusses the nature of rabbinic con-

6. Of interest to the bibliophile are the many observations in these articles indicating where variations in the printed texts of the Pentateuch mirror the divergent customs with regard to vocalization.

tracts. Colleagues in the rabbinate, who may at times feel themselves "enslaved" by their chosen profession, may derive some measure of satisfaction from the realization that this emotion is mirrored in the Halakhah.

The Torah looks upon the institution of slavery with disfavor and permits a Jew to become an indentured servant only when he has no other means of earning a livelihood. Quoting the verse "For unto Me are the children of Israel slaves . . ." (Lev. 25:55), the Gemara, *Baba Meẓi'a* 10a, declares that Jews are the servants of God and hence are not permitted to become "the servants of servants." Taking the view that any form of involuntary labor is a form of servitude, the Talmud states that a workingman may withdraw from employment "even in the middle of the day." In a gloss upon the citation of this halakhah in *Ḥoshen Mishpat* 333:3, Rema quotes definitive authorities who assert that a laborer, or even a teacher or scribe, may not bind himself to an employer for a period greater than three years if the terms of his employment require him to live in the employer's domicile and to accept the employer's board. Permanent employment under such conditions resembles servitude. Service of this type for a period not exceeding three years is sanctioned on the basis of the verse "Within three years, as the years of a hireling . . ." (Isa. 16:14). The individual accepting such service for a period of three years or less is deemed a "hireling"; if he accepts such employment for a period in excess of three years he has entered into a proscribed form of "slavery." *Ḥatam Sofer,* in his collected responsa, *Oraḥ Ḥayyim,* no. 206, indicates that according to some authorities it may be permissible to enter into such contracts for a period of time up to six years in length rather than three.[7]

In another responsum, *Ḥoshen Mishpat,* no. 172, *Ḥatam Sofer* declares that rabbinical contracts are subject to these limitations as well. Although Rema clearly states that such employment is forbidden only if the employee is required to reside in the employer's home, *Ḥatam Sofer* maintains that rabbinic employment is comparable to residing in the employer's household since the rabbi is dependent for his livelihood upon the community employing his services. He is thus a communal employee, whose residence and sustenance are provided by the members of the community cooperatively and who, by virtue of the nature of his employment, is required to live in the employer's domicile, i.e., within

7. See also *Ḥavot Ya'ir,* no. 140.

the community by which he is employed. *Ḥatam Sofer* adds, however, that there is no halakhic impediment to a contract for an extended period of time which permits the rabbi to withdraw from the agreement at any time but prevents him from accepting another rabbinical post other than upon payment of a financial penalty. The rationale of this ruling is that the agreement does not bind the rabbi to his employers but simply provides for a fine in the event that he accepts another position.

In the previously cited responsum, *Oraḥ Ḥayyim,* no. 206, *Ḥatam Sofer* states that there are diverse customs with regard to the terms of rabbinic contracts. In some places a three-year term of service is customary, in others a five-year period; the universal practice is not to draw up an agreement for a period of six years or longer. *Ḥatam Sofer* asserts that a specific period of service is stipulated solely for the benefit of the rabbi. The rabbi, being forbidden to bind himself for a longer period of time, is thus enabled to withdraw from his position, if he so chooses, upon termination of the contract. The congregation, however, "cannot withdraw from the agreement even after the stipulated period has expired unless there is a custom to this effect . . . but it has never been heard or seen in these lands that a rabbi has been removed and deposed from his rabbinical chair and such dare not be done."[8]

Rabbi Reiss advises that a halakhic authority be consulted before drafting a life contract in order to assure that the provisions are in conformity with Halakhah. It is obvious, however, that, where there is no concomitant obligation on the part of the rabbi—as is usually the case—there is no halakhic impediment to conferral of life tenure by a congregation upon its spiritual leader. Indeed, as has been shown earlier, it may be argued that such tenure accompanies every rabbinic appointment.

Seliḥot Services

Traditionally, the penitential season is ushered in by the recitation of *seliḥot* after midnight on Saturday night. Of late, there has been a tendency on the part of synagogues in some areas to introduce *seliḥot* services at an earlier hour for the convenience and, in some cases, the safety of their worshippers.

8. See also *Ḥatam Sofer, Ḥoshen Mishpat,* no. 22, as well as *Iggrot Mosheh, Ḥoshen Mishpat,* I, nos. 76 and 77. Cf. R. Shlomoh Kluger, *Ha-Elef Lekha Shlomoh, Oraḥ Ḥayyim,* no. 38 and *Yoreh De'ah,* no. 253.

A number of considerations which augur against this innovation are cited by *Birkei Yosef, Oraḥ Ḥayyim* 581:1–2. The practice of not reciting *seliḥot* prior to midnight is based upon the kabbalistic teaching surrounding the recitation of the thirteen Divine Attributes. The Divine Attributes are the focal point of the *seliḥot* services and are recited by the congregation in unison following each of the various penitential prayers. The Kabbalists taught that, for mystical reasons, recitation of the Divine Attributes during the latter part of the night awakens divine mercy, whereas recitation of the selfsame Divine Attributes before midnight may, Heaven forfend, have the opposite effect.

A second consideration which precludes recitation of *seliḥot* before midnight on Saturday evening is the fact that due to the sanctity of the departing *Shabbat* it is forbidden to recite the Confession (*vidduy*), which forms an integral part of *seliḥot,* before midnight has passed.

These provisions regarding the recitation of *seliḥot* have become part of Jewish law. Indeed, rabbinic authorities advise that it is preferable not to recite *seliḥot* at all than to recite the Divine Attributes or the Confession before midnight.

There are two possible alternatives to a midnight *seliḥot* service. The first *seliḥot* may be recited early Sunday morning before *shaḥarit,* as is the practice on subsequent days. This is, indeed, the normative practice in German communities on the first day of *seliḥot* as well. If it is absolutely necessary to conduct the *seliḥot* services at an earlier hour on Saturday evening, care should be taken to omit recitation both of the Divine Attributes and of the Confession. The latter procedure is clearly not optimal since, liturgically, recitation of the Divine Attributes constitutes the essence of *seliḥot.*

Dual Bar Mitzvahs

Large synagogues at times find that among their worshippers there are two or more families celebrating the Bar Mitzvah of their respective sons on the same *Shabbat.* Since it has now become *de rigeur* for the Bar Mitzvah to chant the *haftorah,* a problem arises with regard to the accommodation of two young men with the reading of a single prophetic portion. The various feasible solutions to this problem are examined by Rabbi S. Deblitsky in the Nisan–Iyar 5733 issue of *Ha-Ne'eman.*

The matter cannot be resolved simply by allowing both candidates to read the appropriate *haftorah* in succession. Since the congregation has already discharged its obligation upon listening to the first reading of the *haftorah,* the subsequent reading is purely ceremonial and fulfills no liturgical requirement. Accordingly, it is forbidden for the second Bar Mitzvah to recite once again the blessings which accompany the reading of the *haftorah.*

It has been suggested that ten members of the congregation be apprised of the situation and be requested consciously to disavow the fulfillment of their obligation during the first reading of the *haftorah* (*kavanah she-lo lazet*). The second Bar Mitzvah would then be enabled to recite the *haftorah* and the accompanying blessings on their behalf. Rabbi Deblitsky rejects this solution for two reasons:

1. This procedure causes the pronouncement of an "unnecessary blessing" (*brakhah she-einah zerikhah*). The utterance of the Divine Name is viewed by Judaism with the utmost gravity; it is a principle of Halakhah that blessings are not to be multiplied unless specificly mandated. Since there is no impediment preventing those present from having proper intent to discharge their obligation during the course of the first reading, they are not permitted, argues Rabbi Deblitsky, consciously to disavow such fulfillment in order to create the need for additional blessings. Although this latter point may well be disputed, Rabbi Deblitsky further argues that the same consideration also precludes having ten individuals leave the synagogue during the first reading of the *haftorah.*

2. Rabbi Deblitsky points out that many authorities are of the opinion that the reading of both the Torah and the *haftorah* is a congregational rather than an individual obligation. If the obligation is a congregational one, all those present during such readings automatically fulfill the obligation regardless of their intent or attentiveness. Since the obligation is not personal in nature, its fulfillment cannot be disavowed by an individual.

It should be noted that this sensitive issue has previously been discussed at length by two eminent halakhic authorities who reach somewhat different conclusions. Advancing different considerations, Rabbi Eliezer Waldenberg, *Ẓiẓ Eli'ezer,* VI, no. 36, also rules against reading of the Torah by two Bar Mitzvah lads in succession. In the event that the reading of the Torah has been completed and latecomers appear in the synagogue, it is forbidden to read the Torah a second time on their behalf (See *Magen Avraham* 69:9 and *Mishneh Berurah* 69:18). The rationale underlying this ruling is that the observer may not realize why the Torah scroll is being opened anew and may think that the reading is being repeated in a new scroll because an error or flaw was found in the first Torah scroll, rendering it halakhically unfit. Unfounded aspersions upon the fitness (*kashrut*) of a scroll are deemed an indignity to the Torah. Reading the *haftorah* twice would also involve reading the Torah portion for *maftir* twice. It would thus appear that the portion was being reread in a second scroll because the first was found to be unfit, thereby causing an indignity to the Torah scroll. Nevertheless, Rabbi Waldenberg asserts that this provision applies only to individual latecomers, but if ten men have not heard the reading of the Torah, the reading may be repeated on their behalf since ten persons constitute a congregation.

Rabbi Waldenberg strongly advises either that one of the Bar Mitzvah boys be accorded an alternate Torah honor or that the entire reading of the Torah be conducted in two separate places, thereby eliminating all difficulties. Only when such arrangements will cause ill-will and antagonism is Rabbi Waldenberg willing to sanction other modes of accommodation. In such circumstances he advises that ten members of the congregation consciously disavow fulfillment of their obligation during the reading of the first Bar Mitzvah. He further rules that even under these circumstances it is preferable for the second Bar Mitzvah to repeat only the *haftorah* and not to repeat the Torah reading for *maftir*. When it is not feasible to have ten persons disavow fulfillment of their obligation, he permits the second Bar Mitzvah to repeat the *haftorah*, provided that the second Bar Mitzvah himself has not heard the first reading or has consciously disavowed fulfillment of the obligation with regard to the reading of the *haftorah* during the reading of the first Bar Mitzvah.

Rabbi Waldenberg also notes that any congregant may lawfully invoke his halakhic prerogative and protest that repeated reading constitutes an unwarranted encroachment upon his time. Halakhah greatly respects the value of time and provides that the congregation may not be unduly burdened (*tirḥah de-ẓibura*) by encroachment upon its time and patience.

Rabbi Moses Feinstein, *Iggrot Mosheh, Oraḥ Ḥayyim,* I, no. 102, insists upon the requirement of having ten individuals leave the synagogue during the first reading of the *maftir* and *haftorah* and having them re-enter before the second Bar Mitzvah commences the reading of *maftir*. Rabbi Feinstein points out that the Torah reading of *maftir* by the person about to recite the *haftorah* is not an integral part of the Reading of the Torah but was ordained as an "honor to the Torah" since it would be unseemly for the *maftir* to ignore the Torah scroll by reading only a prophetic selection. This consideration, opines Rabbi Feinstein, does not warrant the reopening of an already closed Torah scroll. Therefore, he concludes, the Torah scroll should not be reopened for the reading of *maftir* even if ten persons have not yet discharged their obligation with regard to the reading of the *haftorah.* In order to obviate the indignity to the Torah which would result from opening and unrolling the scroll at second time and, at the same time, accord the second Bar Mitzvah the opportunity of reading *maftir,* Rabbi Feinstein advises that the scroll not be lifted and closed subsequent to the first reading but that it simply be covered and allowed to remain on the reading table. Rabbi Waldenberg, on the other hand, cites several sources which indicate that for a variety of reasons the scroll must be lifted, rolled and closed before the reading of the *haftorah* is begun.

Bat Mitzvah Celebrations

The Bar Mitzvah of a Jewish boy is traditionally marked by festivities. The occasion of the Bat Mitzvah of a girl, on the other hand, is virtually ignored by most segments of Orthodox Judaism. Only following the popularization of Bat Mitzvah ceremonies by the Conservative movement have some modern Orthodox congregations in our country instituted similar rituals. Actually, the institution of some type of ceremony to mark this occasion can be traced to the mid-ninteenth century. It is reported that no less an authority than the renowned R. Jacob Ettlinger sanctioned the institution of such observances in Germany in order to combat the inroads of the early Reform movement, and himself delivered addresses on such occasions.[8a]

Rabbi Moses Feinstein, *Iggrot Mosheh, Oraḥ Ḥayyim,* I, 104, in discouraging Bat Mitzvah practices, declares that there is no source for such celebrations and that a festive meal marking this occasion cannot be viewed as a *se'udat mizvah* (a ritual repast). Discussing a related question, Rabbi Feinstein also maintains that use of the synagogue sanctuary for a Bat Mitzvah ceremony is forbidden by Jewish law. The sanctuary may be used only for sacred purposes. Since Bat Mitzvah rituals have no liturgical basis, the use of the synagogue sanctuary for such purposes, concludes Rabbi Feinstein, is a violation of the sanctity of the synagogue.

Taharat Yom Tov, IX, 40, rules against Bat Mitzvah celebrations on the grounds that they are a Reform innovation. Rabbi Aaron Walkin, *Zekan Aharon,* I, no. 6, deems such ceremonies to be rooted in gentile observances, i.e., the confirmation ritual of various Christian denomina-

8a. See *Ha-Ma'ayan,* Tevet 5732, p. 29 and p. 61, n. 25.

tions, and hence forbidden on the basis of the biblical admonition, *"u-veḥukotehem lo telekhu."* This consideration is dismissed out of hand by Rabbi Yechiel Ya'akov Weinberg in the Nisan 5723 issue of *Ha-Pardes*. Rabbi Weinberg approves of Bat Mitzvah observances when conducted at home or in a congregational hall, but objects to such functions when conducted in the synagogue proper.

Writing in the Tevet 5733 issue of *Ha-Ma'ayan,*[8b] Rabbi Chanoch Zundel Grossberg argues that a festive meal for members of the family on the occasion of a Bat Mitzvah does constitute a *se'udat miẓvah*. In the case of a boy, such a repast is occasioned by the lad's newly assumed obligations with regard to the observance of *miẓvot*. The identical consideration, argues Rabbi Grossberg, should call for a similar observance to mark the Bat Mitzvah of a girl, "even though we have not heard that in previous generations a banquet was made for a girl as for a boy." Rabbi Grossberg, however, advises that for reasons of modesty such a celebration should be limited to members of the family. There is at least one source which serves as a precedent for this view.[9] In *No'am* VII (5724), Rabbi Isaac Nissim, former Chief Rabbi of Israel, quotes an unpublished responsa collection, *Ḥaim ve-Ḥesed,* authored by a Sephardic scholar, Rabbi A. Musapiah, which records that a banquet on such occasions constitutes a *se'udat miẓvah.*[9a] At the same time Rabbi Nissim quotes a divergent view. *Ben Ish Ḥai* (*Re'eh* no. 17), writes, "Even though [a festive meal] is not customary on her behalf, [a girl] should nevertheless rejoice on that day."

Women in a Minyan?

The deliberations and publications of the Rabbinical Assembly do not, in the ordinary course of events, properly come within the purview of a work devoted to Halakhah. Much is to be said in favor of simply ignoring pronouncements with regard to Jewish law issued by those who have placed themselves outside the pale of normative Judaism. Yet from time to time a particular action is erroneously presented as being predicated upon authoritative precedents, and hence as being within the parameters of Halakhah. Since the unwary and unknowledgeable may very easily be confused and misled by such misrepresentations it becomes necessary to take note of the issues involved.

8b. This discussion also appears in *Shma'atin,* Kislev 5734.

9. See also R. Meshullem Roth, *Kol Mevaser,* II, no. 44.

9a. See also R. Ovadiah Yosef, *Yabi'a Omer,* VI, *Oraḥ Ḥayyim,* no. 29.

In a recent pronouncement, the Committee on Jewish Law and Standards of the Rabbinical Assembly declared that men and women may be counted equally for a *minyan* (quorum for public prayer). The concept of a *minyan* as consisting of ten male adults is derived by the Gemara, *Megillah* 23b, from the verse "How long shall I bear with this evil congregation . . . ?" (Num. 14:27). The term "congregation" is here applied to the ten spies who returned from scouting the Holy Land with an unfavorable report. Since the appellation "congregation" is applied by Scripture only to a group of ten individuals, the Gemara declares that a quorum for all matters requiring a "congregation" consists of ten persons. Since the "congregation" referred to by Scripture consisted of ten adult males, it follows that the *minyan* must be composed of adult males.[10] The list of sources which specificly declare that only males are eligible for inclusion in a *minyan* is formidable.

In a paper submitted to the Committee on Jewish Law and Standards advocating the inclusion of women in a *minyan,* Philip Sigal asserts that "before we can declare women qualified to count in a quorum we must be certain that public worship is an absolute requirement, that Jewish public worship requires a specific minimum quorum and that women are obligated equally with men to attend public worship services." Sigal then marshals sources showing that women and men share equal obligations with regard to prayer.[11]

The sources cited would have provided some support for a pronouncement by the Rabbinical Assembly declaring that women are obligated to pray thrice daily. This conclusion is not drawn. Instead Sigal concludes that *public* prayer is mandatory for women. David Feldman, in a paper submitted to the Committee on Jewish Law in opposition to the resolution, correctly points out that an obligation with regard to public prayer on the part of women does not follow from an obligation to engage in private prayer. Indeed, while there is no lack of halakhic authorities who maintain that women are obligated to recite the *amidah* twice daily (*shaḥarit* and *minḥah*), no halakhic authority maintains that women are obligated to pray with a *minyan*. It is patently inconsistent and, based on the sources, contradictory to declare that women are obligated to pray with a *minyan* but to absolve them of the obligation to pray three times each day.

The sole precedent cited in support of this innovation is a statement

---

10. Cf. Rabbi Chaim Hershensohn, *Malki ba-Kodesh,* II, 199–201.
11. See *Arukh ha-Shulḥan, Oraḥ Ḥayyim* 106:5–7.

attributed to Rabbenu Simchah, quoted, but not accepted, by *Mordekhai, Berakhot* 48a. As pointed out by Dr. Feldman, this source is incorrectly cited. Even if his views were not rejected by all other authorities, the opinion of Rabbenu Simchah could not be invoked in support of the position that women may be counted equally with men. Rabbenu Simchah's ruling is much more limited in nature and its application to the question at hand is a distortion of his view.

There is a well-known controversy with regard to whether a *minyan* consists of ten individuals upon whom public prayer is obligatory, or whether it may be formed by nine adults together with one minor. According to the commentary of Rosh on *Berakhot* 48a, it would appear that the authorities who permit the inclusion of a minor maintain that in actuality it is the Divine Presence which is included as the tenth member of the *minyan.*[12] Attention may be drawn to the biblical narrative concerning Abraham's supplication on behalf of Sodom and Gomorrah. Abraham at first prayed that those cities be spared if fifty righteous inhabitants were found. Rashi explains that in actuality five cities were marked for destruction and Abraham prayed that the cities be spared if ten righteous persons—a *minyan*—could be found in each. Subsequently Abraham prayed that the cities be spared even in the event that only forty-five righteous persons could be found. Rashi (Gen. 18:28) comments that Abraham recognized that a *minyan* must be found for each city, but beseeched the Almighty that He include Himself in that number. This would explain why those authorities who sanction the inclusion of a minor as the tenth person require that he hold a written scroll of one of the books of the Pentateuch in his hand. In reality it is the Divine Presence which is symbolized by the scroll of the Law which is included. The presence of a minor is required by virtue of the rabbinic decree which regards him as being already a quasi-member of the *minyan* because the minor will one day share the religious obligations of the rest of the *minyan.*

Rabbenu Simchah maintains that not only a minor but even a woman may be co-opted as the tenth person. According to Rabbenu Simchah, a *minyan* must consist of nine persons obligated to public worship while the tenth individual may be a participant who does not share an equal obligation. Both minors and women are included in this category. Citation of Rabbenu Simchah does not justify the conclusion that women may be counted equally with men since (1) his view rejected by *Mordekhai;*[13] (2)

12. See, however, *Ba'al ha-Ma'or, Berakhot* 48a.
13. See *Be'er ha-Golah, Oraḥ Ḥayyim* 55:4.

most latter-day authorities, including *Pri Megadim, Ḥayyei Adam,* and *Arukh ha-Shulḥan,* maintain that even a minor may not be included in a *minyan;* (3) he sanctions only the inclusion of a single woman. On the basis of the above sources, one can no more contend that a *minyan* may be composed of ten women than that it may be composed of ten minors.

In his paper submitted to the Committee on Jewish Law, and in a carefully worded and well-researched article which appeared earlier in the Summer 1972 issue of *Conservative Judaism,* David Feldman endeavors to explain why women are ineligible for inclusion as part of a *minyan.* He asserts that the non-inclusion of women in a *minyan* is not a form of discrimination against the female sex but simply a concomitant of differing obligations. He explains that the rationale underlying this provision is that only those possessed of an obligation can be numbered in the quorum necessary for the discharge of such obligation. An identical explanation of why women cannot be counted in a *minyan* for communal prayer is offered by *Margaliyot ha-Yam, Sanhedrin* 74b, no. 27. This consideration would explain the fact that an *onen,* who is exempt from prayer, is not eligible to be counted in a *minyan.*[14]

Dr. Feldman further argues that in instances in which a *minyan* is required but in which women share equal obligations with men, Halakhah indeed provides that they may be counted equally with men for purposes of the necessary quorum. Rabbenu Nissim, for example, rules that women, who are obligated to hear the reading of the *Megillah,* may be counted as part of the *minyan* for this purpose. Some authorities maintain that the same is true with regard to the *miẓvah* of sanctification of the Divine Name (*kiddush ha-Shem*). The verse "And I will be sanctified among the children of Israel" (Lev. 22:32) is also understood as meaning that martyrdom is not commanded other than in the presence of at least ten Jews. Rabbi Yosef Engel, *Gilyonei ha-Shas, Sanhedrin* 74b, and *Margaliyot ha-Yam, loc. cit.,* rule that since the obligation with regard to sanctification of the Divine Name is equally incumbent upon both men and women, women are to be counted as part of the quorum for this purpose.

Despite the cogency of this rationale, it serves as a satisfactory explanation only of the authorities cited in its support. Dr. Feldman himself notes

---

14. This explanation may also serve to explain the ruling of a number of authorities to the effect that an *onen* may recite *kaddish* and may, accordingly, be counted toward a *minyan* for that purpose, but for that pupose alone. See R. Yechiel Michal Tucatzinsky, *Gesher ha-Ḥayyim,* I, chap. 18, no. 2, sec. 3.

that *Minḥat Ḥinukh,* no. 296, maintains that women cannot be counted among the ten persons constituting a quorum for sanctification of the Divine Name, despite the fact that women are unquestionably included in this fundamental obligation. More significant in terms of definitive Halakhah is the fact that Rema, *Oraḥ Ḥayyim* 690:18, clearly rejects the view of Rabbenu Nissim. Rema does state that "there is room to question" whether or not women may be counted among the ten. However, Rema's "question" is quoted in the name of *Hagahot Asheri, Megillah,* chap. 1, who explains that this expression of doubt is based on entirely different considerations. *Hagahot Asheri* expresses doubt as to whether a *minyan* in the usual sense of the term is required for the reading of the *Megillah,* in which case women are to be excluded, or whether the requirement of a quorum is not for purposes of constituting a "congregation" but in order to publicize the miracle of Purim. If the latter is indeed the case, the requirement is not at all for the presence of a *minyan* as a "congregation," but for publicizing the miracle, which coincidentally also necessitates the presence of ten individuals. Women are excluded from the constitution of the quorum which is needed to form a "congregation." But in the case of the reading of the *Megillah,* if the requirement is simply that of publicizing the miracle, it follows that this effect is achieved equally whether in the presence of women or of men.

A position which is obviously contradictory to Dr. Feldman's thesis may be found in *Magen Avraham, Oraḥ Ḥayyim* 282:6. *Magen Avraham* cites an opinion which maintains that women are obligated to listen to the Reading of the Law. Yet no authority maintains that women may be counted toward a *minyan* which is required for this purpose.

For these authorities, all that can be said is that women are ineligible for inclusion in a *minyan* simply because in terms of derivation of the concept the term "congregation" applies only to adult males. As such it is not a form of discrimination but simply another instance of Halakhah's recognition of the distinctive roles and obligations of men and women within Judaism.

Serious questions have been raised with regard to the role and function of women in modern society and, accordingly, in religious life as well. An appropriate response to the issues which have been presented may be found *within* the halakhic framework which provides great breadth for the individual self-expression of each man and woman. The teachings and practices of Judaism should certainly not be maligned as being discriminatory in nature. Very much to the point is David Feldman's concluding observation that, quite apart from the fact that "no halakhic basis for counting women is offered," this innovation would make a *"ḥukha u-telula* of traditional forms by appearing to concede to the feminist charge of oppressive discrimination or inequality. The *minyan* is not to be indicted for oppressiveness. It is a technical construct true to its own categories."

It is the pretense of seeking halakhic authenticity and the distortion of sources in order to arrive at preconceived conclusions which is particularly offensive. The motivation for the action of the Rabbinical Assembly is readily apparent. It is a reaction to an enhanced awareness of the role of women in modern society and to the understandable clamor for their inclusion in all phases of religious life. As such, the action with regard to *minyan* is in keeping with the basic philosophy of the Conservative movement. A forthright formulation of the considerations which prompted the innovation is contained in a statement by the chairman of the Committee on Jewish Law in which, *inter alia,* he states: "The approach to Jewish law in Conservative Judaism has always been to change existing norms where they do not further ethical and spiritual values. When an existing norm reflects a world-view or social situation which no longer exists, then the *halakhah* is modified."

These sentiments bespeak a lack of recognition of the fact that Halakhah possesses an enduring validity which, while applicable to changing circumstances, is not subject to change by lobbying or by the exertion of pressure in any guise or form. Nor may independently held convictions, however sincere, be allowed to influence our interpretation of Halakhah. Normative Judaism teaches that Halakhah is not derived from any temporal "worldview" or "social situation" but expresses the transcendental worldview of the Divine Lawgiver.

CHAPTER IV

Kashrut

"For I am the Lord, Who brought you up from the land of Egypt . . ." Had I brought Israel up from Egypt only for this, that they do not defile themselves with swarming creatures it would have been sufficient for Me.

BABA MEẒI'A 61b

The Sages of the Talmud were forthright in their classification of the dietary laws among the *ḥukkim,* the divinely ordained statutes whose rationale cannot full be fathomed by the human mind but which the Jew nevertheless observes by reason of divine fiat. The seemingly arbitrary nature of this class of divine commandments is noted by the Midrash precisely in connection with the dietary laws. "What difference does it make to God whether a beast is killed by cutting the neck in the front or in the back? *Miẓvot* were given solely that people might be purified by means of them." (*Bereshit Rabbah* XLIV, 1).

Despite the great reluctance of the talmudic Sages to offer a rationale for the fundamentals of *kashrut,* others were not similarly reticent. The interpretations which have been advanced over the course of centuries are varied and sundry. The explanation which has probably enjoyed the widest circulation is the one which sees a connection between these laws and physical health and well-being. This concept gained currency in the days of antiquity: it is expressed in the Pseudepigrapha[1] and alluded to in the works of Philo.[2] Although these writings are not necessarily indicative of rabbinic thought, similar concepts are expressed by Maimonides,[3]

1. IV Macc. 5:25–27.

2. *De Specialibus Legibus,* IV, 119. Translated by F. H. Colson (Cambridge, 1939), VIII, 81.

3. *Guide of the Perplexed,* III, chap. 48.

Nachmanides,[4] Gersonides,[5] and others.[6] However, other rabbinic scholars were most emphatic in their denial of a hygienic interpretation of the laws of forbidden foods. Thus, R. Isaac Abarbanel writes, "Heaven forfend that I should believe so. For if that were to be so, the Book of God's Law would be in the same category as any of the brief medical books. . . . This is not the way of God's law or the depth of its intentions." [7] In almost identical language, R. Isaac Arama disparages this explanation, commenting that such an interpretation would "lower the status of divine Law to the status of any brief medical composition." [8]

Of the various other approaches to an understanding of the dietary laws, the one which perhaps strikes a particularly responsive chord, and which has reference to empirically verifiable social phenomena, is the explanation which sees in *kashrut* a vehicle designed to preserve the distinctive identity of Israel as a nation. According to this explanation, dietary regulations are seen as having been designed to restrain untrammeled social intercourse and to serve as a rein against assimilation. Reference to this concept is found in the *Letter of Aristeas* which states: "God has hedged us about on all sides by rules of purity affecting alike what we eat or drink or touch or see. . . . the laws must teach discrimination because we have been distinctly separated from the rest of mankind" (142 and 151). In a similar but somewhat different vein, R. Isaac Arama comments that these regulations were designed to restrict contact between Jews and non-Jews. Dietary restraints serve to create a barrier between them similar to that which exists "between the peasant or provincial and the prince who feasts upon the bread and wine of the king." [9] Just as they are separate in their foods, so must they be different in their thoughts and deeds.

Regardless of which explanation, if any, is accepted, it is clear that the Sages viewed the dietary code as particularly indicative of the unique status of the Jewish people. Jews were singled out from among the nations

---

4. *Commentary on the Bible,* Lev. 11:43.

5. *Commentary on the Bible, Parshat Ekev, To'elet* 26.

6. Abraham ibn Ezra, *Commentary on the Bible,* Exod. 22:30; Rashbam, *Commentary on the Bible,* Lev. 11:3; *Sefer ha-Ḥinukh,* nos. 72 and 147.

7. *Commentary on the Bible,* Lev. 11:13.

8. *Akedat Yiẓḥak, Sha'ar* 60. *See also Kli Yakar,* Lev. 11:1 and Menachem ha-Bavli, *Ta'amei ha-Miẓvot,* negative commandments, no. 84.

9. *Akedat Yiẓḥak, Sha'ar* 60.

of the world and charged with maintaining an enhanced standard of holiness. The Midrash portrays the laws of *kashrut* as the special privilege of the Jewish people and as a mark of the distinction between Israel and other nations. Israel alone among the nations was given the dietary laws, the Midrash observes, for the people of Israel are unique in that as a nation they alone are destined for eternal life.[10] The laws of *kashrut* are designed to enable the Jewish people to achieve the sanctity which is a guarantee of eternity.

Dietary proscriptions include categories of food which are forbidden by their nature and others which are forbidden because of their mode of preparation. Various species of animals, fowl, fish, and creeping things are described in the Torah and declared "unclean" (Lev. 11:1–23 and 41–47, Deut. 14:3–19).

Permitted animals must be slaughtered in accordance with prescribed ritual requirements. Animals which die of themselves, which are improperly slaughtered or which have suffered from certain physiological defects are forbidden. Parts of otherwise kosher animals, such as the blood, certain types of fat (*ḥelev*), located primarily but not exclusively in the hindquarters, and the sciatic sinew, located in the hollow of the thigh, may also not be eaten. Kosher meat must be prepared by a process of soaking and salting in order to drain the blood.

A strict separation must be maintained between meat and dairy products. They may be neither cooked nor eaten together. The stringencies pertaining to this separation necessitate different sets of dishes and utensils for meat and dairy foods.

Single Sterilizer for Both Meat and Dairy Utensils

In an article appearing in the 5728 edition of *Shanah be-Shanah,* Rabbi S. Efratti reports that the following query had been addressed to him: A hospital found it necessary to utilize a sterilizer for all eating utensils used in its pediatric and isolation wings. Since the purchase of two such machines would involve a great expense, could the same sterilizer be used for both meat and dairy utensils, albeit not at the same time? It was to be understood that both dishes and silverware were to be washed properly before being placed in the sterilizer. The apparatus, the interlocutor averred, used cold water and was equipped with its own heating elements, which

10. *Va-Yikra Rabbah* XIII, 2.

were utilized to raise the temperature of the water to the proper degree of heat for purposes of sterilization.

Rabbi Efratti compares this case to that mentioned in *Yoreh De'ah* 94:5 concerning a new pot containing boiling water in which a dairy spoon had been placed. The pot was subsequently emptied and refilled with boiling water, and this time a meat spoon was inserted. The ruling in this situation is that the pot has been rendered unfit for either meat or dairy products and can be used only for neutral foods. If the instance of the sterilizer is analogous to the case cited, use of the machine would be objectionable for either meat or dairy utensils. There is, however, one significant difference. The utensils in question are used by patients in eating meals, but never in the kitchen for the preparation of foods. Thus these dishes never come into contact with hot food while such food is yet in the utensils in which it was originally cooked. The utensils to be sterilized accordingly have the status of a *keli sheni,* a vessel into which cooked food is transferred. Since such vessels possess only the heat transmitted to them by the food they contain, their power of absorption is considerably lessened. Rabbi Efratti points out that in the case under consideration, the "taste" of food goes through three distinct processes of assimilation: from the edibles into the eating utensil, from the eating utensil into the water and from the water into the sterilizing apparatus. Accordingly, he argues, if this analysis does, in fact, take account of all relevant factors, there would be no reason for a stringent ruling so long as the absorption of dairy or meat foods in the eating utensils takes place in the form of a *keli sheni.*

This line of reasoning does not, however, apply to instances where particles of food are permitted to enter the machine. In such an event absorption is directly from the food itself. The situation is then tantamount to actual cooking, and the sterilizer acquires the status of either a dairy or meat utensil depending upon the category of vessels which were sterilized first. Rabbi Efratti states that in the case of the sterilizer it may be anticipated that a fatty residue will remain on at least some eating implements and, accordingly, we must deem the vessel to be one in which food has been cooked.

In cognizance of this additional factor, Rabbi Efratti asserts that it is necessary to *kasher* the sterilizer between meat and dairy and vice versa. This can be done quite easily by simply running the sterilizer for a short period of time while it is empty of dishes and silverware. The machine, heating its own water, will thereby *kasher* itself.

There would still appear to be an impediment to the use of a single sterilizer for both meat and dairy foods even if the machine be *kashered* after each use. *Magen Avraham,* in his commentary on *Oraḥ Ḥayyim* 509:5, states that it is our practice not to *kasher* meat utensils for dairy use or vice versa. *Kashering* procedures are employed only in order to render usable non-kosher utensils which would otherwise not be used for any purpose or in order to prepare utensils for Passover use. The reason for this restriction is apparently the fear that if *kashering* of the utensils be permitted between meat and dairy use there would then be no need for maintaining separate sets of utensils. As a result there might be inadvertent use of such eating implements for both meat and dairy foods without prior *kashering*. Underscoring the fact that the reason for disallowing the *kashering* of a single utensil for meat and dairy use is the danger of forgetfulness, Rabbi Efratti suggests that this fear can be obviated in the case of a sterilizer by requiring separate racks for meat and dairy utensils. The racks would have to be changed constantly and their substitution would serve as a reminder that *kashering* is required as well.

Another reason adduced by Rabbi Efratti for permitting the use of a single sterilizer is based on *Yoreh De'ah* 95:4. According to this source, the addition of ashes to the water before the utensils are placed therein causes the emitted "taste" of milk or meat to become a "spoiled taste." Since the machine then absorbs a "spoiled taste," it does not acquire the status of either a meat or dairy vessel. Rabbi Efratti maintains that addition of chemical substances during the sterilizing process may be considered to have the same effect. However both *Taz* 95:15 and *Shakh* 95:21 express their disagreement with the basic premise concerning a "spoiled taste" arising out of the admixture of ashes and the matter is the subject of considerable discussion in subsequent halakhic literature.

It should be noted that in this article Rabbi Efratti's discussion is limited to the question of sterilizers and no mention is made of dishwashing machines in which different conditions may be operative. For example, the mode of *kashering* a dishwasher, if this process be necessary, requires further clarification since the latter machine does not heat its own water. Furthermore, Rabbi Efratti's permissive ruling is based entirely upon the fact that all utensils to be sterilized had the status of a *keli sheni*. Housewives commonly use cutlery in cooking foods on the stove and any such utensil is considered to be a *keli rishon*.

Garfish and Scad

Identification of the signs of kosher fish is not always a simple matter. The Sivan 5730 issue of *Ha-Pardes* contains an item clarifying some aspects of this problem. Rabbi S. Efratti, who at that time was head of the *Kashrut* Department of the Israeli Ministry of Religions, reports that of late a non-kosher species known as garfish has been imported from Portugal and marketed under the label "Anchovied Fillets of Garfish." The label on this product is misleading in that it may well cause the consumer to believe that he has purchased anchovies, which are known to be kosher, whereas the garfish is not.

Quite apart from misleading labeling, it is possible that erroneous categorization of the garfish as a species of kosher fish may result from either (1) acceptance of the microscopic scales borne by the garfish as a sign of its *kashrut* or (2) reliance upon the split tail of the garfish as conclusive evidence of its status as a kosher fish.

Rabbi Efratti cites the commentary of *Tiferet Yisra'el* on *Avodah Zarah* 2:6, which declares that for a fish to be deemed kosher its scales must be visible to the naked eye. This ruling is based upon two considerations. First, the Gemara, *Niddah* 57b, identifies the biblical term *kaskeset* as the "clothing" of the fish and, accordingly, defines *kaskeset* as "scales." Microscopic scales can hardly be deemed "clothing," and hence cannot satisfy this necessary condition of *kashrut*. Secondly, *Tiferet Yisra'el* establishes the general principle that in all matters contingent upon vision, Halakhah is concerned only with what is visible to the naked eye, not with what is visible under a magnifying glass or microscope. Rabbi Yechiel Michel Epstein reiterates the same principle in his halakhic compendium, *Arukh ha-Shulḥan, Yoreh De'ah* 83:15.[10a] *Arukh ha-Shulḥan* adds that mere perception of the scales is in itself insufficient since it is necessary that scales not only be present but that they be removable as well. This qualification is indicated by Ramban (*Commentary on the Bible,* Lev., 11:10) in his definition of *kaskeset* as a structure "which can be peeled off as one peels a fruit or removes bark from a tree."

Rabbi Efratti points out that even though numerous authorities speak of the split tail as an indication of *kashrut,* it is rather the absence of a split tail which is a definitive indication that the fish is of a non-kosher variety; the presence of a split tail is in itself not a reliable indication of *kashrut*.

In an earlier article, published in the Nisan 5730 issue of the same

---

10a. Cf. also, *Arukh ha-Shulhan, Yoreh De'ah* 84:36.

publication, Rabbi Efratti discusses the *kashrut* of a species known as scad or horsemackerel. [Reference to the dictionary definition of "horse-mackerel" shows that the term may be applied to a number of species. Apparently, some of these are kosher, others not. Its principal usage is as a synonym for tuna, which is, of course, a kosher fish.] These fish have also been marketed in Israel under the label "Anchovied Fillets of Scad." Scads possess a body-covering in the form of bony tubercules: rough, spinous projections, which do not overlap one another. These tubercules do not meet the criteria of the biblical *kaskeset* because they are of a shape markedly different from the shape of scales and are not removable. An informative analysis of the halakhic definition of "scale" by Rabbi Moses Tendler appeared in *Ha-Pardes,* Tevet 5726, and in an article entitled "The Halakhic Status of the Swordfish," which appeared in the April 1968 issue of the *Jewish Observer* and was reprinted in an extended version in *Gesher* (1969), vol. 4, no. 1.

Cold-Water Plucking

The modern housewife has become accustomed to many labor-saving conveniences. In particular, the availability of dressed, eviscerated fowl, completely ready for the pot at the moment of purchase, has been taken for granted for some time.

The preparation of kosher fowl presents a singular problem. In preparing poultry for sale, processing plants commonly remove feathers by means of a machine designed for this purpose. Plants preparing non-kosher fowl routinely immerse the fowl in hot water so that the mechanical feather-plucking process may be performed thoroughly and expeditiously.

The provisions of Jewish law preclude the immersion of unplucked kosher fowl in hot water. Hot-water immersion is not a permissible procedure because in this process the skin and flesh of the fowl become heated. The fowl immersed in this manner is deemed to have been "cooked," albeit briefly. Since, at the time of immersion and plucking, the blood has not yet been removed by means of soaking and salting, the fowl prepared in this manner is deemed to have been cooked together with its blood. This procedure automatically renders the fowl non-kosher.

Accordingly, kosher processing plants have developed a process involving cold-water immersion. The results, however, have not always been optimal. In an item appearing in the Tevet 5734 issue of *Ha-Ma'ayan* and subsequently reprinted in the Nisan 5736 issue of *Ha-Pardes,*[11] Dr. Israel Meir Levinger of the Jerusalem-based Institute for Technology and Halakhah reports on experiments designed to perfect a cold-water feather-removal process. It is Dr. Levinger's hypothesis that it is not heat *per se* which facilitates the removal of feathers, but that any radical change in the body temperature of the fowl causes feathers to adhere less rigidly to the skin, thereby facilitating their removal by machine. His experiments indicate that immersion in very cold water, at temperatures between 32 degrees and 46 degrees, is as effective as immersion in hot water. Immersion in water ranging from 46 degrees to 59 degrees is moderately effective. At higher cold-water temperatures the results are unsatisfactory.

Dr. Levinger does, however, raise one possible halakhic question with regard to processes using water at extremely low temperatures. The process of soaking and salting is designed to assure that the blood will be drained from the fowl. Dr. Levinger raises the possibility that immersion in extremely cold water may constrict the blood vessels, thus interfering with the subsequent draining of blood. However, as Dr. Levinger indicates, this problem may readily be obviated. Poultry immersed in cold water may be restored to normal room temperature before salting. Even frozen meat may be salted after it has been defrosted and restored to normal temperature. With the restoration of normal temperature, the blood vessels again become dilated.

Dr. Levinger also reports that a chemical compound is now available which facilitates the removal of feathers by machine. The compound, produced by Oxford Chemicals of Atlanta, Georgia, is known by the trade name Oxford FSD. According to the producer, the preparation, a slightly viscous liquid, contains organic wetting, emulsifying and defoaming agents. When used in kosher processing the chemical is dissolved in tepid water at room temperature and the fowl immersed in the solution prior to plucking. Dr. Levinger conducted a series of experiments in order to determine whether or not the use of this chemical compound might lead to constriction of the blood vessels and thus interfere with the subsequent draining of blood by means of the salting process. He reports that these experiments demonstrate that Oxford FSD, even when injected intravenously, does not cause vascular constriction.

Dr. Levinger reports that Rabbi S. Efratti notes that there remains

11. A translation of this article appears in the August 1974 issue of *Intercom,* a publication of the Association of Orthodox Jewish Scientists.

one possible complication resulting from the use of Oxford FSD. Use of this solution might conceivably soften tissues and lead to a breakdown of blood vessels. This may cause a subcutaneous collection of blood such as often results from a contusion. When a perceptible subcutaneous collection of blood is present the meat may not be salted unless the skin is first pierced and the blood allowed to drain. Accordingly, notes Dr. Levinger, should such a phenomenon indeed occur subsequent to use of this chemical, the blood should be drained prior to salting. Finding no impediment to its use, Dr. Levinger endorses the addition of Oxford FSD in cold-water processing of kosher fowl.

CHAPTER V

Medical Questions

The Holy One, blessed be He, does not smite Israel unless He has previously created a cure for them.

MEGILLAH 13b

In Jewish law and moral teaching the value of human life is supreme and takes precedence over virtually all other considerations. This attitude is most eloquently summed up in a talmudic passage regarding the creation of Adam: "Therefore only a single human being was created in the world, to teach that if any person has caused a single soul of Israel to perish, Scripture regards him as if he had caused an entire world to perish; and if any human being saves a single soul of Israel,[1] Scripture regards him as if he had saved an entire world" (*Sanhedrin* 37a). Human life is not a good to be preserved as a condition of other values but an absolute, basic, and precious good in its own right. The obligation to preserve life is commensurately all-encompassing.

The obligation to save the life of an endangered person is derived by the Talmud from the verse "Neither shall you stand idly by the blood of your neighbor" (Lev. 19:16). The Talmud and the various codes of Jewish law offer specific examples of situations in which a moral obligation exists with regard to rendering aid. These include the rescue of a person drowning in a river, assistance to one being mauled by wild beasts and aid to a person under attack by bandits.

The application of this principle to medical intervention for the purposes of preserving life is not without theological and philosophical diffi-

1. The phrase "of Israel" is omitted in the Palestinian Talmud and in the Munich MS of the Babylonian Talmud.

culties. It is to be anticipated that a theology which ascribes providential concern to the Deity will view sickness as part of the divine scheme. A personal God does not allow His creatures, over whom He exercises providential guardianship, to become ill unless the affliction is divinely ordained as a means of punishment, for purposes of expiation of sin or for some other beneficial purpose entirely comprehensible to the Deity, if not to man. Thus, while the ancient Greeks regarded illness as a curse and the sick as inferior persons because, to them, malady represented the disruption of the harmony of the body which is synonymous with health, in Christianity suffering was deemed to be a manifestation of divine grace because it effected purification of the afflicted and served as an ennobling process. Since illness resulted in a state of enhanced spiritual perfection, the sick man was viewed by early Christianity as marked by divine favor.

Human intervention in causing or speeding the therapeutic process is, then, in a sense, interference with the deliberate design of providence. The patient, in seeking medical attention, may be seen as betraying a lack of faith in failing to put his trust in God. This attitude is reflected in the teaching of a number of early and medieval Christian theologians who counseled against seeking medical attention. The Karaites, in turn, rejected all forms of human healing and relied entirely upon prayer. Consistent with their fundamentalist orientation, they based their position upon a quite literal reading of Exodus 16:26. A literal translation of the Hebrew text of the passage reads as follows: "I will put none of the diseases upon you which I have put upon the Egyptians, for I am the Lord your physician." Hence, the Karaites taught that God alone should be sought as physician.

This view was rejected by Rabbinic Judaism, but not without due recognition of the cogency of the theological argument upon which it is based. Rabbinic teaching recognized that intervention for the purpose of thwarting the natural course of a disease could be sanctioned only on the basis of specific divine dispensation. Such license is found, on the basis of talmudic exegesis, in the scriptural passage dealing with compensation for personal injury: "And if men quarrel with one another and one smites the other with a stone or with the fist and he die not, but has to keep in bed . . . he must pay the loss entailed by absence from work and he shall cause him to be thoroughly healed" (Exod. 21:18–19). Ostensibly, this passage refers simply to the financial liability incurred as the result of an act of assault. However, since specific reference is made to liability for medical expenses, it follows that liability for such expenses implies biblical license to incur those expenses in the course of seeking the ministrations of a practitioner of the healing arts. Thus the Talmud, *Baba Kamma* 85a, comments, "From here [it is derived] that the physician is granted permission to cure." Specific authorization is required, comments Rashi, in order to teach us that "we are not to say, 'How is it that God smites and man heals?' " In much the same vein *Tosafot* and R. Solomon ben Adret, in their commentaries upon this passage, state that without such sanction, "He who heals might appear as if he invalidated a divine decree."

Nontherapeutic life-saving intervention is talmudically mandated on independent grounds. The Talmud, *Sanhedrin* 73a, posits an obligation to rescue a neighbor from danger, such as drowning or being mauled by an animal. This obligation is predicated upon the scriptural exhortation with regard to the restoration of lost property, "And you shall return it to him" (Deut. 22:2). On the basis of a pleonasm in the Hebrew text, the Talmud declares that this verse includes an obligation to restore a fellow man's body as well as his property. Hence, there is created an obligation to come to the aid of one's fellow man in a life-threatening situation. Noteworthy is the fact that Maimonides,[2] going beyond the examples supplied by the Talmud, posits this source as the basis of the obligation to render medical care. Maimonides declares that the biblical commandment "And you shall return it to him" establishes an obligation requiring the physician to render professional services in life-threatening situations. Every individual, insofar as he is able, is obligated to restore the health of a fellow man no less than he is obligated to restore his property. Maimonides views this as a binding religious obligation.

Noteworthy is not only Maimonides' extension of this concept to cover medical matters but also his failure to allude at all to the verse "and he shall cause him to be thoroughly healed." It would appear that Maimonides is of the opinion that without the granting of specific *permission* one would not be permitted to tamper with physiological processes; obligations derived from Deuteronomy 22:2 would be limited to the prevention of accident or assault by man or beast. The dispensation to intervene in the natural order is derived from Exodus 21:20; but once such license is given, medical therapy is not simply elective but acquires the

2. *Commentary on the Mishnah, Nedarim* 4:4. Cf. *Mishneh Torah, Hilkhot Nedarim* 6:8.

status of a positive obligation.[3] As indicated by *Sanhedrin* 73a, this obligation mandates not only the rendering of personal assistance, as is the case with regard to the restoration of lost property, but, by virtue of the negative commandment, "You shall not stand idly by the blood of your neighbor" (Lev. 19:16), the obligation is expanded to encompass expenditure of financial resources for the sake of preserving life of one's fellow man. This seems to have been the interpretation given to Maimonides' comments by R. Joseph Karo, who, in his code of Jewish law, combined both concepts in stating: "The Torah gave permission to the physician to heal; moreover, this is a religious precept and it is included in the category of saving life; and if the physician withholds his service it is considered as shedding blood."[4]

Nachmanides finds that since the Torah gives permission to seek medical attention the physician's obligation to heal must also be deemed to be inherent in the commandment "And you shall love your neighbor as yourself" (Lev. 19:18).[5] The obligation to heal the sick is an instantiation of the general obligation to manifest love and concern for one's neighbor. As such, the obligation to heal encompasses not only situations posing a threat to life or limb or demanding restoration of impaired health but also situations of lesser gravity warranting medical attention for relief of pain and promotion of well-being.

Nevertheless, in the absence of specific scriptural license to practice the healing arts, Jews would be forbidden to seek the therapeutic benefits of medical science. Accordingly, despite the serious nature of the halakhic imperative with regard to the preservation of life and health, it is not surprising that this imperative is somewhat circumscribed insofar as the practice of medicine is concerned. The limitations, few as they are, serve as a reminder that all healing comes from God.

Sterilization of Women

The halakhic implications of the sterilization of women are the subject of a brief monograph authored by Dayan Grossnass of London which

---

3. Cf. R. Baruch ha-Levi Epstein, *Torah Temimah,* Exod. 21:19 and Deut. 22:2. Cf., also, R. Abraham Danzig, *Ḥokhmat Adam,* 141:25.

4. *Yoreh De'ah* 36:1. See R. Eliezer Waldenberg, *Ramat Raḥel,* no. 21, and *idem, Ẓiẓ Eli'ezer,* X, no. 25, chap. 7.

5. *Torat ha-Adam, Kitvei Ramban,* ed. Bernard Chavel (Jerusalem, 5724), II, 43.

has appeared as number 21 in a series of such responsa published by the London *Bet Din* and has been reprinted in three sections in the Shevat, Adar and Nisan 5732 issues of *Ha-Pardes*. The parents of a mentally incompetent daughter approached Dayan Grossnass with a particularly agonizing problem. Because of her mental condition the young woman in question was repeatedly subjected to sexual abuse and was ultimately found to be pregnant. Although the pregnancy did not pose a danger to her life, medical authorities deemed the pregnancy to be detrimental to her physical health. The parents sought a halakhic ruling with regard to the permissibility of surgical sterilization in order to prevent further pregnancies. Dayan Grossnass rules that an abortion cannot be sanctioned but that, under the circumstances, sterilization is permissible.

The Gemara, *Shabbat* 110b, derives the prohibition against castration of both male human beings and male animals from the verse "And that which is mauled or crushed or torn or cut you shall not offer unto the Lord; nor should you do this in your land" (Lev. 22:24). This verse is understood by the Gemara as having reference to the male sexual organs and hence the latter part of the verse constitutes a prohibition against emasculation. *Tosafot* and *Rashba,* in their commentaries on *Shabbat* 111a, indicate that this prohibition is limited to the removal of male sexual organs, and there exists no biblical prohibition with regard to the sterilization of a female. The terminology employed by Rambam, *Issurei Bi'ah* 16:11, and *Shulḥan Arukh, Even ha-Ezer* 5:11, would seem to indicate that the position of the latter authorities is that surgical sterilization of women, while not an actionable offense, is nevertheless biblically proscribed. Although the reference in Leviticus 22:24 is limited to external male organs, R. Elijah of Vilna, *Bi'ur ha-Gra, Even ha-Ezer* 5:25–26, cites *Sifra* in explaining that the ban against the removal of the internal female sexual organs is derived from the formulation employed in the very next verse, Leviticus 22:25. Nevertheless, other authorities, including *Ḥatam Sofer, Even ha-Ezer* 5:22, maintain that, even according to Rambam, the prohibition against the sterilization of females is rabbinic in nature. *Turei Zahav, Even ha-Ezer* 5:6, goes beyond the position of other authorities in averring that there is no prohibition with regard to female sterilization *per se,* but that it is nonetheless forbidden to subject female animals to this procedure because of the general prohibition against causing pain to animals. Similarly, nontherapeutic sterilization of women would constitute an unlawful act of "wounding"—*ḥavalah.*

In the case at hand, Dayan Grossnass rules that the woman may be sterilized but stipulates that the surgical procedure should be performed by a non-Jewish medical practitioner. *Shulḥan Arukh, Even ha-Ezer* 5:11, expressly declares that a non-Jew may not be requested to castrate an animal belonging to a Jew. Nevertheless, Dayan Grossnass permits sterilization to be performed by a non-Jewish physician in order to preserve the health of the woman. Dayan Grossnass asserts that all rabbinic prohibitions are suspended with regard to matters affecting human health even if no threat to life is involved. Employing this principle, he argues that according to those authorities who maintain that female sterilization is banned only by reason of rabbinic edict, the procedure in question could be performed even by a Jewish physician. There are indeed numerous authorities who are of the opinion that the sterilization of women is forbidden by biblical law. However even those rabbinic scholars who maintain that the sterilization of women is itself biblically forbidden recognize that the prohibition against requesting a non-Jew to perform the action in question is rabbinic in nature. Hence, concludes Dayan Grossnass, even if the ban against requesting a non-Jew to perform sterilization encompasses the sterilization of females, which is itself a matter of some doubt, the prohibition is suspended if the procedure is indicated for therapeutic reasons. Accordingly, Dayan Grossnass rules that a non-Jewish surgeon may be engaged to render this service.

According to Dayan Grossnass' analysis of the case at hand, sterilization may be performed by a non-Jewish surgeon because future pregnancy would be injurious to the health of the young woman in question; the woman's mental incompetence is not a significant factor in the halakhic reasoning which leads to this ruling. It is instructive to compare this recent decision with an earlier ruling recorded by Rabbi Moses Feinstein, *Iggrot Mosheh, Oraḥ Ḥayyim,* II, no. 88. Rabbi Feinstein discusses a closely related situation and arrives at a somewhat different position. Rabbi Feinstein, disagreeing with the view stated by Dayan Grossnass, contends that not all rabbinic prohibitions are suspended for reasons of health.[6] Hence, even according to those authorities who maintain that the prohibition against the sterilization of a female is rabbinic in nature,

6. The identical point is also made by Rabbi Feinstein in *Iggrot Mosheh, Even ha-Ezer,* I, no. 13. While Rabbi Feinstein does not cite a source, this position is clearly espoused by *Teshuvot ha-Rashba Meyuḥasot le-ha-Ramban,* no. 127. See also *Teshuvot R. Akiva Eger,* no. 5. Cf. *Divrei Ḥayyim, Yoreh De'ah,* II, no. 62; *Maharam Schick, Yoreh De'ah,* no. 173; *Teshuvot Sho'el u-Meshiv,* I, no. 210; and R. Eliyahu Klatzkin, *Dvar Eliyahu,* no. 17.

sterilization for therapeutic purposes cannot be sanctioned unless pregnancy poses a threat to the life of the mother. In the case brought before Rabbi Feinstein it was the mentally incompetent woman who initiated acts of sexual misconduct. Rabbi Feinstein asserts that promiscuous conduct on the part of the woman does constitute grounds for sanctioning sterilization because promiscuity constitutes a more serious offense than sterilization. As such, sterilization may be countenanced as the lesser of two evils. Of the two, sterilization is the less serious infraction because sterilization of women carries no statutory punishment. However, as noted earlier, any nontherapeutic surgical procedure entails an act of unlawful "wounding." The latter infraction does carry with it a statutory punishment and hence may not be suspended in order to obviate sexual promiscuity. Rabbi Feinstein permitted sterilization in the case brought to his attention only because pregnancy would also have been injurious to the health of the woman. The prohibition against wounding does not apply to situations in which a therapeutic purpose is served. Although the prohibition against wounding may not be violated if prevention of promiscuity is the sole justification, such sterilization may be performed if there is a therapeutic purpose served as well. Rabbi Feinstein adds that even under such circumstances sterilization should be performed by a non-Jewish physician.

Although Rabbi Feinstein does not spell out the medical details, his responsum is obviously predicated upon the premise that the mode of sterilization to be employed is expected to reduce the desire for sexual gratification, thereby eliminating or reducing the likelihood of sexual advances on the part of the mentally incompetent woman. While there is evidence demonstrating that this effect may be achieved by removal of the adrenal glands, there is no medical evidence that sterilization lessens the sexual drive in women.[7]

It may be noted that in responding to a query involving a situation in which the sole consideration was mental incompetence of the pregnant woman, Rabbi Yechiel Ya'akov Weinberg, *Seridei Esh,* III, *Even ha-Ezer,* no. 21, while not issuing a definitive decision, wrote, "It is possible to say that a woman may undergo sterilization" if pregnancy were to be accompanied by inordinate difficulties.

---

7. See Aleck Bourne, "Gynaecology," in *British Obstetric and Gynaecological Practice,* ed. Aleck Bourne and Sir Andrew Claye, 3rd ed. (London, 1963), p. 883.

Transsexual Surgery

Transsexuals are persons who are born with the anatomy of one sex but suffer from an identification with the other sex which in many instances is total and lifelong. It is claimed by some scientists doing research in this area that this abnormality is the result of hormone disturbances which are quite likely prenatal in origin. In a rapidly increasing number of cases transsexualism is now being treated medically by a combination of hormone therapy and sex-change surgery. While such operations were performed in Europe on an intermittent basis as early as 1930, sex-change operations have become prevalent in our country only since the late 1960s. There are an estimated ten thousand transsexuals in the United States, of whom approximately fifteen hundred have changed their sex by means of surgery. Public awareness of this phenomenon has been heightened by the recent publication of *Conundrum,* an autobiography by Jan (formerly James) Morris, in which the author discusses his own transsexualism with skill and sensitivity.

The growing acceptance of transsexual surgery has made the question of sex-change a topical halakhic issue. A number of rather cursory items dealing with this topic, which are noteworthy primarily on account of the sources cited, have appeared in the 5733 volume of *No'am* and in the Kislev–Tevet and Tammuz–Av 5733 issues of *Ha-Ma'or*. These articles do not treat the unique halakhic problems of hermaphrodites or of individuals born with ambiguous genitalia.

Sex-change operations involving the surgical removal of sexual organs are clearly forbidden on the basis of the explicit biblical prohibition, "And that which is mauled or crushed or torn or cut you shall not offer unto the Lord; nor should you do this in your land" (Lev. 22:24). Sterilization of women is also prohibited, as recorded in *Even ha-Ezer* 5:11.

Rabbi Meir Amsel (*Ha-Ma'or,* Kislev–Tevet 5733) notes that yet another prohibition is also applicable to sex-change procedures, a consideration which may extend as well to hormone treatment for purposes of sex-change. The commandment "A woman shall not wear that which pertains to a man, nor shall a man put on a woman's garment" (Deut. 22:5) is not limited to the wearing of apparel associated with the opposite sex but encompasses any action uniquely identified with the opposite sex, proscribing, for example, shaving of armpits or dyeing of hair by a male. A procedure designed to transform sexual characteristics violates the very essence of this prohibition.

Once a sexual transformation has actually been effected, a host of practical halakhic questions arise. The resolution of these questions hinges upon the crucial conceptual problem of whether or not a change of sex has indeed occurred from the point of view of Halakhah. It should be emphasized that while sexual organs can be removed, medical science is (at least as yet) incapable of substituting functional reproductive organs of the opposite sex. Sex-change procedures involve the construction of simulated sexual organs devoid of reproductive powers.

The most obvious halakhic questions concern the sexual status of such individuals with regard to marriage and divorce and with regard to their status *vis-à-vis* the respective obligations of men and women in the performance of *mizvot*. A related question is discussed by *Teshuvot Besamim Rosh,* a work of questionable authenticity commonly attributed to Rabbenu Asher. *Besamim Rosh,* no. 340, questions whether a man whose genitalia have been completely removed need divorce his wife in order to dissolve their marriage or whether a divorce is unnecessary since the male has been sexually transformed, and hence "a new body has appeared and is comparable to a woman's." *Besamim Rosh* reaches no definitive conclusion with regard to whether or not a divorce is necessary in the event that the operation is performed subsequent to entry into a valid marriage. However, *Besamim Rosh* strongly asserts that, regardless of an individual's sexual status with regard to other matters, once the male sexual organs have been removed the person in question is no longer competent to contract a valid marriage as a man.[8] Although not stated explicitly, it may be assumed, according to *Besamim Rosh,* that such a person is also unqualified to contract a marriage as a woman since true female genital organs remain absent even subsequent to successful completion of the surgical procedure.

For *Besamim Rosh* sexual identity, insofar as marriage is concerned, depends entirely upon the presence of genital organs. No mention is made of the presence or absence of secondary sexual characteristics and indeed it is not difficult to understand why they are deemed irrelevant. Hence, despite the comments of Rabbi Amsel, who asserts that secondary sexual characteristics play a role in sexual identification, there is no

---

8. R. Aryeh Leib Grossnass, *Lev Aryeh,* II, no. 49, takes exception to both the reasoning and the ruling of *Besamim Rosh.* R. Grossnass does, however, express doubt with regard to the necessity for a bill of divorce on the basis of *Minḥat Ḥinukh,* no. 203, but contends that for all other purposes, transsexual surgery has no effect upon sexual identity insofar as Halakhah is concerned.

evidence that the transformation of secondary sexual characteristics affects sexual status in any way.

One contemporary authority has ruled, without citing the ambivalent attitude of *Besamim Rosh,* that no divorce is necessary in order to permit the remarriage of a woman whose husband has undergone a sex-change operation. Rabbi Eliezer Waldenberg, *Ẓiẓ Eli'ezer,* X, no. 25, chap. 26, sec. 6, argues that if the person in question can no longer contract a marriage as a male (as indeed is the stated position of *Besamim Rosh*), the emergence of such a condition automatically terminates any existing marriage. The Gemara, *Yevamot* 49b, declares that although a husband is obliged to divorce an adulterous wife and is not permitted to remarry her, nevertheless, should he subsequently enter into such a marriage, the marriage is, *post factum,* deemed valid and must be dissolved by means of a divorce. Rashi and *Nemukei Yosef, ad locum,* explain that the marriage, when contracted, must be deemed valid, as evidenced by the fact that the original marriage is not automatically terminated upon the commission of adultery by the wife. The clear inference is that if Halakhah recognizes the continued existence of a previously contracted marriage despite a change in pertinent circumstances, a newly contracted marriage under the same circumstances is also valid. Conversely, if under the new circumstances a marriage cannot be contracted, it follows that an already existing marriage must be deemed to have been terminated automatically upon emergence of the new situation.[9] Unlike *Besamim*

---

9. This argument was originally advanced by *Minḥat Ḥinukh,* no. 203, in explanation of an intriguing position taken by *Terumat ha-Deshen,* no. 102. *Terumat ha-Deshen* questions whether the wife of the prophet Elijah was permitted to remarry. According to tradition, Elijah neither died nor divorced his wife but ascended to heaven bodily. *Terumat ha-Deshen* rules that Scripture forbids man to cohabit with "the wife of his fellow" but does not forbid the wife of an angel. (Cf., however, R. Shlomoh Kluger, *Ḥokhmat Shlomoh, Even ha-Ezer,* no. 17, who differs. See also R. Elchanan Wasserman, *Koveẓ Shi'urim,* II, no. 28.) *Minḥat Ḥinukh* explains, on the basis of the previous argument, that since an angel cannot contract a marriage, a marriage to a man who becomes an angel is automatically terminated. (For a different explanation, see *Teshuvot Mahari Asad, Even ha-Ezer,* no. 4. See also *Lev Aryeh,* II, no. 49.)

R. Waldenberg, *Ẓiẓ Eli'ezer,* X, no. 25, chap. 26, sec. 6, and XI, no. 78, maintains that surgical reversal does effect a change in sexual identity in the eyes of Halakhah. He therefore argues that just as cohabitation is forbidden with the wife of his fellow but not with the wife of an angel, so also the concept of the wife of his fellow excludes the concept of the wife of a woman.

Rosh, Rabbi Waldenberg is of the opinion that the surgical removal of male sexual organs effects a change in sexual identity in the eyes of Halakhah. Rabbi Waldenberg, however, cites no evidence whatsoever for this view.

There is at least one early source which apparently declares that a male cannot acquire the status of a woman by means of surgery. Rabbi Abraham Hirsch (*No'am* 5733) cites the comments of Rabbenu Chananel, quoted by Ibn Ezra in his commentary on Leviticus 18:22. Rabbenu Chananel declares that intercourse between a normal male and a male in whom an artificial vagina has been fashioned by means of surgery constitutes sodomy. This would appear to be the case, according to Rabbenu Chananel, even if the male genitalia were removed.[10]

The corollary to this question arises with regard to a woman who has acquired the sexual characteristics of a male as a result of transsexual surgery. A nineteenth-century author, R. Yosef Pelaggi, *Yosef et Eḥav* 3:5, opines that no divorce is necessary in order to dissolve a marriage contracted prior to such transformation. This author goes beyond the position of *Besamim Rosh,* who, as noted, did not reach a definitive conclusion in his discussion of the parallel question with regard to sex change in a male. In opposition to R. Pelaggi's view it may, however, be argued that gender is irreversibly determined at birth and that sex, insofar as Hala-

10. It might be argued against R. Hirsch that citation of Rabbenu Chananel is not conclusive in showing that Halakhah does not recognize reversal of sexual identity. The situation depicted by Rabbenu Chananel, after all, refers to a homosexual act with a male in whom an artificial orifice has been constructed; Rabbenu Chananel clearly does not describe a situation in which sex reversal has also been undertaken by means of removal of the male genitalia. Nevertheless, in context, the argument has not lost its cogency. If surgical changes in sexual identity are recognized for purposes of Halakhah, it would stand to reason that just as male-female changes effect a change in sexual identity, the construction of female organs, when unaccompanied by removal of male organs, should similarly be recognized as effecting a change in sexual identity from male to hermaphrodite. Rabbenu Chananel, as is evident from the text of these remarks, does not view penetration of the female organ of a hermaphrodite by a male as constituting a homosexual act (although he does allow for such a position in subsequent remarks). Yet, according to Rabbenu Chananel, intercourse via the artificially constructed vagina does constitute sodomy. This, then, indicates that the individual is regarded as a male rather than a hermaphrodite. Therefore it follows that if surgical procedures do not effect a change in status from male to hermaphrodite, such procedures cannot create a change of status from male to female in the eyes of Halakhah.

khah is concerned, cannot be transformed by surgical procedures. This position is particularly cogent in view of the fact that fertile organs of the opposite sex cannot be acquired by means of surgery. The view that sexual identity cannot be changed by means of surgery would appear to be the position of Rabbenu Chananel. According to Rabbenu Chananel, this principle would appear to govern all halakhic questions pertaining to sexual identity.

Parenthetically, it is of interest to note that various courts in the United States have ruled that, in the eyes of the law, surgery to transform genitalia has no effect upon the gender of the person upon whom such procedures are performed (*Anonymous* v. *Anonymous,* 67 Misc. 2d 982; *Baker* v. *Nelson,* 291 Minn. 310, 191 N.W. 2d 185; 409 U.S. 810, 93 Supreme Court, 37; *Jones* v. *Hallahan,* Ky., 501, S.W. 2d 588). Recently, a justice of the New York State Supreme Court ruled that a woman who underwent surgery to become a man and subsequently married could not seek a divorce since a valid marriage had, in fact, never existed. The decision states that a marriage contract entered into by individuals of the same sex, one of whom has undergone sex-reversal surgery, has no validity either in fact or in law (*New York Law Journal,* April 30, 1974, p. 17, col. 4).

Another interesting question arises with regard to circumcision. In female-to-male transformations a simulated male organ is often created by means of skin grafts and silicone forms. In some cases this effect is achieved by freeing the clitoris from its connective tissue. There is no question that this newly fashioned organ need not be circumcised. This is abundantly clear from the conclusion reached by *She'elat Ya'avez,* I, no. 171, in the discussion of a similar question arising with regard to a congenital defect. *Yosef et Eḥav* cites the comments of *Yad Ne'eman,* who maintains that circumcision would be unnecessary even if the new organ were physiologically similar to that of a male in every respect. In the opinion of the latter authority, the phraseology employed by Scripture, "uncircumcised male" (Gen. 17:13), applies solely to an individual who is a male at the time of birth.

A peripheral halakhic question which arises in cases of sexual transformation concerns which of the blessings included in the morning service should be recited by an individual who has undergone a transsexual procedure. Is the person in question to recite the blessing "Who has not made me a woman" or the blessing "Who has made me in accordance with His will"? The question is a compound one involving two separate issues. The first question is identical with the issue previously discussed:

Is the individual's gender deemed to have been changed or is it deemed to have remained unchanged? Secondly, assuming that surgical transformation is to be recognized as indeed having effected a transformation from the point of view of Halakhah, there exists a halakhic controversy with regard to whether the blessings to be recited each morning are determined by the individual's status at birth or by his status at the time the blessings are pronounced. This difference of opinion is reflected in the controversy with regard to the recitation of the blessing "Who has not made me a gentile" by a proselyte. Rambam maintains that since the convert was born a gentile, it follows that he cannot truthfully pronounce the blessing "Who has not *made* me a gentile." Rashi disagrees and maintains that the blessing is fundamentally an expression of thanksgiving for being bound by the commandments of the Torah incumbent upon members of the Jewish faith and hence may be pronounced by the proselyte, since at the time of the recitation of the blessing he is indeed a Jew and subject to all *mizvot*. The blessings "Who has not made me a woman" and "Who has made me in accordance with His will" reflect the differing status of men and women with regard to the performance of *mizvot*. Hence, if the surgical transformation effects a change in the eyes of Halakhah, the proper blessing should, according to the opinion of Rashi, reflect the changed status, whereas, according to the opinion of Rambam, the usage "Who has made" or "Who has not made" in this context would express a falsehood.

It has been suggested that the entire question may be obviated by composing a text which would be more appropriate to such situations. According to this view, the proper blessings would be "Who has transformed me into a male" and "Who has transformed me in accordance with His will." Quite apart from the unwarranted assumption regarding divine approbation implied by this phraseology, it may be objected that in the absence of any liturgical formulation pertaining to "transformation" the proposed texts do not constitute rabbinically ordained formulae and hence cannot serve as valid substitutes for statutory blessings.

Although Judaism does not sanction the reversal of sex by means of surgery, transsexualism is a disorder which should receive the fullest measure of medical and psychiatric treatment consistent with Halakhah. Transsexuals should be encouraged to undergo treatment to correct endocrine imbalances, where medically indicated, and to seek psychiatric guidance in order to alleviate the grave emotional problems which are frequently associated with this tragic condition.

Host-Mothers

Any parent who has at one time or another been exposed by his children to the captivating Dr. Seuss fantasy, *Horton Hatches the Egg,* will recall the dilemma around which that tale centers: to whom does the offspring rightfully belong, the irresponsible mother who abandoned it, or the faithful elephant who guarded and protected the egg over a span of months? The fictional solution may be both too facile—and too equitable—for real life. Preposterous and farfetched as the situation may appear to be the problem it poses may be upon us before long. We find ourselves in an age in which the science fiction of yesterday is rapidly becoming the reality of today; the hypothetical curiosity of today may well become the commonplace of tomorrow. These unfolding *realia* often carry in their wake hitherto unexamined moral and religious questions. Perhaps in no area is this more evident than in the field of embryology. Recent experimental developments indicate that it may soon become possible to remove a naturally fertilized ovum from the womb of a pregnant mother and reimplant it in the uterus of another woman. The embryo would then remain in the womb of the "host-mother" throughout the period of gestation until birth.

In a statement released by his office, Rabbi Immanuel Jakobovits, Chief Rabbi of Great Britain, aptly characterizes such practices as offensive to moral sensitivities when resorted to as a convenience in order to avoid the encumbrances of pregnancy. Certainly all will agree that "to use another person as an 'incubator' and then take from her the child she carried and delivered for a fee is a revolting degradation of maternity and an affront to human dignity."

Convenience is, however, not the only conceivable motive which might prompt a procedure of this nature. Medical factors may well make it impossible for the natural mother to carry her baby to term. Would Halakhah sanction the use of a "host-mother" for the purpose of saving the fetus? If such a procedure is performed, with or without halakhic sanction, who is regarded as the mother in the eyes of Halakhah: the natural mother or the host-mother?

As yet, very little has been written on this subject, although a related question has received some attention in rabbinic literature. The 5731 edition of *No'am* features an extensive and wide-ranging paper by Rabbi Isaac Liebes dealing with the various halakhic questions associated with organ transplants. *Inter alia* Rabbi Liebes cites sources bearing upon the problems posed by ovarian transplants. The question of ovarian transplants was raised by Rabbi Yekutiel Aryeh Kamelhar in a Torah journal published in Warsaw in 1932 and was subsequently reprinted in his *Ha-Talmud u-Mada'ei ha-Tevel,* pp. 45–45.[11] Rabbi Kamelhar relates that a paper was read at a medical conference held in Chicago some twenty-one years earlier in which it was alleged that in at least one instance sterility was successfully corrected by an ovarian transplant. The ovary of a fertile woman was transplanted into the body of a previously barren woman in an attempt to enable her to become pregnant and bear children. Rabbi Kamelhar examines the question of which of the two women is to be considered the mother of the child in the eyes of Jewish law. Cases involving a donor who is a married woman pose yet another question. Is the husband of the woman receiving the transplant thereafter permitted to engage in intercouse with his wife? Is the husband who has sexual relations with a wife carrying a transplanted reproductive organ of another married woman guilty of adultery? Rabbi Kamelhar dismisses the latter question by demonstrating that the source of specific organs has no bearing upon the halakhic definition of adultery.

Furthermore, maintains Rabbi Kamelhar, a transplanted organ is deemed to have become an integral part of the body of the recipient. For this reason, the recipient of an ovarian transplant must also be considered the mother of any child subsequently conceived. Despite a lack of relevant sources dealing with human transplants Rabbi Kamelhar endeavors to establish this point by drawing upon regulations governing the classification of plants and animals. The fruits of a seedling are forbidden as *orlah* during the first three years following its planting. *Sotah* 43b declares that a seedling which is grafted to a mature tree loses its independent identity and hence the fruit of the seedling is not deemed to be *orlah.* The same principle, argues Rabbi Kamelhar, applies with regard to the transplantation of organs; namely, a transplanted organ acquires the identity of the recipient. A second argument is based upon laws pertaining to hybrid animals. *Ḥullin* 79a, in discussing the classification of the offspring born as a result of the interbreeding of different species, records one opinion which maintains that the identity of the male parent is to be completely disregarded in determining the species of the offspring. According to this view, since it is the mother who nurtures and sustains the embryo, it is the female parent alone who determines the species of the offspring. It is thus the identity of the mother which is transferred to members of an inter-species. There

11. See R. Yekutiel Greenwald, *Kol Bo 'al Avelut,* I, chap. 3, sec. 21.

is, however, a conflicting opinion which asserts that "the father's seed is to be considered." Rabbi Kamelhar asserts that even proponents of this latter view will concede that with regard to ovarian transplants the identity of the donor need not be considered in establishing maternity. "The father's seed is to be considered" because the father plays a dynamic role in the birth of the offspring. The ovary alone, Rabbi Kamelhar points out, is an inert organ and incapable of reproduction were it not for the physiological contributions of the recipient. In conclusion, Rabbi Kamelhar notes that Rabbi Meir Arak, one of the foremost halakhists of the day, accepted the cogency of this argument.[12]

To a significant degree, the identical argumentation may be applied in determining the maternity of a child born of a fertilized ovum implanted in the womb of a host-mother. It is the host-mother who nurtures the embryo and sustains gestation. However, the role of the natural mother in the determination of identity is a dynamic one and analagous to that of "the seed of the father." It may therefore be argued according to those who assert with reference to the classification of hybrids that "the seed of the father is to be considered" that, in the case of an already fertilized ovum, the maternal relationship between the child and the donor mother is to be "considered" no less than "the seed of the father." Consideration must also be given to the possibility that perhaps two maternal relationships may exist simultaneously, just as maternal and paternal relationships exist at one and the same time. The child would then, in effect, have two "mothers," the donor-mother and the host-mother.

According to some authorities, however, the donor-mother alone may be viewed as the mother in the eyes of Jewish law. There are those who maintain that the prohibition against feticide is applicable from the moment of conception and deem the fetus to be a nascent human being even in the the earliest stages of gestation. According to this view, the zygote may perhaps be viewed as having already acquired identity and parentage.

The discussion thus far applies only to the transplantation of a fertilized ovum removed shortly after conception. Transplantation of an embryo in later stages of development presents a rather different question. What has preceded is based upon fragmentary sources and is but one aspect of a

12. See also R. Binyamin Aryeh Weiss, *Even Yekarah,* III, no. 29; *Teshuvot Rabaz, Even ha-Ezer,* no. 5; R. Eliezer Waldenberg, *Ẓiẓ Eli'ezer,* VII, no. 48, chap. 5, sec. 16; R. Yeshayahu Silverstein and R. Eliezer Deutsch, *Tel Talpiot,* 5668; R. Menasheh Klein, *Mishneh Halakhot,* IV, no. 249; and R. Yosef Schwartz, *Va-Yelaket Yosef,* nos. 22, 32, 54 and 77.

topic whose many ramifications have yet to be examined. There is indeed a great need for such examination and analysis for the transformations which may soon be wrought by scientific advances in this field touch upon the very foundations of the sanctity of the family.

Tay-Sachs Disease

Only recently has the general Jewish community become aware of the existence of a genetic disorder, Tay-Sachs disease, having a high incidence of Jewish victims. Tay-Sachs disease is a fatal, inherited condition. A child afflicted with this disorder appears normal at birth and may develop normally until five or six months of age. At that point normal development of the nervous system ceases. Over the next few months the infant gradually loses the ability to sit and in time becomes unable to hold up his head. As physical deterioration progresses, the child becomes blind, becomes subject to frequent convulsive seizures, loses the ability to swallow food and its limbs become stiff. Death usually occurs in the third or fourth year of life.

Although there are clinical descriptions of this disorder dating back to 1881, an explanation of the nature of this mysterious disease was not found until 1969. Medical research has discovered that the disease is caused by the absence of an enzyme which normally assists in the breakdown of fatty substances known as gangliosides. The missing enzyme is hexosaminidase A (HEX A). Since the requisite enzyme is absent these gangliosides accumulate in the cells and tissue of the affected Tay-Sachs child and ultimately lead to the destruction of brain cells.

Tay-Sachs disease is caused by a genetic mutation. The disease appears only in a child who has inherited a pair of genes both of which are defective. One of the pair is inherited from the mother; the other from the father. The parents, each the carrier of a defective gene which may be transmitted to their offspring, are themselves perfectly normal both physically and mentally.

Diseases resulting from genetic mutation are often limited to specific ethnic groups. Tay-Sachs is such a disease and is prevalent among children of Ashkenazic Jews. On the other hand, phenylketonuria, a defective gene common among white gentiles, is very rare among Jews. Similarly, sickle-cell anemia is prevalent among Negroes. The carrier-rate of Tay-Sachs disease among Jews of Central and East European ancestry is believed to be about one person in thirty. Since both persons must be carriers for the child to be affected it may be assumed that statistically one in nine hundred Jewish couples may have a Tay-Sachs child. Should two such people marry and have children the risk that they will have an infant afflicted with Tay-Sachs disease is one in four with each pregnancy. This is so because each normal parent possesses two genes, one of which is normal, the other defective. The child inherits only one of these genes, giving him a fifty percent chance of inheriting the abnormal gene from each of his parents. If a defective gene is inherited from one parent but a normal gene from the other the child will be normal. The statistical probability of his inheriting two defective genes, one from each parent, is 1/2 x 1/2, or 1/4. Since one individual in thirty is a carrier, one in thirty-six hundred babies (1/30 x 1/30 x 1/4) will be a victim of Tay-Sachs disease. In the non-Jewish population only one individual in three hundred is a carrier. Hence statistically only one marriage in ninety-thousand is between two carriers and only one baby in 360,000 is a victim of Tay-Sachs disease.

During the past several years medical science has discovered ways of identifying potential victims, and medical centers in a number of cities, notably Johns Hopkins University in Baltimore, Montreal Children's Hospital and the Hospital for Sick Children in Toronto, have initiated large-scale campaigns in a massive attempt to eliminate the disease. A carrier can be identified by means of a simple blood test. The enzyme responsible for the condition normally leaks from cells into the circulating plasma. The absence of this enzyme in the plasma indicates that the individual is a carrier. The absence of the enzyme can also be detected in cells shed from skin of the fetus into the amniotic fluid. It is thus possible to make a diagnosis of an affected fetus in-utero by means of amniocentesis, which involves tapping the amniotic fluid in the uterus and examination of fetal cells.

Physicians in the above-mentioned communities now urgently recommend that rabbis refer prospective brides and grooms to a local testing center so that a blood test may be performed in order to identify carriers of Tay-Sachs disease. As a result of the test the following recommendations are made by the medical personnel involved:

1. If the screening test for the carrier state is positive in only one member of the couple no danger exists with regard to the offspring of that marriage. Such individuals are counseled with regard to the significance of the mutation and are urged to have their own offspring tested for future reference and counseling.

2. If both members of the couple are carriers:
   a) The couple is warned that the risks of bearing a Tay-Sachs child are one in four with each pregnancy.
   b) The couple are counseled with regard to the alternatives to having their own natural children.
   c) They are admonished that should they proceed to have their own children, fetal monitoring should be undertaken. If a Tay-Sachs fetus is identified the common medical practice is to recommend an abortion.

The elimination of Tay-Sachs disease is, of course, a goal to which all concerned individuals subscribe. However, the means by which this desideratum is to be attained require halakhic review, all the more so because the active participation of the rabbinate has been solicited by concerned medical authorities. An article by the present writer, outlining the halakhic ramifications of the testing program, appears in the Tammuz 5732 issue of *Or ha-Mizraḥ*.

The obligation with regard to procreation is not suspended simply because of the statistical probability that some children of the union may be deformed or abnormal. While the couple may quite properly be counseled with regard to the risks of having a Tay-Sachs child, it should be stressed that failure to bear natural children is not a halakhically viable alternative.[12a]

Of at least equal, if not graver, concern is the proposal that fetal monitoring be performed with a view toward termination of the pregnancy if the fetus be identified as a victim of Tay-Sachs disease.

The fear that a child may be born physically malformed or mentally deficient does not in itself justify recourse to abortion. At present amniocentesis cannot be performed prior to the fourth or fifth month of pregnancy. Most rabbinic decisors agree that at so late a stage in pregnancy abortion is permissible only if continuation of pregnancy constitutes a threat to the life or, according to many, to the health of the mother.[12b] In situations where amniocentesis is performed for purposes of diagnosing a condition for which a medical remedy is available, e.g., blood-group incompatibility which can be treated by exchange transfusion, the physician is not only permitted but is obligated to perform amniocentesis, even repeatedly. However, amniocentesis carried out solely for the purpose of diagnosing

12a. See *Iggrot Mosheh, Even ha-Ezer,* no. 62.
12b. See below, p. 346, n. 42.

severe genetic defects, such as Tay-Sachs disease, serves no therapeutic purpose. Since the sole available medical remedy following diagnosis of severe genetic defects is the abortion of the fetus, which is not sanctioned by Halakhah in such instances, amniocentesis, under these conditions, does not serve as an aid in treatment of the patient and is not halakhically permissible. Initiation of this procedure in the absence of a therapeutic goal poses a pointless medical risk to both mother and fetus and also constitutes an act of *ḥavalah*—an unwarranted assault upon the mother.

Blood-testing programs as a screening method for the identification of carriers of Tay-Sachs disease are certainly to be encouraged. However, sensitivity to the dictates of Halakhah, which precludes both abortion and a sterile union, would indicate that the most propitious time for such screening is childhood or early adolescence.[12c] Early awareness of a carrier state, particularly when determination can be made on mass scale and accompanied by a public-information campaign, would contribute greatly to alleviating the gravity of the situation.

Tay-Sachs Re-examined

The Falk-Schlesinger Institute of Jerusalem's Sha'arei Zedek Hospital has for the past several years sponsored the publication of *Assia,* a journal devoted to topics of medical halakhah. The Adar 5736 issue of this periodical contains an important responsum authored by Rabbi Eliezer Waldenberg dealing with the grave and emotion-laden question of abortion of a Tay-Sachs fetus.

Until very recently virtually all rabbinic authorities who have addressed themselves to the question of the permissibility of destroying a defective fetus have ruled that the presence of physical or mental abnormality does not, in itself, constitute sufficient halakhic grounds for sanctioning termination of pregnancy. Heretofore the most lenient opinion given serious

12c. Possible psychological consequences of carrier identification are discussed by E. Beck, S. Blaichman and C. R. Scriver, "Advocacy and Compliance in Genetic Screening," *New England Journal of Medicine* 291: 1166–1170, 1974; M. M. Kaback, R. S. Zeiger, L. W. Reynolds *et al,* "Tay-Sachs Disease: A Model for the Control of Recessive Genetic Disorders," *Proceedings of the Fourth International Conference,* Vienna, Austria, Sept. 2-8, 1973 and *Excerpta Medica,* 1974, pp. 248–262; M. D. Kuhr, "Doubtful Benefits of Tay-Sachs Screening," *New England Journal of Medicine* 292: 371, 1975; and by L. Schneck, A Saifer and B. W. Volk, "Benefits of Tay-Sacks Screening" *New England Journal of Medicine* 292: 758, 1975.

consideration in rabbinic circles has been that of R. Eliezer Waldenberg, whose views are recorded in *Ẓiẓ Eli'ezer,* IX, no. 51, ch. 3. In that work Rabbi Waldenberg rules that abnormality of the fetus is sufficient justification for termination of pregnancy within the first trimester provided there is as yet no fetal movement. While this ruling is significant in the case of an expectant mother who has contracted rubella, it has little practical application with regard to termination of a pregnancy in which the fetus is afflicted by Tay-Sachs disease or by some other genetic abnormality. The presence in the fetus of Tay-Sachs disease, or of any of some seventy-odd other genetic disorders, can be diagnosed only by amniocentesis which, at present, can be performed no earlier than the fourth or fifth month of pregnancy. According to the opinion recorded in *Ẓiẓ Eli'ezer* abortion cannot be performed at such an advanced state of gestation.

Rabbi Waldenberg's decision is based upon the configuration of several considerations: 1) the view that there is no prohibition against destruction of a fetus during the first trimester of pregnancy; 2) the view of R. Joseph Trani, *Teshuvot Maharit,* I, nos. 97 and 99, who states that feticide is forbidden as an act of "wounding" and, accordingly, is permitted for any therapeutic purpose; and 3) the position of R. Ya'akov Emden, *She'elat Ya'aveẓ,* no. 43, who sanctions abortion in cases of "grave necessity."[12d]

R. Emden's thesis is based upon two novel concepts. In disagreement with most other authorities, R. Emden (following *Ḥavot Ya'ir,* no. 31) espouses the view that feticide is proscribed because it is a form of "destruction of the seed." Destruction of the seed is prohibited as being tantamount to onanism which, in turn, is defined as emission of the seed "for no purpose." The term "for no purpose" is usually understood as restricting every emission of semen with the exception of ejaculation for purposes of procreation or, more broadly, any ejaculation which occurs in the context of natural intercourse. R. Ya'akov Emden, however, defines the term *"le-vatalah*—for no purpose" quite literally. According to this view, any ejaculation which serves a useful and licit purpose is not *"le-vatalah."* Accordingly, R. Emden rules that, since feticide involves only the "destruction of the seed," the fetus may be destroyed if there exists a "grave need" to do so. The presence of a "grave need" renders the act purposeful and hence not *"le-vatalah."* On these grounds R. Emden permits the destruction of a bastard fetus. R. Emden takes cognizance of the pain and anguish of the mother which is attendant upon a pregnancy of this

12d. These positions are discussed in greater detail in Part II, chap. XV, "Abortion in Halakhic Literature," pp. 336–339, 341 and 354–356. It should be noted that *Teshuvot Binyan David,* no. 60, regards Maharit as permitting an abortion only when the mother's life is in danger. See below, p. 356, n. 61.

nature and asserts that relief of such anguish constitutes a "grave need." In a similar fashion Rabbi Waldenberg recognizes that the difficulties engendered by the birth of an abnormal child may render abortion a grave necessity.

Rabbi Waldenberg is, however, aware that the vast majority of rabbinic decisors are in disagreement with this view.[12e] Accordingly, he rules that this opinion may be relied upon only during the first three months of pregnancy during which time there are other grounds for leniency. The distinction between the first trimester of pregnancy and subsequent stages of gestation is cited by Rabbi Waldenberg in the name of *Pri ha-Sadeh,* IV, no. 50. That authority, in turn, attributes the distinction to *Ḥavot Ya'ir.* Elsewhere, this writer has noted that this distinction was made by *Ḥavot Ya'ir* only as a hypothetical distinction which must be rejected for lack of substantiation.[12f] *Ḥavot Ya'ir* concludes his prefatory remarks with the statement that it is not his goal to adjudicate such matters on the basis of "inclination of the mind or reasoning of the stomach" but rather on the basis of "law of the Torah." *Ḥavot Ya'ir* thus dismisses the possibility of any distinction between various stages of pregnancy as being without precedent in rabbinic sources. Indeed, on the basis of *Ḥavot Ya'ir's* thesis that feticide is a form of destruction of the seed such a distinction would be quite illogical. The distinction between the first three months of pregnancy and later stages of gestation was apparently erroneously transmitted and subsequently cited by a number of authorities who did not have the original source before them.[12g] R. Chaim Chizkiyahu Medini, author of *Sedei Ḥemed,* for example, carefully notes that he did not have access to this work.[12h]

The grave question of aborting a defective fetus has now been examined anew by Rabbi Waldenberg in his contribution to *Assia.* Rabbi Waldenberg now notes that the distinction frequently attributed to *Ḥavot Ya'ir* is spurious. There is thus no source for a distinction between the first trimester and later stages of pregnancy. Since in *Ẓiẓ Eli'ezer* Rabbi Waldenberg permitted abortion of a defective fetus only during the first trimester at

---

12e. See below, p. 346 and p. 367.

12f. See below, p. 340, n. 31 and p. 346, n. 41.

12g. There are, of course, other authorities who assert that the prohibition against feticide does not apply during the first forty days of pregnancy, but that is an entirely different matter. See below, pp. 339–347.

12h. See R. Solomon Abraham Rezechte, *Bikkurei Shlomoh* (Pietrokow, 5665), no. 10, sec. 5; see also, below, p. 340, n. 31.

which time such an abortion is purportedly sanctioned also by the weight of *Ḥavot Ya'ir's* opinion it might be concluded that, subsequent to discovery that there exists no authority who views the prohibition against abortion as inoperative during the first trimester, permission to abort an abnormal fetus should be withheld. Rabbi Waldenberg, however, reaches the opposite conclusion. In this recent responsum he relies entirely upon the opinions of R. Emden and Maharit and permits abortion of a Tay-Sachs fetus during later stages of pregnancy as well. In doing so Rabbi Waldenberg rules contrary to the decisions of other contemporary rabbinic scholars and contrary to his own previously expressed position. Rabbi Waldenberg's presently held view is that abortion of a defective fetus may be sanctioned until the end of the second trimester of pregnancy provided that the abortion itself poses no danger to the mother. He refuses to permit abortion beyond this period because a seven-month abortus may be viable. He further recommends that, if possible, the abortion should be performed by a female physician since, according to many authorities, women are not bound by the prohibition against "destruction of the seed."

In the same responsum Rabbi Waldenberg affirms the view that if Tay-Sachs screening is carried out before marriage and both prospective bride and groom have been identified as Tay-Sachs carriers they should be counselled that Judaism does not sanction a sterile union and they should be dissuaded from marrying one another.

It cannot be overemphaized that this advice pertains only to a contemplated marriage in which *both* partners are Tay-Sachs carriers. Since Tay-Sachs is a genetically recessive abnormality there is absolutely no possibility whatsoever that a child may suffer from Tay-Sachs disease if only one of his parents is a carrier. Children born of a union between a carrier and a non-carrier are at risk only of themselves being carriers. Since a Tay-Sachs carrier is in no way less healthy than a non-carrier such a child suffers no disadvantage save the advisability of exercising prudence in determining that his or her marriage partner is a non-carrier. Thus there is no reason for any stigma to be associated with the carrier state.

Temporary Crowns

In order to secure adequate protection of teeth prepared for single crowns or bridge retainers it is common dental practice to insert a temporary crown which then remains in place during the interval between preparation and final cementation of the restoration. This interval may vary in length from several days to several months. The temporary crown serves to protect the margins of preparation from damage and fracture, to maintain proper occlusal relationship between the teeth and also to protect the dentine and pulp from thermal, chemical and medicinal irritants. A temporary crown of aluminum or plastic is cemented in place either with an inert substance or with a medicinal agent which is sedative in nature. Such temporary restorations are later removed with the aid of dental instruments and normally cannot be removed by the patient himself.

Temporary crowns of this nature pose a halakhic problem with regard to ritual immersion by female patients. Immersion must be performed by submerging the entire body in water; the interposition of an intervening object constitutes a *ḥaẓiẓah* and invalidates the immersion. Do such crowns constitute a *ḥaẓiẓah* and must they therefore be removed before immersion, or may immersion be performed with the temporary crown in place? In general, a foreign substance permanently affixed to the body (e.g., a permanent filling in a tooth) is halakhically considered to be part of the body and hence does not constitute a *ḥaẓiẓah*. The plastic crown, although securely affixed with cement, must eventually be removed. Hence the problem: is a foreign substance which is now attached but eventually to be removed to be deemed a part of the body, or is it to be considered an entity distinct from the body and hence a *ḥaẓiẓah?* Rabbi Aaron Zlotowitz, writing in the Iyar 5731 issue of *Ha-Pardes,* cites a similar question which had been referred to *Ḥatam Sofer*. The case discussed deals with the initial immersion of the bride prior to her marriage. It was the custom in Hungary to cut the bride's hair after the wedding ceremony. Since it was soon to be cut, was the hair to be considered a foreign object and hence a *ḥaẓiẓah* in immersion? Quoting *Tosafot, Baba Kamma* 76b, *Ḥatam Sofer* declares that, while under certain circumstances Halakah considers an anticipated act to have taken place even prior to its actualization, this principle applies only if such actualization follows without interruption or delay. Since the bridal custom was to delay cutting the hair until the day following the wedding the hair did not constitute a *ḥaẓiẓah*. Similarly, concludes Rabbi Zlotowitz, since the temporary crown must remain in place until the time set by the dentist for its removal, such a crown does not constitute a *ḥaẓiẓah*.

Although Rabbi Zlotowitz formulates the problem of temporary crowns as a new question, the issues involved have been investigated previously in responsa literature in connection with related problems. Rabbi Moses Feinstein, *Iggrot Mosheh, Yoreh De'ah,* I, no. 97, advances a number of arguments, on the basis of which he rules that certain types of temporary fillings do not constitute a *ḥaẓiẓah.* Many of those considerations are equally applicable with regard to temporary crowns.

There is a general rule that a foreign object which is not an item of "concern" (*aino makpid*), i.e., its presence is not a source of annoyance and there is no "concern" to remove it, does not constitute a *ḥaẓiẓah.* Items which are a source of "concern", i.e., with regard to which there does exist a desire for removal, do constitute a *ḥaẓiẓah.* Rabbi Feinstein seeks to demonstrate that a foreign substance which is to remain attached to the body for a specific period of time does not constitute a *ḥaẓiẓah* even though there is definite reason and desire for removal at a later period. This is certainly the case if there is a positive reason for desiring the object to remain attached in the interim. This decision is based upon clarification of the halakhic provision that a foreign substance whose presence is not a matter of "concern" (*aino makpid*) does not invalidate the immersion. Rabbi Feinstein maintains that this rule is not predicated upon the rationale that the object in question acquires the status of an integral part of the body, but is based upon the facile explanation that something which is not an object of "concern" simply does not constitute an "interposition." Therefore, even though a temporary filling cannot be deemed to be a permanent part of the body, it nevertheless does not constitute a *ḥaẓiẓah.* If a definite date has been set for removal of the filling, the patient is "unconcerned" with its presence in the interim. On the contrary, he is "concerned" that it remain in place until the time set for its removal by the dentist.[13]

Rabbi Feinstein advances a second reason for ruling that a temporary filling does not constitute a *ḥaẓiẓah.* Although the filling is to be removed, the patient's "concern" is not that it be removed in order that the cavity be exposed. On the contrary, the patient wishes the cavity to be filled, his sole "concern" being that the temporary filling be replaced with a filling which is permanent in nature. Thus, a temporary filling may be deemed to have become part of the body because, even though the particular filling now in the tooth is eventually to be replaced, nevertheless, *a* filling will always be utilized to close the cavity. Both reasons advanced by Rabbi Feinstein apply to temporary crowns no less than to temporary fillings.[14]

Rabbi Feinstein cautions that an improperly inserted filling—or crown—

13. See also R. Yitzchak Ya'akov Weisz, *Minḥat, Yiẓḥak,* I, no. 23, and V, no. 111; and R. Ya'akov Breish, *Ḥelkat Ya'akov,* I, no. 137, and II, no. 173.

14. See also R. Meir Ze'ev Goldberger, *Ha-Ma'or,* Elul 5733.

which causes toothache or which interfers with mastication does constitute a *ḥaẓiẓah* and hence a toothache at the time of immersion involving a tooth which has already been filled poses a halakhic problem.

Earlier responsa are replete with questions concerning individual false teeth, apparently of ivory or wood, which had to be removed from time to time for cleansing. R. Shalom Mordecai Schwadron, *Da'at Torah, Yoreh De'ah* 198:24, and R. Pinchas Horowitz, *Pitḥa Zuta* 198:41, cite several authorities who maintain that, despite their periodic removal, such teeth do not constitute a *ḥaẓiẓah* if either of two conditions are present: (1) the tooth can be removed only by a dentist or (2) removal of the tooth by the patient causes pain.

Many scholars maintain that since false teeth serve a cosmetic purpose they do not constitute a *ḥaẓiẓah* because there is a definite desire that they remain in place in order that personal appearance not be marred. Such false teeth must, however, be of a type which cannot easily be removed.[15] Rabbi David Spector, *Ha-Pardes,* Tammuz 5732, notes that false teeth located in the rear of the mouth also do not constitute a *ḥaẓiẓah.* Although such teeth do not serve a cosmetic purpose, they are designed to aid in mastication of food. Since they serve a functional purpose, there is a definite desire that they remain in place and hence the same line of reasoning applies.

It has been brought to the writer's attention that some Orthodox dental practitioners are careful to use a medicinal cement in preparing temporary crowns for female patients. Apparently, these dentists are under the impression that such cement does not constitute a *ḥaẓiẓah* simply by virtue of the fact that it serves as a therapeutic agent. This assumption is, however, erroneous. Numerous authorities indicate that foreign substances serving a therapeutic function, such as powder or salve, do constitute a *ḥaẓiẓah* unless applied to alleviate a threat to the very life of the patient.[16] Accordingly, there is no halakhic preference for the use of medicated rather than inert cement. The previously cited arguments serve to establish the fact that neither the crown nor the cement with which it is affixed constitutes a *ḥaẓiẓah.*

---

15. See R. Abraham Danzig, *Binat Adam, Sha'ar ha-Nashim,* no. 12; R. Ya'akov Ettlinger, *Binyan Ẓion ha-Ḥadashot,* no. 57; and R. Ya'akov Breish, *Ḥelkat Ya'akov,* III, no. 33.

16. See *Mishneh Aḥaronah, Mikva'ot* 9:9; *Shakh, Yoreh De'ah,* 198:14; *Binat Adam, Sha'ar ha-Nashim,* 12; and *Iggrot Mosheh, Yoreh De'ah,* I, no. 97.

Plastic Surgery

Judaism recognizes divine proprietorship over all objects of creation, including the human body. Judaism expressly teaches that the individual has no proprietary rights with regard to his own body, and hence is forbidden to mutilate or wound his own body (see Rambam, *Hilkhot Ḥovel u-Mazik* 5:1).[16a] A person's body is committed to him for safekeeping, and hence self-mutilation or any form of assault upon the body is viewed as a breach of this stewardship. Dispensation for intervention in physiological processes for therapeutic purposes is granted in the biblical directive, "and he shall cause him to be thoroughly healed" (Exod. 21:19). Thus, a surgical operation to correct a deformed or malfunctioning organ is specifically excluded from the prohibition against "wounding."

The perfection of highly sophisticated medical techniques has led to the development of a wide range of elective surgical procedures. As a result, cosmetic surgery is becoming increasingly more commonplace in our society. From the perspective of Halakhah, elective cosmetic surgery gives rise to a number of significant questions. Plastic surgery undertaken solely for cosmetic or esthetic purposes differs significantly from other corrective procedures. The obvious halakhic problem associated with plastic surgery is whether or not such procedures involve infractions of the law against wounding (*ḥavalah*). A further, more general question is raised by the risk to life involved in such procedures. Any form of surgery, particularly when performed under general anesthesia, poses at least a minimal, but nevertheless significant, threat to life. Is it permissible, according to Halakhah, to expose oneself to such danger for cosmetic purposes? A third question is posed by cosmetic surgery performed upon male patients. The prohibition "a man shall not put on a woman's garment" (Deut. 22:5) extends not only to the wearing of female clothing by a male but also to the application of cosmetics or to any act of beautification usually associated with women. Dyeing of the hair and removal of armpit or pubic hair are specifically enumerated acts of this nature. Are such forms of plastic surgery as facelifting, nasoplasty, etc., so widely associated with women as to constitute a form of "female dress," or may men avail themselves of such methods for purposes of improving their appearance?

The problems posed by plastic surgery are discussed by Rabbi Chanoch Grossberg in a cursory manner in the context of a more comprehensive

---

16a. Cf. R. Joseph Babad, *Minḥat Ḥinukh*, no. 48; and R. Chaim Chizkeyahu Medini, *Sedei Ḥemed*, I, *Ma'arekhet ha-Alef, Pe'at ha-Sadeh*, no. 40.

treatise devoted to topical medical issues appearing in the 5733 edition of *No'am*. Rabbi Grossberg cites the earlier, more extensive analyses of these questions by Rabbi Yechiel Ya'akov Breish, *Ḥelkat Ya'akov,* III, no. 11, and Rabbi Menasheh Klein, *Mishneh Halakhot,* IV, nos. 246 and 247. Of importance in this regard is the responsum of Rabbi Eliezer Waldenberg, *Ẓiẓ Eli'ezer,* XI, no. 4, secs. 8–9, in which Rabbi Waldenberg forcefully advances the argument against surgery which is purely cosmetic in nature.

Rabbi Klein draws a distinction between plastic surgery undertaken for cosmetic purposes in order to improve personal appearance or to reverse the normal manifestations of the aging process and surgery designed to remedy a *mum,* or "blemish," which may be either congenital in nature or the result of accidental disfigurement. *Ketubot* 72b states that if a man contracts a marriage on the condition that the bride be free of blemishes, and it is subsequently discovered that a blemish is present, the marriage is deemed to be invalid. The Gemara further declares that since the marriage is considered to be invalid from its inception, subsequent removal of the blemish cannot validate the marriage. Rabbi Klein argues that since the Gemara, in the course of the discussion of this question, makes specific reference to the woman seeking medical help "to heal" the blemish, it may be inferred that a physician is permitted to correct such blemishes. According to this argument, the treatment of such conditions constitutes an act of healing included in the dispensation "and he shall surely heal" and is accordingly excluded from the proscription against "wounding."

The term "blemish" is defined by the Gemara by means of specific enumeration. Priests marred by "blemishes" are forbidden to participate in the sacrificial rituals. A total of 140 different blemishes are listed. Among these are are included a crooked nose, a nose longer than the small finger of one's hand and inordinately large breasts. Rabbi Klein argues that the reversal of any condition constituting one of the specifically enumerated "blemishes" does not constitute an act of wounding. Although this thesis may not be an unreasonable one Rabbi Klein adduces no convincing evidence that "wounding" is permissible other than for purposes of healing a malady. There is no specific evidence that members of the priestly family were permitted, much less obliged, to remove such blemishes by means of surgery in order to become qualified to participate in the offering of sacrifices.[16b] Nor does the Gemara, in speaking of a woman seeking the re-

16b. Indeed, *Tosafot, Pesaḥim* 28b, states explicitly that a person whose genital organs have not appeared externally (a *tumtum)* need not submit to corrective surgery in order to fulfill the *miẓvah* of circumcision.

moval of a blemish, state that the condition was remediable by means of surgery or that such surgery was indeed permissible. Be that as it may, Rabbi Klein, in the second of his two responsa dealing with this topic, ignores his own distinction, but indicates that plastic surgery is warranted in order to alleviate certain forms of psychological distress, as will be indicated later.

Rabbi Breish cites evidence showing that "wounding" is permissible not only for purposes of curing a physiological disorder but also for purposes of alleviating pain. *Shulḥan Arukh, Yoreh De'ah* 241:3, states that a son should not "wound" his father even for medical reasons. Hence he should not remove a splinter, perform blood-letting or amputate a limb. Rema adds that if no other physician is available and the father is "in pain," the son may perform blood-letting or an amputation on behalf of his father. A similar statement is made by Me'iri, *Sanhedrin* 84b. Since the phraseology employed by these sources indicates that the contemplated procedures were designed to mitigate pain rather than to effect a cure, Rabbi Breish concludes that alleviation of pain is included in the pronouncement "and he shall cause him to be thoroughly healed" and hence excluded from the prohibition against "wounding."

The halakhic definition of pain is significantly expanded by *Tosafot, Shabbat* 50b. *Tosafot* states that a state of mind which prevents a person from mingling with people constitutes "pain" within the halakhic definition of that term. Accordingly, both Rabbi Breish and Rabbi Klein conclude that if an individual shuns normal social intercourse as a result of a deformity or other disfigurement, the condition causing distress may be corrected by means of plastic surgery.

Writing in the sixth volume of *No'am* (5723), Rabbi Immanuel Jakobovits opines that plastic surgery would also be permissible in order to rectify conditions as a result of which the afflicted individual experiences difficulty in finding employment or a marriage partner, but indicates that he has not marshaled halakhic sources substantiating this conclusion. Indeed, *Tosafot, Baba Kamma* 91b, clearly states that "wounding" is forbidden even when undertaken for purposes of pecuniary advantage. Quite obviously the desire for financial gain is not in itself sufficient grounds upon which to justify "wounding." Nevertheless, it would appear that the psychological anguish normally attendant upon not being able to find gainful employment or a suitable marriage partner is a form of "pain" no less severe than distress at not feeling free to mingle socially with other people. It would follow that, in such circumstances, cosmetic surgery is permissible in order to alleviate this anguish.

Although the prohibition concerning wounding does not apply in these limited situations, is it permissible to place one's life in danger in order to alleviate psychological anguish? Citing the above-mentioned comments of Rema, Rabbi Breish argues that even the amputation of a limb is permissible in order to alleviate pain. The Gemara, in a number of instances (*Shabbat* 129b, *Avodah Zarah* 30b, *Niddah* 31a and *Yevamot* 72a), indicates that a person may engage in commonplace activities even though he places himself in a position of danger in so doing. In justifying such conduct the Gemara declares, "Since many have trodden thereon 'the Lord preserveth the simple' (Ps. 116:6)." The talmudic principle is that man is justified in placing his trust in God, provided that the risk involved is of a type which is commonly accepted as a reasonable one by society at large. Rabbi Breish apparently feels that any accepted therapeutic procedure falls into this category.[16c]

This position may perhaps, be justified on the basis of yet another argument. Both Ramban, in his *Torat ha-Adam* (*Kitvei Ramban,* ed. Bernard Chavel, II, 43), and Ran, in his commentary to *Sanhedrin* 84b, comment that all modes of therapy are potentially dangerous. Ran declares, "All modes of therapy are a danger for the patient, since it is possible that if the physician should err with regard to a specific drug, it may kill the patient." Ramban states even more explicitly, "With regard to cures, there is nought but danger; what heals one, kills another." Nevertheless, it is beyond dispute that a physician may treat even those illnesses which are not life-threatening in nature. Since an aggressor is clearly liable for medical expenses, even if the wound inflicted is not potentially lethal, it may be argued that the verse "and he shall cause him to be thoroughly healed" conveys blanket dispensation for any sound medical practice. Although every therapy is fraught with danger, the hazards of treatment are specifically sanctioned when incurred in conjunction with a therapeutic protocol. Accordingly, the practice of the healing arts may be permitted even if designed simply for the alleviation of pain.[16d]

A diametrically opposed view is expressed by R. Ya'akov Emden in his *Mor u-Keẓi'ah Oraḥ Ḥayyim* 328, R. Ya'akov Emden speaks of persons

16c. Cf. *Darkei Teshuvah, Yoreh De'ah* 155:2; *Levushei Mordekhai, Yoreh De'ah,* II, no. 87; and R. Eliezer Waldenberg, *Ẓiẓ Eli'ezer,* X, no. 25, chap. 17, sec. 1.

16d. See also *Ẓiẓ Eli'ezer,* X, no. 25, chap. 17, sec. 1.

who place their lives in jeopardy in order to alleviate pain, such as those "who allow themselves to be operated upon in order to remove a stone in the 'pocket' etc.," and states that if there is no danger associated with the pain, such individuals "do not act correctly." Similarly, *Avnei Nezer, Yoreh De'ah,* no. 321, permits the application of a cast for purposes of correcting an orthopedic condition but adds that he would not have approved an operation as a proper therapeutic procedure since all surgical procedures involve some danger. Rabbi Klein also rules that cosmetic surgery is not permissible if it poses any danger to life.

Rabbi Breish and Rabbi Klein both rule that cosmetic surgery, when permissible, is permissible not only for women but for men as well. As has been indicated, cometic surgery is not permitted simply for purposes of beautification but is sanctioned only in order to alleviate psychological anguish. *Tosafot, Shabbat* 50b, states that males are permitted to use cosmetics if such cosmetics are applied for purposes of alleviating pain. It follows, therefore, that other forms of beautification commonly associated with women are also permitted to males, provided they are designed primarily for purposes of alleviating pain. Rabbi Klein further notes that in the United States cosmetic surgery is not a uniquely feminine form of beautification but is widely practiced by males as well and, accordingly, does not constitute an infraction of the prohibition against the wearing of female garments.

Post-Mortem Caesareans

The medical feasibility of a post-mortem Caesarean section in order to save the fetus after the mother has died in labor was not only known in talmudic times but was regarded as an obligatory procedure in order to preserve the life of the unborn child. The Gemara, *Erukhin* 7a, declares that if a woman dies in childbirth on the Sabbath, a knife may be brought through a public domain in order to make an incision into the uterus for the purpose of removing the fetus. It is thus evident that not only is this procedure compatible with halakhic principles, but that Sabbath regulations may be violated in order to save the life of the unborn fetus. This ruling is authoritatively cited by *Shulḥan Arukh, Oraḥ Ḥayyim* 330:5. However, R. Moses Isserles, in a gloss to this ruling, indicates that this provision, while valid in theory, is nevertheless inoperative in practice. Rema declares that quite apart from the problems related to desecration of the Sabbath, it is forbidden to attempt a post-mortem Caesarean for other reasons. Such attempts are forbidden on weekdays as well as on the Sabbath, according to Rema, because we lack the competence to determine with exactitude the precise moment of maternal death. Since one may not even move a limb of a moribund person lest this action hasten his death, it is obvious that an incision into the womb cannot be made until such time as death has been established with absolute certainty. The requirement that death be established conclusively necessitates a significant delay following the manifestation of clinical symptoms of death. Rema declares that it is a foregone conclusion that the fetus will no longer be viable after this period has elapsed. This procedure, if performed after the required delay, serves no medical purpose and consequently constitutes an unwarranted violation of the corpse.

Rema's position is that what may appear to be cessation of respiratory activity cannot be accepted as an absolute criterion of death. Our lack of competence is due to an inability to distinguish between death and a fainting spell or swoon. In the latter cases respiratory activity does continue to occur, although respiration may be so minimal that it cannot be perceived.

Writing in the Tammuz 5731 issue of *Ha-Ma'ayan,* Dr. Jacob Levy, an Israeli physician and frequent contributor to halakhic journals, argues that in light of the clinical aids now available to the physician, the considerations raised by Rema are no longer relevant. Rema's declaration that the ruling of the *Shulḥan Arukh* is not followed in practice is based upon the fear that a fainting spell or swoon may be misdiagnosed as death. Dr. Levy points out that in many cases the possibility of such errors can be eliminated by the use of a sphygmomanometer to determine that no blood pressure can be detected in conjunction with an electrocardiagram to ascertain that all cardiac activity has ceased. Accordingly, Dr. Levy strongly recommends that rabbinic authorities declare that the original ruling of the *Shulḥan Arukh* now be followed in practice.

Dr. Levy adds that this proposal should not be construed as an abrogation of Rema's ruling since many authorities recognize that Rema's statement is based upon empirical considerations and admits to exceptions. For example, R. Ya'akov Reischer, *Shevut Ya'akov,* I, no. 13, in discussing the bizarre case of a pregnant woman who had been decapitated on *Shabbat,* states unequivocally that the physician who had the presence of mind to incise the abdomen immediately in order to remove the fetus need have no pangs of conscience since in this instance the mother's prior death is established beyond cavil. Similarly, concludes Dr. Levy, Rema's statement should not be viewed as normative under changed circumstances which enable medical science to determine that death has already occurred. This argument is cogent because Rema himself remarks that it had become necessary to disregard the earlier authoritative decision of the *Shulḥan Arukh* solely because of a lack of medical expertise.

This question is essentially part of a much broader problem; namely, the establishment of an exact definition of death in Jewish law, a topic which has received much attention of late. Rema does not indicate how much time must elapse after the apparent cessation of respiration before the patient may be pronounced dead. Various later authorities establish a twenty-minute waiting period, others a period of thirty minutes. Several contemporary halakhic scholars who have addressed themselves to this issue fail to abrogate this waiting period. The problem of determining the halakhic definition of death will be discussed in a later chapter.

Autopsies with Consent of the Deceased

The regular appearance of *Talpiot,* a quarterly devoted to all areas of Jewish scholarship and published under the auspices of Yeshiva University, has been suspended since the death in 1966 of its editor, the late Professor Samuel K. Mirsky. Prior to his demise, Professor Mirsky had been engaged in the compilation of material to be included in yet another volume of this publication. This task was brought to completion by his son, Rabbi David Mirsky, dean of Yeshiva University's Stern College for Women.

This issue of *Talpiot,* bearing the date Elul 5730, contains a hitherto unpublished responsum by the renowned scholar, the late Rabbi Yechiel Michal Tucatzinsky, dealing with a timely issue pertaining to the general question of autopsies. The question concerns individuals who have willed their bodies to institutions engaged in medical research or who, while yet alive, have given permission for autopsies to be performed upon their bodies. Rabbi Yekutiel Yehudah Greenwald, in his *Kol Bo 'al Avelut*—a twentieth-century compendium which has gained wide acceptance as a standard work on the laws of mourning and related topics—cites R. Ya'akov Ettlinger, *Binyan Ẓion,* nos. 170 and 171, and declares that dissection may be performed without transgression if such was the wish of the deceased. This ruling is predicated upon the rationale underlying the Halakhah forbidding desecration of a dead body. Halakhah demands that every honor be accorded the human corpse; dissection constitutes a violation of the dignity of the deceased body. The claim to honor and dignity is essentially a personal prerogative and may be renounced at will. If prior consent is obtained during an individual's lifetime, claims with regard to honor and dignity after death can no longer be entertained. Accordingly, the person who performs dissection under such circumstances commits no transgression.

Rabbi Tucatzinsky contests this thesis. It is an established verity that, from the point of view of Judaism, man has no proprietary rights with regard to his body. A person's body has been committed to him for safekeeping only, and must be returned to the Creator as it was received. Thus, self-mutilation, or any assault upon the body other than for therapeutic purposes, is forbidden by Halakhah. The prohibition against desecration of the dead, points out Rabbi Tucatzinsky, is based upon similar considerations. The Torah declares, "You shall not cause his body to remain all night upon the tree . . . for a reproach unto God is hanged" (Deut. 21:23) and thereby indicates that even after life has ebbed it is forbidden to commit indignities against the human body which is created in the "image of God." Rabbi Tucatzinsky argues that since all laws pertaining to violation of the corpse are predicated upon this verse, man has no rights of "proprietorship" with regard to the disposal of his body after death, just as he enjoys no rights of ownership over his body during his lifetime. Violation of the body is then essentially a crime against God rather than a crime against man. Since the crime is against God, prior permission of the person whose body is to be dissected is of no significance. We may note that a similar view is recorded in *Teshuvot Ḥatam Sofer, Yoreh De'ah* no. 336, and in *Teshuvot Maharam Schick, Yoreh De'ah,* no. 347.

Medical Experimentation Upon Severed Organs

A recurrent question in rabbinic literature concerns the status of organs and limbs removed from living persons during the course of surgery. At times there is a need for protracted examination of such organs in conjunction with medical research. Such experimentation poses two halakhic questions: (1) Is the commandment to bury the dead applicable only after death has occurred, or does it also include an obligation to bury limbs and organs removed from living persons? (2) A corpse is deemed to be *assur be-hana'ah,* i.e., it is forbidden to derive benefit from the body of the deceased (other than in face of immediate danger to human life). Is this prohibition limited to the body of a deceased person, or does it also encompass lifeless organs and limbs which have been removed from a living person?

The tenth volume of *Ẓiẓ Eli'ezer* deals extensively with a multitude of pertinent medical questions. In no. 25, chap. 8, of this work, Rabbi Eliezer Waldenberg discusses in detail the halakhic problems attendant upon medical experimentation utilizing severed organs. Two issues of *Kol Torah* (Adar–Iyar and Sivan–Elul 5730) contain a further discussion of this important topic by Rabbi David Cohen of Yeshivat Chevron.

The *Yad ha-Melekh*, commenting on Rambam, *Mishneh Torah, Hilkhot Avel* 2:14, declares that there exists an obligation to bury parts of the body removed from a living person. The Halakhah prohibits a *kohen* from defiling himself through contact with severed organs even when these are removed from the persons of those close relatives whose burial requires his participation and defilement. The implication, argues *Yad ha-Melekh,* is that such limbs and organs require burial even though a *kohen* may not defile himself in conjunction with their interment. Rabbi Waldenberg rejects this contention, arguing that burial is required not as a fulfillment of the commandment concerning interment of the dead, but simply as a means of preventing inadvertent defilement of *kohanim* who may come into contact with such limbs or organs. Quoting *Maharil Diskin, Kuntres Aḥaron,* no. 188, who describes the interment of severed organs as a practice mandated by custom rather than by law,[17] Rabbi Waldenberg concludes that there exists no prohibition against deriving benefit from such organs. Were this not the case, burial would be obligatory as a matter of law rather than custom, as is the Halakhah with regard to all substances from which it is prohibited to derive benefit (*issurei hana'ah*). Accordingly, Rabbi Waldenberg rules that there is no halakhic objection to medical experimentation upon organs and limbs removed from living persons.

Rabbi Waldenberg draws a sharp distinction between the status of an aborted fetus and that of removed organs. The preponderance of halakhic opinion is that burial of a fetus is halakhically mandated as a matter of law. In his analysis of this subject, Rabbi Cohen seizes upon this point and contends that the status of removed organs is identical with that of a fetus. The halakhic obligation to bury a fetus is derived by inference from the stipulation that a *kohen* may not defile himself in order to bury

17. This is also the position of *Noda bi-Yehudah,* II, *Yoreh De'ah,* no 209. R. Moses Feinstein, *Iggrot Mosheh, Yoreh De'ah,* I, no. 231, rejects this view and rules that all parts of the body require burial as a matter of law.

his own fetal progeny. From this it is deduced that although a *kohen* may not defile himself, interment of the fetus is obligatory (*Magen Avraham, Oraḥ Ḥayyim,* 526:2). This obligation with regard to the fetus is deemed to be included in the obligation to bury the dead and is not regarded as a precautionary stipulation designed to prevent *kohanim* from inadvertently defiling themselves through contact with the fetus. This line of reasoning parallels that of *Yad ha-Melekh* with regard to separated organs. Thus, Rabbi Cohen argues, the halakhah forbidding a *kohen* to defile himself through contact with organs removed from close relatives should be viewed as establishing an obligation with regard to the interment of organs removed from living persons. Furthermore, contends Rabbi Cohen, those authorities who view burial of organs separated from a living person as a mere custom similarly maintain that burial of individual organs separated from a corpse is a custom, not an obligation. In terms of definitive Halakhah this latter opinion is rejected and the accepted view deems it obligatory to bury individual organs of the deceased. Therefore, Rabbi Cohen concludes that, with regard to burial, there is no distinction between organs separated from a corpse and those separated from a living person.[18]

In practice, when such organs are utilized for purposes of scientific research, they should be accorded dignified burial upon completion of the necessary pathological procedures.

18. Of interest with regard to this discussion is *Bereshit Rabbah* LX,3, which reports that Jephthah was punished for his arrogance and was afflicted with a debilitating disease which caused his limbs to fall off. This occurred over a period of time during which Jephthah journeyed through many cities. Each limb, the Midrash indicates, was interred in the city in which it became separated from his body. Judges 12:7 reads, ". . . and Jephthah the Gileadite died and was buried in the cities of Gilead." Since his limbs were buried in different locales, Jephthah is spoken of as having been buried in the *cities* of Gilead.

CHAPTER VI

Medical Questions and Shabbat

Violate one Sabbath on his behalf that he may observe many Sabbaths.

YOMA 85b

Every ethical system posits a given number of stated or implied moral values. Yet these values cannot all be regarded as absolute values since when they are applied to real-life situations, irresolvable conflicts may occur. For example, preservation of human life is universally regarded as a moral value; so is, in most moral systems, respect for ownership of property as reflected in the injunction "Thou shalt not steal." However, it may not always be possible to act in a manner which allows for simultaneous preservation of both values. If a person is bleeding profusely, is it morally proper to make use of the most readily available object in order to improvise a tourniquet, e.g., a shirt or sheet belonging to a third party? The moral dilemma posed by such a situation calls for a choice between preservation of life and respect for the property rights of others. This is the obvious moral of the Robin Hood story. Robin Hood steals from the Sheriff of Nottingham in order to save the lives of starving children. Friar Tuck plays the role of the professor of moral theology and bestows tacit approval. Jewish teaching, in terms of normative Halakhah, sanctions the appropriation of property belonging to another when absolutely necessary for the preservation of life, but stipulates that financial restitution must be made at such time as possible.

In any moral system there must exist a hierarchy of values or a set of rules which enables a person to determine which of two or more conflicting principles must be subordinated to another. Jewish law bestows a privileged position upon the preservation of human life as a moral value. As a moral desideratum it takes precedence over virtually all else. Excepted are the three cardinal transgressions: murder (hardly an exception), idolatry and sexual offenses such as incest and adultery. All purely ritual laws are suspended for purposes of conservation of life. Even the mere possibility of saving human life mandates violation of such laws "however remote the likelihood of saving human life may be" (*Oraḥ Ḥayyim* 329:3). The quality of the life which is thus preserved is never a factor to be taken into consideration. Neither is the length of the survivor's life expectancy a controlling factor. Judaism regards not only human life in general as being of infinite and inestimable value, but regards every moment of life as being of infinite value.

Even Sabbath regulations, despite their status as testimony to the doctrine of divine creation, are suspended when life is in danger. The Gemara, *Yoma* 84b, declares, " 'For it is holy unto you' (Exod. 31:13)—the Sabbath is given over into your hands, but you are not given over into its hands." One talmudic explanation of the subordination of other laws to the preservation of life is based on the line of reasoning that it is preferable to violate one Sabbath in order that the patient be enabled to observe many Sabbaths (*Yoma* 85b). Implicit in this formulation is the notion that the observance of divine law must be maximized. In effect, a calculus of observance is established. Hence, temporary abrogation may be sanctioned for the sake of subsequent observance.

Consistent with this position, Jewish law requires that the abrogation of Sabbath laws be as minimal as possible compatible with the needs of conserving life. Minimalization of infraction is a factor not only with regard to frequency of occurrence, but also with regard to the severity of the violation. Thus it is readily understandable that rabbinic scholars are frequently called upon not only to determine whether Sabbath laws are to be disregarded in certain situations but also the manner in which therapeutic procedures are to be carried out in order to minimize any necessary infractions.

Medical Questions Concerning Shabbat

Over the centuries countless editions of the *siddur* have been published, many of which were designed for specific scholarly or pragmatic purposes. Several years ago another edition was added to this evergrowing list. The *Siddur Minḥat Yerushalayim,* edited by Rabbi Y. A.

Dvorkes, and published in Israel under the aegis of the prestigious *Oẓar ha-Poskim,* is in a class by itself by virtue of its success in combining so many diverse features in one volume. Published in a small format with a soft plastic cover, the *siddur* is pocket size despite its twelve hundred–odd pages. Apart from its comprehensiveness in anticipating the worshipper's every need, the *siddur* abounds in illustrations and tables ranging from detailed, diagrammed instructions for the construction of a *Shabbat eruv* to step-by-step illustrations of the procedure to be followed in fashioning the special knots of the phylacteries. One part of the work contains numerous pictures of fruits and vegetables, both common and exotic, identified and classified in terms of the appropriate blessing to be pronounced before partaking of them and includes a chart from which the reader can determine at a glance the proper order in which such blessings are to be recited. Several sections are devoted to practical *halakhot* with special emphasis on the laws concerning the Holy Places and the *miẓvot* unique to the Land of Israel. For the attentive, merely leafing through the pages of this *siddur* can become a valuable educational experience.

Particularly noteworthy is an appendix entitled *Divrei Refu'ah be-Shabbat,* dealing with the care of the sick on *Shabbat.* This material was compiled by Rabbi Joshua Neuwirth, the author of *Shemirat Shabbat ke-Hilkhatah*, a work which, in the few short years that have elapsed since its publication, has already become a modern classic. Indeed, much of the material incorporated in this section is culled from chapter 19 of the latter work. The title page indicates that the definitive opinions contained therein have received the approbation of Rabbi Shlomoh Zalman Auerbach, the dean of Yeshivah Kol Torah and one of Israel's foremost halakhic authorities.

The halakhic section of this fascinating treasure-trove-cum-prayerbook has an interesting literary sequel. Appended to the *Divrei Refu'ah be-Shabbat* is a series of footnotes written by the late Rabbi Pinchas Epstein, who served as head of Jerusalem's *Edah ha-Ḥaredit,* in which the latter disagees with many of the opinions expressed by Rabbi Neuwirth and Rabbi Auerbach. With the publication of these opposing views, Rabbi Auerbach felt constrained to defend his own conclusions and to present the halakhic reasoning upon which they are based. The Sivan–Tammuz 5731 issue of *Moriah* features a lengthy article by Rabbi Auerbach in which he replies in great detail to a number of Rabbi Epstein's glosses. This article was subsequently reprinted in the 5732 edition of *Torah She-*

be-'al Peh. The specific hypothetical questions which constitute the subject of these disputes are, in effect, paradigm cases having wide ramifications with regard to the treatment and care of the sick on *Shabbat.*

1. Rabbi Auerbach rules that it is permissible to perform such services as lighting a fire or boiling water on behalf of a patient who is seriously ill, even though a kindled lamp or boiled water could be secured from a neighbor, if obtaining these items from the neighbor would cause the latter some deprivation or inconvenience. Thus, if the neighbor is asleep and would have to be awakened or requires the water for his own use, one need not impose upon the neighbor but may do whatever is necessary on behalf of the patient. Rabbi Eliezer Waldenberg, *Ẓiẓ Eli'ezer,* VIII, no. 15. chap. 11, sec. 7, has similarly stated that a person need not give his lamp to a sick neighbor in order to prevent infringement of *Shabbat* laws and himself remain bereft of illumination.

Rabbi Epstein takes issue with this ruling and argue that each and every individual is obligated to do whatever may be necessary to preserve the life of his fellow even though this may involve inconvenience to himself. Accordingly, the neighbor is himself under the obligation to provide a lamp or hot water if needed by the patient. There is, therefore, no reason for others to violate *Shabbat* law in order to do so since the same results may be achieved by the neighbor without violation. This conclusion may also be inferred as being the position of *Divrei Malki'el,* I, no. 28, whose views will be examined later.

In defending his position Rabbi Auerbach establishes an interesting thesis according to which the commandment "You shall not stand idly by the blood of your fellow" (Lev. 19:16) obligates an individual to (1) whatever personal action is necessary in order to preserve life, even though such action may involve transgression of other biblical ordinances, and (2) financial expenditures if preservation of the life of one's fellow is impossible otherwise. However, the commandment does not obligate financial expenditures in order to obviate the necessity for a physical act which itself constitutes a violation of Jewish law. Such expenditures, maintains Rabbi Auerbach, are mandated only if the patient is one's own young child or wife. One must incur financial loss in order to avoid desecration of the Sabbath only if one bears general financial responsibility for the care of the patient in question. Such general responsibility is recognized by Halakhah only with regard to one's wife and young children.

There is yet another consideration which must be taken into account.

It is evident from the comments of Rema 328:11 and *Mishneh Berurah* 328.35 that, in providing for the needs of a seriously ill person, only minimal delay is permitted in order to secure alternate modes of providing such needs which do not involve Sabbath desecration. More than minimal delay is forbidden, even if the danger to life is not immediate. Accordingly, concludes Rabbi Auerbach, if any significant lapse of time would be involved in arousing the neighbor from his sleep or in transporting the required article, there is no question at all that it is mandatory immediately to do everything necessary on behalf of the patient even if infringement of Sabbath laws is involved.

2. The same principles may be applied to the resolution of a second question. If a larger number of gravely ill patients than anticipated are admitted to a hospital on *Shabbat,* are the nurses and other hospital employees obliged to make their own food available to the patients in order to avoid the necessity of cooking on behalf of those newly admitted patients, or may they consume their own previously prepared food and cook additional food on behalf of such patients? On the basis of the previously stated considerations, Rabbi Auerbach rules that the hospital employees need not surrender their own food in order to prevent desecration of the Sabbath. Rabbi Auerbach further adds that since it is not a halakhic requirement, such employees should not be asked or advised to relinquish their own food on behalf of the patients. Rabbi Auerbach points out that in numerous instances the Sages express fear that if subjected to hardship on a given occasion, a person may be remiss in fulfilling his obligation under similar circumstances in some future emergency. An employee requested to accept undue discomfort may well react by refusing *Shabbat* duty in the future.

3. If the patient is himself incapable of visiting the physician's office but is able to telephone the doctor, are others obligated to go by foot to request the doctor to visit the patient?

A comparable question discussed by *Divrei Malk'iel,* I, no. 28, concerns provision of kosher food for the sick. If the patient has only non-kosher food available to him, are relatives and friends obligated to extend themselves in order to provide kosher meals at their own expense? This problem arises quite frequently, since patients are often confined in hospitals which do not make provisions for kosher meals. If, for psychological reasons, the patient finds himself incapable of consuming such food or if the food is regurgitated because the patient is revolted by non-kosher food, there is no question that one must provide food which the patient can digest. *Divrei Malki'el* rules that even in the absence of such considerations, kosher food must be provided. All persons are obligated to do whatever is necessary in order to cure the patient and no dispensation permitting non-kosher food is halakhically recognized if kosher food can be provided. Following *Divrei Malki'el*'s line of reasoning it may be inferred that, if no undue delay is involved, others must go by foot to call a physician in order to spare the patient the need to telephone on *Shabbat*. By the same token, they must make available their own lamp or boiled water in order to obviate the necessity for the patient to light a fire or to cook.

Rabbi Auerbach notes the views of *Divrei Malki'el* and also cites the apparently similarly dissenting view of *Teshuvot Radbaz,* II, no. 130. Rabbi Auerbach himself, however, disagrees. In the first place, as noted earlier, Rabbi Auerbach maintains that a person is not obligated to ask another to provide for the needs of a patient in order to obviate the necessity for violating *Shabbat* laws. Secondly, he argues, even given a negative answer to the question posed in the first section and granting that a neighbor must give his own lamp in order to obviate the necessity for someone else to kindle a lamp on behalf of the patient, the neighbor is obliged to do so only if the patient is incapable of lighting the fire himself. If the patient is unable to perform a service for himself, others must provide him with his needs. Since all are under equal obligation, the primary responsibility falls upon the person who can do so without transgression. However, if the patient can perform the service for himself, no obligation whatsoever devolves upon others. The injunction "You shall not stand idly by the blood of your fellow," Rabbi Auerbach claims, implies only that one is obligated to preserve the life of one who cannot save himself; there is no such obligation if the person has the ability to save himself but willfully refuses to do so. Hence, Rabbi Auerbach rules that, in the case at hand, if the patient is himself able to telephone the doctor, others have no responsibility in the matter and are, therefore, not obligated to suffer inconvenience in order to prevent an act of Sabbath violation by the patient.

4. A closely related but not directly medical question involves exposed electrical wiring on *Shabbat*. Rabbi Neuwirth rules that fallen lines or exposed wires which may endanger the lives of persons coming into contact with them constitute a hazard to life. Accordingly, any necessary measures may be taken to eliminate the danger. Rabbi Epstein adopts an opposing view and declares that no violation of the Sabbath may be

sanctioned in such an instance since the situation can be remedied by affixing a "Danger" sign or, if necessary, by standing guard and warning unwary individuals that touching the exposed wire is dangerous.

A precedent for the resolution of this problem is found by Rabbi Auerbach in *Shulḥan Arukh, Oraḥ Ḥayyim* 334:27, in the ruling that a glowing coal, found in a location where the public may be harmed thereby, may be extinguished on the Sabbath. There is no mention of an obligation to stand guard over the coal in order to eliminate the necessity for extinguishing the burning coal on *Shabbat.* In view of the absence of such provision, Rabbi Auerbach claims that it may be concluded that in instances in which it is permissible to violate the Sabbath laws in order to save another person's life there is no obligation to incur a financial loss or to undergo undue inconvenience in order to eliminate the necessity for such *Shabbat* desecration. The arguments applicable with regard to the first of this series of questions are, of course, germane with regard to this problem as well. In Rabbi Auerbach's opinion, in each of the cases under discussion acceptance of financial loss or inconvenience in order to eliminate the necessity of *Shabbat* violation is not a halakhic obligation but is nevertheless a commendable act of piety.

The general principles which emerge from these decisions are of significance in the resolution of many similar problems which arise with regard to care of the sick on the Sabbath. Comparable situations in which these rulings may be applied are often encountered by the observant physician in the course of his practice. The particular details of each question of this nature will, of course, require further analysis.

Emergency Use of an Automobile on Shabbat

The Tammuz 5733 issue of *Moriah* contains a valuable article dealing with a tangential aspect of care of the sick on the Sabbath contributed by Rabbi Joshua Neuwirth, author of the popular compendium of Sabbath laws, *Shemirat Shabbat ke-Hilkhatah.* Although it goes without saying that an automobile may be used on *Shabbat* by a physician called upon to attend a gravely ill patient, or for the transportation of such a patient to a hospital or physician's office, there are a number of halakhic strictures governing such use. Rabbi Neuwirth outlines the proper procedure to be followed under such circumstances.[1]

---

1. See also R. Eliezer Waldenberg, *Ẓiẓ Eli'ezer,* VIII, no. 15, chap. 7, and R. Yisrael Aryeh Zalmanowitz. *No'am,* IV (5721).

The basic principle with regard to all aspects of the treatment of patients on *Shabbat* is that Sabbath regulations are suspended only insofar as the actual treatment of the patient is concerned. Considerations arising out of regard for the convenience of the physician or others engaged in the care of the patient do not constitute a basis for the setting aside of Sabbath laws unless failure to heed such concerns will in some manner compromise the treatment or care of the patient.

Continual acceleration of a combustion engine in the operation of a motor vehicle involves repeated actions which are ordinarily forbidden on *Shabbat*. Since any prolongation of the journey necessarily involves the repeated pumping of additional fuel into the engine, any travel beyond what is of absolute necessity to the patient is not sanctioned. Furthermore, the driving of an automobile under usual conditions involves a number of activities not directly relevant to the operation of the vehicle *per se* which are themselves forbidden on *Shabbat*. Dome lights illuminating the interior of the car, lights on the instrument panel, signal lights and brake lights are integral components of the electrical system of most automobiles. Since the use of these lights is not usually pertinent to the efficient transportation of the physician or patient they should not be turned either on or off on *Shabbat* when it is possible to avoid doing so. In view of the fact that many of these lights operate automatically, it is often impossible to provide for the needs of the patient other than by at the same time also causing such lights to be turned on or to be extinguished. One is, however, required to avoid any action which would cause such lights to be activated unnecessarily. Rabbi Neuwirth presents a number of ways in which such infractions may be obviated. The following are a number of salient points which serve to indicate how these general principles are applicable in practice:

1. The shortest route should be taken in order to minimize infractions of *Shabbat* regulations insofar as possible. However, a patient may be transported to a more distant hospital, even though adequate facilities are available close by, if the medical facilities or patient care in the distant hospital are superior. Since *Shabbat* regulations are suspended not only for the actual treatment of illness but also in order to alleviate the fear, aggravation or anxiety of a seriously ill person, the patient may be taken to the hospital of his choice even if he is mistaken in his belief that the facilities or the quality of the medical care in that hospital are superior. Similarly, a physician may drive on *Shabbat* in order to visit a seriously ill patient if the patient has confidence in him and requests his presence,

even though other equally competent medical personnel are available close by or, indeed, even if such physicians are already in attendance. Financial considerations, however, do not warrant traveling greater distances. Therefore, the minimalization or avoidance of hospital charges or medical fees does not justify infractions which are medically unnecessary.

2. All other considerations being equal, Rabbi Neuwirth advises that the lightest available vehicle be used in order to minimize, insofar as possible, the pumping of gasoline in the operation of the automobile. For the same reason, time permitting, any heavy object which may be in the car should be removed. This should be done even if the object is *mukẓah,* and/or the automobile is standing in a public thoroughfare (*reshut ha-rabbim*).

It should be pointed out that Rabbi Neuwirth's comments are not at all prompted by a consideration of the total amount of fuel consumed. Rabbi Neuwirth expressly declares that Jewish law is concerned solely with the number of acts of "kindling" performed but that the amount of fuel burned as a result of each act of combustion is of no halakhic significance. Rabbi Neuwirth reports that he has been informed by knowledgeable persons that the number of times an automobile must be accelerated in the course of any given journey varies in proportion to the weight of the vehicle being propelled.

This writer has received contradictory information with regard to this crucial technical point. Dr. Jonathan Wachtel, a professor of physics at Yeshiva University's Belfer Graduate School of Science, advises that frequency of acceleration is by no means solely a function of the weight of the automobile. In addition to vehicle mass, frequency of acceleration will depend upon such factors as engine power, engine compression, transmission ratio and sequence in automobiles equipped with automatic transmission, rear-axle gear ratio, tire size and inflation and suspension characteristics. Furthermore, other variable factors, such as traffic and road conditions and personal driving habits, may be the dominant determining factors in any actual driving situation. Professor Wachtel is of the opinion that even if the latter factors were to remain constant it would be impossible to predict the relative number of accelerations required since the high number of mechanical variables make it impossible to treat the problem on a qualitatively analytical basis.

Indeed, Professor Wachtel argues that a heavy vehicle may, under certain conditions, require fewer individual accelerations. The reason for this phenomenon follows from an examination of the man-machine interaction which occurs during acceleration. The operator desiring a specific speed cannot compute the amount of gas to be fed into the engine at every future instance in order, asymptotically, to reach a predetermined speed. The process is more properly viewed as a sequence of positive and negative increments which lead to a convergence to the desired speed. These increments probably occur more quickly with a light car than with a heavy one and, as a result, a greater number of such increments may occur in a lighter vehicle. The greater number of positive increments, of course, involves a correspondingly greater number of accelerations. In heavier vehicles the inertial mass of the vehicle serves to average the result of a sequence of short accelerator depressions over a longer period of time and the driver would therefore tend toward fewer but longer accelerations due to the futility of short bursts. While high engine power in a heavier vehicle may produce an effect similar to light-car behavior, this qualitative analysis is certainly valid when comparing an overpowered light vehicle with an underpowered heavy one.

On the basis of this information, one may conclude that it is virtually impossible to determine which of any two vehicles will require a greater number of accelerations and, accordingly, Rabbi Neuwirth's specific findings would seem to be founded upon erroneous premises. Comparisons between any two vehicles, light or heavy, can be made, according to Professor Wachtel, only on the basis of an empirical test and, in light of individual differences in driving habits, such comparisons are valid only insofar as the individual operator is concerned.

3. Brakes should be applied only in order to avoid danger, since pressure on the brake pedal automatically causes the brake lights to be illuminated. When feasible, the hand brake should be used in order to avoid activation of the brake lights, provided, however, there is no danger that the lack of smoothness occasioned by use of the hand brake will have a negative effect upon the patient.

4. When possible, hand signals should be used in order to avoid use of signal lights.

5. In most automobiles the dome light operates automatically when either of the front doors is opened. A physician anticipating that occasions will arise requiring driving on *Shabbat* should disconnect the interior light in advance. Alternatively, it may be possible to enter and leave the car via a back door and to gain access to the driver's seat by climbing over the front seat. If it is necessary to open the door in a

manner which causes the light to be turned on, the inside switch governing the interior light should be turned to an "on" position before the door is closed in order to prevent the light from being extinguished with the closing of the door. If this is not feasible, then, if possible, the bulb should be removed while driving before the door is opened at the conclusion of the journey. This procedure serves to prevent the light from being activated a second time upon the opening of the door. If this is not feasible, the door should be allowed to remain open at the conclusion of the journey in order to prevent the extinguishing of the interior light.

6. When the use of headlights is necessary, the low beam should be used whenever possible in order to circumvent the need for raising and lowering the beam. Headlights should not be turned off at the close of the journey. This last point does not apply in the case of a physician who must use the same vehicle to visit yet another seriously ill patient if continued burning of the headlights will deplete the battery charge.

7. At the conclusion of the journey and at any other time when it is necessary to bring the car to a halt, the driver should, if possible, remove his foot from the accelerator and permit the car to coast to a stop. This procedure serves to prevent the activation of the brake lights. If braking is necessary, and if it is feasible to do so without jolting the patient, the automobile should be stopped at the end of the journey by means of the hand brake.

8. The ignition switch should be turned off by a non-Jew. If possible, he should not be asked to do so explicitly but should be apprised of the situation so that he will be prompted to turn off the ignition of his own accord. If the non-Jew fails to take the hint, he may be asked to do so directly. Quoting an oral directive of the *Ḥazon Ish,* Rabbi Neuwirth states that in the absence of a non-Jew this task may be performed by a minor or, in the event that a minor is not available, even by an adult Jew. If possible the ignition should be turned off in an unusual manner (*shinuy*). However, an adult may turn off the ignition only if no lights will be extinguished in the process, unless, of course the automobile is so situated that the continued running of the engine constitutes a danger. However, fear of financial loss due to possible damage to the mechanical system of the automobile resulting from continued running of the engine is not sufficient grounds for permitting the ignition switch to be turned off when such action also causes electric lights to be extinguished.

9. In bringing the car to a halt, care should be taken, for obvious rea-

sons, not to block the hospital entrance. However, once the automobile has been stopped it may not be driven again other than for reasons of actual *pikuaḥ nefesh.* Avoidance of a summons for a parking violation is not sufficient reason for moving the car.

10. In places where it is forbidden to carry on *Shabbat,* the key should not be removed from the car. Furthermore, if the key is designed to fit only the ignition switch it is *mukẓah* and should not be handled once the automobile has been stopped. The ignition key, however, is not *mukẓah* if it also serves as the key with which to lock and unlock the car door.

Of course, any or all of these points should be ignored by a driver who feels that preoccupation with such concerns will hamper him in providing life-saving assistance to the patient. If the driver is not well versed in the relevant *halakhot* or is unused to the physical manipulations involved, deliberation with regard to the proper procedure to be followed will undoubtedly cause delay. Since the driver's overriding obligation is to provide speedy care for the patient, such delay is unconscionable. Nevertheless, the physician who may reasonably anticipate that such emergencies will arise in the course of his practice of medicine should be advised to prepare himself for such contingencies in advance by means of study and practice. It is heartening to note that there is now a growing cadre of observant physicians who combine the highest standards of conscientious medical practice with scrupulous and meticulous concern for *shemirat ha-miẓvot.* Physicians such as these will find a careful study of Rabbi Neuwirth's article highly rewarding.

Accompanying a Patient on Shabbat

A related question which frequently arises with regard to the use of an automobile in the transportation of patients on *Shabbat* is whether or not a relative or friend may accompany the patient in an automobile or taxi. There is no question that another person may accompany the patient if assistance is required or in the event that the patient will experience fear or aggravation in traveling or in being admitted to the hospital alone. *Ḥazon Ish, Koveẓ Iggrot,* I, no. 141, urges that a woman in labor be accompanied on her trip to the hospital. *Ḥazon Ish* does not furnish explanatory remarks but the reasons for his decision are self-evident.

However, at times the presence of another person is not required for any reason directly relating to the needs of the patient and the trip is undertaken simply in order to be together with a loved one in a time of stress. The halakhic question posed by this situation is whether it is permissible for a healthy individual to travel in a vehicle being driven on *Shabbat* on behalf of a sick person. Addressing himself to the question of the inherent permissibility of riding in a motor vehicle which is being driven on the Sabbath on behalf of a patient, Rabbi Moses Feinstein, *Iggrot Mosheh, Oraḥ Ḥayyim,* I, no. 132, remarks, "I do not know of any clear prohibition . . ." and accordingly rules that it is permissible to accompany the patient if the latter will feel more comfortable as a result, even if there is no real need for the patient to be accompanied. However, Rabbi Feinstein notes that in some circumstances an ancillary problem arises, unrelated to the question of the use of an automobile *per se* but pertaining to the question of the distance traversed. It is forbidden to travel on the Sabbath beyond the *teḥum Shabbat* —a distance of two thousand cubits beyond a populated area. Since other forms of transportation are generally proscribed on *Shabbat,* this restriction is usually associated with travelling by foot on the Sabbath. However, in actuality, this limitation applies to any form of transportation. Hence, when the journey involves travel beyond the *teḥum Shabbat* and there is no cogent reason for the presence of an escort, the journey is not permissible simply for purposes of accompanying the patient.[2]

Rabbi Zevi Pesach Frank, *Har Ẓevi, Yoreh De'ah,* no. 293, assuming that the amount of fuel needed to propel a motor vehicle increases with the weight of the automobile and its occupants, discusses the ramifications of this phenomenon with regard to the laws of *Yom Tov*. Rabbi Frank notes that the presence of an additional passenger increases the frequency with which fuel must be burned by the engine. Thus the presence of an additional passenger in the car leads to an increased number of infractions of *Shabbat* laws on the part of the driver. Rabbi Neuwirth, both in *Shemirat Shabbat ke-Hilkhatah* chap. 19, n. 140, and in the above-cited article (*Moriah*, Tammuz 5733), quotes the opinion of "experts" who distinguish between heavy and light vehicles and states that while in a light vehicle an additional passenger will cause added infractions on the part of the driver, this is not the case in a "heavy" vehicle. The same distinction is drawn in *Divrei Ẓavah u-Milḥamah* (no. 231), a compendium devoted to *halakhot* pertaining to military service. The High Holy Day 5734

---

2. See also R. Abraham Chaim Noeh, *Keẓot ha-Shulḥan* 140:1; and R. Chanoch Zundel Grossberg, *Shevilin,* Tevet–Adar 5725.

edition of *Morashah,* a relatively new Israeli periodical, contains an article by Rabbi Israel Rosen in which some of the broader aspects of this question are discussed. Rabbi Rosen notes that, in point of fact, any additional weight is likely to increase the frequency of acceleration.

The validity of these conclusions must, of course, be reevaluated in light of the aforementioned information supplied by Professor Wachtel. It may, however, be stated that even the possibility of the need for additional acceleration due to the added weight of the passenger would augur against the transportation of any additional person. Any actions performed on behalf of the patient are permissible; hence, even if the total number of accelerations is increased as a result of the lighter weight, all such accelerations are performed expressly for the benefit of the patient. On the other hand, any acceleration which might be necessitated by the increased weight of the passenger constitutes an act which is not performed on behalf of the patient.

It should be reiterated that all such considerations are clearly irrelevant in the event that the gravely ill patient requires a companion for either medical or psychological reasons, even if such a need is not explicitly voiced by the patient.

Induced Labor

Occasionally, during the final stages of pregnancy, when medically indicated, labor is induced either chemically or by rupturing the membrane surrounding the amniotic fluids. Moreover, it is common practice to administer a drug to a woman already in labor in order to speed the birth process. This procedure is designed to minimize the period of labor and to reduce the danger of subsequent hemorrhaging.

The late Rabbi Y. E. Henkin, nestor of the American rabbinate and one of its foremost halakhic authorities, published a short item in the Tishri 5732 issue of *Ha-Pardes* in which he states that, in his opinion, children whose delivery has been speeded by means of medical intervention should not be circumcised on the Sabbath or the Day of Atonement. Unfortunately, Rabbi Henkin, in his brief remarks, does not include the rationale upon which his innovative decision is based.

Two possible lines of reasoning which might lead to this conclusion are formulated and presented in another article appearing in the Kislev 5732 edition of the same periodical. The author, Rabbi Moshe Bunim Pirutinsky, himself a *mohel* by profession, has written many erudite articles concerning various aspects of circumcision and is the author of *Sefer ha-Brit,* a comprehensive work dealing with the laws of *milah.* In his present article, Rabbi Pirutinsky outlines and rejects the arguments which might lead to a ruling prohibiting circumcision on *Shabbat.* When delivery is hastened, the possibility exists that the child may be sufficiently premature for the embryo not to have been fully developed prior to birth. Halakhah stipulates that an infant whose viability is in doubt may not be circumcised on the Sabbath. This consideration does not apply to the case at hand, observes Rabbi Pirutinsky, since the medical procedures in question are generally performed during or after the ninth month. In any event, the child may be examined for physical signs of fetal maturation, such as the presence of hair and nails, which are accepted by Halakhah as evidence of viability.

Another possible factor militating against circumcision on *Shabbat* in the cases under discussion is the element of artificiality in the birth process. Children whose birth occurs as a result of Caesarean section may not be circumcised on the Sabbath. It may be argued that children born following medically induced labor may be equated in status with children delivered by means of Caesarean section. Rabbi Pirutinsky dismisses this contention as being unfounded. The provision forbidding *Shabbat* circumcision of children born by Caesarean section is not predicated upon the fact that this procedure constitutes an "unnatural" form of childbirth. The Gemara, *Shabbat* 135a, cites Leviticus 12:2–3, "If a woman conceive and give birth to a male child, she shall be unclean seven days. . . . And on the eighth day the flesh of his foreskin shall be circumcised." On the basis of the juxtaposition of these two verses the Gemara concludes that only in cases when the mother is subject to the laws of impurity associated with childbirth is there an overriding necessity for circumcision to be performed on the eighth day even when that day coincides with the Sabbath. Since Caesarean delivery in and of itself does not result in the ritual impurity which follows normal chilbirth, the child born in this manner may not be circumcised on *Shabbat.* There is no question whatsoever that artificially induced delivery does result in such ritual impurity. Hence the element of artificiality present in medically induced delivery does not preclude circumcision on the Sabbath. Rabbi Pirutinsky concludes that there is no reason to postpone *Shabbat* circumcision of infants whose delivery has either been hastened or induced by medical means.

Circumcision on Shabbat

It is a sad fact that, unfortunately, many circumcisions performed on *Shabbat* become the occasion for desecration of the Sabbath on the part of guests traveling to the *brit milah* and in the preparation of the circumcision repast.[3] In the Tishri 5732 issue of *Ha-Pardes,* Rabbi Simon Schwartz opines that the performance of a circumcision under such circumstances borders upon the transgression "Thou shalt not place a stumbling block before the blind." He bolsters this argument by citing Rabbi A. Yudelevitz, *Bet Av Ḥamisha'i, Yoreh De'ah,* no. 280, who records that "some rabbis among the scholars of Galicia and Hungary" forbade circumcision on the Sabbath of children whose parents were known to be willful *Shabbat* violators.

Rabbi Pirutinsky, in the previously quoted article, rejects this position as well. The Sages abrogated fulfillment of the commandments concerning the *shofar* and the four species when *Rosh ha-Shanah* or the first day of *Sukkot* occurs on a Sabbath lest an individual intent upon the performance of these precepts violate the Sabbath laws by transporting the requisite ritual objects through a public thoroughfare. The identical consideration may be applied to circumcision on *Shabbat;* namely, fear lest the *mohel* transport the circumcision knife through a public thoroughfare. Yet circumcision on *Shabbat* was never proscribed. A variety of reasons have been advanced in explanation of why the Sages did not feel prompted to forbid circumcision on the Sabbath. Citing *Magen Avraham, Oraḥ Ḥayyim* 301:58, Rabbi Pirutinsky argues that since no such edict was issued in days of yore, despite the perfectly obvious basis for such a pronouncement, we, in our day, are not empowered to forbid circumcision on *Shabbat.*

A similar query was addressed to Rabbi Moses Feinstein by a *mohel* who sought permission to decline an invitation to officiate at a circumcision on *Shabbat*. The *mohel* explained that he did not wish to witness desecration of the Sabbath. Rabbi Feinstein, *Iggrot Mosheh, Yoreh De'ah,* I, no. 156, agrees that the sentiments of the *mohel* are well founded. Indeed, the Gemara, *Yoma* 70a, states that merely being present at the performance of a *miẓvah* is meritorious because "in the multitude of people is the king's glory" (Pro. 14:28). By extension, the more individuals present at the

---

3. See also R. Shalom Mordecai Schwadron, *Teshuvot Maharsham,* II, no. 156; R. Ya'akov Breish, *Ḥelkat Ya'akov,* I, no. 47; R. Eliezer Waldenberg, *Ẓiẓ Eli'ezer,* VI, no. 3; and R. Shlomoh Schneider, *Ha-Ma'or,* Iyar-Sivan 5733.

commission of a transgression, the greater the dishonor to the King. Hence, being present when a transgression occurs is itself an infraction. However, the *miẓvah* of circumcision constitutes an overriding obligation and cannot be suspended or postponed because of transgression on the part of the nonobservant. Accordingly, Rabbi Feinstein directed the *mohel* to perform the circumcision but to depart immediately thereafter.

CHAPTER VII

Marriage, Divorce and Personal Status

If a husband and wife are worthy, the Divine Presence is in their midst; if they are not worthy, a fire consumes them.

SOTAH 17a

The purity of the family unit is the cornerstone of the sanctity of the community of Israel. The Gemara, *Kiddushin* 70a, declares, "The Divine Presence does not rest other than upon genealogically pure families of Israel." In that succinct statement the Sages eloquently underscore the importance of the family and its genealogical purity in the Jewish system of values. At the very inception of the Jewish faith-community in the wilderness of Sinai our ancestors "declared their pedigrees according to their families" (Num. 1:8) and the family assumed its position as the most fundamental of Jewish institutions.

The marriage bond, in particular, must remain inviolate if legitimacy of birth is to be preserved and the continued manifestation of the Divine Presence to be assured. A marriage can be terminated only by death or by means of a *get,* a properly executed bill of divorce. This realm of Halakhah is singled out for the most stringent safeguards. Lest the ignorant wreak untold havoc, the Sages admonish that one who is not proficient in the laws of marriage and divorce should have no traffic with the performance of marriage or, most emphatically, with the execution of a bill of divorce. The bill of divorce must be drawn up by the husband, or his proxy, and delivered to the wife (Deut. 24:1). Jewish law is quite specific with regard to the formula to be employed in this instrument and with regard to its mode of execution. A woman who remarries without benefit of a *get* (religious divorce) is guilty of adultery. Children born of such a union bear the stigma of bastardy,

Polygamy is not banned by Scripture but was forbidden among Western

Jews following an edict proscribing plural marriages promulgated in approximately the year 1000 by the renowned Ashkenazic authority, Rabbenu Gershom. This authority further decreed that, except in certain limited extenuating circumstances, a woman may not be divorced against her will. Hence, in practice, neither a husband nor a wife may remarry unless a bill of divorce is executed by mutual agreement.

Jewish law pertaining to divorce, remarriage and the legitimacy of children may appear to some to be overly harsh. However, this stringency has served as a prophylactic measure; it has been a guarantee against promiscuity and the breakdown of the family. In this Judaism has achieved remarkable success. Throughout the centuries Jews could point with pride to the beauty and sanctity of their family life. In his home the Jew found personal happiness and spiritual fulfillment. Moreover, the Jewish home served as a vehicle for religious expression, as the institution which preserved and transmitted intact the myriad details of Jewish law, ritual and custom. Despite the vicissitudes of exile and dispersion, the integrity of the family remained the hallmark of the Jew.

Surnames in Marriage Contracts and Bills of Divorce

The important question of the necessity of including the surnames of the various parties in bills of divorce is discussed in a significant work, recently republished, the *Ḥelkat Ya'akov,* collected responsa of Rabbi Jacob Breish of Zurich. The earliest mention of this matter is to be found in a work entitled *Seder Gittin,* cited in the *Darkei Mosheh* of R. Moses Isserles, *Even ha-Ezer* 129:19. According to the *Darkei Mosheh,* family names should not be included as a cognomen in these documents. Rabbi Shalom Mordechai Schwadron, in vol. I, no. 83, of his *Teshuvot Maharsham,* contends that this ruling was valid only in earlier days when family names were not widespread, but now that people are invariably known by their surnames, these names must be included in legal documents. In an addendum, published together with volume III of these responsa, Maharsham adds that since positive identification of the individuals named must be possible on the basis of the content of the document itself (*mukhaḥ mi-tokho*), the absence of a surname in an age when persons are identified primarily by last names renders the bill of divorce invalid. Yet Maharsham's ruling was never accepted as normative practice. Rabbi Breish, in vol. I, no. 161, of his *Ḥelkat Ya'akov,* advances several considerations which, in his opinion, explain the nonimplementation of the Maharsham's decision. In the first place, a bill of divorce commonly contains all names, cognomens, nicknames, aliases, etc., including those in the vernacular, of both husband and wife and their respective fathers. Accordingly, there is no question of absolute identification of the parties named. Furthermore, inclusion of the surname may lead to confusion, for while at the time of divorce husband and wife share the same surname, the wife's family name will change upon remarriage. Therefore, there is no need to deviate from the recorded opinion of the *Darkei Mosheh.*

Rabbi Moses Feinstein, *Iggrot Mosheh, Even ha-Ezer,* I, 178, states that surnames are not included in a bill of divorce lest an error be made in Hebrew spelling as a result of incorrect transliteration and thus render the divorce invalid. Were this to be the case, consequent marriages contracted by the divorcee would, in fact, constitute adultrous relationships. Since this consideration does not apply to marriage contracts, there is no impediment to the inclusion of surnames in such documents. However, it goes without saying that even with regard to the execution of a marriage contract the officiating rabbi should familiarize himself thoroughly with the halakhic forms governing transliteration. Rabbi Feinstein adds that there may be a positive reason for the inclusion of surnames in marriage contracts because in such documents cognomens are not commonly included. In large cities, where many individuals may have identical Hebrew names, positive identification of the principals would, perhaps, not be effected by means of the document itself and hence it might be advisable that the surname be utilized for this purpose.

When the surname *is* included, care should be taken that it not be identified as a personal cognomen and the term *ha-mekhuneh* should not be employed. *Darkei Mosheh,* quoting *Seder Gittin,* states that the term *ha-mekhuneh* denotes the use of the appellation as a *personal* name. Thus the use of *ha-mekhuneh* in conjunction with a surname is erroneous and renders the document invalid. In point of fact, the individual to whom reference is made bears no such personal name and the document is therefore faulty by virtue of misidentification. For this reason, Rabbi Feinstein declares that the surname, when used, must be introduced by a term identifying it as such. Rabbi Feinstein recommends use of the term *le-mishpaḥat* ("of the family") followed by the surname.

Employment During the Postnuptial Week

Among the halakhic prerogatives of a bride is the privilege of rejoicing with, and being gladdened by, her new husband. A previously unmarried bride is entitled to enjoy the undivided attention of her groom for a period of seven days. Rambam, *Hilkhot Ishut* 10:12, indicates that it is because of this obligation that the groom may not engage in labor or in commercial activity. *Bet Yosef, Even ha-Ezer* 64, cites a somewhat different rationale for the restrictions enjoining the groom from engaging in work. *Pirkei de-Rabbi Eli'ezer,* chap. 16, records: "A groom is likened unto a king—just as a king does not go to the marketplace and performs no labor, so also a groom [does not go to the marketplace, etc.]."

Ḥelkat Meḥokek, Even ha-Ezer 64:2, points out that the acceptance of this rationale, as cited by *Bet Yosef,* serves to prohibit gainful employment on the part of the groom in circumstances under which such employment would otherwise be deemed permissible. Save for *Bet Yosef* it would be assumed that the obligation with regard to "rejoicing" during the seven-day period is designed to guarantee satisfaction of a prerogative of the bride. Accordingly, if the bride voluntarily surrenders her privilege the groom is relieved of his responsibility to "gladden" the bride. Were this line of reasoning the sole basis for the prohibition against work—as indeed seems to be Rambam's position—the groom would then be permitted to engage in gainful employment as well. However, the reason advanced by *Bet Yosef* serves to prohibit work under such circumstances. The groom is always "compared to a king" and even if the bride forgoes her privilege of "rejoicing," the groom, by virtue of his "royal" status, may not engage in activity unbecoming to a kingly personage. In this light it is understandable that Rema, *Even ha-Ezer* 64:1, finds it necessary to append a statement embodying a blanket prohibition against a groom engaging in work.

Of interest in these days when so many women are employed outside of the home, is the question of work on the part of the bride during the postnuptial week. This issue is raised by Rabbi Ephraim Grunblatt in the Adar 5734 issue of *Ha-Pardes.* The question concerns a bride who was unable to obtain leave from her job for the entire seven-day period and wished to know whether, according to Jewish law, she might report to work during the week following her wedding. Since the previously cited sources speak only of a prohibition against work on the part of the groom it would appear that there is no explicit ban with regard to employment on the part of the bride. *Teshuvot Maharsham,* III, no. 206, does permit a bride employed as a seamstress to work at her trade during this period, but stipulates that she may do so only with the acquiescence of her husband. *Maharsham,* however, does not explain why he deems permission of the husband to be necessary, *Maharsham*'s position may perhaps be understood in light of comments by Rabbi Simchah Elberg, *Shalmei Simḥah,* I, no. 70. Citing the verse "on the day of his wedding and the day of the rejoicing of his heart" (Song of Songs 3:11), Rabbi Elberg argues that the groom is bound by a two-fold obligation, viz., to gladden his bride and also himself to rejoice. *Maharsham* may well have reasoned that the bride may engage in work only with the acquiescence of the groom since it may be assumed that her employment will mar the groom's own joy. It should be noted that one source, *Pesikta de-Rav Kahana,* no. 22, while giving no reason, clearly indicates that a bride may not engage in labor for a period of seven days following her wedding.

Not cited by Rabbi Grunblatt is the comment of R. Meir Arak, *Minḥat Pittim, Even ha-Ezer* 64:1, who, while not issuing a definitive ruling, indicates that on the basis of the codification of the *Shulḥan Arukh,* it would appear that there is no restriction whatsoever on work by the bride. According to this position, prior permission of the husband would be unnecessary.

Parenthetically, students frequently ask whether they are permitted to attend *shi'urim* during the week following their wedding. R. Chaim Joseph David Azulai, *Teshuvot Ḥayyim Sha'al,* no. 38, sec. 60, declares that a scholar should not engage in studies requiring intensive concentration during this period in order that he not be distracted from fulfilling his obligation with regard to gladdening his bride. A similar statement is recorded in *Ḥina ve-Ḥisda*, I, 74a. It would appear, however, that with the consent of his bride, the groom may be permitted to attend classes and to engage in study. While labor is indeed forbidden to the groom because he is "compared to a king," this status in no way prevents him from engaging in study. Labor is antithetical to royal status but Torah study is indeed a kingly pursuit. Of course, time devoted to study cannot be spent in festivities or other activities designed to gladden the bride, but the bride may, at her option, forgo this prerogative in whole or in part. Accordingly, if the bride does not object, there is no halakhic impediment to attendance at *shi'urim* by the groom.

The Agunah Problem

The problem of the *agunah,* a woman whose husband has disappeared or is otherwise unable to terminate the marriage by executing a bill of divorce, has long been the source of much hardship and heartache. In addition to the toll taken in human lives, war has the disastrous side-effect of increasing the incidence of *agunot*. Since Halakhah does not sanction remarriage in the absence of positive proof of death, the wife of a soldier missing in action may become bereft of her husband yet forbidden to remarry.

Judaism has always been keenly aware of the anguish suffered by the *agunah*. The tragic plight of the *agunah* has spurred rabbinic authorities throughout the generations to seek every possible means of remedying such grievous situations. This entire subject is one of the utmost gravity and it is of importance to examine the methods that have been advocated as a means of avoiding this tragic situation while yet remaining within the letter and spirit of the law. The measures taken during the course of Jewish history in order to alleviate this problem are reviewed by Rabbi Shiloh Rafael in a contribution to the 5729 edition of *Torah She-be-'al Peh*.

The earliest attempts to mitigate the *agunah* problem date to biblical times. The Gemara, *Ketubot* 9b, states that participants in the wars of King David delivered bills of divorce to their wives before leaving for battle. According to Rashi such divorces were conditional—becoming effective retroactively in the event of the husband's failure to return; according to Rabbenu Tam these divorces were absolute—the couple, of course, having the prerogative of remarrying upon the husband's release from military service. The Gemara, *Shabbat* 56a, cites this practice in explanation of the dictum, "One who claims that David was a sinner is naught but mistaken." Bat-Sheva, according to the Talmud, was no longer the wife of Uriah since Uriah had followed the usual procedure and presented his wife with a bill of divorce before undertaking his military assignment.

Ba'al ha-Turim, in his commentary to Numbers 32:21, presents the novel view that this practice was not King David's innovation but was originally introduced by Moses prior to the military engagements leading to the conquest of the land of Canaan. However, the purpose of the practice as instituted by Moses was somewhat more limited and was employed merely to obviate the necessity for levirate marriage or *ḥaliẓah* in the case of a childless widow. *Ba'al ha-Turim*'s argument is predicated upon the philological relationship of *ḥaluẓ ha-na'al* ("unshod") of Deuteronomy 25:10 and the similar term *ḥaluẓ* ("armed warrior") in the previously cited passage. A warrior, according to this commentator, is called a *ḥaluẓ* because his occupation often necessitates the ceremony of *ḥaliẓah* entailing the removal of a shoe.

Throughout the years conditional divorces were at times granted in order to obviate other causes of the *agunah* situation. We find this remedy utilized in the case of a childless couple in instances in which the husband was gravely ill and the wife wished to avoid the difficulties of *yibum* and *ḥalizah.* Rabbi Rafael notes that one of the *Ba'alei ha-Tosafot,* R. Yechiel of Paris, decreed that the husband execute an unconditional bill of divorce in such instances. This course of action was advocated by R. Yechiel because the halakhah governing the formulation of stipulations is extremely complicated, and he wished to preclude invalidation of the divorce due to lack of expertise in effecting a conditional divorce. In order to assuage the husband, and to eliminate any hesitancy on his part lest in the event of his recovery the wife refuse to remarry her former husband, R. Yechiel provided for a formal sworn acceptance of this obligation upon pain of anathema.

At a later date a question arose with regard to the prerogatives of the wife under this arrangement. The widespread controversy surrounding the famed "Divorce of Vienna" centers around this problem. The details were as follows: A young man, sixteen years of age, became afflicted with a severe illness and agreed to present his wife with a bill of divorce in order to avoid the eventuality of *ḥalizah.* At the time of the divorce proceedings the husband's consent was obtained by convincing him that the divorce was being executed solely for the purpose of exempting his young wife from *ḥalizah* but that upon his recovery his wife would return to him. The young man was restored to health but his wife refused to resume the marital relationship. The matter was brought before the renowned Maharam of Lublin, who ruled that in light of this understanding the husband's recovery invalidated the original divorce.[a]

An intriguing and unprecedented argument forbidding the woman to remarry was forwarded by R. Mordecai Jaffe, the author of the *Levush.* Scripture states, "and if it come to pass that she does not find favor in his eyes . . . and he should write her a bill of divorce and give it into her hand and send her out of his house. And she shall go out of his house and became a wife to another man . . ." (Deut. 24:1–2). R. Mordecai Jaffe contended that a woman may "become a wife of another man" only if she has been divorced by her husband because "she does not find favor in his eyes." A bill of divorce whose presentation is not motivated by a loss of "favor" but by other considerations—a "divorce of love" is the term coined by R. Mordecai Jaffe—is not effective as an instrument empowering marriage to another.

These opinions notwithstanding, a synod of the Polish and Russian rab-

a. See *Teshuvot Maharam Lublin,* nos. 102–106.

binate, convened by R. Shmuel Eliezer Edels, of renown as the author of the talmudic commentary, *Maharsha,* upheld the validity of the "Divorce of Vienna." The issue developed into a *cause célèbre* with the controversy continuing unabated for many years.

In modern times this form of divorce was again employed as a means of curtailing the instances of *agunot.* Changing circumstances and the need to find measures adaptable to large numbers of conscripted soldiers gave rise to added halakhic complications. In times of mass conscription it was difficult for inductees to appear before a rabbinic court in person in order to appoint court functionaries as scribes and witnesses for the drawing up of a bill of divorce. *Divrei Malki'el* sanctions the appointment of scribes and witnesses in the presence of any two individuals even though the functionaries named are not present in person. To avoid error, he advises that a general designation be made appointing all residents of the city as agents of the husband so that any one of them may be the scribe and any two may serve as witnesses. This proposal has an added advantage in that the bill of divorce itself need not be executed until a question of remarriage becomes actual. Forms incorporating the formula proposed by *Divrei Malki'el* were prepared by the Chief Rabbinate of Palestine and used in that country during World War II. In the United States a formula containing the names of individuals designated to serve as scribes and witnesses was prepared by the *Agudat ha-Rabbanim* and published in *Ha-Pardes,* Iyar 5702.

In recent years a further difficulty arose with regard to this procedure in view of the fact that soldiers now receive frequent furloughs. Both Rambam and *Shulḥan Arukh* state that if the husband and his spouse are secluded together before a bill of divorce is delivered to the wife, the divorce is invalidated. The act of seclusion gives reason to suspect that the husband may have annulled the previously prepared document. In a letter to Rabbi Herzog, Rabbi Chaim Ozer Grodzinski of Vilna wrote that in his city he required each soldier to renew the appointment of proxies at the close of each furlough. Similar provisions were made in Palestine by Rabbi Herzog.[1] Rabbi Yechezkel Abramsky, then head of the London *Bet Din,* maintained that these provisions were unnecessary. Dayan Abramsky argued that since the husband grants such a divorce for the sole purpose of precluding the eventuality of his wife becoming an *agunah,* there is no reason to suppose that he will annul his proxy while on leave.

While these procedures received the approbation of most halakhic au-

---

1. See also, R. Meshullam Roth, *Kol Mevaser,* II, no. 14.

thorities, one scholar of world repute expressed dissent. The *Ḥazon Ish* was strongly opposed to the accepted mode of appointing proxies and court functionaries but devised an alternate method of effecting such divorces.

In concluding his summary, Rabbi Rafael notes that for psychological reasons this practice has fallen into disuse and is no longer the standard procedure in the Israel Defense Forces. But the realities of life continue. Unfortunately, Israel is enveloped in a seemingly endless state of warfare, and the *agunah* problem is both real and heart-rending. Under these circumstances every possible measure should be taken to prevent any such unfortunate occurrence. The formula adopted in the past is one which may understandably generate feelings of distaste and hesitation. In reality it represents an emergency measure expressing the acme of forethought, concern, and devotion—a veritable "divorce of love." Any precaution is clearly worthwhile if only to avoid a single case of anguish and tragedy.

Refusal to Grant a Religious Divorce

According to Jewish law, matrimonial bonds can be severed in only one of two ways: by the decease of one of the parties, or by means of a *get,* a bill of divorce written at the specific behest of the husband and delivered by him, or by his proxy, to the wife. Rabbinic literature is replete with references to cases of insufficient or inadequate evidence of the death of the husband. Unless such evidence is forthcoming, the woman is forbidden to remarry.

In our time, *agunah* situations arise most frequently not from instances of unprovable death but from the refusal of the husband to execute a *get,* or religious divorce. In such cases, even though a civil divorce may have been obtained, the marital bonds continue to remain intact in the eyes of Halakhah and the woman is forbidden to contract a second marriage until she has obtained a religious divorce.

Over the years, a number of proposals have been advanced in attempts to ameliorate this problem. These include a suggestion that all marriages be made conditional by incorporating a clause in the marriage ceremony stipulating that if the marriage is subsequently dissolved by a civil court the marriage be deemed null and void *ab initio.* It has also been suggested that the parties take a solemn oath to seek a religious divorce should they become estranged. Yet another proposal called upon the groom to obligate himself to the payment of a fine or penalty for failure to execute a religious divorce in the event that the need for one should arise. Each of these proposals has been rejected in turn by the consensus of recognized halakhic experts as being incompatible with the dictates of Halakhah.

The most widely publicized proposal of this nature is a formula promulgated by the Conservative movement. The couple bind themselves to submit any marital disputes which may arise to an ecclesiastical court established by the Conservative rabbinate and to abide by any decisions of that body. Implicit in the agreement is an obligation to pay any penalty which may be imposed upon failure to issue a *get* when it is so ruled by that court. A clause to this effect is incorporated in the text of the Conservative *ketubah*. The Orthodox rabbinate strongly opposed this innovation for several reasons. In the first place, there is serious doubt with regard to whether the proposed penalty can be legally or halakhically imposed. Secondly, many authorities reject the threat of financial penalty for nonconformity with the edict of a *Bet Din* as constituting a form of unlawful coercion which may invalidate the *get*. An even more fundamental objection focuses upon the competence of the proposed *Bet Din*. Normative Judaism does not recognize the authority of a Conservative *Bet Din.*[2] Persons who deny the authority of Halakhah, in whole or in part, are disqualified from serving as members of a rabbinical tribunal charged with interpreting and enforcing Jewish law.

In a paper appearing in the Tammuz–Sivan 5731 issue of *Sinai,* Rabbi Elyakim Ellinson advances an interesting suggestion which, if accepted, would resolve the problem of *igun* in a significant number of cases. Opposition to previous proposals that every groom obligate himself to pay a fine or penalty for failure to execute a *get* when warranted centers upon the coercive nature of such a stipulation. Halakhah requires that the bill of divorce be presented to the wife by the husband of his own free will. The threat of punitive measures, according to many authorities, constitutes coercion, which may invalidate the divorce. There are, however, certain financial responsibilities which devolve upon the husband as a matter of statutory obligation. The husband is bound by Jewish law to support his wife. This obligation ordinarily remains in force until such time as the marriage is dissolved. In Israel, where rabbinic tribunals have jurisdiction over domestic matters, the husband can be held liable for the support of his wife until such time as he executes a bill of divorce. A decree ordering the husband to provide for the sustenance of his estranged wife will, in most cases, effect a change of heart in even the most recalcitrant of husbands.

2. See R. Moses Feinstein, *Iggrot Mosheh, Yoreh De'ah,* I, no. 160; *Even ha-Ezer,* I, no. 135; and *Even ha-Ezer,* II, no. 17.

Desire for release from further financial obligation usually prompts the husband to terminate the relationship voluntarily by executing a religious divorce. This method of gaining compliance with the edict of a *Bet Din* is identical to the procedure outlined by *Bet Me'ir, Even ha-Ezer* 154:1, as a means of persuading an apostate to execute a bill of divorce.

In the Diaspora the problem is more complex. Civil courts view a marriage as having been dissolved upon the issuance of a divorce decree and, barring an alimony award, the husband is released from further obligation with regard to financial support. Rabbi Ellinson proposes that prior to the wedding ceremony each groom be asked to enter into a legally binding civil contract providing for the support of his bride and stipulating that the extent of this obligation be in accordance with the provisions of Jewish law. The contract would be drawn up as a legal document enforceable in the civil courts. The husband would then be legally obligated to support his wife until a religious divorce has been executed since Jewish law recognizes an ongoing obligation to support one's wife until the union has been dissolved by a *get*. This arrangement would provide ample motivation for the otherwise uncooperative husband to comply in granting a religious divorce.

A precedent for this innovation may be found in *Naḥalat Shivah* 9:14, which reports that it was customary in certain German communities to draw up an engagement contract which contained a clause providing that in case of domestic strife, a specific sum be paid to the wife for her support until such time as the couple appear before a *Bet Din* which would then make a final determination with regard to all matters at issue.

It is quite possible that a remedy along the lines suggested by Rabbi Ellinson already exists. Were this point to become a matter of litigation, it is conceivable that the court would rule that no additional contract to this effect is necessary since the *ketubah,* or marriage contract, drawn up prior to the wedding ceremony specifically contains a clause providing for support of the wife in accordance with Jewish law. In at least one case dating back to 1926 (*Hurwitz* v. *Hurwitz,* 216 A.D. 362, 215 N.Y. Supp. 184) the court recognized the *ketubah* as constituting a binding legal contract and on that basis upheld certain claims of a widow against the estate of her deceased husband. More recently, in a decision handed down in March 1972, the New York State Supreme Court (*Kaplan* v. *Kaplan,* 329 N.Y.S. 2d 750) invoked the provisions of the *ketubah* in an award for support and maintenance. Whether or not the provisions of the *ketubah* are enforceable in a court of law is a matter to be determined by legal experts. In any event, it would appear that any legal deficiencies in the *ketubah* could indeed be remedied by introducing a separate contract such as that outlined by Rabbi Ellinson.

In terms of Halakhah, the basic premise upon which the proposal rests is open to question. There is some uncertainty concerning a husband's obligation under Jewish law with regard to financial support of an estranged wife. Rema, *Even ha-Ezer* 70:12, rules that the husband's obligations cease when the wife leaves his home. However, *Baba Meẓi'a* 12b declares that in all instances in which there are unresolved halakhic questions surrounding the efficacy of a particular bill of divorce the financial obligations of the husband remain in force. Although the woman no longer shares his bed and board, the husband must provide for her sustenance since she is "bound to him" and is not free to remarry. Various Israeli rabbinical courts have issued conflicting rulings with regard to this question. There are recorded decisions in which the *Bet Din* has decreed that the husband is not obligated to provide for the support of his estranged wife. On the other hand, in at least some instances, *Batei Din* have ruled that if the wife is prepared to accept a bill of divorce, the husband is bound to provide for her maintenance should he be unwilling to execute a *get*. Opinions to this effect by the late Chief Rabbis Herzog and Uziel are to be found in notes appended to *Oẓar ha-Poskim,* II, p. 8 and p. 16. Since Rabbi Elinson's proposal hinges upon this fundamental point the issue clearly requires further investigation and analysis.

The proposal under discussion also has a number of practical drawbacks which detract from its effectiveness in certain cases. For example, there is no halakhic obligation on the part of the husband to support his wife if she earns her own livelihood. However, in the event that the husband refuses to accede to the wife's desire for a religious divorce, a working woman who would have to resort to a claim of maintenance as a means of securing a *get* could be advised to cease working temporarily. Similar problems arise in the case of a woman who derives an independent income from invested capital. According to Halakhah, such funds accrue to the husband, who may then claim that the income, if paid to the wife and sufficient for her needs, discharges his obligation with regard to maintenance. In order to obviate this contingency, Rabbi Ellinson suggests that every groom be required to enter into an agreement renouncing his right to such monies.

The most serious deficiency with regard to this proposal arises from the fact that an alimony award frequently accompanies a divorce decree. When such is the case, it is difficult to perceive how the proposed document would influence the husband to execute a religious divorce. Of course, in such eventualities the wife does retain the option of offering to forgo alimony rights in return for a religious divorce.

It is hoped that ultimately the various halakhic and practical difficulties involved can be overcome. With refinement and modification, perhaps there will emerge a proposal which may serve to relieve the agony and anguish of such modern-day *agunot*.

In point of fact, it appears to this writer that there does exist an alternate method not subject to the aforementioned objections and deficiencies. In every marriage, the husband, by virtue of the conditions of the *ketubah* and of rabbinic legislation, is obliged to provide for the needs of his wife. The style in which a husband is obligated to support his wife and the extent of this obligation are carefully spelled out in *Shulḥan Arukh, Even ha-Ezer* 70:1–3. However, there is nothing to prevent the husband from voluntarily obligating himself to a more generous level of support. Rashi, Genesis 26:7, cites the midrashic comment which points out that the food brought by Jacob to his father was not stolen but was the lawful property of his mother. The Midrash declares that Isaac included a clause in Rebeccah's *ketubah* obligating him to provide her with a daily allowance of two goats.

Similarly, it may be proposed that the groom obligate himself to provide his wife with a certain sum of money each day for her expenses, either by including an additional clause in the *ketubah* or by drawing up a separate document. It would be clearly stipulated that this obligation remains binding under any and all circumstances, regardless of the wife's own earnings, as long as a marital relationship continues to exist under Jewish law. For a variety of reasons, it would be best to limit this obligation to periods during which the wife does not share her husband's board but to allow the wife the option of electing to receive the stipulated allowance in lieu of board. Thus the wife's claim to a monetary allowance, practically speaking, would be limited to periods of separation. However, for technical halakhic reasons, in order that it be binding, it might be necessary for this obligation to encompass amicable separations, such as separate vacations, as well as periods of estrangement. The husband would be unable to escape this financial liability other than by executing a *get*. Since the obligation is derived from a voluntary contract drawn broadly enough to encompass even those contingencies in which the husband would be exempt from support mandated by Halakhah, the objections raised earlier do not seem to be applicable. Indeed, this proposal closely parallels the practices referred to by *Naḥalat Shivah* cited earlier. Of course, to be fully effective, the sum stipulated at the time of marriage should be significantly greater than any likely alimony award.

Mamzerut: I

Problems associated with marriage and divorce are recurring sources of irritation within Israeli society. Questions of personal status fall under the exclusive jurisdiction of the rabbinate, with the result that many secularists feel themselves deprived of basic freedoms. The problem of *mamzerut* is a particularly painful one and threatens to create a major rift between the religious and nonreligious sectors of the Israeli populace. According to Halakhah, a bastard is defined as a child born of an adulterous or incestuous relationship and may marry only a person of similar birth or a convert; a *mamzer* is forbidden to marry a Jew of legitimate birth. Since in Israel marriage is entirely within the domain of the rabbinate, restrictions upon *mamzerim* are not merely matters of personal observance but are enforced as the law of the land. Unquestionably, problems associated with *mamzerut* may occasion deep anguish. Many of those who are troubled by the ramifications of this issue, particularly those who have no personal commitment to the halakhic ethic, have called upon the Israeli government to institute a system of civil marriage. In turn, such proposals have aroused the concern of members of the Orthodox community. Their counterargument is that since, according to Jewish law, a child born to a *mamzer* has the same status as the parent, a policy of civil marriage will ultimately lead to a situation in which free intermarriage between different groups of Jews will be severely restricted.

Professor Moshe Silberg, formerly a justice of the Israeli Supreme Court, has advanced an interesting proposal which, in his opinion, would obviate this problem. His written views on this matter were published in the now defunct Israeli weekly, *Panim el Panim*, 5 Iyar and 4 Sivan, 5731. Justice Silberg recommends a form of civil marriage to be restricted to bastards. This proposal, he contends, is compatible with the provisions of Halakhah concerning liaisons with bastards. His suggested innovation centers around Rambam's ruling, *Hilkhot Issurei Bi'ah* 15:2, to the effect that sexual intercourse between a bastard and a person of legitimate birth is a culpable offense only within the framework of a matrimonial relationship. Rambam maintains that the prohibition "A bastard shall not enter into the assembly of God" (Deut. 23:3) refers solely to validly contracted marriages. *Migdal Oz, ad locum,* explains that Rambam renders the term *lo yavo* as "he shall not enter," the form of "entry" to which reference is made being marriage. Rabad, in a gloss to this ruling, disagrees sharply with Rambam and asserts that all cohabitation with a bastard is proscribed by this prohibition. Rabad apparently translates the term *"lo yavo"* literally as referring to the sexual act (*bi'ah*). Professor Silberg urges rabbinic authorities to accept Rambam's position as authoritative. This would open the way for a form of civil marriage to be contracted in a manner which would regularize the relationship in the eyes of civil authorities, but would not constitute a halakhically valid marriage. From the point of view of Halakhah, the woman entering into such a relationship would have the status of a concubine.

Professor Silberg himself notes a number of objections which may be raised with regard to his proposal but expresses the hope that rabbinic scholars will somehow resolve these difficulties. In the first place, Rabad and other authorities take issue with the basic premise and assert that all forms of sexual intercourse between *mamzerim* and those of legitimate birth are proscribed. According to *Migdal Oz,* Rambam merely rules that the statutory forty lashes are not to be inflicted as punishment for cohabitation outside of the marital relationship; Rambam does not declare such cohabitation to be permissible. *Migdal Oz* asserts that, according to Rambam, such cohabitation is forbidden by rabbinic edict. Thirdly, Rambam himself maintains that the prohibition "There shall be no harlot among the daughters of Israel" (Deut. 23:18), encompasses fornication with unmarried women. Finally, it is not at all clear that concubinage can be sanctioned within the framework of Halakhah. Professor Silberg notes that the late Sephardic scholar, Rabbi Ya'akov Moshe Toledano, at one time advocated reinstitution of concubinage as a means of ameliorating certain social and halakhic problems but subsequently withdrew this recommendation. Actually, a similar suggestion was originally formulated by R. Ya'akov Emden, *She'elat Ya'avez,* II, no. 15, in response to the threat posed by the licentiousness of the Sabbatians. Needless to say, this proposal never gained wide acceptance within the community of rabbinic scholars.

Professor Silberg's views are carefully analyzed and refuted by Rabbi Judah Dick in the Tishri 5732 issue of *Ha-Pardes*. Rabbi Dick is a member of the staff of the corporation counsel of New York City and an officer of the National Jewish Commission on Law and Public Affairs (COLPA). In his article, Rabbi Dick points out that Silberg's thesis contains an inherent self-contradiction. Rambam indeed maintains that cohabitation with a *mamzer* outside of marriage does not constitute an infraction of the prohibition against entry by a bastard into the "assembly of God." Yet it is Rambam himself, *Hilkhot Melakhim* 4:4, who maintains that concubinage is a royal prerogative and is forbidden to commoners. Moreover, Rabbi Dick notes that, according to Rambam, any form of sexual intercourse outside of marriage is biblically forbidden. There is some question as to whether the basis for this ban is the prohibition "There shall be no harlot among the daughters of Israel" since *Leḥem Mishneh, Hilkhot Melakhim* 4:4, maintains that this prohibition is limited to intercourse with a promiscuous woman who dispenses her favors indiscriminately.[3] In any event, the verse "When a man takes a wife" (Deut. 24:1) is understood by Rambam, *Hilkhot Ishut* 1:1, as constituting a positive commandment regarding marriage and as a prohibition against fornication outside of matrimony. On the other hand, those authorities who disagree with Rambam and permit concubinage nevertheless maintain that all forms of sexual intercourse between a *mamzer* and a person of legitimate birth are forbidden.

Rabbi Dick claims that a logical connection exists between Rambam's ruling that the prohibition with regard to *mamzerim* is limited to sexual relations within marriage and his prohibition of concubinage. According to those authorities who permit concubinage, this relationship, no less than matrimony, is included in the meaning of the term "assembly of God" and hence is forbidden to a *mamzer*. Rambam maintains that concubinage is forbidden and hence cannot be deemed an "assembly of God." It is precisely because concubinage is forbidden that the prohibition devolving upon intercourse with a *mamzer,* according to Rambam, is restricted to cohabitation within a marital relationship. Rabbi Dick concludes that Professor Silberg's proposal, intriguing as it may be, lacks halakhic validity.

Furthermore, in the opinion of this writer, Professor Silberg's proposal proves to be untenable on other grounds as well. In *Perushei Ivra,* no. 4, Rabbi Y. E. Henkin presents a fundamental analysis of the essence of the matrimonial relationship.[4] In a far-reaching ruling, he declares that civil marriage results in a relationship identical to that which follows upon the traditional nuptial ceremony and cannot be dissolved other than by means of a bill of divorce. This relationship can in no way be equated with concubinage. The essence of marriage, asserts Rabbi Henkin, is a permanent and exclusive conjugal relationship. When such a relationship is established,

3. Cf., however, *Kesef Mishneh* and *Maggid Mishneh, Issurei Bi'ah* 15:2.

4. See also the comments of R. Henkin published in the addenda to *Oẓar ha-Poskim,* XI, 396f.

the woman has the status of a wife and not of a concubine, whether or not the relationship has been formalized by means of a religious ceremony. The type of civil marriage proposed by Professor Silberg would, according to this analysis, constitute marriage rather than concubinage and hence is of no avail in alleviating the problem of *mamzerut.*

Mamzerut: II

Rabbinic authorities have always sought ways and means of alleviating the plight of unfortunate individuals stigmatized by *mamzerut* in order to permit such individuals to marry within "the community of God." Their efforts consisted of examining the loopholes which would have the effect of removing the onus of bastardy. Perhaps the most famous of these proposed remedies is a tentative suggestion advanced by Rabbi Shalom Mordecai Schwadron in his *Teshuvot Maharsham,* I, no. 9.

The Mishnah, *Gittin* 32a, states that in former times a husband could appoint a proxy to deliver a bill of divorce to his wife and yet retain the prerogative of annulling the proxy and thereby invalidating the divorce. Originally, the husband was not required to inform the proxy of his change of heart. This practice was later banned by Rabban Gamaliel the Elder in order to promote "the better ordering of society" (*tikkun ha-'olam*). In defining the concept of *tikkun ha-'olam,* R. Yochanan maintained that the measure was designed to prevent the proliferation of *mamzerim.* A messenger, unaware of the fact that his authority to deliver the bill of divorce had been nullified might, in good faith, present the bill of divorce to the woman in question. The woman, equally unaware that the proxy had been annulled and her divorce nullified, would feel free to remarry. Under such circumstances, any issue of a subsequent union would be a *mamzer* in the eyes of Jewish law. R. Yochanan states that it was to prevent such unfortunate occurrences that Rabban Gamaliel forbade annulment of the proxy other than in the presence of the messenger.

In the event that the husband transgresses the injuction of Rabban Gamaliel and annuls the proxy other than in the presence of the messenger, R. Simeon ben Gamaliel ordained that the act of annulment itself be null and void so that the bill of divorce may retain its validity. In discussing Rabban Gamaliel's decree the Gemara raises an obvious objection. It is axiomatic that a bill of divorce which is invalid according to biblical law cannot be validated by rabbinic decree. In response to this objection, the Gemara enunciates the well-known dictum: "Everyone who betroths [a wife] does so in accordance with the intention of the Sages, and they annulled his betrothal." The import of this statement is that while the Sages have no power to validate a bill of divorce which is not valid under biblical law, they do have the power to annul the marriage itself retroactively. Since they do not acquiesce to the marriage under such circumstances, the stipulated condition has not been fulfilled and the marriage itself is null and void. The status of the woman in these circumstances is not that of a divorcee but that of a single woman who had been consorting with a male without benefit of a nuptial ceremony. Accordingly, as a result of Rabban Gamaliel's decree, annulment of a proxy other than in the presence of the messenger and subsequent delivery of the *get* to the wife become the occasion for the retroactive annulment of the marriage.

Tosafot points out that Rabban Gamaliel's decree could be utilized in furthering certain ends which Rabban Gamaliel would certainly not have sought to promote. By invoking this decree, acts of adultery could be legitimized with the cooperation of the husband and both the adulterer and the adulteress might be enabled to escape punishment. This could be effected by having the husband draw up a bill of divorce, appoint a proxy to deliver it to his wife and subsequently annul the proxy other than in the presence of his messenger. The resultant effect would be annulment of the marriage *ab initio,* which would then mean that subsequent intercourse with another male was in the nature of fornication rather than adultery. *Ri,* cited by *Tosafot,* maintains that this procedure is perfectly legal.

Maharsham, quoting *Tosafot,* points out that a *mamzer* could also be legitimized retroactively in precisely the same manner. If the husband is yet living and willing to cooperate, he could simply appoint a proxy to deliver a bill of divorce to his wife and then proceed to annul the proxy other than in the presence of the messenger. Since the marriage is annulled retroactively, the liaison between his wife and another man does not constitute adultery and hence the issue of that union are not *mamzerim.*

The innovative suggestion of Maharsham has been the subject of several recent articles of note. The proposal was brought to the attention of readers of *Tradition* by Rabbi Dr. Louis Rabinowitz, Spring 1971, pp. 5–15.[4a] *Moriah,* Elul 5730–Tishri 5731, featured an article by Rabbi Shlomoh Zalman Auerbach, the eminent Israeli halakhic authority, containing a lengthy and exhaustive analysis of Maharsham's position. In *Panim el Panim,*

4a. See also Rabbi Aaron Rakeffet-Rothkoff, "Annulment of Marriage within the Context of Cancellation of the *Get*", *Tradition,* Spring-Summer 1975, pp. 173–185.

Shevat 2 and I Adar 13, 5733, the Israeli scholar and jurist Professor M. Silberg discusses practical proposals to eliminate incidences of *mamzerut*. Professor Silberg's views are challenged by Rabbi Judah Dick in *Panim el Panim,* I Adar 13, 5733.

Maharsham's language, "Had you consulted me before the bill of divorce was executed by the first husband, I would have made a suggestion *le-halakhah vo-lo le-ma'aseh* (according to theoretical halakhah but not for practical application)" clearly indicates that Maharsham viewed his innovative proposal as relegated to the realm of theory and not for actual implementation. Maharsham's use of the subjunctive phrase "had you consulted me" demonstrates that his answer, even at that time, would not have been intended for practical application. Rabbi Auerbach presents numerous reasons, many highly technical, in explaining why practical implementation of this proposal is precluded. The most salient of these considerations are the following:

1. The major argument against the implementation of Maharsham's proposal is that Ramban, *Shitah Mekubeẓet* and Me'iri, in their commentaries on *Ketubot* 3a, state clearly that any children born of an adulterous relationship prior to the retroactive annulment of the marriage are *mamzerim* by virtue of rabbinic decree. According to these authorities, the rabbinic decree providing for annulment of the marriage was accompanied by a decree declaring such issue to be legitimate precisely because the Sages did not want the decree regarding retroactive annulment of the marriage to serve as a tool in the hands of evildoers. This opinion is followed by many latter-day authorities.[5] *Oneg Yom Tov,* no. 169, states explicitly that "it is for this reason that this solution is not mentioned by any authority."

2. Retroactive annulment of the marriage renders all preceding acts of coitus acts of fornication. An individual is not permitted retroactively to transform his actions into transgressions and certainly should not be advised to do so and abetted in such a course of action by a *Bet Din.*

3. It is not certain that when the husband is counseled by a *Bet Din* to annul the proxy the marriage itself *is* in fact annulled retroactively. The phraseology employed by the Gemara in explaining why such annulment

---

5. See *Ketav Sofer, Even ha-Ezer,* no. 51; *Oneg Yom Tov,* no. 169; and R. Shlomoh Kluger, *Ha-Elef Lekha Shlomoh, Even ha-Ezer,* no. 34; *Pitḥei Teshuvah, Even ha-Ezer* 144:1 also cites *Brit Avraham, Even ha-Ezer,* no. 49, sec. 5. See also Rashba, *Ketubot* 3a; and R. Yitzchak Elchanan Spektor, *Ein Yiẓḥak,* I, *Oraḥ Ḥayyim,* no. 28, sec. 23.

was legislated is "He acted with impropriety." When acting upon the advice of a *Bet Din* the husband can hardly be said to have acted with impropriety and hence there are no grounds for annulling the marriage.

4. A number of early authorities, including Ramban, Re'ah, and Rashba, maintain that in point of fact the original marriage is never annulled. According to this interpretation, the husband, cognizant of the statutory provision for such annulment, recognizes that annulment of the proxy is of no avail and hence never actually intends to annul the proxy. *Pnei Yehoshu'a, Ketubot* 3a, offers a different interpretation in agreement with the basic premise that in actuality no annulment takes place.

Both Dr. Rabinowitz and Professor Silberg assert that the late Chief Rabbi Herzog did, in fact, invoke Maharsham's proposal in practice. Rabbi Herzog does indeed discuss Maharsham's responsum in his *Heikhal Yiẓḥak,* II, nos. 17–19. However, Rabbi Herzog's ruling in the specific case brought to his attention was based on different grounds. As is often the case in halakhic responsa, considerations which are themselves insufficient to warrant the conclusion advanced are adduced as a *snif,* or secondary line of reasoning, in order to strengthen the ultimate decision.

Rabbi Auerbach reports that *dayyanim* in Israel have on numerous occasions refrained from following Maharsham's suggestion precisely because the latter stated explicitly that his words were not intended for practical implementation.

Apart from the halakhic objections which have been advanced, the proposal as formulated by Maharsham suffers from one practical drawback, viz., it requires the active cooperation of the original husband. Needless to say, the cooperation of an estranged husband is often difficult to obtain. Professor Silberg suggests that this defect can be remedied by requiring that, at the time of marriage, every groom designate specific rabbinic officials as his proxies for the writing and delivery of a bill of divorce to his wife and also grant the individuals named the power to appoint other persons as proxies to act in their stead. The groom would at the same time grant his designated proxies concomitant power to annul any further proxies they may subsequently appoint. Confronted with a situation involving *mamzerut,* these rabbinic officials, acting on behalf of the husband, would proceed to appoint a proxy and annul that proxy other than in his presence, thereby dissolving the marriage *ab initio* and retroactively removing the stigma of bastardy.

Professor Silberg's proposal presents exactly the same problem as a similar suggestion with regard to the resolution of the *agunah* problem which has been advanced at various times in the past. In order to solve the problem of a recalcitrant husband who refuses to issue a religious divorce, it has been suggested that every groom appoint a proxy to execute a bill of divorce on behalf of his wife in the event that at some future date the *Bet Din* should rule that the wife is entitled to a religious divorce under Jewish law. Both Rambam and *Shulḥan Arukh* state that if husband and wife are secluded together after appointment of a proxy and before the bill of divorce is delivered, the divorce is invalidated. The act of seclusion gives reason to suspect that the husband may have annulled the previously executed proxy.

Rabbi Dick raises a novel and intriguing objection with regard to Professor Silberg's proposal. He argues that were Maharsham's suggestion to become standard procedure in all cases of adultery, a Pandora's box of halakhic problems would be opened. In order to establish that a husband has died and his wife is permitted to remarry, the halakhic canons usually applicable require the testimony of two reliable witnesses. In a desire to alleviate the problems of *agunot* insofar as possible in cases in which the husband is missing and presumed dead, the Sages modified the rules regarding the admission of evidence and permitted acceptance of the testimony of a single witness as well as of certain forms of circumstantial evidence. At the same time they decreed that should the husband prove to be alive, the woman in question would be forever forbidden to both the first husband and the second. The purpose of this decree was to assure that a woman confronted by a situation in which she would not be able to live with either of her spouses would herself investigate the matter thoroughly and would not marry unless every shadow of a doubt with regard to the decease of her first husband were removed. The resultant assumption, *ishah daika u-minsiva* ("it is presumed that a woman will investigate prior to marriage") is sufficient to counterbalance the presumption (*ḥazakah*) that she is a married woman. This meticulousness on the part of the woman, coupled with the testimony of her witness, is accepted as the equivalent of the testimony of two witnesses in establishing her eligibility to remarry. However, argues Rabbi Dick, if every woman were to know that a sexual liaison may be legitimized by subsequent retroactive annulment of her original marriage there would no longer be any reason for her to be particularly meticulous in her investigation into the circumstances of her husband's disappearance since she would suffer no adverse consequences were her first husband subsequently found to be alive. This would, then, negate the presumption that a woman's own declaration may be relied upon with regard to her eligibility to remarry. This, in turn, would lead to the reinstitution of a requirement for the testimony of two reliable witnesses attesting to the death of the husband before remarriage would be permitted. Thus, virtually all leniencies which were incorporated into the structure of the Halakhah in order to alleviate the plight of the *agunah* would be eliminated.

Although Professor Silberg, in his response to Rabbi Dick, does not refute this basic objection, this particular problem could presumably be overcome if, as Professor Silberg recommends, every bridegroom were to appoint rabbinic officials as his proxies for the drawing up of a bill of divorce. If their power were to be broadened sufficiently, they could, in an instance of *igun,* simply draw up such a divorce and thereby circumvent the need for two witnesses to attest to the death of the husband. However, as has been previously indicated, this aspect of Professor Silberg's proposal is not halakhically acceptable on the basis of other considerations.

The Langer Case

One cannot fail to sympathize with the plight of Miriam and Chanoch Langer. These two children of Otto and Chava Langer were declared to be *mamzerim* by the Rabbinical Court of Tel Aviv in November 1955 and, as is the stipulation of Halakhah, were forbidden to contract marriage with any naturally born Jew of legitimate parentage. The recent decision by Rabbi Goren removing the stigma of *mamzerut* from the Langers has become the subject of great controversy. Regrettably, passions were aroused in a manner that has obscured the genuine halakhic issues involved. A discussion of the emotional and political overtones, either of the decision itself or of the subsequent controversy, is irrelevant insofar as an understanding of the halakhic questions is concerned. Accordingly, the discussion will be limited to a review of the basic facts and a survey of the halakhic issues which have been raised and which are the legitimate subject of halakhic analysis and discussion.

One further observation should be made. The issues involved are not matters which have direct applicability to other unfortunate cases of *mamzerut.* Rabbi Goren's decision was based entirely upon the unique factors presented by the Langer case which have no bearing upon virtually any other case of *mamzerut.* This ruling is limited to a specific incident and cannot possibly be viewed as a panacea for the vexing problem of *mamzerut*.

Chava Ginsburg was born in Lukov, a small town in Poland, in the early 1920s. While yet a young girl of fourteen or fifteen, she met a non-Jewish lad by the name of Borokovsky, ran away, and lived with him in a neighboring village. Subsequently, the young man was said to have converted to Judaism in Warsaw and was known in Lukov by the name of Avraham Borokovsky. In 1933 the Borokovskys emigrated to Israel, where they shared an apartment with Mrs. Borokovsky's parents. The Borokovskys subsequently separated without obtaining a religious divorce. Later Chava Borokovsky met a Jewish soldier serving in the British forces named Otto Langer and married him in April, 1944. The ceremony was performed by the late Rabbi Ya'akov Levitsky, who at the time served as rabbi of Givat Rambam. According to her own testimony, given before a *Bet Din* in 1955, Mrs. Borokovsky failed to disclose her previous marriage and informed Rabbi Levitsky that she was unmarried and that her name was Chava Ginsberg. Two children, Chanoch and Miriam, were born to Otto and Chava Langer.

In August 1951, Avraham Borokovsky and Chava Borokovsky-Langer appeared before a *Bet Din* in Tel Aviv for the purpose of executing a religious divorce, apparently because Avraham Borokovsky desired to remarry. In the course of those proceedings, the liaison between Chava and Otto Langer became known to the *Bet Din*. Even subsequent to obtaining a divorce from her lawful husband, Jewish law forbids a woman to consort with a man with whom she has previously had adultrous relations. Thus, in view of their previous adultrous relationship, the *Bet Din* issued a decree forbidding Chava and Otto Langer to live as man and wife.

Otto Langer died in 1952. Some three years later Mrs. Langer applied to the *Bet Din* in Tel Aviv for permission to remarry. In the course of an investigation prior to the issuance of a marriage license, the *Bet Din* became aware of the birth of Chanoch and Miriam Langer. On November 11, 1955 the regional *Bet Din* in Tel Aviv issued a decree declaring the Langer children to be *mamzerim*.

There the matter rested until May, 1966, when Chanoch Langer became affianced and applied for permission to marry. The *Bet Din* before whom the matter was presented refused to issue the necessary license because of the earlier decree of 1955. In an appeal to the Supreme Rabbinical Court of Appeals, the Langers contended that Avraham Borokovsky's conversion was invalid, hence no marriage existed between him and their mother and consequently their own birth was legitimate. The Supreme Rabbinical Court, noting that one of the judges who had signed the original decree was now serving as head of the Petach Tikvah *Bet Din,* remanded the case to the *Bet Din* of Petach Tikvah for review. Testimony was heard by that *Bet Din* and a decision affirming the original ban on the marriage of the Langer children was handed down on October 7, 1967. The decision was then appealed to the Supreme Rabbinical Court. This tribunal, upon deliberation, again returned the case to the *Bet Din* of Petach Tikvah with instructions to conduct further investigations into Avraham Borokovsky's status as a convert. On June 4, 1969 the *Bet Din* of Petach Tikvah reaffirmed the original ruling. This decision was subsequently reviewed and confirmed by the Supreme Rabbinical Court. A decree to that effect, signed by Rabbis Yosef Eliashuv, Sha'ul Israeli and Ovadiah Yosef, was issued on January 20, 1970.

Upon his election as Chief Rabbi, Rabbi Shlomoh Goren sought to have the case reheard by a panel of the Supreme Rabbinical Court consisting of the two Chief Rabbis and a third member to be selected jointly by both Chief Rabbis. Rabbi Yosef refused to accede to this proposal, noting that he had already sat as a member of a *Bet Din* which had issued a negative ruling and that Rabbi Goren, while yet Chief Chaplain of the Israeli Armed Forces, had authored and circulated among selected individuals a pamphlet in which he had argued that the Langers were not to be regarded as *mamzerim.* In view of their prior involvement Rabbi Yosef felt that both Chief Rabbis should disqualify themselves. He instead proposed that an impartial *Bet Din* be appointed to be composed of *dayanim* who had not previously ruled on the matter. This suggestion was not acceptable to Rabbi Goren, who subsequently, on November 19, 1972, issued a ruling in his own name and in the name of eight other rabbis, whose names he declined to reveal, permitting the Langers to marry. The reasons for this decision and the documents supporting it were published by Rabbi Goren in a two-hundred-page book bearing the imprimatur of the Chief Rabbinate of Israel.

Rabbi Goren, claiming to have had additional evidence not available to the rabbinical courts which had previously held hearings on the matter, bases his decision on the following considerations:

1. There exists no admissible evidence attesting to Avraham Borokovsky's conversion to Judaism,

2. In the event that a valid conversion ceremony did take place, the conversion was nullified by virtue of the fact that Borokovsky continued

to live as a practicing Christian. Rabbi Goren cites *Ẓofnat Pa'aneaḥ,* a commentary on the *Mishneh Torah* authored by the late Rabbi Yosef Rosen, in which Rabbi Rosen interprets Rambam as maintaining that subsequent idolatry on the part of a convert is tantamount to proof that the original conversion was insincere and hence invalid.

3. The original wedding ceremony between Chava Ginsberg and Avraham Borokovsky took place in a church. There is no evidence, argues Rabbi Goren, that they were subsequently married in accordance with the law of Israel.

4. The conversion of Avraham Borokovsky, if it indeed did take place, was the result of coercion on the part of Chava Ginsberg's father and hence is null and void.

5. Even if the conversion were to be accepted as valid, Borokovsky, since he subsequently reverted to the practice of Christianity, would have the status of an apostate. *Ba'al ha-Ma'or* maintains that an apostate is not biblically qualified to issue a bill of divorce; according to *Ba'al ha-Ma'or,* a divorce executed by an apostate is valid only by virtue of rabbinic decree. It is, however, axiomatic that rabbinic legislation cannot validate a divorce which is biblically invalid. The formula invoked in such situations is an annulment of the original marriage. Such annulment is within the province of rabbinic jurisdiction, since all marriages are conducted according to "the law of Moses and Israel." The term "law of Moses" refers to biblical law, while "law of Israel" encompasses rabbinic legislation. Rabbi Goren argues that since Borokovsky is to be deemed an apostate, the bill of divorce which he ultimately delivered to Chava Langer had the effect of retroactively annulling their marriage. As a result, she was yet an "unwed woman" in the eyes of Jewish law at the time of her involvement with Otto Langer and hence the issue of that union are not to be considered bastards.

A rebuttal of Rabbi Goren's arguments, authored by Rabbi Bezalel Zolti, senior member of the Supreme Rabbinical Court, appeared in several Israeli newspapers and was reprinted in the Adar and Nisan 5733 issues of *Ha-Pardes.* In opposing Rabbi Goren's action in the Langer case, Rabbi Zolti argues both that the substance of the halakhic reasoning on which it was based is erroneous and that the method employed in arriving at the decision violated the canons of judicial procedure. Rabbi Goren's arguments are marred by the inclusion of a number of points which are basically extraneous but are nevertheless misleading. [For example, Rabbi Goren states that according to Rambam, marriages contracted in the usual manner, viz., by conveyance of a ring from the bridegroom to the bride, have no biblical validity but are valid solely by virtue of rabbinic decree, "as the commentators have written." In actuality, virtually all commentaries on Rambam indicate that such marriages are biblically valid. *Maggid Mishneh, Hilkhot Ishut* 3:20, quotes a responsum written by Rambam himself in which he unequivocally affirms the biblical validity of such marriages.] Many of the inaccuracies noted by Rabbi Zolti are not crucial to the substance of Rabbi Goren's decision. There are, however, three crucial points which do affect the substance of the halakhic reasoning and three major points with regard to questions of judicial procedure which merit analysis.

1. Rabbi Goren argues that there is no evidence that a conversion ceremony did in fact take place. Rabbi Zolti counters that if a person identifies himself as a Jew, conducts himself as a Jew, and is accepted as such, no further evidence is required. It is an established halakhic principle that the general conduct and deportment of an individual is sufficient presumptive evidence with regard to the determination of matters of personal status. Thus, for example, deportment manifesting maternal solicitude and filial response between a woman and an infant is sufficient to establish that a mother-child relationship exists between the two. With regard to conversion, Rambam, *Issurei Bi'ah* 13:9, declares, "similarly a proselyte who comports himself according to the ways of Israel . . . and performs all the commandments is assumed to be [*beḥezkat*] a righteous convert." Rabbi Goren cites numerous authorities in an effort to establish that conduct and deportment are insufficient to establish presumption of conversion, particularly when the individual concerned is unable to identify the rabbis who performed the conversion. On the other hand, *Ḥazon Ish, Yoreh De'ah* 158:6–9, unequivocally asserts that deportment as a Jew extending over a period of thirty days is sufficient in and of itself to establish identity as a Jew and requires no further evidence or declaration on the part of the convert. Rabbi Zolti demonstrates that this is the position of *Teshuvot R. Akiva Eger,* no, 121, as well. It is noteworthy that Rabbi A. I. Kook, *Ezrat Kohen,* no. 13, expresses an identical view.

Rabbi Zolti asserts that there is ample evidence confirming the fact that Avraham Borokovsky conducted himself as a Jew and was publicly known as such. The documents which he utilized in immigrating to what was then Palestine refer to him as a proselyte, It is beyond dispute that Borokovsky, declaring himself to be a convert, divorced his wife in the presence of a *Bet Din* and subsequently remarried as a Jew.

2. Rabbi Goren contends that Borokovsky continued to be a practicing Christian following his conversion. His evidence is based in part upon the

written report of a social worker. Rabbi Zolti notes that the report itself indicates that the information gathered was not based on the social worker's own observation but was supplied by Chava Borokovsky, who had a self-serving interest in conveying negative information regarding her first husband. The testimony of two other witnesses is adduced by Rabbi Goren to the effect that Borokovsky ate pork, did not fast on the Day of Atonement, attended church services, and in general did not conduct himself as a Jew. These allegations were vehemently denied by Borokovsky. This testimony had not been accepted by the *Bet Din* which had earlier heard the case because the witnesses were themselves guilty of the very practices ascribed to Borokovsky; one of the witnesses was married to a Catholic woman and regularly escorted her to church. The *Bet Din* ruled that the testimony of witnesses guilty of such infractions could not be admitted in evidence.

Press reports have made much of the fact that when Borokovsky was asked by the *Bet Din* to conclude the sentence *"Shema Yisra'el . . ."* he was unable to do so correctly. Borokovsky completed *"Shema Yisra'el"* with the phrase *"Ha-Shem Elokeinu melekh ha-olam,"* which would have been the proper response had he been asked to give the formula used in the various blessings. He did, however, reply correctly that prayer is obligatory thrice daily, that phylacteries are worn on the upper part of the left arm, and that they are donned on weekdays but not on Sabbaths or festivals. Evidence had been introduced before the original *Bet Din* indicating that Borokovsky conducted himself as a practicing Jew in his daily life. In addition to the testimony of several relatives, the *gabbai* (warden) of the Rambam Synagogue in Tel Aviv testified that Borokovsky attended services regularly, was called to the Reading of the Torah, arranged a Bar Mitzvah ceremony for his son, and conducted himself as an observant Jew. Rabbi Goren argues that the testimony of a single qualified witness is not sufficient to substantiate Borokovsky's claim to be recognized as a Jew.

3. Although *Ẓofnat Pa'aneaḥ*'s interpretation of Rambam's *Hilkhot Issurei Bi'ah* 13:14 can readily be accommodated by the language of the text, this interpretation is apparently contradicted elsewhere by Rambam himself. In *Issurei Bi'ah* 13:17 Rambam writes, "A proselyte who has not been investigated [with regard to his motive for conversion] . . . is a convert, and even if he subsequently serves idols he is a Jewish apostate and a marriage contracted by him is valid." Rabbi Zolti, apparently in an effort to resolve this obvious contradiction, argues that even according to *Ẓofnat Pa'aneaḥ*'s analysis of Rambam's position, the conversion is to be regarded as null and void only if the would-be convert reverts immediately

to non-Jewish practices without at all conducting himself as a Jew. Under such circumstances the conversion is deemed to have been insincere and invalid at the time that it was performed. However, even according to this latter interpretation, the conversion of a proselyte who conducts himself as a Jew even for a brief period must be considered as valid, since there is no evidence that the conversion was insincere at the time of its performance. The testimony cited by Rabbi Goren regarding Borokovsky's alleged lack of observance refers to events which took place many years after his conversion.

Moreover, in a similar case brought to the attention of the first Chief Rabbi of Israel, the late Rabbi Abraham I. Kook, concerning a convert who had reverted to non-Jewish practices and married a gentile woman, Rabbi Kook, *Mishpat Kohen,* no. 14, refused to declare the conversion null and void. In yet another case, Rabbi Avraham Ya'akov Horowitz, *Ẓur Ya'akov,* no. 24, ruled that a woman who converted and apparently reverted immediately to Christian practices was nevertheless to be considered a Jewess and her husband forbidden to marry another wife without first executing a bill of divorce,

In adition to these arguments concerning the substance of the decision, Rabbi Zolti contends that a number of procedural irregularities occurred which affect the validity of the ruling.

1. One rather irregular aspect of the decision issued by Rabbi Goren's *Bet Din* is the fact that his signature alone appears on the decree which was issued. In a departure from the usual practice, the eight other members of the rabbinical court remain anonymous. Rambam, *Hilkhot Sanhedrin* 22:8, states, "neither the names of the acquitting [judges] nor the names of the convicting [judges] are mentioned, but rather the court of so-and-so, on the basis of their deliberations, so-and-so was acquitted." On the basis of Rambam's phraseology, Rabbi Goren argues that only the signature of the presiding judge is required.

In disputing this point, Rabbi Zolti cites a well-known controversy with regard to whether or not a dissenting judge is required to affix his signature to a decree with which he disagrees.[6] The fact that there is a dispute with regard to the necessity for the signatures of the dissenting judges is evidence that the names of the entire court, or, at the very minimum, the

6. See *Teshuvot Mabit,* nos. 172 and 173; *Knesset ha-Gedolah, Ḥoshen Mishpat* 19:7, *Birkei Yosef, Ḥoshen Mishpat* 19:2; and *Pitḥei Teshuvah, Ḥoshen Mishpat* 19:4.

names of a majority of the judges sitting on the *Bet Din* are required. Rabbi Zolti further contends that the previously cited passage of Rambam indicates only that no identification is to be made of which judges voted for acquittal and which voted for conviction; Rambam does not imply that the litigants are to remain unaware of the identity of the judges sitting in their case.[7]

2. Rabbi Zolti maintains that in view of Rabbi Goren's claim to have uncovered new evidence, proper procedure would require that the case be referred back to the *Bet Din* which had heard the matter originally. The Mishnah, *Sanhedrin* 31a, declares, "Whenever new evidence is adduced, the verdict is rescinded." Rashi, in his commentary, clearly indicates that it is the original *Bet Din* which must issue a new decision. *Birkei Yosef, Ḥoshen Mishpat* 17:11, demonstrates that it is mandatory that the new evidence be heard by the original *Bet Din.*

3. It is a fundamental principle of Jewish law that the testimony of witnesses may be heard by a *Bet Din* only in the presence of the litigants. Testimony affecting an individual's personal status may be heard only in the presence of that person. Rema, *Even ha-Ezer* 11:4, rules that testimony with regard to adultery can be accepted only in the presence of both the woman concerned and her husband; since a woman who has committed adultery and her husband are forbidden to live together as man and wife, they are both deemed parties to the proceedings. In the case at hand, the nullification of Borokovsky's conversion makes it forbidden for him to consort with a Jewess. Hence, argues Rabbi Zolti, testimony with regard to his conversion cannot be accepted other than in his presence.

In anticipation of this argument, Rabbi Goren writes that the regulation regarding the presence of the litigants does not apply to testimony concerning conversion. It is Rabbi Goren's contention that this procedure applies only to litigants of the Jewish faith; testimony regarding non-Jews, argues Rabbi Goren, may be heard even in the absence of the non-Jewish party. Therefore, Rabbi Goren contends, the presence of the convert is not required during hearings for the purpose of invalidating his conversion. He argues that upon acceptance of the testimony the litigant is judged to be a non-Jew, and the presence of a non-Jew is not required for the acceptance of testimony.

Rabbi Zolti counters with two arguments. First, it is precisely the ques-

---

7. See also R. Meir Blumenfeld, *Mishnat Yisra'el,* commentary on *Pirkei Avot* 4:8.

tion of whether the party concerned is or is not a Jew which is the subject of the proceedings, Since the individual has been regarded as a Jew, and it is this presumption which is being challenged, the regulations concerning judicial proceedings which are to be applied are those which apply to Jewish litigants. Rabbi Zolti further challenges the basic assumption that testimony may be accepted in the absence of a non-Jewish party. Observing that Rabbi Goren cites no sources for his contrary assertion, Rabbi Zolti argues that Jewish courts must follow the identical procedure with regard to both Jews and non-Jews who appear before them. Many authorities, among them *Teshuvot Ḥelkat Ya'akov,* II, no. 14, rule that although non-Jewish courts, in administering the Noachide Code, may rely upon the testimony of a single witness, nevertheless, a Jewish court may judge a non-Jew only on the basis of the testimony of two qualified witnesses. Similarly, it may be concluded, argues Rabbi Zolti, that the canons of judicial procedure followed by Jewish *Batei Din* are one and the same for both Jewish and non-Jewish litigants appearing before them.

Furthermore, the rationale underlying the rule that testimony must be given in the presence of the litigants is that a potential perjurer may find it easier to bear false witness in the absence of those who are aware of the false nature of the testimony.[8] *Minḥat Ḥinukh,* no. 75, declares that testimony inadmissible in a Jewish court on grounds of suspected perjury is unacceptable under the Noachide Code as well. Hence, concludes Rabbi Zolti, even gentile courts are required to hear testimony only in the presence of the parties concerned.

It is of interest to note that, upon a petition submited to the Israeli High Court of Justice by Avraham Borokovsky requesting clarification of his status as a Jew, the court, in a decision handed down on April 3, 1973, invoked the civil counterpart of the halakhic principle that evidence must be given in the presence of the litigants. The court held that the basic law of natural justice—*audi alteram partem*—demanded that Borokovsky should have been given a hearing by Rabbi Goren's *Bet Din.* The High

8. This explanation is offered by a host of authorities, including *Teshuvot ha-Rif,* no. 200; Ramah, *Shitah Mekubeẓet, Baba Kamma* 112a; *Teshuvot Maharash,* no. 33; *Tumim, Ḥoshen Mishpat* 28:15; and *Imrei Binah, Ḥoshen Mishpat* 9. *Teshuvot ha-Rashba,* II, no. 376, and *Netivot ha-Mishpat* 28:6 disagree with this explanation. A further discussion of this point by R. Meir Blumenfeld appears in the Sivan 5733 issue of *Or Torah,* a journal published by the Sephardic community in Israel and in his work on Psalms, *Sha'ar ha-Melekh,* III, 202–203.

Court also directed Rabbi Goren to pay one thousand pounds toward the legal fees incurred by Avraham Borokovsky.

Of course, the pros and cons of the halakhic arguments, however important they may be, are not the crucial issues. The dispute, in its bitterness, served to widen the rifts between the religious and nonreligious elements of the Israeli populace and within the Orthodox camp itself. The sad spectacle of a deeply divided people was revealed for all to see. The passions aroused by the Langer affair go far beyond the immediate concerns. Proponents of the Langer ruling argued that extrajudicial procedures circumventing the established rabbinic courts were warranted in order to forestall proposals for the institution of civil marriage which had been tabled in the Knesset. Others feared that the methods employed in the issuance of the Langer ruling posed a threat to judicial process in the future and that the remedy might prove more dangerous than the malady it was purported to cure. The real issues are the relationship between synagogue and state, concern for the integrity of the judicial process and the abyss between observant and nonobservant in Israel. It is to these fundamental problems that the religious community must direct its constructive energies.

Children of Mixed Marriages: Their Status as Levites

In a well researched and clearly reasoned article appearing in the 5729 Adar-Nisan issue of *Ha-Pardes,* Rabbi Meir Just discusses one interesting ramification of the many problems resulting from mixed marriages. The *Bet Din* of Amsterdam had been consulted with regard to the halakhic status of a child born of a union between a Levite mother and a gentile father. As the first-born son of a Levite woman, the child is exempt from the obligation of redemption of the first-born (*Yoreh De'ah* 305:18). Halakhah clearly provides that maternal Levite parentage carries with it such statutory exemption even in instances when the child himself is not a Levite, as is indeed the case with regard to the issue of all marriages between a Levite mother and an Israelite father. In the case under consideration, the question to be resolved is whether such exemption extends also to a future first-born son of the issue of a Levite mother and a gentile father. The question is raised only with regard to the first-born son of a Levite mother. The son of the daughter of a *kohen* who cohabits with a gentile is not exempted from redemption (*Yoreh De'ah* 305:18).

The Gemara, *Bekhorot* 47b, states that the progeny of a union between a Levite woman and a non-Jew has the status of a *levi pasul*—a disqualified

Levite. Although paternal parentage is the controlling factor in the determination of tribal status, this principle applies only as long as there exists a recognized genealogical relationship between a father and son. Since, however, Halakhah does not recognize the existence of a genealogical relationship (*yiḥus*) between a gentile father and a son sired by him, in such instances the tribal status of the mother devolves upon her children. Rabbi Chaim Soloveitchik, in his novellae on *Mishneh Torah, Isurei Bi'ah* 15:9, explains the appellation *levi pasul* as referring to an individual who, while disqualified from performing the functions of a Levite in conjunction with the Temple service, retains the familial status of a Levite. As such he is exempt from the precept concerning redemption of the first-born because he himself is a Levite, genealogically speaking, notwithstanding the fact that he is barred from fulfilling the function of a Levite in the Temple service. According to this analysis, exemption from redemption of the first-born extends to succeeding generations, even in the case of the progeny of a *levi pasul* who is himself the issue of a mixed marriage.

Dayan Just points out that the first discussion of this question appeared in one of the earliest Torah journals, the *Shomer Zion ha-Ne'eman,* which was published in Altona in the mid-nineteenth century under the editorship of R. Jacob Ettlinger and Samuel Joseph Enoch. In his treatment of this problem in issues no. 98 (36 Nisan, 5610) and no. 99 (14 Iyar, 5610), R. Samuel Bondi of Mainz reached a similar conclusion but hesitated to implement his ruling pending a concurring opinion on the part of prominent halakhic authorities. These responsa evoked a contrary opinion penned by R. Moses Schick, which appeared in issue no. 110 (22 Elul, 5611) of the same journal, and was later reprinted in a more comprehensive form in *Teshuvot Maharam Schick*, *Yoreh De'ah,* no. 299. A similarly dissenting view is expressed by *Ḥazon Ish, Even ha-Ezer* 6:7 and 16:17. According to this opinion, a child can never acquire the tribal identity of its mother because the paternal genealogical relationship does not merely supersede that of the mother and hence become the governing factor in the determination of tribal identity, but serves as the sole operative relationship with regard to tribal status. Hence the first-born issue of a mixed marriage does not have the tribal status of a Levite and is exempt from redemption as a first-born solely by virtue of the fact that he is a son of a female Levite. Accordingly, *Ḥazon Ish* defines the term "disqualified Levite" employed by the Gemara as having reference to one who is the progeny of a Levite but who himself lacks any such tribal identity. A similar interpretation is to be found in the commentary of the *Rit Algazi* on *Bekhorot*. In support of the view of these authorities, Rabbi Just cites the commentary of Nachmanides on the verse "and the son of an Israelite woman and a son of Israel strove together in the camp" (Lev. 24:11). Nachmanides remarks that despite his unquestioned status as a Jew, Scripture speaks of the child of an Israelite mother and Egyptian father as the "son of an Israelite woman" and not as an Israelite in his own right as an indication that such progeny lacks tribal identity. We are, then, confronted by the odd case of an individual who is unquestionably a Jew by birth but is not a member of any of the twelve tribes and hence lacking in tribal status. The halakhic ramifications of this anomalous status precludes such individuals from encampment around the banners in the wilderness and from inheritance in the Land of Israel.

Insofar as being called to the Reading of the Torah as a Levite is concerned, there is no question that a son of a mixed marriage is disqualified from being accorded this honor since the Gemara deems such a child to be a "disqualified Levite."

CHAPTER VIII

Social Problems

A person should always associate himself with the community.

BERAKHOT 30a

Personal liberty and the rights of the individual are strongly rooted as cardinal values of Western philosophy. Systems of thought which view the rights of individuals as paramount and inalienable find it difficult to accommodate the concept of a state which requires its citizens to surrender basic freedoms and to sublimate individual self-interest for the sake of the welfare of society. Much of Western social and political philosophy is devoted to the formulation of an intellectual matrix designed to justify the extension of the powers of the body politic to spheres beyond the simple protection of its members against evildoers. Thus, eighteenth- and nineteenth-century European thought gave rise to various forms of a social-contract theory. Inherent in many such theories is the concept that, at least ideally, the state should maintain a *laissez-faire* attitude toward its citizens insofar as possible.

Jewish thought—and law—is based upon an entirely different set of premises. Man is bound by divinely imposed imperatives which oblige him to be concerned with the needs of his fellow. Some of these obligations are entirely personal. Others either could not possibly be discharged by any person acting independently or, if directed to individuals, would constitute an inordinate burden. Hence such obligations become the responsibility of society at large. According to Nachmanides,[1] the very first divinely commanded system of law, the Noachide Code, contains a single positive commandment, *dinim,* which translates into a general obligation to

1. *Commentary on the Bible,* Gen. 34:13.

promulgate laws and to establish standards regulating the manifold areas of interpersonal intercourse. Jewish law recognizes not only the reciprocal dependency of members of the human race, but also that the human condition requires that the governing authority, acting as the representative of society as a whole, be endowed with the broad powers necessary for the promotion of social welfare.

Judaism views every man as his brother's keeper. Since furtherance of the common good is not simply an ideal but is, in many instances, a positive obligation, government need not necessarily derive its authority from the consent of the governed. In fact, Judaism does not view the social order as being predicated upon consent at all. "Inhabitants of a city may coerce one another" is the phrase commonly employed in rabbinic writings in introducing a description of the services or amenities which society must provide for its citizens. From the moral right of one citizen to force another to discharge obligations *vis-à-vis* his fellow citizen arises the positive coercive power of the state designed to achieve the same end. The state in such instances simply acts as the agent of its individual citizens in assuring that all the citizens contribute to the promotion of social welfare and well-being. Indeed, the power of coercion is vested not only in governmental entities but in more limited social units as well. Thus, artisans may organize themselves into guilds and are empowered to impose binding regulations upon all practitioners of their craft. The individual may not refuse to accept restrictions designed to enhance the common welfare.

In any system of law conflicts are bound to arise between personal liberty and social needs. The respective rights of society and of the individual require careful elucidation in order that conflicts between the two be resolved. While the general principles of Jewish law in this area are incorporated in the various codes, subsequent responsa literature is replete with examples of how Jewish law strives to strike an equilibrium between the rights and prerogatives of society and those of the individual.

War and Peace

There are few social issues on which more popular attention has been lavished than the moral problems surrounding the Vietnam conflict. As the moratorium movement swept the United States during the late 1960s, problems of conscience previously buried deep within the recesses of heart and mind were subjected to probing analysis in the harsh spotlight of public controversy. There was a general heightening of moral consciousness which aroused feelings of abhorrence to all forms of warfare. It was an unfortunate accident of history that at precisely such a juncture uncontrollable circumstances conspired to project a warlike image of the Israeli. Harsh and tragic facts of life caused an unprecedented degree of attention, pride and even adulation to be focused upon the Israeli soldier. This phenomenon was, of course, understandable and indeed well founded. Yet it is imperative that at no time do we allow ourselves to lose sight of the striving for peace which lies at the very core of Judaism.

It was, no doubt, sentiments such as these which prompted the editors of the engaging Israeli army magazine, *Maḥanayim,* to devote an entire edition to the theme of peace in Jewish sources. The issue of Adar 5729 contains a wide range of articles dealing with halakhic, historical, literary and liturgical aspects of this topic. Although primarily in the nature of a general précis, of special interest are Rabbi Shlomoh Goren's discussion of "Army and Warfare in the Light of the Halakhah" and Rabbi Mordechai ha-Kohen's "Peace in the Wars of Israel in the Light of the Halakhah."

Rabbi Goren presents a general discussion of the classical distinction between obligatory wars, permissible wars and wars of defense. More noteworthy is his presentation of sources pertaining to the establishment of minimum and maximum ages with regard to the conscription of soldiers. The chief difficulty in establishing a minimum age is that although Rashi, in his commentary on the Pentateuch (Exod. 30:14 and Num. 1:3), states that warriors must be "twenty years old and upward," Rambam, in his *Mishneh Torah,* is silent with regard to any such provision. The question of a maximum age limit centers upon the proper textual reading of the *Sifre,* Numbers 197, which establishes an upper limit of either forty or sixty years of age, depending upon which of the variant readings is accepted as accurate. Another problem to be resolved is whether these limits pertain only to permissible wars (*milḥemet reshut*) or are applicable to obligatory wars (*milḥemet ḥovah*) as well.

Rabbi Mordechai ha-Kohen demonstrates that it is mandatory that peace terms be set forth before engaging in hostilities. In this article the author endeavors to prove that normative Halakhah requires the initial proffering of peace terms even in the case of obligatory wars in accordance with the ruling of Rambam, *Hilkhot Melakhim* 6:1, and concurring authorities in contradiction to the ruling of the *Sifre,* Deuteronomy 199, and Rashi in his commentary on Deuteronomy 20:10. The latter sources regard this provision as being operative only in the case of permissible wars to the exclusion of obligatory wars.

While we cannot but regret that cogent questions such as these must yet be classified as *contemporary* halakhic problems, we should perhaps recall that "All that is recorded in the Torah is written for the sake of peace; and although warfare is recorded in the Torah, even warfare is recorded for the sake of peace" (*Tanḥuma, Ẓav* 3).

Changing Neighborhoods

The observation that conditions of life on the American continent are markedly different from those encountered in European countries in days gone by is a commonplace truism. One aspect of the American scene which is of the utmost significance in terms of Jewish communal life is the phenomenon of changing neighborhoods. In previous habitations Jews tended, whether by necessity or by choice, to form their own ethnic enclaves and to establish themselves in residential areas which retained their Jewish identity over a period of centuries. The permanence and stability of these Jewish sectors permitted the erection of synagogues, the development of networks of schools and the founding of communal institutions with the surety that population shifts would not render them obsolete. Jews residing in such areas could not but acquire a strong sense of belonging which, in turn, naturally fostered a strong sense of communal responsibility. Life in such surroundings had a distinctive Jewish flavor; the very air became permeated with *Yiddishkeit*. All of this was of inestimable value in terms of fostering a feeling of Jewish identity and solidarity and in transmitting these emotions to subsequent generations.

At least a portion of the responsibility for the malaise of American Jewish life may be attributed to the uniquely American phenomenon of population shifts and changing neighborhoods. Synagogues, schools and communal institutions must be relocated or rebuilt—at phenomenal cost in terms of both finances and human energy. Feelings of transience and anonymity born of this unprecedented degree of domiciliary mobility contribute to a general shirking of communal responsibility. The lack of Jewish atmosphere causes feelings of Jewish identification to become dull and commitment to pall.

For decades, rabbinic authorities, in company with lay leaders of the Jewish community, simply wrung their hands in grief and bemoaned what appeared to be an irreversible sociological trend. However, several years ago a significant attempt was made to halt migration from Jewish neighborhoods by showing that such action is not contraindicated solely by social desiderata but frequently entails violation of halakhic precepts as well. In a noteworthy article on this topic appearing in the Iyar 5728 issue of *Ha-Pardes,* Rabbi Menachem Mendel Schneerson, the Lubavitcher Rebbe, points out that the sale of a dwelling within a Jewish neighborhood is subject to rigid halakhic limitations.

Ḥoshen Mishpat 156:1 stipulates that if an objection is entered by any one of the residents, householders sharing a common courtyard may not rent a dwelling to a physician, blood-letter, weaver, notary or teacher of secular subjects. Since the practice of these professions would increase traffic in the courtyard, objections to such rental are legitimate. Rema adds that sale of a dwelling—in contradistinction to rental—to Jewish members of these professions is permitted. As explained by *Sema,* a standard commentary on *Ḥoshen Mishpat,* rental is presumed to be for personal domicile and therefore is forbidden to members of the aforementioned professions; purchase, however, may be motivated by other purposes, such as subsequent lease to a tenant not practicing these professions or personal use at a later date following retirement from these offending pursuits. In any event, activity counter to the interests of other residents can be curtailed by the *Bet Din* if the purchaser is a Jew subject to halakhic jurisdiction. A non-Jew engaged in one of these professions is not similarly bound. Hence, sale of such property to members of these professions who are not subject to Jewish law can be prevented by neighborhood residents since it is possible that their interests will be jeopardized. Citing these sources, Rabbi Schneerson reasons that property owners may, in accordance with Halakhah, prevent the sale of property if such sale would depress property values or would result in the lowering of existing housing standards.

Indeed, Halakhah imposes restrictions upon the sale or lease of property to non-Jews. Fearful that persons not bound by the dictates of Jewish law will use the property for purposes not sanctioned by such law, Halakhah demands that the original owners assume liability for any resultant damages. *Ḥoshen Mishpat* 175:40 states, on the basis of *Baba Kamma* 114a, that the original owner is subject to excommunication unless he assumes responsibility for any loss incurred or unless the gentile purchaser or tenant agrees that all disputes arising from use of such property be adjudicated in accordance with Jewish law. Although *Shulḥan*

Arukh cites an opinion of Rosh to the effect that these restrictions are relaxed in instances where no Jewish purchaser or tenant is willing to offer an equivalent sum, real estate owners are nevertheless forbidden to engage in profiteering. The property owner is expressly enjoined from accepting a sum significantly higher than the fair market value of the property when such an offer is malevolently tendered for the specific purpose of destroying the Jewish character of the neighborhood.

Taking into consideration the fact that the lives and safety of the remaining Jewish residents are often endangered as a result of neighborhood deterioration, Rabbi Schneerson even goes so far as to argue that there may be grounds for demanding that neighborhood emigres return to their previous homes. Jewish law requires an individual to do everything in his power to prevent or remove any source of potential communal harm. Rema, *Ḥoshen Mishpat* 155:22, cites an intriguing ruling of *Hagahot Mordekhai* regarding the case of a certain feudal lord who desired to move Jews living in scattered villages throughout the countryside to an area within his suzerainty. In order to secure compliance with his wishes, he sought to enlist the judicial aid of the large Jewish community already within his jurisdiction and threatened that *kehillah* with expulsion from his domain were they not to cooperate. The ruling issued in this particular case was that, in light of the grave communal threat, Jews residing in far-flung settlements were indeed obligated to alleviate the danger to their coreligionists by changing their places of residence. In some circumstances, the people compelled to relocate would be entitled to claim financial compensation. Following this line of reasoning, Rabbi Schneerson argues that nowadays Jews may perhaps be obliged to return to their former abodes in order to prevent deterioration of a neighborhood if continued deterioration would effectively result in the expulsion of remaining residents. Regardless of the applicability of this particular parallel, the considerations advanced by Rabbi Schneerson underscore the gravity of the problem.

Rabbi Moses Feinstein, in a letter published in the Sivan 5728 issue of the same journal, indicates general agreement with Rabbi Schneerson's views and adds that had the latter's article not appeared he would himself have authored a similar responsum.

Without doubt the Jewish community has a vested interest in areas where it has built religious centers and educational institutions at a high expenditure of communal funds and a priceless investment of human effort. These halakhic opinions serve to reemphasize the importance of neighborhood preservation. Of course when actual physical danger to residents is involved the situation is totally different and other considerations become paramount. Therefore, pragmatically speaking, it may not be feasible to legislate with regard to moribund neighborhoods. However, before the fabric of existing Jewish neighborhoods becomes hopelessly unraveled, we would be wise to take the proverbial stitch in time and exercise imagination and foresight in communal planning.

Mendicants

The 5730 issue of *Shanah be-Shanah* contains a short item from the pen of the octogenarian scholar, Rabbi Shlomoh Yosef Zevin, who in addition to his many and varied scholarly pursuits serves as general editor of the *Encyclopedia Talmudit.* An official of the Israeli Ministry of the Interior referred a proposal of the Tel Aviv municipal government to Rabbi Zevin, in the latter's capacity as a member of the Chief Rabbinate Council, for his evaluation of the request from the point of view of Halakhah.

As every tourist is painfully aware, Israel has an inordinate number of paupers who openly solicit alms not only in synagogues but on the public streets as well. There is no gainsaying that such practices are socially undesirable and do not reflect creditably upon a country in which they are so widespread. The municipality of Tel Aviv therefore requested the Minister of the Interior to initiate legislation which would effectively ban such mendicants from the streets. The official soliciting Rabbi Zevin's views emphasized that no one had suggested restraining the poor from requesting charity from worshippers in synagogues; the proposed ban was to be limited to solicitation in public thoroughfares.

Rabbi Zevin quotes chapter 17 of the Chafetz Chaim's *Ahavat Ḥesed,* a work devoted to the *mizvah* of charity, in which the author reports the innovative move of establishing "federations" for the purpose of conferring stipends upon itinerant beggars in order to preclude them from soliciting alms from individual householders. The Chafetz Chaim frowns on this practice and among his sources cites the negative view expressed in the Gemara, *Baba Batra* 7b, with regard to the building of a walled enclosure around one's courtyard because the wall prevents the cry of alms-seekers from being heard.

The well-known anecdote concerning the reaction of Rabbi Levi Yitzchak of Berditchev to a similar proposal is also noted by Rabbi Zevin in this context. The Berditchiver sarcastically remarked that the idea is not at all novel; such a communal edict was long ago promulgated by the Council of Four Lands: Sodom, Gomorrah, Admah and Zeboiim. Clearly, Berditchev—and hopefully Tel Aviv also—would not want to be included in such an infamous grouping.

In conclusion Rabbi Zevin suggests that many such paupers would cheerfully desist from these activities if their needs would be provided for by an adequate social-welfare allotment. Nevertheless, he agrees that steps may be taken to prevent beggars from accosting people on public thoroughfares, but argues that they should not be restrained from adopting a mendicant posture at a fixed location. In the final analysis, while undignified forms of public solicitation are to be deplored, it is unthinkable that a Jewish community bar any individual from seeking charity. "If there be among you a needy man, one of your brothers, within any of your gates, in your land which the Lord your God gives you, you shall not harden your heart, nor shut your hand from your needy brother" (Deut. 15:7).

Organized Labor

Industrialization has given rise to many issues which are not directly discussed in earlier rabbinic literature. Not a few of these are in the area of labor relations. Writing in the 5732 edition of *Shanah be-Shanah*, Rabbi K. Tchursh reports that some forty years earlier Mr. S. Z. Shragai, acting on behalf of the executive of the Hapoel Hamizrachi, placed the following questions before the then Chief Rabbi of Israel, Rabbi Abraham I. Kook:

1. Are strikes permitted when an employer seeks to lower wages or to extend working hours? Are they also permitted in an attempt to improve working conditions, to obtain higher wages or to shorten working hours?
2. Assuming that strikes are sanctioned by Halakhah, at least under certain conditions, what is the status of the strikebreaker? Does Halakhah construe his activity as constituting illicit interference with the striking workers' attempts to earn a livelihood? May such individuals be restrained from strikebreaking activities?
3. Does a labor union have the halakhic right to force the employer to engage in collective bargaining with the union? Does a labor union have the right to force individual workers to become members of the union, thereby establishing a union shop, in order to

prevent the employer from utilizing nonunion labor to the detriment of the union members?

The oral ruling issued by Rabbi Kook with regard to each of these questions was reported in the press at the time but was not subsequently recorded in the form of a formal responsum. According to Rabbi Tchursh, Rabbi Kook declared that basically Halakhah grants labor unions the prerogatives in question. Rabbi Kook expressed the opinion that unions are nevertheless halakhically obligated to submit all labor disputes to a *Bet Din* for adjudication before taking any direct action. He ruled, however, that workers are permitted to strike in the event that the employer refuses to accept the jurisdiction of the *Bet Din* or refuses to abide by its decision. When strikes are warranted, strikebreaking is forbidden. Demands that all workers be compelled to enroll in a union, Rabbi Kook maintained, may be enforced only following a decision of a *Bet Din* in each individual case.

Mr. Shragai evidently presented the same set of questions to Rabbi Waldenberg as well, for we find a responsum addressed to this official in *Ẓiẓ Eli'ezer,* II, no. 23. Rabbi Waldenberg answers in a similar vein but significantly limits the role of the *Bet Din* in matters involving malfeasance on the part of the employer. According to Rabbi Waldenberg, workers are under no obligation to seek intervention by a *Bet Din* and may go on strike without prior approval if their grievance results from the failure of the employer to fulfill his obligations toward his employees, provided, however, that the union is absolutely certain of the justice of its grievance. Otherwise the workers are not absolved from their obligation to bring the matter before a *Bet Din.*

The Gemara, *Yoma* 38a, in what may well be the first recorded instance of a "strike" in order to obtain higher wages, relates that at one point the bakers of the shewbread refused to perform their assigned duties. The shewbread were very thin and fragile and extraordinary skill was required to keep them fresh and well-tasting. The methods employed in the difficult task of baking the shewbread in accordance with their precise specifications and in removing them from the oven without breaking them were jealously guarded secrets of the House of Garmu. Indeed, the Mishnah decries the refusal of these individuals to divulge this information. In an attempt to destroy the monopoly of the House of Garmu other craftsmen were brought from Alexandria. Unfortunately, the latter were unable to perform this intricate task with competence. Ultimately, after their wages were doubled, the bakers of the House of Garmu were prevailed upon to return to their posts.

The right of workers to organize and to formulate binding regulations is codified by Rambam, *Hilkhot Mekhirah* 14:10. Rambam states that artisans may regulate the periods during which individual craftsmen may engage in gainful employment; they may also establish fines and similar sanctions for the punishment of violators. Such regulations, however, must, wherever possible, have the approval of competent rabbinic authorities. The prerogatives of organized labor are further discussed by Rabbi Tchursh in an earlier version of the same article, *Shanah be-Shanah* 5723, and in his *Keter Efrayim,* no. 19. This subject is also dealt with by R. Eliezer Waldenberg, *Ẓiẓ Eli'ezer,* II, no. 23; R. Ben Zion Uziel, *Mishpetei Uziel, Ḥoshen Mishpat,* III, no. 41; Rabbi M. Findling, *Teḥukat ha-Avodah,* pp. 61–64 and 119–126; and R. Moses Feinstein, *Iggrot Mosheh, Ḥoshen, Mishpat,* I, no. 58. Rabbi Feinstein opines that rabbinic approval is required only for the establishment of sanctions to punish violators but not for the promulgation of regulations which are to be binding upon the members of a labor union.

Rabbi Tchursh points out that Halakhah embodies safeguards to protect the interests of the employer as well as those of the employee. Perhaps the clearest example is a limitation of what Halakhah deems to be the most fundamental privilege of the worker, viz., the right of a laborer to terminate his employment "even in the middle of the day." Halakhah forbids coercion of a laborer to work against his will. In so doing the Sages equated this situation with involuntary servitude and forbade such practices, declaring, " 'For they are My servants'—and not servants of servants." Yet even this basic prerogative is suspended if such action would result in financial loss to the employer. In explicating the term "financial loss," Rema, *Ḥoshen Mishpat* 333:5, extends this concept to encompass nonperformance of any task which could not be performed by the employer himself.

Rabbi Tchursh further contends that under certain conditions striking workers may legitimately demand compensation for the period during which they were on strike. Citing Rosh, *Baba Kamma,* chap. 6, no. 6, Rabbi Tchursh argues that, in the absence of a disclaimer on the part of the employer, rehiring of the workers signifies agreement to pay back-wages covering the period of work stoppage. Rabbi Tchursh agrees, however, that the strikers need not be paid full wages; the employer may deduct that amount which it may reasonably be assumed an employee would agree to forgo in return for not being required to report for work. A decision to this effect is contained in *Tashbaz,* I, no. 64. It may be argued that this conclusion is valid for countries such as Israel, which apparently has a tradition of compensating workers for periods of work stoppage, but not in countries where this practice is unknown. The presumption that an agreement of this nature has been accepted is valid only if such agreement is in accordance with local custom. Accordingly, if local labor-relations practices do not provide for payment of wages covering the strike period, rehiring of striking workers, in and of itself, should not be taken as constituting agreement to pay such wages.

The situation is somewhat clearer if the strike resulted from violation of a labor agreement on the part of the employer. In such cases *Tashbaz* rules that since the strike resulted from malfeasance on the part of the employer, he is obliged to compensate the workers for their loss. A similar conclusion is reached by Rabbi Moses Feinstein, *Iggrot Mosheh, Ḥoshen Mishpat,* I, no. 59.

Tenure

Traditionally, communal and synagogal functionaries enjoy tenure in their positions as long as they are not remiss in the performance of their duties. This arrangement serves to protect the livelihoods of persons whose talents and specialized skills have been devoted to public service. Thus it precludes the ignominious possibility that an individual who has sacrificially devoted years of service to the community may be discharged due to frivolous whim or personal animosity. But, most significantly, tenure serves to preserve the independence and integrity of religious leadership, much in the same manner that academic tenure serves as the single most potent safeguard of academic freedom.

Tenure in communal office is a well-established provision of Jewish law and references to this prerogative may be found in many diverse sources. As is the case with regard to any area governed by legal codes, questions have arisen through the ages with regard to fine points of application. Which officials are considered to be tenured? May the right to tenure be waived? Upon what grounds may a tenured official be removed? While references to these questions are to be found scattered throughout rabbinic and responsa literature, a systematic and comprehensive treatise dealing with these questions is lacking. Several years ago a dispute arose between the administration of a religious school in Israel and a number of the members of its faculty. The administration sought to discharge the teachers while the latter contended that, according to Jewish law, they were entitled to tenure in their positions. The case was heard by a rabbinic district court in Tel Aviv composed of Rabbis S. Tena, Y. Nesher, and A. Horowitz. The *Bet Din*'s written decision, which runs to over thirty printed pages, is not limited solely to the resolution of the questions raised in the particular case before the court. Incorporated in the decision is a fairly comprehensive review of the entire matter of tenure in Jewish law. This decision was included in the current volume of the published decisions of the Israeli rabbinical courts, *Piskei Din Rabbaniyim,* VIII.

The underlying concept upon which the right to tenure is predicated is an intriguing one. Jewish law provides that succession to the monarchy be from father to son, provided that the son is qualified to discharge the duties of this high office. The right of inheritance is not limited to the royal throne but extends to all positions of *serarah,* or communal authority. (See Rambam, *Hilkhot Melakhim* 1:7.) *Or Zaru'a,* no. 65, remarks that since a son has precedence over all others aspiring to such office, "most certainly the person himself has precedence as long as he has not been remiss." The identical rationale is formulated by *Mabit,* no. 4, and *Bet Yiẓḥak, Yoreh De'ah,* no. 34. *Rivash,* no. 271, finds the halakhic concept of tenure to be based upon the statement of the Palestinian Talmud, *Horiyot* 3:5, to the effect that care was exercised in taking apart and reassembling the Tabernacle to assure that boards used for the different walls on the various sides of the courtyard not be interchanged. Even an inanimate piece of wood, once it has been accorded the "privilege" of occupying a position of honor, cannot be removed and assigned an inferior position. Other authorities cite the talmudic principle "In matters of sanctity one enhances but does not diminish" and interpret it as prohibiting the diminuation of "sacred" responsibility by removal from office.

The *Bet Din,* noting that automatic tenure, according to Halakhah, is a prerogative only of those occupying positions of "authority," carefully draws a distinction between teachers engaged in the education of young children and *roshei yeshivah* to whom is entrusted the training of more mature students. Teachers are considered to be communal employees rather than communal officials. *Roshei yeshivah,* even though they exercise authority only within their individual classrooms and perform no formal administrative function, are "heads" of the yeshivah, as evidenced by their title and their relationship vis-à-vis their students.

This distinction may be traced to *Nidrei Zerizin* as cited by *Divrei Ge'onim,* no. 94.

Interestingly, the rabbinic court found grounds to differentiate between institutions administered by the community at large and institutions sponsored by an individual or a small group of people, even though the latter may also be funded by philanthropic sources.[2] In this decision religious and educational institutions sponsored by individuals are viewed as private institutions even though their services are freely available to the entire community and, accordingly, the usual employer-employee relationship exists between the administration and members of the staff.

Probably the most important issue with regard to tenure is the question of whether this prerogative may be surrendered by means of a contract specifically limiting the term of office. At least one authority, *Ḥikrei Lev, Oraḥ Ḥayyim,* no. 50, maintains that the right to tenure, where it exists, cannot be waived by prior stipulation. *Yoma* 12b discusses a contingency in which the High Priest becomes temporarily disqualified from performing the sacrificial ritual on Yom Kippur and a substitute must be appointed to perform the service on that day. What is the status of the newly appointed High Priest after the temporarily disqualified High Priest is again able to return to the performance of the duties of his office? There is a dispute between R. Meir and R. Yosi as to whether or not the temporarily appointed High Priest retains the status of a High Priest but both concur that one who has filled the office of High Priest, even temporarily, can no longer function as an ordinary priest. The rationale adduced by the Gemara is the principle that "in matters of sanctity one enhances but does not diminish." Now, reasons *Ḥikrei Lev,* it would be quite simple to stipulate in advance that the appointment as High Priest be only temporary in nature, and that the individual so designated revert to his prior status upon the lapse of his temporary appointment. Since this was obviously not viewed by the Gemara as a viable procedure it may be concluded, argues *Ḥikrei Lev,* that tenure is a divinely bestowed prerogative which cannot be waived. Any contractual agreement to this effect constitutes a stipulation contrary "to that which is written in the Torah" and hence is *ipso facto* null and void.

Other authorities disagree and point out that the High Priest did not

---

2. See also *Teshuvot Maharam Schick, Ḥoshen Mishpat,* nos. 18 and 19; and R. Ya'akov Kanefsky, *Kehillot Ya'akov al Mesekhtot Baba Kamma u-Baba Batra* (B'nei Brak, 5725), addenda, no. 11, sec. 6.

simply discharge a religious function; rather, inauguration into this exalted office conferred a unique sanctity upon the occupant by virtue of the holy oil with which the High Priest was annointed. These authorities argue that appointment to other communal offices does not confer any specific sanctity upon the designee, and hence such appointment may be for a specific period of time. This is the view of *Ḥemdat Shlomoh, Oraḥ Ḥayyim,* no. 7, who has been understood as ruling that a cantor may be discharged upon the expiration of the term of his contract. *Be'er Yiẓḥak, Yoreh De'ah,* no. 3, following *Ḥemdat Shlomoh,* rules that the same is true with regard to the removal of a ritual slaughterer. With regard to the adjudication of the case at hand, the Israeli *Bet Din* followed the latter authorities in ruling that the contract of a teacher or *rosh yeshivah* engaged for a provisional period need not be renewed since the period of service has been stipulated in advance by means of a written contract. The acceptance of a stipulation with regard to a specific period of service is viewed as constituting a waiver of the right to tenure.

It should be pointed out that an apparently contradictory ruling was issued by Rabbi Moses Feinstein, *Iggrot Mosheh, Ḥoshen Mishpat,* I, no. 77. Rabbi Feinstein declares that a teacher engaged for a period of one year cannot be denied reappointment other than for justifiable cause. The Israeli court takes notice of Rabbi Feinstein's responsum and attempts to show that its decision does not contradict the position adopted by *Iggrot Mosheh* since the latter deals with the case of a teacher who had been dismissed by a board of directors, whereas in the case before the Israeli *Bet Din* the dismissal was initiated by the school's principal. However, a careful reading of *Iggrot Mosheh* shows that this analysis is erroneous. Rabbi Feinstein declares that despite an express stipulation to the effect that the individual may be dismissed upon expiration of the contract period, "it is greatly to be doubted" that employment may be denied other than for a halakhically acceptable cause. *Iggrot Mosheh* argues that since the directors and principals do not act in individual capacities, but are representatives of the community, it is self-understood that they are empowered to act only in accordance with the criteria of Jewish law and may not substitute their own subjective judgment for halakhically established criteria. It should be emphasized that, contrary to the assertion of the Israeli *Bet Din,* Rabbi Feinstein specifically refers to both "directors and principals." Moreover, Rabbi Feinstein declares that the argument need be invoked only if the contract expressly stipulates that continued employment may be denied even without just cause. In an earlier responsum, *Ḥosen Mishpat,* I, no. 76, Rabbi Feinstein rules that in the more usual event that the contractual agreement makes no reference to employment beyond the date of expiration, but simply specifies a period of employment, the contract is automatically renewable and may not be terminated other than for just cause. *Iggrot Mosheh* goes beyond other authorities in asserting that this principle applies not only to communal employees but to private employees as well. Rabbi Feinstein maintains that no employee may be dismissed without cause as long as there remains a need for the services he was engaged to perform. His argument is that since contracts are customarily renewed, provided there is no cause for dismissal, it must be assumed that renewal of the contract is an implied condition of employment. This would, of course, not be the case if this implied condition were to be nullified by inclusion of a clause specifically reserving to the employer the power of arbitrary dismissal upon termination of the contract period.

The situation with regard to dismissal of a rabbi upon the expiration of his contract is somewhat different. In this decision, the *Bet Din,* citing *Ḥatam Sofer, Oraḥ, Ḥayyim,* no. 206,[3] affirms that, under existing practice, a rabbi cannot be dismissed through failure to renew his contract. More recently, in 1974, an attempt by officials of the Jewish community of Rotterdam to terminate the tenure of their rabbi by refusing to renew his contract elicited a number of statements regarding rabbinic tenure. In separate declarations, the Israeli Chief Rabbinate, the Union of Orthodox Rabbis of the United States and Canada and the Dutch Board of Chief Rabbis affirmed the principle of rabbinic tenure and indicated that any dispute between a community and its spiritual leader must be submitted to a qualified *Bet Din* since only a *Bet Din* is competent to render a decision with regard to grounds for termination of rabbinic tenure.[4]

The halakhic aspects of dismissal of a teacher *within* the contract period are also considered in the published decision of the Israeli rabbinic court. The *Bet Din* found no difficulty in permitting the removal of a teacher for malfeasance and ruled that in such cases the teacher need be compensated only for time actually served. At times, however, there is a de-

3. See also *Ḥatam Sofer, Ḥoshen Mishpat,* no. 22.

4. See also R. Shlomoh Kluger, *Ha-Elef Lekha Shlomoh, Oraḥ Ḥayyim,* no. 38, and *Yoreh De'ah,* no. 253. The earlier mentioned considerations advanced by *Iggrot Mosheh, Ḥoshen Mishpat,* I, nos. 76 and 77, are, of course, fully applicable to rabbinic tenure as well.

sire to replace a teacher during the contract period, not because of the latter's negligence in performance of his duties, but simply because a more qualified person has been found. Under such conditions the employee's claim to full compensation for the term of employment specified in the contract is not questioned by the *Bet Din.* The *Bet Din,* however, cites conflicting opinions with regard to whether the teacher may lawfully be replaced during the term of the contract even if under such conditions the school is willing to compensate the dismissed teacher in full. No attempt was made by the *Bet Din* to issue a definitive judgment with regard to this point.

The final issue discussed in this decision is the question of the legitimacy of strike action on the part of teachers in religious schools as a means of forcing a resolution of disputes between faculty and administration. The *Bet Din,* citing *Iggrot Mosheh, Ḥoshen Mishpat,* I, no. 59, who rules that strikes against a yeshivah can be sanctioned only under extraordinary circumstances, emphatically declares that interruption of Torah study cannot be countenanced as a means of resolving issues which should properly be adjudicated by a *Bet Din.*

Cannibalism

There are few things more abhorrent to civilized man than partaking of the flesh of a fellow human being. Feelings of repugnance and revulsion were evoked in the course of widespread press coverage in recent years of two instances of cannibalism on the part of survivors of airplane crashes. The first case involved an accident in which a plane crashed in the Andes Mountains in Chile. For ten long weeks until their rescue, a number of the victims managed to survive by feeding upon the flesh of their dead fellow passengers. In a later incident the Canadian pilot of a small aircraft which met with an accident in the far reaches of the North kept himself alive by eating portions of the body of a dead passenger. Following these gruesome events theologians of diverse religious persuasions were queried with regard to the propriety of sustaining life by means of cannibalism in these and similar unfortunate circumstances. There are occasions when such bizarre questions become removed from the realm of abstract theory. Life at times presents us with tragic situations in which the most unpalatable and most unpleasant of eventualities must be faced forthrightly. What, indeed, is the attitude of Jewish law with regard to this agonizing question?

A cursory discussion of this subject by Rabbi Avraham Meir Israel appears in the Tevet–Kislev 5733 issue of *Ha-Ma'or*. The pertinent sources may be found in *Darkei Teshuvah* 79:15. Surprising as it may appear, there is no explicit biblical injunction against partaking of human flesh. Nevertheless Rambam's position, *Ma'akhalot Assurot* 2:3, is that a biblical prohibition may be inferred from Leviticus 11:2. The general statement "These are the living things which you may eat among all the beasts that are on the earth" is followed by an enumeration of specific categories of permitted animals. Since, of course, no mention is made of human flesh it may be inferred, declares Rambam, that cannibalism is forbidden. Ritva, in his commentary on *Ketubot* 60a, is also of the opinion that human flesh is biblically forbidden, but for an entirely different reason. According to Ritva, the flesh of a deceased individual is subsumed under the general prohibition against partaking of "unslaughtered" flesh, a prohibition which applies to the meat of any animal not slaughtered in the manner required by Jewish law.

Many authorities, including Rosh, *Ketubot* 5:19, *Teshuvot ha-Rashba,* I, no. 364, and Ramban, commentary on Leviticus 11:3, maintain that there is no specific biblical prohibition against eating human flesh. These authorities would nevertheless agree that partaking of the flesh of a dead person is forbidden on other, more general, grounds. *Yoreh De'ah* 349:1 records a general prohibition against deriving any benefit from a corpse; using the flesh of a corpse for food is, of course, a forbidden "benefit." [5]

There is, however, nothing in any of these sources to suggest that the prohibition against eating human flesh is not suspended in cases of imminent danger to life, as is the rule with regard to all prohibitions with the exception of the three cardinal sins. There are two precedents in responsa literature which are applicable to the case at hand. *Teshuvot Radbaz,* no. 979 (III, no. 548), reports that in his day mummies were thought to possess medicinal properties. These properties were apparently believed to be derived from the drugs and spices used in the embalming process. Radbaz permits consumption of parts of the mummy, even when the life of the patient is not threatened, because the corpse is completely

---

5. The prohibition with regard to deriving benefit from a Jewish corpse is biblical in nature. There is some disagreement as to whether the prohibition against deriving benefit from the corpse of a non-Jew is biblical or rabbinic in nature. See *Pitḥei Teshuvah, Yoreh De'ah* 349:1; *Mishneh, le-Melekh, Ma'akhalot Assurot* 2:3 and *Hilkhot Avel* 14:21; and *She'elat Ya'aveẓ,* I, no. 41.

dried and "unfit for consumption [even] by a dog." It may be inferred that edible flesh would be permitted only if the patient's life were in danger.

Also germane, although dealing with flesh from a living person rather than a corpse, is *Teshuvot ha-Rashbash,* no. 518. As Rashbash indicates, the situation with regard to a living person is somewhat different from that of a corpse. As opposed to Rambam and Ritva, Rashba, in his previously cited responsum, declares that there is no specific biblical prohibition against eating flesh removed from a living person but asserts that the practice is forbidden by rabbinic edict. Rashba cites the decree forbidding an adult to suckle a nursing woman and argues that the prohibition includes an injunction against consuming any portion of the human body. *Pri Ḥadash, Yoreh De'ah* 79:6, specifically negates this point, contending that the prohibition is limited to nursing. Consequently, *Pri Ḥadash* maintains that there is not even a rabbinic prohibition against consuming flesh removed from a living human being. Rashbash was informed that some women believed that barrenness could be remedied by swallowing the foreskin removed from an infant in the course of circumcision. Rashbash dismisses the contention as an old wives' tale but adds, hypothetically, that he would have been willing to sanction the practice, not as a fertility measure, but as a cure for actual illnesses if there would indeed be demonstrative evidence that the procedure was of therapeutic value.

To return to the case at hand, it is apparent that, when confronted by actual danger to life, preservation of human life takes precedence over the prohibition against eating human flesh. Judaism manifests singular concern for the dignity of the dead body. The Torah requires that the dead body be accorded dignity and respect because human beings are created *be-ẓelem Elokim*—in the divine image. The numerous stipulations and restrictions incorporated in the laws of burial are designed to safeguard the honor and sanctity of the corpse. But, in the final analysis, the corpse itself remains bereft of life. Therefore, when confronted with questions involving the survival of living human beings questions of the honor due to dead bodies become secondary. Preservation of actual life quite obviously takes precedence over regard and concern for life that was.

CHAPTER IX

Miscellaneous Questions

Ben Bag-Bag said, "Delve into it over and over again, for everything is contained in it."

AVOT 5:22

Divine service, for the Jew, consists not simply of worship and the performance of prayer rituals but pervades every facet of his existence. The mode of worship prescribed by Judaism is not limited to specific times, places or actions. No aspect of human life is removed from the service of God. In the Torah man finds a paradigm for every aspect of human conduct.

The ultimate goal of man, asserts Maimonides, is the attainment of the knowledge of God insofar as it is possible for mortal man to know Him.[1] This, according to Maimonides, is the essence of divine service and constitutes man's paramount duty. Ideally, all of man's actions should be directed to this end. Every word and deed should be weighed in order to determine whether or not it furthers this goal. Man's aim, even in purely mundane activities, should be the preservation of his bodily health so that he may be able to acquire moral and intellectual virtue, thereby furthering his ultimate purpose, that of serving God.

This ideal is, to be sure, only rarely attained and, indeed, Maimonides places one who has achieved this exalted state of human perfection "in a rank not lower than that of the prophets." Although he may fall short of reaching this goal, the Jew is bidden to strive for its attainment. The commandments of the Torah are designed to maximalize the natural pro-

1. *The Eight Chapters,* chap. 5. Cf. *Guide of the Perplexed,* III, chap. 51; and Abraham ibn Daud, *Emunah Ramah,* III.

pensity for divine service which is present in every man and, insofar as is possible for ordinary mortals, to consecrate all human activity to the worship of God.

To this end, the Torah ordained manifold precepts and laws governing virtually every aspect of human conduct. "*Mizvot* were given solely that people might be purified by means of them," declared the Sages (*Bereshit Rabbah* XLIV, 1). In the performance of *mizvot* man finds existential fulfillment. The actions required of him are designed to produce both physical and intellectual perfection so that man, insofar as he is capable of doing so, may turn his attention to matters of the spirit and achieve a knowledge and awareness of the divine.

The miscellaneous and varied *halakhot* governing human conduct are all manifestations of divine beneficence toward the people of Israel. As the Mishnah, *Makkot* 23b, declares, "The Holy One, blessed be He, desired to bestow merit unto Israel; therefore He increased unto them Torah and commandments."

Delayed Burial

The cemetery strike which affected the New York City metropolitan area in 1969 caused untold anguish to the many bereaved who were unable to bury their dead. For observant Jews bound by the halakhic requirement of speedy burial this grief was compounded by distress at violation of religious scruples. Fortunately, a court order was forthcoming assuring that no attempt would be made to interfere with private arrangements for the digging of a grave by individuals who demanded immediate burial as a matter of conscience.

Jewish law clearly stipulates that every possible effort be made to assure immediate interment. However, there were cases where, for whatever reason, such arrangements were not made and burial was perforce postponed until the resolution of the labor dispute. The bodies were turned over to the custody of the cemetery officials who assumed responsibility for interment. In such instances questions of when the laws of mourning become applicable and when recitation of the *kaddish* is begun are germane.

The precedents for conduct in such circumstances are reviewed by Rabbi Meir Amsel, the editor of *Ha-Ma'or,* in the Kislev–Tevet–Shevat 5730 issue of that journal. Rosh, in his comments on the third chapter of *Mo'ed Katan,* records that Rabbenu Kalonymos died during a period of siege.

Since his body could not be transported to the cemetery outside the city his coffin was placed in the ritualarium for the duration of the hostilities. Rosh records that the ritual of mourning commenced immediately upon deposit of the body in the ritualarium despite the intention of the family to effect proper burial upon the lifting of the siege. Even though, in accordance with Halakhah, mourning is deemed to begin only after burial has actually taken place, in this case the sealing of the coffin and its deposit in a specific shelter are tantamount to burial with regard to the laws of mourning. This ruling is cited by the *Shulḥan Arukh, Yoreh De'ah* 375:44.

There is yet another consideration that would mandate immediate observance of mourning. In cases where the mourners do not accompany the bier—for example, when burial takes place in a distant locale—the laws of mourning become effective as soon as the coffin has been "delivered to the porters," i.e., mourning commences immediately after the mourners have completed all funeral arrangements and are no longer personally responsible for funeral procedures. The status of the deceased during the period of the strike is literally that of having been "delivered to the porters" since the family has already completed all funeral arrangements and has left the body in the custody of the cemetery authorities and empowered them to make the actual burial.

The following issue of *Ha-Ma'or* contains an article on the same topic by Rabbi Chananyah Yom-Tov Lippa Dreisinger. Rabbi Dreisinger states that his responsum was originally written in reply to identical questions raised during an earlier strike on the part of gravediggers in 1967. The sources cited and conclusions reached parallel those of Rabbi Amsel. *Chavrusa,* April 1967, published by the Rabbinic Alumni of Yeshiva University, contains an article entitled "The Cemetery Strike—Some Halakhic Considerations," by Rabbi Fabian Schonfeld, in which the author presents a conflicting view.[2]

Sounding the Trumpets

It is of singular interest that after a lapse of millennia the opportunity now present itself for the performance of a virtually forgotten *mizvah.* All are familiar with the *shofar* and the *mizvot* attendent upon it. There is yet a second wind instrument associated with *mizvot* with which we are less well acquainted. Scripture commands the fashioning of two trum-

---

2. See also R. Shmuel Hubner, *Ha-Darom,* Tishri 5728; and R. Yechiel Michal Tucatzinsky, *Gesher ha-Ḥayyim,* I, chap. 18, no. 1, sec. 4.

pets of hammered silver to be blown by the *kohanim* for purposes of assembling the congregation and as a signal to continue on the journey through the wilderness. These trumpets were also to be blown on festivals in conjunction with the sacrificial offerings. Furthermore, in the event of warfare, the trumpets were to be sounded in order that ". . . you shall be remembered before the Lord your God and you shall be saved from your enemies" (Num. 10:9). The possibility that this latter exhortation be applicable in our own day in face of the dangers besetting the State of Israel is discussed in two articles which appeared recently. Rabbi Judah Gershuni, in the Tevet 5730 issue of *Or ha-Mizraḥ,* and Rabbi Chaim Shrage Frank, in the Tammuz 5730 issue of *Ha-Ma'ayan,* cover much the same ground and reach similar conclusions.

Although the *Sefer Miẓvot Gadol* does not include the commandment to sound the trumpet in time of war in his enumeration of the 613 commandments, both Rambam, *Sefer ha-Miẓvot, miẓvot 'aseh,* no. 59, and *Mishneh Torah, Hilkhot Ta'anit* 1:1, and *Sefer ha-Ḥinukh, miẓvah* 384, view the sounding of trumpets as a positive commandment obligatory not merely in time of war but in the event of any potential misfortune, such as famine, plague or pestilence. The sounding of trumpets under these circumstances is an appurtenance of prayer and serves as a summons to repentance. The commandment to sound the trumpet in time of danger is binding, according to these authorities, not merely while the Temple is in existence but subsequent to its destruction as well.

Many authorities are of the opinion that there exists no obligation to sound the trumpets in the event of a calamity in the Diaspora. *Magen Avraham, Oraḥ Ḥayyim* 576, queries why this practice has lapsed even though it appears to be a biblical obligation. Various commentators, including *Pri Megadim, Oraḥ Ḥayyim* 575:2, and *Mishneh Berurah* 575:1, answer that the fulfillment of this commandment is limited solely to the Land of Israel. Both express doubt as to whether the commandment is obligatory even in *Ereẓ Yisra'el* when that country is not under Jewish sovereignty. In any event, it is clear, according to all authorities, that there is a clear-cut obligation to sound these instruments in times of trouble when the Land of Israel *is* under Jewish dominion.[3] Thus the question of whether this *miẓvah* should be performed nowadays becomes germane.

There is considerable discussion and controversy among early authorities with regard to the details of the performance of this *miẓvah* and as to

---

3. Cf. *Arukh ha-Shulḥan, Oraḥ Ḥayyim* 576:4.

when the trumpets are to be blown alone and when together with the *shofar* as indicated in Psalms 98:6, "With trumpets and the voice of the *shofar* shall you sound the *teru'ah* before the King, God." Some authorities maintain that the trumpets together with the *shofar* are to be sounded only on the Temple Mount; in other locales the *shofar* alone is to be blown. Rabbi Frank explains that this opinion is based upon Numbers 10:9, ". . . and you shall be remembered before the Lord your God." According to this line of reasoning, only the Temple site is considered to be "before God." Nowadays, considerations of ritual purity preclude entry onto the Temple Mount. Rabbi Frank, however, brings evidence that all of Jerusalem is considered to be an extension of the Temple with regard to the sounding of trumpets. He adds that the *shofar* need not be sounded together with the trumpets other than at the actual site of the Temple, since the relevant passage in Psalms indicates that both instruments are employed simultaneously only "before the King, God." Rabbi Frank maintains that while the entire city of Jerusalem is "before God," nevertheless the site of divine kingship is limited to the Temple Mount proper. Hence the rest of Jerusalem is not "before the King, God." Therefore, argues Rabbi Frank, trumpets unaccompanied by the *shofar* must be sounded in Jerusalem in the event of impending misfortune.

It should be noted that the silver trumpets must be sounded by *kohanim*. Indeed, R. Jacob Emden, *Mor u-Keẓi'ah, Oraḥ Ḥayyim* 576, states that this commandment has lapsed in our day because the genealogical purity of *kohanim* is now subject to doubt. Rabbi Gershuni objects to this line of reasoning because, in any event, there is no transgression involved in the blowing of the trumpets should it transpire that one who does so is not of priestly lineage, while the biblical commandment must be observed even in the case of doubt.

In the following issue of *Ha-Ma'ayan,* Tishri 5731, Rabbi Kalman Kahane notes that at least one authority maintains that this *miẓvah* can no longer be fulfilled. Rabbi Moses Feinstein, *Iggrot Mosheh, Oraḥ Ḥayyim,* I, no. 169, is of the opinion that only trumpets fashioned for use in the Temple proper may be used for fulfillment of the *miẓvah* of sounding the trumpets in time of peril. For this reason Rambam, in his enumeration of the 613 *miẓvot,* views the commandment to blow the trumpets at the time of sacrificial offerings and the commandment to sound the trumpets when confronted by impending misfortune to be a single *miẓvah* rather than two distinct commandments. Rabbi Kahane himself argues that, practically speaking, trumpets may be fashioned in an infinite number of sizes and shapes. However, for fulfillment of the *miẓvah* a specific shape and form was ordained. The exact form in which the trumpets are to be made is now unknown to us since the tradition with regard to their proper shape has lapsed. Accordingly, adds Rabbi Kahane, it has been the custom of the Ashkenazic community in Jerusalem to sound the *shofar* rather than trumpets on fast days and in times of trouble.

Rabbi Frank nevertheless reports that in light of the serious threat of war which existed at that time the *Bet Din* of Jerusalem decreed that trumpets be sounded and accordingly, on 12 Iyar, 5730, *kohanim* sounded trumpets of hammered silver before the Western Wall.[4] We join in the prayer expressed by Rabbi Frank that these trumpets sounded in time of grave danger lead to the fulfillment of the divine promise "and you shall be remembered before the Lord your God and you shall be saved from your enemies" and that we may speedily be privileged to fulfill the second *mizvah* associated with these trumpets: "And on the day of your rejoicing, and on your festivals and on your New Moons, and you shall sound the trumpets on your burnt offerings and your peace offerings and they will be for you a remembrance before the Lord your God."

The Names of God

In any halakhic study, it is necessary to clarify whether a particular practice is mandated as a halakhic requirement, is to be followed on the basis of *minhag,* or is to be dismissed as being grounded upon superstition and ignorance. Undoubtedly, in the course of Jewish history—particularly in areas having little contact with centers of Torah scholarship—many folk-customs did arise which diverge from the original Halakhah to so great a degree as to constitute a farcical distortion thereof. On the other side of the coin are the many time-hallowed practices followed by knowledgeable Jews which *are* founded upon authentic halakhic considerations.

A case in point involves practices related to the writing and vocalization of the Names of God. The Tishri–Cheshvan 5730 issue of *Kol Torah* features an article by Rabbi A. Steinsalz in which he examines the widespread tendency to avoid writing the letters of the Divine Name even when such letters occur in a secular context.[5] This practice is most commonly encountered in the writing of proper names in which one of the Divine

---

4. Cf. however, R. Eliezer Waldenberg, *Ẓiẓ Eli'eẓer,* XI, no. 16.
5. See also R. Menasheh Klein, *Mishneh Halakhot,* V, nos. 117–122.

Names is incorporated as part of the cognitive meaning of the appellation, e.g., Azaryah ("God helped") or Netanel ("God gave"). Many individuals also refrain from employing such letter combinations even in words totally disassociated from reference to the Deity. Thus, for example, when a Hebrew word ends in the letter *he* preceded by a *yod* either the final letter is dropped or the word is written with a dividing mark between the two letters.

The Gemara, *Shevu'ot* 35a, states that it is forbidden to erase the name of God and for that reason care is taken not to write the Divine Name upon any document or paper which might be destroyed. *Megillat Ta'anit* 7a and the Gemara, *Rosh Hashanah* 18b, report that during the Hasmonean period promissory notes bore the legend, "In such and such year in the reign of Yochanan, High Priest of the most high God." The Sages, upon hearing of this innovation, exclaimed: "Tomorrow the debtor will repay his debt, with the result that the note will be cast away with the refuse!" Accordingly, they abrogated the practice and declared the day on which they did so to be a holiday. On the basis of this source, Rema, *Yoreh De'ah* 276:13, rules that it is forbidden to write the Divine Name "other than in a book, for it may come to dishonor. Therefore, we take heed not to write the Divine Name in a letter." The prohibition against erasing the Name of God is, however, limited to the specifically enumerated Divine Names which possess intrinsic sanctity. *Mesekhet Sofrim* 4:4 states clearly that even these names may be erased when they do not stand independently but form an integral part of the name of a mortal.

Rabbi Steinsalz notes that examination of early rabbinic manuscripts shows that words combining letter combinations spelling a Divine Name were written out in their entirety. Although it is now universal practice to employ the combination *tet-vav* for the number fifteen rather than a *yod* followed by a *he,* this custom is of comparatively recent origin. The usage of *yod* followed by *he* to represent fifteen would appear to be particularly objectionable since these two letters standing alone constitute the complete spelling of one of the sanctified names. Yet in earlier times there appears to have been no objection to this practice. One may conclude that since these letters are not intended to stand for a Divine Name their mere juxtaposition does not endow them with sanctity.

The same point is made by Dr. Louis Rabinowitz, former Chief Rabbi of South Africa, in an article entitled "On the Names of God," which appeared in the *London Jewish Chronicle,* April 10, 1970. Rabbi Rabinowitz also discusses the status of the term *shalom.* Rabbi Rabinowitz comments with amazement that he has been told of "one distinguished rabbi who never writes the word *shalom* in full, but writes only the first three letters and an apostrophe—because the Talmud states (*Shabbat* 10b) that *shalom* is one of the names of God." It is indeed true that *Teshuvot ha-Rosh* 3:15 declares, "We have found no one who forbids the erasure of *shalom*." Rabbi Rabinowitz, however, fails to mention the many authorities who insist that *shalom* may not be erased. *Tosafot, Sotah* 10a, comments that the list of seven Divine Names which may not be erased is not exhaustive and that *shalom* is to be included in this category. Writing only the first three letters of this word is a time-honored custom. *Birkei Yosef, Oraḥ Ḥayyim* 85:8, quotes Rabbenu Yechiel who asserts that, since it is one of the Divine Names, the word *shalom* is not spelled out in a greeting. Rema, *Yoreh De'ah* 276:13, also cites this practice.

Another question requiring clarification is the permissibility of writing the name of God in the vernacular. This question is, of course, relevant only with regard to correspondence or other forms of writing which are likely to be discarded heedlessly. As previously noted, Rema states explicitly that the name of God may be written out in full in printed works which presumably will be treated with respect. The prohibition against obliterating the name of God is limited to the specifically enumerated Divine Names; other cognomens are regarded as adjectival descriptions rather than as names of the Deity and as such are not included in the prohibition against erasure. Both *Shakh, Yoreh De'ah* 179:11, and R. Akiva Eger, *Yoreh De'ah* 276:9, state definitively that the name of God occurring in languages other than Hebrew is regarded as a cognomen and hence the prohibition with reference to erasure does not apply.

Although the prohibition against erasure is not applicable, proper respect must nevertheless be paid to the name of God even when it occurs in languages other than Hebrew. *Nedarim* 7b states: "Every place where the unnecessary mention of the Divine Name is found, there poverty is to be found." This is deduced from the biblical verse ". . . in every place where I cause My name to be mentioned I will come unto thee and bless thee" (Exod. 20:21), indicating that the pronunciation of the Divine Name in a sacred manner is rewarded with blessing and prosperity. From this the converse is also deduced, viz., that the pronunciation of the Divine Name in vain leads to poverty.

Two renowned authorities, R. Yonatan Eibeschutz, *Urim ve-Tumim* 27:2, and R. Ya'akov of Lissa, *Netivot ha-Mishpat* 27:2, maintain that reverence must also be accorded to written occurrences of the Divine

Name, whether in Hebrew or in the vernacular. Both scholars decried even the use of the French *adieu* (the root meaning of which is "with God") in written communications because of the dishonor of the Divine Name resulting from careless disposal of such correspondence. These authorities maintain that poverty follows not merely improper vocalization of the Divine Name but also failure to accord proper respect to written occurrences of the Divine Name even in the vernacular. Rabbi Rabinowitz errs in describing scrupulousness with regard to the writing of the Divine Name in languages other than Hebrew as a recent development and in contending that mention of this prohibition appears for the first time in the comparatively recent *Arukh ha-Shulḥan, Ḥoshen Mishpat* 27.

Another practice questioned by Dr. Rabinowitz is constraint in pronouncing the terms *Shaddai* and *Ẓeva'ot.* The prohibition against vocalizing the name of God other than in the reading of Scripture, prayer, or recitation of blessings is derived from the positive commandment "The Lord your God shall you fear" (Deut. 6:13). Restraint in not mentioning the name of God in vain is a manifestation of fear and awe. Rav Aḥai Ga'on, *She'iltot, Yitro, She'ilta* 53, deems this to be a transgression of the negative prohibition "Thou shalt not take the name the Lord your God in vain" (Exod. 20:7). According to numerous authorities, e.g., Rambam *Hilkhot Shevu'ot* 12:11 (see *Teshuvot R. Akiva Eger,* no. 25), this prohibition embraces all of the seven names of God. Since both *Shaddai* and *Ẓeva'ot* are enumerated among the seven names of the Deity common practice is to use the assonant forms *Shakai* and *Ẓevakot* respectively as substitutes for these names. Dr. Rabinowitz' incredulity at this "strange mispronunciation of Hebrew" is misplaced.

Utterance of the Divine Name in languages other than Hebrew is discussed by *Nimukei Yosef* in his commentary on *Nedarim* 7b. This authority declares that while needless mention of the name of God in secular languages is not encompassed by the biblical prohibition, nonetheless, "*go'arin bo*—the one doing so is to be admonished and chastised." It should be noted that Rabbi Moses Feinstein, *Iggrot Mosheh, Yoreh De'ah,* I, no. 172, states that this statement of *Nemukei Yosef* regarding inappropriate vocalization of the name of God in the vernacular is limited to the proper name of the Deity in such languages (e.g., "God") and not to adjectival cognomens (e.g., "Almighty").[6]

6. Cf. *Ḥiddushei Ḥatam Sofer, Nedarim* 2a, and *Teshuvot R. Akiva Eger,* no. 25.

In conclusion, it is quite apparent that regardless of the final adjudication of these questions, the meticulousness with which God-fearing Jews have always conducted themselves in the writing and vocalization of the Divine Name is grounded upon a deeply rooted reverence for Halakah in all its ramifications. Improper understanding of the halakhic bases of such practices may at times lead to their being treated with a levity which is unwarranted. To paraphrase a famous dictum, *afilu ketivat ḥullin shel talmidei ḥakhamim ẓerikhah limmud*—even the idle *writing* of Torah scholars bears studious attention.

Religiously motivated forms of conduct practiced by devout Jews over a span of generations are but seldom without a firm basis. Our Sages long ago counseled in this regard, "Even if they are not prophets, they are the sons of prophets." Those who inveigh in caustic tones against the manner in which their coreligionists spell the name of God not only err in their preconceptions but fail to realize that such time-hallowed customs acquire a meaning and significance of their own. The Jew who inserts a dash in spelling the Divine Name is filled with an all-pervasive sense of the immanence of the Almighty. His action demonstrates that he feels no inhibition in expressing his reverence for the divine in all aspects of his daily life. Whether or not one chooses to adopt this practice, whether one regards it as well-grounded or as ill-founded, the usage "G-d" should, at the very minimum, command a dash of respect.

Residence in Spain

The permission granted in 1968 by the Franco government for the repair of an ancient synagogue in Madrid brought to the fore the question of whether permanent Jewish settlement in Spain is proper. An article by Rabbi Judah Gershuni in the Tishri 5731 issue of *Ha-Darom* deals with this topic, as do a prolonged series of brief items appearing in *Ha-Ma'or* over a period of several months. The Kislev–Tevet 5729 issue of *Ha-Ma'or* contains a note bearing the initials of the editor stating that although no source can be cited, it is well known that following the expulsion of Jews from Spain the rabbinic authorities of that generation placed the country under an interdict forbidding any Jew to establish residence there upon pain of anathema. It is alleged that this prohibition was originally promulgated for a period of only four hundred years but was voluntarily accepted by later generations as a permanent decree. The editor further asserts, in light of the fact that this prohibition has been accepted by "all of Israel," that no subsequent *Bet Din* may annul the decree.

The latter point is disputed both by Rabbi Shlomoh Wahrman, writing in the following issue of *Ha-Ma'or,* and more recently by Rabbi Gershuni. Rabbi Wahrman cites a discussion of this prohibition in *Teru'at Melekh,* no. 13. This authority, Rabbi Joseph Susmanovitz, son-in-law of the renowned R. Moshe Mordecai Epstein of Slobodka, states clearly that the decree did not extend to "all of Israel" but merely to those who were expelled from Spain and therefore can be rescinded by subsequent authorities. Furthermore, the prohibition was not promulgated in the form of a decree but was proclaimed as a *ḥerem* (interdict), which may be annulled by another *Bet Din.*

Rabbi Gershuni cites *Iggrot Re'iyah,* II, no. 632, of Rabbi Abraham I. Kook, in which the latter voices his doubts with regard to the nature of this prohibition, but declares that the ban is surely no more stringent than the biblical prohibition against returning to Egypt. Accordingly, only permanent settlement is forbidden; temporary residence for purposes of commerce is permissible. Rabbi Gershuni argues that the ban may have been merely against the establishment of Jewish settlements, but once such communities are established in violation of the ban there may be no prohibition against an individual subsequently establishing residence in Spain. Others have suggested that the ban was applicable only during the period of the Spanish monarchy but lapsed with the establishment of the republic. One who vows not to enter a certain house is bound by the vow only as long as the owner has not died or sold the dwelling. Similarly, it has been argued, Spain, following the establishment of the republic, may be deemed to be a new country against which an interdict was never pronounced. Since the text of the ban is not available, Rabbi Gershuni argues, such conjecture serves only to establish a doubt. Violation of this ban may involve a biblical transgression. The governing canon is *safek de'oraita le-chumra*—actions involving even the *possibility* of a biblical violation must be eschewed. Hence Rabbi Gershuni concludes that permanent residence in Spain cannot be permitted.

An item in the Av–Elul 5729 issue of *Ha-Ma'or* reports that at least one authority did permit Jewish settlement in Spain. Rabbi Chaim Elazar Schapiro, popularly known as the Munkatcher Rebbe, published a responsum in *Tel Talpiot,* Tishri 5691, in which he granted permission for residence in Spain provided that the Jewish nationals of that country be granted full religious freedom. To this may be added the discussion of this topic by Rabbi Shlomoh Aaron Wertheimer in his *She'elat Shlomoh.* II, no. 53, in which he concludes that no *ḥerem* was ever issued against residence in Spain. Moreover, it is evident from a responsum contained in *Teshuvot Mabit,* I, no. 307, that the author, R. Moshe di Trani, was unaware of any such ban. It is most unlikely that a *ḥerem,* had it existed, would have been unknown to this sixteenth-century scholar.

Nevertheless, it is clear that residence in Spain was discountenanced. Mr. Tovia Preschel, in an article which appeared in the Israeli newspaper *Ha-Modi'a,* 30 Tishri, 5714, and in a subsequent article in *Ha-Do'ar,* 11 Tevet, 5731, reports that the archives of the Sephardic community of Hamburg contain a document indicating that in 1658 the community adopted a regulation which provided that "whoever visits Spain or Portugal may not be called to the Torah or honored with any other *miẓvah* for two years."[7]

Professor Cecil Roth, *Jewish Life,* Adar 5717, cites religious sanctions imposed upon visitors to Spain and Portugal. These sanctions were incorporated in the regulations of the "Society for Dowering the Brides" promulgated in Leghorn in 1727. In 1785 similar sanctions were included in the *"Ascamot"* of Congregation Sahar Asamaim of London.[8] Roth states that such sanctions were based upon earlier regulations of the Sephardic communities of Amsterdam and Venice.

In a study published in *Talpiot,* III (5708), nos. 3–4, Professor Abraham Shalom Yahuda offers an interesting explanation of the opprobrium associated with travel to Spain. The text of the edict of expulsion issued by Ferdinand and Isabella stated that any Jew found in Spain after the stipulated date of expulsion would be obliged to convert to Christianity or suffer death by hanging. Thus, subsequently, any Jew who wished to visit the country would have found it necessary to pretend to be a Christian. Since Halakhah forbids a Jew to pretend to be a Christian, return to Spain was effectively banned, not by virtue of the promulgation of a *ḥerem* but because of the prohibition involved in the subterfuge of pretending to be a Christian. The transgression would have been sufficiently odious to warrant communal sanctions. A somewhat similar explanation is also offered by Cecil Roth. According to Yahuda, following the dis-

7. *Jahrbuch* of the *Juedisch-litterarische Gesellschaft* of Frankfurt, VIII (1911), 231.

8. See also Tovia Preschel, *"Al Ḥerem Sefarad," Ha-Do'ar,* 22 Kislev 5732.

bandment of the Inquisition in 1834 there no longer exists any reason for Jews not to visit Spain or even to establish residence there since they are no longer compelled to disguise their Jewish identity.

The Southern Hemisphere

The Tishri–Cheshvan 5730 edition of the Israeli journal, *Kol Torah,* contains a hitherto unpublished responsum by Rabbi Zevi Pesach Frank, the late Chief Rabbi of Jerusalem. The same material also appears in the Kislev 5731 issue of *Ha-Pardes.*[8a] This responsum, addressed to the Chief Rabbi of Argentina, Rabbi S. Y. Glicksberg, deals with a halakhic question arising from the climatic variations of the Southern Hemisphere.

Leviticus 19:23 stipulates that the fruit of newly planted saplings is forbidden for the first three years of the tree's growth. The three-year period is counted not from the date of planting but from the fifteenth of Shevat, the "New Year of Trees." Those fruits which are formed and show a distinct shape before the fifteenth of Shevat of the fourth year are forbidden as *orlah;* those formed afterwards are permitted. The question posed by the interlocutor is whether, in view of the reversed seasons in the Southern Hemisphere, the fifteenth of Shevat marks the termination of the period of *orlah* in those lands as well.

The Gemara, *Rosh Hashanah* 14a, explains that the fifteenth of Shevat was ordained as the New Year of Trees because by this date "most of the year's rains have been exhausted." Rashi explains the Gemara quite simply by stating that by this date the major portion of the rainy season has elapsed and hence the fruits are already formed. *Tosafot,* however, maintains that despite the reference to the fifteenth of Shevat, it is really the first day of Tishri which is the New Year of Trees. Fruit nurtured by rain falling prior to the first of Tishri is considered to be the produce of the previous year even though the fruit itself is formed after the New Year. All fruit formed before the fifteenth of Shevat must have been nurtured by precipitation occuring before Tishri; growth after this date cannot be attributed to rains falling before Tishri. Hence, for practical

---

8a. This item was subsequently included in R. Zevi Pesach Frank's recently published responsa collection, *Har Ẓvi, Oraḥ Ḥayyim,* II, no. 29. A shorter item addressed to the inhabitants of New Zealand appears in *Har Ẓvi, Oraḥ Ḥayyim,* I, no. 56.

purposes, the fifteenth of Shevat marks the boundary between the old crop and the new.

Rabbi Frank notes that, according to *Tosafot,* the date ordained as the New Year of Trees quite obviously does not depend upon the local rainy season. Fruit nurtured by rain falling before the first of Tishri is deemed to be of the previous year's growth even though the fruit appears at a later date. According to *Tosafot,* the talmudic reference to the rainy season is merely an observation of the agricultural phenomenon that rains falling before the first of Tishri are capable of producing fruit only until the fifteenth of Shevat. Hence this date is observed as the New Year of Trees in every locale regardless of local seasons of precipitation. The question at hand, then, arises only according to Rashi's interpretation: Is the date signaling the beginning of a new year with regard to *orlah* statutory, with the fifteenth of Shevat marking the beginning of the New Year of Trees because it coincides with the close of the rainy season in the Land of Israel, or are these yearly periods contingent upon the local growing season?

Rabbi Frank quotes Rabbi Y. Cohen, currently a member of the Jerusalem *Bet Din,* in ruling that the New Year of Trees is to be universally observed on the fifteenth of Shevat. Rabbi Cohen advances two reasons for his decision. First, *Turei Even,* in his commentary on *Rosh Hashanah,* indicates that the phraseology of the talmudic passage in question indicates that by this date most of the rainy season has passed and therefore the major portion of the crop has assumed a distinctive forum. The fifteenth of Shevat is hence the New Year in only a majority of cases, but since it is a valid date for the major portion of the crop, it becomes the standard date for all trees. Similarly, the general rule remains valid for countries subject to diverse growing seasons.

Secondly, Halakhah accepts the conditions prevailing in *Ereẓ Yisra'el* as constituting the norm. For example, with regard to the prayer for rain included in the daily *Shemoneh Esreh* during the winter months, the *Shulḥan Arukh, Oraḥ Ḥayyim* 117:2, states that even if the conditions prevailing are such that an entire country is in need of rain during the summer months, the prayer for rain is not recited other than in the winter. The justification is that this prayer was instituted on the basis of the needs of the Land of Israel. Similarly, argues Rabbi Cohen, the laws of *orlah* were established on the basis of agricultural conditions prevailing in Israel and are applicable without variation throughout the world.

Miẓvot on the Moon

As is clearly underscored by the popular witticism regarding "the Elephant and the Jewish Problem," the Jew tends to examine every phenomenon, whether natural, social, political or scientific, in the light of his own particular interests. Little wonder, then, that the contemporary preoccupation with the conquest of space should be reflected in halakhic writings. One of the more intriguing topics in the current literature is the question of the extent to which *miẓvot* are binding upon Jews who may happen to find themselves in the vast regions of outer space. There has now appeared, for the first time, a serious discussion of man's religious obligations on the moon. Undoubtedly, the subject will become a recurrent one and rabbinic literature dealing with this topic will be considerably enriched in the months and years to come.

Among the opinions published thus far, the most extreme position is advanced by Rabbi Ben-Zion Firrer in the 5730 issue of *No'am*. Rabbi Firrer maintains that *miẓvot* are incumbent upon man only in his terrestrial habitat. The sole supporting evidence for this radical point of view, which is described by its proponent as being "only in the nature of first thoughts; a modest beginning in investigation of this question," is an argument based upon a statement in *Kiddushin* 37a. Asserting that commandments which are personal in character are binding not only in *Ereẓ Yisra'el* but in the Diaspora as well, the Gemara quotes the verse ". . . all the days which you are alive on the earth" (Deut. 12:1). Rabbi Firrer argues that since a pleonasm, "on the earth," is required to establish this obligation, such obligation must be limited to what is specified in this verse. Therefore, man is exempt from performance of *miẓvot* in places other than those which are "on the earth."

In a report of an interview granted by Rabbi Shlomoh Goren, published in *Ha-Ẓofeh,* 10 Av, 5729 (and cited by Rabbi Firrer in *No'am*), Rabbi Goren is quoted as asserting that theoretically *miẓvot* contingent upon "time" cannot be performed on the moon, since "time" as measured by twenty-four hour day-night sequences does not exist on this celestial body. *Keri'at shema,* for example, is obligatory only during certain time periods. Since these periods are defined in terms of terrestrial cycles of light and darkness, it is not clear when *keri'at shema* should be recited on the moon where the lunar "day" is equal to a month (which, on the average, is 29 days, 12 hours, 44 minutes and 2.78 seconds in length). The same question arises with regard to determining the occurrence of the seventh day which is to be hallowed as the Sabbath. However, argues Rabbi Goren, in practice man is obligated to perform such *mizvot*. Since natural atmospheric conditions on the moon cannot support human life, man will be able to exist only by creating an artificial atmosphere composed of elements transported from earth. In light of his continual dependence upon Mother Earth, man living on the moon will continue to be governed by the laws operative on earth.

Rabbi Firrer contests the assumption that dependence upon terrestrial materials renders such dependents subject to "Earth-Halakhah," arguing that once such materials come into contact with the moon they are accorded the same status as lunar material. The Gemara, *Gittin* 7b, declares that bodies of water in *Erez Yisra'el* are not part of the Land of Israel and that a ship plying the lakes and rivers of *Erez Yisra'el,* as long as it does not scrape bottom, is considered to be outside the borders of the Land of Israel. When the vessel does touch bottom, its passengers and cargo, even while submerged, are considered to be within the confines of *Erez Yisra'el*. Rabbi Firrer observes that the ship acquires the halakhic status of the underlying river-bed simply by coming into physical contact with it. Similarly, argues Rabbi Firrer, Earth material coming into contact with lunar substance acquires the halakhic status of the moon itself.

Another article in the same issue of *No'am* takes sharp issue with Rabbi Firrer's thesis. In direct contradiction to the opinion of Rabbi Firrer, Rabbi Menachem Kasher declares that halakhic obligations are personal ones and are incumbent upon Jews in any and all places where they may find themselves. Hence, the contention that the observance of *mizvot* is abrogated in the celestial spheres cannot be entertained. Rabbi Kasher adds that since Rabbi Firrer has described his words as "first thoughts," he is certain that the latter's "second thoughts" will reflect a change of heart. Insofar as the reckoning of time is concerned, Rabbi Kasher opines that this situation is no different from the situation which prevails in the earth's polar regions, which have days and nights of many months' duration. Rabbi Kasher has long been of the opinion that under such circumstances the day must be reckoned on a twenty-four-hour basis with alternating twelve-hour periods of "day" and "night" regardless of the presence or absence of solar illumination. The same practice, contends Rabbi Kasher, should be followed by man on the moon.[9]

---

9. On this topic see also R. Meir Blumenfeld, *Peraḥ Shoshanah,* no. 67.

Comets

The anticipated appearance of the comet Kohoutek was much heralded as potentially the most spectacular astronomical occurrence of the century. Although the predicted celestial extravaganza failed to materialize, the abundant publicity preceding the anticipated event occasioned a discussion of questions concerning blessings associated with this and similar phenomena.

The first question which presents itself is whether the appearance of a comet is included among the specifically enumerated occurrences which, when witnessed, occasion the recitation of a unique blessing expressing praise to God as Creator of the universe. Rabbi Abraham Israel, writing in the Kislev–Tevet issue of *Ha-Ma'or,* quotes the Gemara, *Berakhot* 58b, which states that the appearance of a *kokhava de-shavit* occasions such a blessing. This term is translated as "a star with a tail"—an obvious reference to comets. In accordance with the view of Rambam, *Hilkhot Berakhot* 10:14, and *Shulḥan Arukh, Oraḥ Ḥayyim* 227:1, when experiencing phenomena such as thunder or lightning, the viewer has the option of reciting either the blessing "Whose power and might fill the universe" or the blessing "Who created the works of creation." Rambam explicitly states that the same choice is open to one who witnesses "a star which has a tail." However, *Taz, Oraḥ Ḥayyim* 227:1, records that it is customary to pronounce the blessing "Whose power and might fill the universe" when hearing thunder since the phenomenon of thunder is a demonstration of divine power, whereas lightning evokes praise of God as the Creator "of the works of creation." It would therefore follow, according to this custom, that the blessing "Who creates the works of creation" would be appropriate upon the sighting of a comet.

Another question which has been raised is whether a blessing is required if the comet is not visible to the naked eye but is seen through a telescope. It is of interest to note that some type of optical instrument seems to have been extant in the days of the Gemara. *Eruvin* 43b[10] re-

10. Me'iri, commenting on this statement in his *Bet ha-Beḥirah, ad locum,* quotes Rav Hai Ga'on as offering two alternate explanations: (1) that the tube was a tube *simpliciter* without glass and was used as an ordinary measuring instrument; and (2) that the tube was an astrolabe, to which, in fact, he refers by name. In his other work on *Eruvin, Ḥiddushei ha-Me'iri,* Me'iri refers obliquely to Rav Hai Ga'on's comments but dismisses them, stating that these interpretations are "difficult to understand" and that Rashi's interpretation "is sufficient."

ports that Rabban Gamaliel had a "tube" through which he could see a distance of two thousand cubits. There is some question as to whether, from the halakhic perspective, a visual phenomenon perceived through a telescope is deemed to be a veridical perception of the object itself or whether such perception is deemed to be a form of optical distortion rather than a true visual perception of the object *per se*. This question is discussed by various authorities in a number of different contexts. Rabbi Isaac Schmelkes, *Bet Yiẓḥak, Even ha-Ezer,* II, no. 86, demonstrates, on the basis of talmudic sources, that witnesses may testify only to matters which they have perceived directly, but may not testify to events which they have observed through the lens of a telescope. More comparable to the issue at hand is the question of whether the sanctification of the New Moon may be recited in the event that the moon is perceivable only through a telescope. *Devar Shemu'el,* no. 242 (cited by *Be'er Heitev, Oraḥ Ḥayyim* 426:1), declares that one who sees the moon through a telescope or glass instrument should not recite the blessing "for it is not a proper visual perception" (*re'iyah gemurah*). However, this view is challenged by *Shevut Ya'akov,* I, no. 126, and by *Sha'arei Teshuvah, Oraḥ Ḥayyim* 426:1. The latter authority declares that the sanctification of the New Moon may be recited by a person who requires the aid of eyeglasses even if he is totally unable to see the moon without glasses. Rabbi Israel, citing these sources, draws an analogy between the sanctification of the New Moon seen through a telescope and the recitation of the appropriate blessing upon the occasion of the sighting of a comet by means of a telescope and asserts that the halakhic determination should be the same in both instances. However, any conclusions with regard to the blessing upon the sighting of a comet by means of a telescope predicated upon sources pertaining to sanctification of the New Moon are specious since the rationale underlying the halakhah with regard to the sanctification of the New Moon is not applicable to the sighting of a comet. The very source cited, *Sha'arei Teshuvah,* indicates that the sanctification of the New Moon may be recited despite the fact that the New Moon is not visible to the naked eye because even a blind person is obligated to pronounce the sanctification and hence it is not necessary actually to "see" the moon. This is certainly not the case with regard to the recitation of a blessing upon the sighting of a comet.

Rabbi Israel adduces further evidence drawn from the discussion of a similar question pertaining to the obligation to rise in the presence of a Torah scholar. *Halakhot Ketanot,* I, no. 274, rules that one must rise even if the scholar is seen through an intervening pane of glass. Similarly, *Shulḥan Arukh, Oraḥ Ḥayyim* 75:5, states that the restriction against reading the *shema* in the presence of "nakedness" encompasses such utterances even if the "nakedness" is covered by glass. However, Rabbi Israel's conclusion that there is no halakhic distinction between perception by means of the naked eye and perception by means of an optical instrument is unwarranted. The sources dealing with rising in the presence of a scholar and the recitation of the *shema* in the presence of nakedness speak of intervening windows or sheets of glass which in no way magnify or distort vision. Under such conditions Halakhah deems the perception to be a true one. However, on the basis of these sources, the question of whether or not the perception of an object artificially magnified by means of a glass prism is the equivalent of "seeing" remains an open question. Evidence that it is not deemed a proper visual perception may be found in the previously cited statement of *Sha'arei Teshuvah.* As noted, this authority rules that the viewing of a telescopically magnified moon occasions the recitation of the sanctification of the New Moon precisely because that moon need not be actually seen, as evidenced by the obligation of a blind person *vis-à-vis* the sanctification of the New Moon. The clear implication of *Sha'arei Teshuvah*'s discussion is that telescopic magnification does not result in *re'iyah gemurah* insofar as Halakhah is concerned and accordingly no blessing would be occasioned unless the comet is seen without magnification. However, *Sha'arei Teshuvah* does not cite *Shevut Ya'akov's* discussion in its entirety. Deuteronomy 25:9 prescribes that *ḥaliẓah* must be performed "before the eyes of the judges." *Shevut Ya'akov* addresses himself to the question of whether or not the members of a *Bet Din* convened for purposes of *ḥaliẓah* must be capable of seeing the performance of this rite without benefit of eyeglasses. *Shevut Ya'akov* concludes that inability to see without eyeglasses does not serve to disqualify a person from serving as a member of a *Bet Din* for this purpose. Not mentioned by these authorities is a possible distinction between eyeglasses, which simply correct a distortion caused by a malfunction of the eye thereby restoring normal vision to the wearer, and magnification by means of a telescope or other instrument which results in a vision not perceivable under normal conditions.

Part II

"Now these are the ordinances which you shall set before them." It should not enter your mind to say "I shall teach them a section of Torah or a halakhah twice or thrice . . . but I shall not trouble myself to cause them to understand the reasons for the matter and its explanation . . ."

RASHI, EXODUS 21:1

CHAPTER X

Electricity

Be conscientious in kindling the lights in my honor and I shall light a great light on your behalf in the world to come.

TANḤUMA, BE-HA'ALOTKHA 2

Electric Substitutes for Chanukkah and Sabbath Lights

The suitability of electric lights for use in place of the usual Sabbath candles and as a substitute for the traditional Chanukkah *menorah* has been a recurrent theme in halakhic literature since the invention of the incandescent bulb. Numerous responsa expressing conflicting viewpoints have been written on this topic. One of the earliest authorities to discuss the matter, R. Yitzchak Schmelkes, *Bet Yiẓḥak, Yoreh De'ah,* no. 120, sec. 5, ruled that electric bulbs may be utilized in fulfilling the *miẓvah* of kindling the Sabbath lights but not in discharging the obligation with regard to Chanukkah lights. Later, R. Abraham Steinberg, *Maḥazeh Avraham,* I, *Oraḥ Ḥayyim,* no. 41, concurred in the opinion that electric bulbs may be used as *Shabbat* lights. More recently, Rabbi Y. E. Henkin, *Edut le-Yisra'el,* p. 122, adopted a similar position. In *Ha-Ḥashmal le-Or ha-Halakhah,* a work devoted exclusively to the halakhic implications of electricity, the author, Rabbi S. A. Yudelevitz, also endorses this position. On the other hand, Rabbi Elazar Lev, *Pekudat El'azar, Oraḥ Ḥayyim,* nos. 22–23, Rabbi Ben-Zion Uziel, *Mishpetei Uziel,* I, *Oraḥ Ḥayyim,* no. 7, and, as we shall see, Rabbi Zevi Pesach Frank all ruled that incandescent bulbs cannot be used in fulfilling the *miẓvah* of kindling Sabbath lights. None of the aforementioned authorities sanctions the use of electric bulbs as Chanukkah lights.

A renewed discussion of this topic is to be found in two contemporary Israeli periodicals. The Tevet 5732 edition of *Ha-Ma'ayan* features a responsum on this theme by Rabbi Zevi Pesach Frank, the late Chief Rabbi of Jerusalem. A section of another paper on the same topic, authored by Rabbi Mordecai L. Katzenellenbogen, appears in the Cheshvan–Kislev 5732 issue of *Moriah*. Every practicing rabbi can attest to the frequency with which this question is posed and the interest it evokes. Although definitive answers to some aspects of the problem remain clouded by controversy, the complex nature of the considerations involved requires elucidation and merits a somewhat fuller discussion.

1. *Chanukkah Menorah*

The halakhic principle governing the lighting of the Chanukkah lamp is the dictum, "Kindling constitutes performance of the *mizvah.*" For this reason, the lights, once properly kindled, need not be relit should they become extinguished. But, on the other hand, if the lamp, at the time of kindling, contains an insufficient quantity of fuel, additional fuel should not be added; rather the lamp must be extinguished and relit. On the basis of this principle, Rabbi Frank peremptorily dismisses consideration of the halakhic feasibility of an electric Chanukkah *menorah*. Electric current is not stored for future use but is consumed as it is generated. Thus the requisite amount of "fuel" is not immediately available at the moment the lamp is turned on. The lamp is dependent upon continuous generation of power to remain lit. Hence the act of kindling in itself is insufficient to cause the lamp to burn for the prescribed period of time. An identical line of argument is advanced by Rabbi Shlomoh Zalman Auerbach in the third chapter of his *Me'orei Esh,* a classic monograph on the halakhic ramifications of electricity.

Elsewhere in his published responsa, *Har Zevi, Orah Hayyim,* no. 143, Rabbi Frank raises yet another objection. He questions whether the turning on of an electric switch constitutes an act of kindling. He expresses doubt as to whether this is to be deemed a direct action or an "indirect action" (*gerama*) and enters into a further discussion of whether a direct action is indeed required or whether an "indirect action" is sufficient with regard to the fulfillment of *mizvot*. This point is also discussed by Rabbi Eliezer Waldenberg, *Ziz Eli'ezer,* I, no. 20, chap. 12, and is the subject of one section of Rabbi Katzenellenbogen's paper in *Moriah*.

Objections to the use of electric bulbs in place of the Chanukkah *menorah* have been advanced by other authorities on the basis of different considerations. Rabbi Yitzchak Schmelkes mantained that since electricity is in common use throughout the year, the use of electric lights on Chanukkah does not constitute "publicizing the miracle." Rabbi Eliyahu Klatzkin, *Dvar Halakhah,* no. 36, and Rabbi Henkin both assert that the Chanukkah *menorah,* since it is modeled upon the candelabrum used in the Temple, must contain fuel and a wick. Electric bulbs do not incorporate these features and hence, in their opinion, cannot be used as Chanukkah lights. Both Rabbi Waldenberg and Rabbi Katzenellenbogen disagree and present evidence supporting their contention that neither wick nor fuel is essential for fulfillment of this obligation.[1] Rabbi Waldenberg nevertheless expresses doubt with regard to the utilization of electric bulbs for this purpose on the basis of a consideration which will be examined in the following section. While there is some disagreement with regard to the specific grounds for its disqualification, none of the above authorities approves the use of an electric Chanukkah *menorah* for fulfillment of the *mizvah.*

2. *Sabbath Lights*

The factors involved in determining the suitability of electric bulbs for use as a substitute for the customary Sabbath candles are more complex. *Magen Avraham, Oraḥ Ḥayyim* 263:11, rules that a woman who reminds herself after sunset that she has not as yet kindled the Sabbath lights should request a non-Jew to perform this service on her behalf but should pronounce the blessing herself. Subsequent commentators question *Magen Avraham*'s rationale in directing that the mistress of the house pronounce the blessing. There is a fundamental halakhic principle that a non-Jew, who is himself exempt from such duties, cannot serve as a proxy in the performance of ritual obligations. If, then, the obligation is not fulfilled through the agency of a non-Jew, why is the woman in question instructed to pronounce the blessing? The explanation is that, in contradistinction to the *mizvah* of kindling the Chanukkah lamp, the precept concerning Sabbath lights is fulfilled, not in the act of kindling, but in the subsequent benefit derived from the illumination. According to Rabbi Frank, if this were the sole consideration, electric bulbs would be eminently suitable for use as Sabbath lights because the "benefit" derived from their illumination is at least equal, if not superior, to that derived from candles. Rabbi Yudelevitz, *Ha-Ḥashmal le-Or ha-Halakhah,* no. 3, chap. 6, concurs in this analysis. Rabbi Katzenellenbogen disputes the basic premise and asserts that the act

1. See also *Bet Yizḥak, Yoreh De'ah,* II, no. 131.

of kindling constitutes the essence of the *miẓvah* with regard to Sabbath lights just as is the case with regard to the Chanukkah *menorah.* This position has previously been held by *Mishneh Berurah* 675:1. In disagreeing with *Mishneh Berurah* on this point, Rabbi Waldenberg demonstrates that early authorities viewed the principle "Kindling constitutes the performance of the *miẓvah*" as having been formulated solely with regard to the Chanukkah lamp. Rabbi Uziel endeavors to show that the applicability of this principle to the *Shabbat* lights has long been the subject of dispute. According to his analysis, Rambam maintains that no direct act of kindling is required while Rabbenu Tam and *Tur* maintain that such an act is essential with regard to this *miẓvah.*

Rabbi Frank finds electric bulbs unacceptable on other grounds. He argues that an electric bulb is not the type of "lamp" designated by the Hebrew term *ner.* A *ner,* by definition, claims Rabbi Frank, implies the presence of a flame. The source of illumination in an electric bulb is a heated filament; there is neither fuel nor a burning flame within the glass bulb. Since the halakhic requirement stipulates lighting of a *ner* in honor of the Sabbath, Rabbi Frank concludes that a glowing filament may not be substituted.[2] A similar point is raised by Rabbi Klatzkin, who observes that the term *ner* connotes a lamp containing both fuel and wick. Rabbi Klatzkin does not assert that the absence of fuel or wick invalidates fulfillment of the *miẓvah* but advises that it is preferable not to use electricity wherever the Sages specify use of a *ner.* Parenthetically, Rabbi Klatzkin is the one authority who also discusses the use of an electric lamp as a *yahrẓeit* light. In this case as well, he advises against the use of electricity for the identical reason.[3]

A somewhat far-fetched argument against the use of electricity for Sabbath lights was advanced by Rabbi Uziel. Doubtless this line of thought was prompted by the rather frequent power failures to which the inhabitants of the early *Yishuv* were accustomed. The Mishnah, *Shabbat* 24b, records R. Yishmael's pronouncement that *itran* (a type of resin) may not be used as fuel for the Sabbath lamp. The Gemara explains that since this fuel is foul-smelling, there is a distinct possibility that the householders may abandon their residence in order to escape the odor. The resultant state of affairs is, of course, the opposite of the "Sabbath delight" which the Sages

2. A similar view attributed to R. Yosef Rosen of Dvinsk is recorded by Rabbi Frank in his *Mikra'ei Kodesh,* I (Jerusalem, 5735), p. 47.

3. See also R. Yekutiel Yehudah Greenwald, *Kol Bo al Aveilut,* p. 397, n. 30; and R. Menasheh Klein, *Mishneh Halakhot,* V, no. 70.

sought to promote by promulgating a decree requiring the kindling of a Sabbath lamp. Rabbi Uziel argues that since there is a strong likelihood that power failure will occur as a result of mechanical malfunction, electricity cannot be used for the Sabbath lamp. The inconvenience and discomfort resulting from a power failure is antithetical to the "Sabbath delight" which the Sabbath light is designed to provide. Rabbi Waldenberg dismisses the analogy between resin and electricity as drawn by Rabbi Uziel. According to Rabbi Waldenberg, the Sages forbade the use of *itran* because when this substance is used as fuel, it is the lamp itself which causes discomfort. Electricity, on the contrary, carries with it no inherent inconvenience as long as it provides light. Rabbi Yudelevitz, more cogently, compares the situation to the lighting of candles in a windy place, a practice which is forbidden by *Oraḥ Ḥayyim* 673:2 because of the likelihood that the candles may be extinguished. Switching on an electric light, which may well become extinguished because of power failure, argues Rabbi Yudelevitz, is akin to lighting a lamp in a windy place. Obviously, this consideration is germane only under conditions in which uninterrupted electric power is not to be assumed as a matter of course.

Yet another objection to the use of electricity in kindling both Sabbath and Chanukkah lights is raised by Rabbi Waldenberg. The filament used in incandescent bulbs is constructed in the shape of an arc. Rabbi Waldenberg suggests that the arc-shaped filament has the halakhic status of a *medurah* ("blaze of fire") and thus does not fulfill the requirement for a *ner*. In opposing this contention, Rabbi Yudelevitz maintains that the definitive characteristic of a *medurah* is a large flame, whereas the filament in a light bulb produces no flame whatsoever. Furthermore, argues Rabbi Yudelevitz, even granting that the filament is a *medurah,* it is not therefore rendered unsuitable for use as a Sabbath light. A *medurah* was excluded by the Sages from use as a Chanukkah *menorah* solely because the latter serves as a commemoration of the candelabrum kindled in the Temple. The Sabbath lights are designed for illumination alone and therefore the enhanced illumination provided by the *medurah,* concludes Rabbi Yudelevitz, augurs in favor of its use for this purpose.[4]

Even those authorities who permit the use of electric bulbs as Sabbath lights do not necessarily sanction the use of neon lights or fluorescent bulbs. Rabbi Yudelevitz notes that the latter are significantly different from incandescent bulbs in that their light is produced by means of the activation

---

4. See also R. Meir Blumenfeld, *Peraḥ Shoshanah,* no. 54.

of a gas or fluorescent coating rather than through heating a filament or bulb. Consequently, neon and fluorescent lights provide a "cold light," remaining cold to the touch even when lit. The rabbinic edict calls for a *ner,* which implies a light which is produced by fire and generates heat. Accordingly, Rabbi Yudelevitz rules that neon (and fluorescent) bulbs are not acceptable for this purpose.[5]

3. *Havdalah Flame*

The suitability of an electric bulb for use in conjunction with the *havdalah* service marking the conclusion of the Sabbath is also a matter of dispute. Rabbi Yudelevitz recounts that the renowned R. Chaim Ozer Grodzinski of Vilna was wont to pronounce this blessing upon an electric light.[6] Moreover, R. Chaim Ozer is said to have preferred to use electricity for this purpose in order to indicate dramatically that one may not use electricity on *Shabbat.* By utilizing an electric light as an integral part of the *havdalah* ceremony he sought to emphasize that the use of electricity was forbidden throughout the Sabbath day.

Rabbi Frank, however, declares that electric lights cannot be used for this purpose. Employing the same line of reasoning cited earlier, he argues that a heated filament is not a fire. Accordingly, he rules that the blessing rendering praise to the "Creator of lights of fire" cannot be pronounced over an electric bulb.

Rabbi Auerbach advances two other reasons militating against the use of an electric light in the *havdalah* ceremony. According to tradition, upon the conclusion of the first Sabbath Adam struck two stones one against the other and, for the first time, man enjoyed the benefits of fire. The blessing over fire is included in the *havdalah* service as an expression of thanksgiving for the gift of fire bestowed upon man at the close of the first Sabbath. In view of the commemorative aspect of this blessing, many authorities rule that it may be recited only upon a flame and not, for example,

5. For additional sources discussing the use of electricity for Sabbath lights see R. Zevi Pesach Frank, *Har Ẓvi, Oraḥ Ḥayyim,* I, no. 143; *Ha-Ma'ayan,* Tevet 5732; and *Moriah,* Cheshvan-Kislev 5732; R. Ovadiah Yosef, *Yabi'a Omer,* II, no. 17; R. Binyamin Silber, *Oz Nidberu,* III, nos. 1–2 and VI, no. 68; R. Menasheh Klein, *Mishneh Halakhot,* V, no. 41; R. Shmuel Singer, *Ha-Ma'or,* Elul 5733; R. Raphael Soloveitchik cited in *Ha-Pardes,* Nisan 5735, p. 9; R. Abraham Schlesinger, *Ha-Ma'or,* Kislev-Tevet 5735; and R. Aaron Zlotowitz, *Ha-Pardes,* Tammuz 5736.

6. A similar view is attributed by Rabbi Frank to R. Yosef Rosen of Dvinsk. See *Mikra'ei Kodesh,* I, 47.

upon glowing coals. The heated filament, Rabbi Auerbach argues, is comparable to a glowing coal and hence cannot be used for this purpose. Secondly, *Mishneh Berurah, Bi'ur Halakhah* 298, rules that, since the fire produced by Adam was an uncovered flame, the blessing cannot be recited upon a flame which is covered by a glass. Accordingly, an electric bulb cannot be used because the filament is encased within a glass, Both Rabbi Yudelevitz and Rabbi Waldenberg dispute this finding. Rabbi Waldenberg cites a variant version of this narrative as recorded in *Midrash Shoḥar Tov,* Psalms 92, which relates that Adam recited the blessing over a fire that had descended from heaven for his benefit. The identical version is found in *Pirkei de-Rabbi Eli'ezer* and is followed by a statement to the effect that the blessing may be pronounced upon the light cast by stars. Rabbi Waldenberg maintains that the authorities who do not sanction the use of glowing coals and glass-covered flames for the blessing in conjunction with the *havdalah* service do not base their ruling upon the midrashic narrative. Rather, he claims, their decision is based upon the contention that such illumination is inferior to that provided by an open flame, However, light emanating from an electric bulb is at least equal, if not superior, to that of burning candles. Rabbi Waldenberg permits the use of an electric light in conjunction with the *havdalah* ceremony when no other flames are available but, on the basis of *Oraḥ Ḥayyim* 298:2, advises that a special lamp be used rather than one ordinarily employed for illumination.

The Microphone Controversy

A recent halakhic dispute involving a ruling issued by an Israeli Chief Rabbi to a South African Jewish community and subsequently challenged by other authorities in Israel, the United States and Great Britain was amplified by the press and developed into a controversy whose echoes quickly reverberated around the globe. Unfortunately, the extended press coverage of the more dramatic aspects of this issue generated more heat than light. In reality the matter is one of significant practical concern to many rabbis and their congregations and merits detailed examination.

Over the years, rabbis and cantors serving synagogues having large seating capacities have experienced difficulties in making themselves heard by worshippers, particularly since many such edifices are plagued by inordinately poor acoustical conditions. These difficulties have, over and over again, prompted halakhic investigations of the permissibility of employing microphones and other types of public-address systems on the Sabbath and

Yom Tov. The preponderance of heretofore recorded halakhic opinion has been in the negative. Some time ago, Rabbi I. Y. Unterman was queried as to whether new scientific discoveries and recent technological advances might not be employed in order to obviate the halakhic problems associated with the use of such an apparatus on the Sabbath. Rabbi Unterman in turn enlisted the aid of Dr. William Low, a professor of physics at the Hebrew University and director of the Institute for Science and Halakhah, who drew up detailed plans for a transistorized public-address system which was accepted by Rabbi Unterman as being in accordance with Halakhah. Rabbi Unterman signified his approval in an official communication dated the eighth day of Chanukkah 5730 and addressed to Rabbi B. M. Casper, Chief Rabbi of the Federation of Synagogues of South Africa. In this letter, which unfortunately does not include the halakhic reasoning upon which his decision is predicated, Rabbi Unterman stresses that his approval is limited to devices constructed in strict accordance with the detailed plans of Professor Low. In an *obiter dictum* Rabbi Unterman declines to sanction the use of amplifying devices in Israeli synagogues because of his concern lest scrupulous attention not be paid to the construction of such microphones in meticulous conformity to all the details of the blueprints prepared by Professor Low. A report on the discussions between himself and Rabbi Unterman as well as a non-technical description of the Low system was published by Rabbi Casper in the July 1970 issue of the *Federation Chronicle*. A description of the proposed system appears in a pamphlet published by the Institute for Science and Halakhah entitled *Shimmush be-Mikrofon be-Shabbat,* dated Tammuz 5729. The writer is indebted to Rabbi Casper for making available to him additional information regarding the nature of the system. The following are the salient features of the system devised by Professor Low:

1. The microphone and public address system must be completely transistorized. There must be neither electron tubes nor electric pilot lights in the system. The device should contain no metal or other material which may become heated in the course of amplification.
2. The microphone must be of the condenser or capacitor type. In utilization of the condenser type microphone the voice does not create energy, as is the case with other microphones, but merely manipulates the energy already stored in it.
3. The system must be operated by batteries and not be connected to any other electricity supply.
4. The batteries should be charged before the onset of *Shabbat* or *Yom*

Tov and should hold at least twice the amount of current required for use during the *Shabbat* or *Yom Tov* period.

5. The transistorized system should remain open during the entire *Shabbat* or *Yom Tov* period or be switched on and off automatically by means of a time clock.
6. There must be no possibility of increasing or decreasing the volume of amplification on *Shabbat* or *Yom Tov*. Accordingly, the storage batteries and other equipment must be enclosed in a locked case or closet in order to preclude the possibility of any person adjusting or otherwise tampering with the system on *Shabbat* or *Yom Tov*.

These provisions are designed to eliminate various infractions of the laws concerning forbidden acts on *Shabbat* and *Yom Tov* and, accordingly, Rabbi Unterman stresses that *any* deviation from the details of the Low system will result in the violation of halakhic restrictions. Rabbi Casper reports that some authorities have expressed objections on the grounds that obvious and readily discernible amplification may lead individuals to draw erroneous inferences regarding the use of electricity on *Shabbat*. Because of ignorance of the technical nature of the amplification system in use, some individuals may assume that ordinary use of electrical devices and appliances is permissible. Accordingly, the system, as designed by Professor Low, provides for several loudspeakers to be installed throughout the synagogue in order to reproduce a voice which is not unduly loud and is as natural in tone as possible. Furthermore, it is directed that steps be taken to inform congregants that the system does not function through utilization of the usual sources of electrical current and that the special arrangements are under rabbinic supervision.

Despite the innovations introduced by Professor Low in devising his system, many rabbinic authorities took sharp issue with the permissive ruling issued by Rabbi Unterman in approving this device. A negative ruling dated 27 Elul, 5730 was issued and signed by Rabbi Moses Feinstein in his capacity as president of the *Agudat ha-Rabbanim*. This ruling specifically bans the use of transistorized systems as constituting desecration of *Shabbat and Yom Tov*.[7] It is interesting to note that while Rabbi Unterman relies upon technical information supplied by the Institute for Science and Halakhah, the Institute itself issued a contrary opinion with regard to the use of transistorized systems. The conclusions of the Institute were published in the previously cited pamphlet, which may presumably be re-

7. Cf. R. Eliezer Waldenberg, *Ẓiẓ Eli'ezer*, IX, no. 21.

garded as an expression of the collective view of the Fellows of the Institute since the pamphlet does not bear the name of an individual author or authors.

Moreover, in recent communications addressed to individuals and synagogues seeking his guidance, Rabbi Unterman himself has narrowly circumscribed the scope of his original ruling. In a letter dated 21 Iyar, 5731, a copy of which is in the possession of this writer, Rabbi Unterman declares that he had granted permission for the use of the system devised by Professor Low "only in communities where, to our regret, desecration of the Sabbath through [use of] the electrical microphone became so deeply rooted that it was as if they had completely forgotten that turning on electricity is a serious form of 'labor' on the Sabbath. But in a place where this did not previously exist we did not permit the installation of the improved [apparatus] because there are questions with regard to it which cannot be resolved."

The apparatus designed by Professor Low successfully eliminates questions of forbidden "labor" arising from sparking, heating of metal elements, creation of a finished utensil and "giving birth" to newly created electric current (*molid*). The controversy centers around various other considerations: [8]

1. The playing of musical instruments (*mashmi'a kol*—"causing a sound to be heard") on *Shabbat* or *Yom Tov* is rabbinically forbidden, lest one be tempted to repair the instrument and thereby transgress a biblical prohibition. Rema (*Oraḥ Ḥayyim* 338:1) declares that causing the emission of any sound by a utensil designed for this purpose falls within this category and is forbidden. Consistent with his view that this edict is not limited to musical instruments, Rema declares that the use of door-knockers is forbidden on *Shabbat*. Similarly, it is argued, a microphone constitutes a device specifically designed for the production of sound. Microphones do

8. Various aspects of the halakhic questions pertaining to the use of the microphone are discussed by R. Ovadiah Hadaya, *Yaskil Avdi,* no. 29; R. Zevi Pesach Frank, *Har Ẓvi, Oraḥ Ḥayyim,* I, no. 183; R. Meshullam Roth, *Kol Mevaser,* II, no. 25; R. Moses Feinstein, *Iggrot Mosheh, Yoreh De'ah,* II, no. 5, and *Oraḥ Ḥayyim,* III, no. 55; *Peraḥ Shoshanah,* no. 58; R. Yitzchak Ya'akov Weisz, *Minḥat Yiẓḥak,* I, no. 107, and III, no. 38; R. Shmuel Hubner, *Ha–Darom,* Elul 5721; R. Shmuel Rubinstein, *Torah She-be-'al Peh,* IX (5727); and R. Chaim Regensberg, *Ha-Darom,* Nisan 5734. The permissive view of R. Simchah Levy, former chairman of the Halakhah Commission of the Rabbinical Council of America, is recorded in *Ha-Pardes,* Iyar 5712 and in his *Simḥat ha-Levi,* no. 26.

not simply amplify an already existing human voice; rather, through the use of a transducer, the human voice utilizes electric current which in turn creates audio-tones resembling the human voice but higher in volume. The perceived sound is not that of the human voice but a totally different sound produced by electric current. Rabbi Yitzchak Schmelkes (*Bet Yiẓḥak, Yoreh De'ah,* II, *Maftehot,* no. 31) declares that the act of speaking on a telephone is forbidden on *Shabbat* because the electric current creates a new sound. Some writers (Rabbi Joseph Tumim, *Ha-Pardes* Sivan 5705, and Rabbi Menachem Poliakov, *Ha-Darom,* Nisan 5718) dismiss these arguments on the erroneous assumption that a microphone merely amplifies the human voice, whereas, in reality, the microphone, through the intermediary of electric current, converts the voice into a totally new sound. Even if the microphone were designed merely to amplify the human voice it is not entirely clear that the use of such a device would be permissible. Rabbi Samuel Hubner (*Ha-Darom,* Nisan 5719) accepts the premise that in electronic amplification it is the human voice which is heard but nevertheless argues that in the eyes of Halakhah the amplification of an existing sound constitutes the creation of a new "voice." The prohibition against "causing a sound to be heard," which applies to transistor microphones no less than to conventional amplification systems, is sufficient reason in and of itself for disallowing the use of microphones on *Shabbat* and *Yom Tov.* Numerous halakhic authorities cite this explanation in ruling against the use of microphones.[9] There is, however, no explicit discussion by any of these authorities with regard to the question of whether or not the rabbinic injunction against "causing a sound to be heard" is a blanket prohibition encompassing instruments and utensils which are so designed that they cannot readily be adjusted or repaired on the Sabbath.

The ban against the use of microphones, if predicated upon the prohibition against "causing a sound to be heard," may apply not only to speaking or singing into a microphone but also to listening to such amplified voices. According to some authorities, the prohibition against use of musical instruments applies not merely to those producing the music but also to those listening to it. R. Yechiel Michal Epstein (*Arukh ha-Shul-*

9. See R. Yosef Rosen, *Ẓofnat Pa'aneaḥ,* II, no. 19; R. Yosef Eliyahu Henkin, *Edut le-Yisra'el,* p. 122; R. Eliezer Waldenberg, *Ẓiẓ Eli'ezer,* IV, no. 26; R. Ben-Zion Uziel, *Mishpetei Uziel,* I, *Oraḥ Ḥayyim,* no. 13; *Minḥat Yiẓḥak,* III, no. 38; R. Yitzchak Glick, *Yad Yiẓḥak,* III, no. 268; R. Shlomoh Zalman Braun, *Sha'arim ha-Meẓuyanim be-Halakhah,* II, 80:78; and R. Yissachar Dov Bergman, *Ha-Pardes,* Kislev 5712.

ḥan 378:5) rules that it is forbidden to allow a radio to remain playing during the Sabbath or to have it turned on and off by means of an automatic clock.[10] According to *Arukh ha-Shulḥan,* the prohibition against playing musical instruments encompasses situations in which the "voice" is emitted automatically "for since the prohibition is [based upon the fear] that perchance he will repair the musical instrument, what difference is there if it plays through human action or of its own accord?" In either event there remains a possibility that a malfunctioning instrument may be repaired.

There are, however, other authorities who clearly maintain that the edict forbidding the creation of sound does not apply to the approximation of the human voice by means of electric current. Rabbi Judah Leib Zirelson (*Aẓei Levanon,* no. 10), in a responsum dealing with the permissibility of the use of the telephone on the Sabbath, lists a number of reasons prohibiting the use of this device. Enumerated among these are "giving birth" to an electric circuit, sparking and causing a bell to ring on the other end of the line. Since consideration is given only to the sound produced by the bell, while the question of production of the voice itself is ignored, it may be assumed that this authority did not view the voice produced by electric current as being included in the prohibition against "causing a sound to be heard." Similarly, Rabbi Shlomoh Zalman Auerbach (*Sinai,* Adar II 5723) maintains that the prohibition against creating a "voice" or sound is limited to sounds produced by direct human action and does not include sounds indirectly produced by the human voice. A similar position is adopted by *Teshuvot Maharshag,* II, no. 118, and *Ẓlaḥ he-Ḥadash, Kuntres Aḥaron,* no. 1.[11]

2. Rabbi Auerbach, however, forbids the use of a microphone on other grounds. R. Yechezkel Landau (*Noḍa bi-Yehudah,* II, *Oraḥ Ḥayyim,* no. 30) writes that a parasol opened before the Sabbath may not be used on the Sabbath because the beholder has no way of knowing that the parasol has not been opened on the Sabbath. Rabbi Auerbach argues that the same line of reasoning may be applied to the use of amplification systems since most individuals are not scholars and will not understand the technical differences between a microphone and other electrical appliances and hence may easily be led to biblical transgressions.

---

10. R. Waldenberg, *Ẓiẓ Eli'ezer,* III, no. 16, chap. 12, and IX, no. 21, also forbids listening to a radio on *Shabbat* for this reason.

11. See also R. Simchah Levy, *Ha-Pardes,* Iyar 5712; R. Menachem Poliakov, *Ha-Darom,* Nisan 5718; and R. Shlomoh Goren, *Maḥanayim,* 26 Iyar 5718.

3. Rabbi Joseph Tumim (*Ha-Pardes, Sivan* 5705 and Sivan 5706) presents the interesting argument that microphones may not be used in conjunction with prayer because the microphone constitutes a "musical instrument" and as such its use is forbidden, just as, for example, the use of an organ is forbidden in conjunction with prayer.

4. There is yet another reason cited by numerous authorities in forbidding the use of a microphone on *Shabbat* and *Yom Tov*. Rema (*Oraḥ Ḥayyim* 252:5) states that it is forbidden to place wheat in a water mill prior to the Sabbath in order that the wheat may be ground during the Sabbath. This is forbidden even though it is publicly known that the grain was placed therein prior to the Sabbath and that the grinding of the wheat takes place automatically. This activity is rabbinically forbidden despite the absence of human labor because *avsha milta* ("the thing grows loud"). The accompanying noise draws attention to the activity taking place, thereby degrading the Sabbath since passersby may believe that the sounds emanating from the mill signal the performance of acts forbidden on the Sabbath. The prohibition of *avsha milta* is limited to activities accompanied by sound but encompasses all activities forbidden on *Shabbat* when accompanied by sound even if performed automatically. Rabbi Auerbach cites authorities who forbid a radio to be turned on before *Shabbat* or to be regulated by means of a time clock for the same reason. Thus, Rabbi Auerbach argues, even if it be publicized that the radio or microphone is operated automatically, such devices may not be permitted to operate on *Shabbat*.[12] This consideration applies to all amplification systems, even to those which cannot possibly be adjusted or repaired on the Sabbath.

The preceding has been limited simply to the question of the permissibility of the use of microphones on Sabbath and Holy Days without consideration of the uses to which the microphone might be put. The overwhelming majority of halakhic authorities rule that a microphone cannot be used for the fulfillment of such *mizvot* as blowing the *shofar,* reading the Torah, reading the Megillah, etc., since the sound heard is an artificial one rather than the requisite sound of the *shofar* or human voice.[13]

The microphone question is indeed a highly technical matter and it is

---

12. Other authorities who cite this reason in ruling against the use of microphones include R. Ovadiah Yosef, *Yabi'a Omer,* I, no. 20, sec. 12; *Ẓiẓ Eli'ezer,* IV, no. 26; *Minḥat Yiẓḥak,* II, no. 38; and R. Yissachar Dov Bergman, *Ha-Pardes,* Kislev 5712.

13. Cf., however, *Ẓiẓ Eli'ezer,* VIII, no. 11; and *Iggrot Mosheh, Oraḥ Ḥayyim,* II, no. 108.

most unfortunate that the publicity surrounding this controversy tended to obfuscate the issues. The implication that negative rulings on such matters stem from a reactionary stance and that Orthodox rabbis are stubbornly opposed to all innovation is a lamentable distortion. In actuality, Judaism steadfastly refuses to sacrifice religious observance for the sake of convenience but is happy to welcome any scientific advance which satisfies the requirements of Halakhah.

CHAPTER XI

Daylight Saving Time and Morning Prayer

There is no nation in the world like unto them. . . . They arise from their sleep as lions and make haste to recite the shema and proclaim the kingship of the Holy One, blessed be He . . . [only then] do they embark upon [their] affairs and business pursuits.

BEMIDBAR RABBAH XX, 19

Prior to the energy crisis of the winter of 1973–74, perennial proposals for the adoption of year-round daylight saving time were successfully opposed by Jewish groups motivated by concern for their constituents' need to recite morning prayers at the time prescribed by Jewish law. The adoption of daylight saving time as an emergency conservation measure brought with it considerable inconvenience for observant Jews. Under year-round daylight saving time, sunrise occurs as late as 8:20 in New York City for a period of several weeks and occurs even later in some major Jewish population centers such as Miami Beach. Since, normally, *shemoneh esreh* is not recited until after sunrise, the implementation of daylight saving time poses problems for persons who must be at their offices or places of employment at an early hour.

Of course, the problems which arise with regard to determining the earliest permissible time for morning prayers may be obviated by advising individuals who must leave their homes at an early hour to pray at downtown synagogues, to organize *minyanim* near their places of work or to pray without benefit of a *minyan*. However, many rabbis are quite correctly concerned lest the adoption of such a policy have a negative effect upon the spiritual welfare of the community at large. At stake is not only the survival of the daily *minyan* in suburban areas but also participation in prayer by countless numbers of Jews. The observant Jew committed to the halakhic discipline will be meticulous in the recitation of prayer under all conditions, no matter how trying. However, many a less committed worshipper may cease to pray entirely unless a *minyan* is readily accessible. The marginal worshipper who attends synagogue in order to recite *kaddish,* or only on special occasions, will find that even these tenuous links with Jewish observance are severed. It is little wonder, then, that leading rabbinic authorities have devoted much time and effort to delineating the procedures to be followed so that the maximum possible number of people be enabled to pray with a *minyan* each morning,

The halakhic problems attendant upon the recitation of prayers at an early hour are by no means new. Although sources and precedents are readily available, and perhaps precisely because of the accessibility of this material, a comprehensive treatment of the question does not appear in responsa literature until comparatively recent times. It is interesting to note that a large number of the previously published responsa dealing with this question are addressed to a single interlocutor who was prompted by varied circumstances to raise the question on different occasions. Under the collectivization programs fostered by the Communist regime, citizens of the Soviet Union were assigned specific jobs and forced to accept government-dictated conditions of employment upon pain of imprisonment. The hours of work were long and often spanned the entire daylight period. Workers were not permitted to engage in prayer, nor were they afforded leisure to don *talit* and *tefillin* during the working hours. In 1941, Rabbi Samuel Meir Hollander of Tzernovitz sought the advice of Rabbi Aaron Walkin with regard to how such individuals should be guided. The response appears as a foreword preceding the preface to the first volume of Rabbi Walkin's responsa collection, *Zekan Aharon.* Some ten years later, Rabbi Hollander, then living in Israel, found that the work schedule in certain areas, presumably dictated by reasons of climate, presented similar problems with regard to morning prayers. Thereupon, Rabbi Hollander again submitted queries to the Slutzker Rav, the late Rabbi Zalman Sorotzkin, and to the Chief Rabbinate of Israel. Rabbi Sorotzkin's reply appears in his *Moznayim la-Mishpat,* no. 3, while the responses of various members of the Israeli rabbinate, as well as his own reply, were published by Rabbi Kasriel Tchursh in his *Keter Efrayim,* no. 21. Additional brief items dealing with this topic were collected by Rabbi Chananyah Yom Tov

Deutsch and published in his *Taharat Yom Tov,* VII, 85–96.[1] The implementation of daylight saving time on a year-round basis in 1974 occasioned an article by Rabbi Moses Feinstein which appears in the third of a series of publications entitled *Le-Torah ve-Hora'ah* (Winter 5734), published by Rabbi Feinstein's *Bet Medrash le-Torah ve-Hora'ah.* In addition, two mimeographed pamphlets recently appeared which are designed to serve as practical guides for meeting these problems. These brochures also contain tables giving the proper time for donning the *talit,* recitation of *shema* and *shemoneh esreh,* etc., for each day of the year. The first of these pamphlets was authored by Rabbi Aryeh Katz of Mesivta Torah Vodaath; the second, by Rabbi Mordecai Willig, is a publication of the Student Organization of Yeshiva University.

1. *Shemoneh Esreh*

Shulḥan Arukh, Oraḥ Ḥayyim 89:1, declares that, under ordinary circumstances, *shemoneh esreh* should not be recited prior to sunrise, but adds that if the morning prayer is recited any time after "the face of the East is illuminated"—*he'ir pnei ha-mizraḥ*—the obligation with regard to morning prayer is discharged thereby and the prayer need not be repeated at a later hour. Some authorities (including *Eliyahu Rabbah, Matteh Yehudah, Shenot Eliyahu* of R. Elijah of Vilna and *Derekh ha-Ḥayyim*) maintain that under no circumstances may *shemoneh esreh* be recited at an earlier hour. Other authorities (including *Magen Avraham, Pri Ḥadash,* and *Pri Megadim*) disagree and maintain that in cases of necessity morning prayers may be recited as early as *alot ha-shaḥar*—"the crack of dawn."[2]

The determination of the phenomenon constituting *alot ha-shaḥar* and the precise time at which it occurs is a matter of considerable dispute. It is accepted that *alot ha-shaḥar* precedes sunrise by a period of time equivalent to the length of time it would take an average person to walk a distance of four *mil.* There is, however, some disagreement with regard to how long a period of time is necessary in order to traverse a distance of four *mil* by foot. Some authorities maintain that the period of time required to travel a single *mil* is 24 minutes (Rambam and Bertinoro in their respective commentaries on the Mishnah, *Pesaḥim* 3:2; *Pri Ḥadash, Kuntres de-Bei Shimsha; Shulḥan Arukh ha-Rav, Oraḥ Ḥayyim* 459:10). Others

1. Cf. also R. Yekutiel Yehudah Greenwald, *Oẓar Neḥmad,* pp. 14–21.
2. For a definition of *alot ha-shaḥar,* see *Bi'ur Halakhah, Oraḥ Ḥayyim* 89:1, and cf. *Bi'ur Halakhah, Oraḥ Ḥayim* 58:4; see also *Oẓar Neḥmad,* pp. 14f.

maintain that the period of time defined as a *shi'ur mil* is 22.5 minutes (*Ḥok Ya'akov, Oraḥ Ḥayyim* 459:10; *Bi'ur ha-Gra* and *Bi'ur Halakhah, Oraḥ Ḥayyim* 459:2; *Teshuvot Ḥatam Sofer, Oraḥ Ḥayyim,* no. 80). Yet others maintain that this period is only 18 minutes in length (*Terumat ha-Deshen,* no. 167; *Shulḥan Arukh, Oraḥ Ḥayyim* 459:2 and *Yoreh De'ah* 69:6; Rema, *Yoreh De'ah* 261:1). The time of *alot ha-shaḥar,* which is reckoned as preceding sunrise by the length of time necessary to walk a distance of four *mil,* would thus occur, according to these respective opinions, 96 minutes, 90 minutes, or 72 minutes prior to sunrise. Contemporary practice, at least for purposes of stringency (*le-ḥumra*), is based on the calculation of the *shi'ur mil* as 18 minutes. [There is general agreement that *alot ha-shaḥar* occurs at a time equivalent to the *shi'ur* of four *mil* prior to sunrise. There should be no confusion between the determination of *alot ha-shaḥar* and *ẓet ha-kokhavim*—night as heralded by the appearance of stars. The exact time of *ẓet ha-kokhavim* is the subject of a celebrated controversy between Rabbenu Tam and the Ge'onim. Rabbenu Tam maintains that *ẓet ha-kokhavim* occurs at a time equivalent to the *shi'ur* of four *mil* following sunset, while the Ge'onim maintain that this phenomenon occurs at a time equivalent to the *shi'ur* of three-fourths of a *mil* after sunset.]

A further complication is introduced by yet another controversy. There is a dispute as to whether the period of four *mil* is standard in the sense that *alot ha-shaḥar* is universally deemed to occur a given number of minutes before sunrise, regardless of the locale or the season of the year, or whether the precise determination varies according to seasonal astronomical conditions. According to the latter view, the time span of four *mil,* which is given as the means of determining the moment of *alot ha-shaḥar,* applies only when the day and night are equal in length; the exact moment of *alot ha-shaḥar* fluctuates in accordance with the season and is closer to sunrise during the winter period, when the period of daylight is shorter, and earlier in the summer, when the daylight hours are longer. Accordingly, 72 minutes is not a fixed time span for the determination of *alot ha-shaḥar,* but should be understood as the equivalent of one-tenth of the period of daylight when the day is exactly 12 hours in length (*sha'ot zemaniyot*). Accordingly, *alot ha-shaḥar* would be ascertained for other times during the year by calculating one-tenth of the time period spanned by sunrise and sunset on any given date. *Alot ha-shaḥar* occurs on that day at a time earlier to sunrise equivalent to one-tenth of the time between sunrise and sunset. [According to the authorities who reckon four *mil* as 90 minutes, the 90 minute period between *alot ha-shaḥar* and sunrise is equivalent to one-eighth of the day when the day is 12 hours in length. A corresponding fraction may be calculated for those who reckon the interval as 96 minutes.] Accordingly, it has been argued by some that *alot ha-shaḥar* occurs much less than 72 minutes prior to sunrise during the winter months when the period of daylight is relatively shorter. However, it would appear that if the *shi'ur* of four *mil* is not a fixed one, but fluctuates proportionately in accordance with the relative period of daylight, it may be assumed that the measurement is not an arbitrary one, but that the proportionate calculation reflects the thesis that the appearance of a certain level of illumination marks the beginning of the "day." Thus the number of minutes prior to sunrise at which such a degree of illumination is reached varies according to the season. However, it also follows that not only seasonal variations must be considered in calculating the moment at which such illumination occurs but that other astronomical factors must be weighed as well. It is empirically observable that the length of twilight increases in accordance with distance from the equator. Darkness falls very quickly in the tropics, whereas the period of dusk is of a much greater duration in the northern regions. At our latitude, this phenomenon has the effect of canceling any diminution of the *shi'ur* of four *mil* which might be anticipated in light of the shorter span of daylight during the winter months. This was clearly recognized by R. Elijah of Vilna who writes, ". . . in our countries it [the period of twilight] is not equal in all latitudes and at all times" (*Bi'ur ha-Gra, Oraḥ Ḥayyim* 459:2). Citing this source, *Bi'ur Halakhah, Oraḥ Ḥayyim* 261:2, writes: "For the *shi'urim* of the Gemara were set only for the latitude of Babylonia; however, in our countries extending to the north, twilight is always of greater duration."

According to calculations made a number of years ago by a group of graduate students at Beth Medrash Elyon in which this writer participated, the time of *alot ha-shaḥar* in New York City fluctuates between 80 and 111 minutes prior to sunrise. In preparing these calculations, this group was guided by information received from the United States Naval Observatory. Subsequently there appeared a comprehensive work by Professor Leo Levi, entitled *Jewish Chrononomy—Zemanei ha-Yom be-Halakhah,* in which virtually identical tabulations of the time of *alot ha-shaḥar* may be found. According to Professor Levi, the degree of illumination manifest 72 minutes before sunrise in Israel and Babylonia on the date of the equinox is reached in New York City no later than 80 minutes prior to sunrise and, on some occasions during the year, as early as 109 minutes before sunrise.

On the basis of these calculations, it follows that acceptance of the position that the four *mil* are to be measured in *sha'ot zemaniyot* does *not* lead to the conclusion that *alot ha-shaḥar* occurs even later (in the United States) than 72 minutes prior to sunrise. On the contrary, acceptance of this position yields the conclusion that *alot ha-shaḥar* occurs at a somewhat earlier hour,

Although their opinion is rejected by all codifiers of Halakhah, classical as well as modern, three early authorities do maintain that *shemoneh esreh* may be recited even before *alot ha-shaḥar*. Rashi, *Berakhot* 30a, Rabad, cited in *Sefer Hashlamah, Berakhot* 24, and Raban, no. 176, permit a person about to embark upon a journey to pray before *alot ha-shaḥar*. Curiously, however, these authorities fail to specify how much earlier one may do so. Rabbi Sorotzkin, in analyzing the rationale underlying this view, raises the obvious question that since the morning service parallels the regular morning sacrifice offered in the Temple in times of old, it would stand to reason that the time ordained for *shaḥarit* prayers should not be earlier than the earliest moment at which the morning sacrifice could be offered in the Temple. Since the *korban tamid* may not be sacrificed before the *alot ha-shaḥar,* it should follow that *shaḥarit* may also not be recited earlier than the *alot ha-shaḥar*. Rabbi Sorotzkin, in an attempt to resolve this difficulty, points out that the daily ritual in the Temple actually commenced with the *terumat ha-deshen*—the removal of the ashes which accumulated during the night as a result of the burning of the previous day's sacrifices. This took place much earlier than the offering of the morning sacrifice. Ordinarily this task was performed at the time of *keri'at ha-gever* (variously defined in *Yoma* 20b as the "crowing of the rooster" or as the "call of the man" summoning the officiants to commence the Temple rites), but on *Yom Kippur,* when the entire sacrificial order was carried out by the High Priest alone, *terumat ha-deshen* was performed at midnight. Hence, concludes Rabbi Sorotzkin, the aforementioned authorities presumably reasoned that the morning prayer may be recited as early as the hour at which the sacrificial rites of the new day began in the Temple, i.e., at midnight. Rabbi Sorotzkin cautions, however, that the opinion of these authorities may be relied upon only under conditions of emergency which render prayer later in the day an absolute impossibility. Rabbi Sorotzkin adds that, even in such situations, since the view that *shemoneh esreh* may be recited before the *alot ha-shaḥar* is rejected by all authorities other than those earlier named, the individual offering such a prayer should mentally stipulate that if the time for the obligatory morning prayer has indeed not arrived (as is the opinion of the vast majority of halakhic authorities) his prayer be accounted a "voluntary" one. Accordingly, as is the rule with regard to all "voluntary" prayers, prayer under such conditions should include a personal supplication which is not an integral part of the formal liturgy. It further follows that such prayers may be offered only privately but not publicly with a *minyan* since Halakhah makes no provision for a "voluntary" communal recitation of *shemoneh esreh.* When this procedure is followed, the reading of the *shema* should be repeated later in the day, some time after the earliest time that *keri'at shema* may properly be recited; i.e., after it has become light enough to recognize a casual friend at a distance of four cubits (see *Oraḥ Ḥayyim* 58:1 and 58:4). Rabbi Sorotzkin states emphatically that this procedure may be followed only in situations similar to those prevailing in Iron Curtain countries where the authorities will not permit prayer in places of employment. Otherwise, prayers should be recited during a break in the work schedule even if, as a result, the individual will be exposed to ridicule and derision. Despite these stringent limits upon the applicability of his ruling, Rabbi Sorotzkin stipulates that, even in cases of emergency, his ruling should not be followed in practice unless at least two other rabbinic authorities signify their assent. It may be noted that Rabbi Walkin fails to concur in this decision, and in his reply rules that under absolutely no condition may the *shemoneh esreh* be recited before *alot ha-shaḥar*.

Rabbi Sorotzkin's advice with regard to a mental stipulation to the effect that the *shemoneh esreh* be deemed a "voluntary" prayer is disputed in an opinion written by Rabbi D. Rosenthal and cited in *Keter Efrayim,* pp. 330–31. A similar course of action was rejected by *Ḥayyei Adam* at a much earlier date. Earlier authorities had suggested that a person who is in doubt as to whether or not he has recited one of the obligatory daily prayers might repeat the *shemoneh esreh* with the stipulation that, in the event that he had not prayed earlier, the present *shemoneh esreh* be deemed a fulfillment of his statutory obligation, but in the event that he had in fact already prayed and had thereby discharged his obligation, the new prayer be accounted a "voluntary" one. *Ḥayyei Adam* 27:17 rules that this position is not viable and maintains that since we, "in our day," are incapable of proper *kavanah* (concentration), one should not recite a "voluntary" *shemoneh esreh* prayer. According to *Ḥayyei Adam,* one should not offer a conditional "voluntary" *shemoneh esreh* even in cases where there is doubt with regard to whether or not one has recited the obligatory prayer.

None of the authorities cited sanctions recitation of *shaḥarit* prayers earlier than *alot ha-shaḥar* under the conditions prevailing in our country and indeed every effort should be made not to recite the *shemoneh esreh* earlier than the time of *he'ir pnei ha-mizraḥ*.

The phenomenon of *he'ir pnei ha-mizraḥ* occurs some time after *alot ha-shaḥar* but before sunrise.[3] It is, however, difficult to define the time of this occurrence with exactitude. According to *Pri Megadim,* one is able to recognize a casual acquaintance 6 minutes after *alot ha-shaḥar,* or 66 minutes prior to sunrise. *He'ir pnei ha-mizraḥ* would then presumably occur a bit earlier. *Pri Megadim*'s basic position is sharply disputed by *Bi'ur Halakhah* 58:1 but the latter fails to give a precise definition of when these phenomena occur. However, since *talit* and *tefillin* should be donned before prayer, a precise determination of the time of *he'ir pnei ha-mizraḥ* is not a matter of pressing concern. As will be demonstrated, *talit* and *tefillin* should not be donned until it is light enough to recognize a casual acquaintance at a distance of four cubits. This phenomenon occurs subsequent to the time of *he'ir pnei ha-mizraḥ*.

2. *Recitation of the Shema*

Keri'at shema should not be recited until such time as there is illumination sufficient to enable one to recognize a casual friend at a distance of four cubits (*Oraḥ Ḥayyim* 58:1). Nevertheless, in cases of necessity, the *shema* may be recited as early as *alot ha-shaḥar* (*Oraḥ Ḥayyim* 58:3–4). However, a number of authorities (*Magen Avraham, Pri Megadim,* and *Mishneh Berurah*) maintain that while this is the rule with regard to the *shema* itself, the blessing "Who creates light" (*yoẓer or*), which is normally recited prior to the *shema,* should not, under any circumstances, be pronounced until such time as there is sufficient illumination by which to recognize a casual acquaintance at a distance of four cubits. (See *Bi'ur Halakhah* 58:1 and 58:4.)

3. *Talit*

Insofar as the proper times for *keri'at shema* and *shemoneh esreh* are concerned, one could quite properly begin the morning service at an early hour and time oneself not to reach the blessing of "Who creates light" until such time as there is sufficient light to recognize a friend at the distance of four cubits, and thereafter recite the *shemoneh esreh* after "the face of the

3. Cf., however, *Bi'ur Halakhah, Oraḥ Ḥayyim* 58:4.

East has become illuminated." There is, however, another consideration, which pertains to the donning of the *talit*. Although Rema, *Oraḥ Ḥayyim* 18:3, rules that one may pronounce the blessing over *ẓiẓit* as early as the time of *alot ha-shaḥar,* R. Elijah of Vilna, in agreement with the position recorded in the *Shulḥan Arukh* itself, rules that the blessing over the *ẓiẓit* should not be recited until such time as there is sufficient light to enable a person to distinguish between blue (*tekhelet*) and white. As a practical matter, the problem with regard to the recitation of the blessing over the *ẓiẓit* can be circumvented without difficulty by donning the *talit* before beginning the morning service and later fingering the *ẓiẓit* and pronouncing the blessing after *yishtabaḥ*. In accordance with Rema, *Oraḥ Ḥayyim* 54:3, when praying with a *minyan,* the blessing should be pronounced after *yishtabaḥ* but before *kaddish.*

4. *Tefillin*

The prescribed time for donning the *tefillin* is no earlier than such time as one can recognize a casual friend at a distance of four cubits (*Oraḥ Ḥayyim* 30:1). There are varying opinions with regard to how long before sunrise this is possible. As previously noted, *Pri Megadim* maintains that this occurs 66 minutes before sunrise but this opinion is rejected by subsequent authorities. Opinions vary from as early as 60 minutes before sunrise (Rabbi Joseph Gruenwald, cited in *Taharat Yom Tov,* VII, 92) to as late as 35 minutes before sunrise (Rabbi Moses Feinstein, *Le-Torah ve-Hora'ah,* no. 3, p. 7).

It might appear that when it is necessary to begin services at an earlier hour, the same procedure might be applied with regard to *tefillin* as was earlier suggested with regard to the *talit;* i.e., that the *tefillin* be donned before the commencement of prayer and that one later finger the *tefillin* after *yishtabaḥ* and pronounce the blessing at that time. There is, however, one consideration militating against this procedure; viz., the rabbinic prohibition against donning *tefillin* during the nighttime hours lest one fall asleep while wearing the *tefillin* (*Oraḥ Ḥayyim* 30:2). An exception to this restriction is provided for an individual who embarks upon a journey at an early hour. This provision is based upon the presumption that it is unlikely that an individual will again fall asleep once he has commenced his journey. Under such circumstances, the *tefillin* may be donned but the blessing may, of course, not be recited until after the proper time. Rabbi Tchursh, as well as the Tzelemer *Rav,* Rabbi Levi Yitzchak Gruenwald, and Rabbi Yonatan Steif (both cited in *Taharat Yom Tov,* VII, 88–89),

Rabbi Yekutiel Yehudah Greenwald (*Oẓar Neḥmad,* p. 17), and Rabbi Moses Feinstein (*Iggrot Mosheh, Oraḥ Ḥayyim,* I, no. 10)[4] argue that those rising at an early hour in order to be at work at a specified time fall into the same category as a person embarking upon a journey. These writers fail to mention that many authorities, including *Magen Avraham* and *Mishneh Berurah,* maintain that the dispensation provided for those embarking upon a trip applies only to individuals who pray while walking or riding, but not to those who pray while sitting in a wagon or carriage.[5] These authorities are of the opinion that it need not be feared that the traveler will fall asleep as long as he is in an upright position, whereas if he is in a sitting position, he may become drowsy and, since it is yet night, he may well fall asleep. Hence, according to these authorities, if *tefillin* are donned at an early hour, care should be taken to pray in a standing position. Rabbi Naftali Henig, *Rav* of Sharmash (cited by *Taharat Yom Tov,* VII, 91) argues that dispensation to don *tefillin* at an early hour is granted only to a person who has actually begun his journey, but that one may not don the *tefillin* prior to the prescribed time while yet at home.

5. *Breakfast*

It is permitted to eat until the time of *alot ha-shaḥar*. However, if one wishes to eat or drink more than the equivalent of an egg, the meal must begin at least one half hour before the *alot ha-shaḥar*. The meal must be completed before the time of *alot ha-shaḥar* regardless of when it was begun or how little one wishes to eat.

6. *Conclusions*

In light of the differing opinions with regard to the precise time at which "a casual friend can be recognized at a distance of four cubits," it is preferable that *talit* and *tefillin* should not be donned prior to 35 minutes before sunrise. If necessary, prayers may begin earlier, but the donning of the *tefillin* should be delayed until after *yishtabaḥ,* by which time it should be no earlier than 35 minutes prior to sunrise. The *talit* may either be donned before the beginning of the service and the blessing delayed until after *yishtabaḥ,* or alternatively, the *talit* may be donned after *yishtabaḥ* together with the *tefillin.*

If absolutely necessary, prayer may begin at an even earlier hour but

4. Rabbi Feinstein is inclined to permit recitation of the blessing as well.
5. See, however, *Ateret Zekenim, Oraḥ Ḥayyim* 30:3, who disagrees.

the blessing over the *talit* and *tefillin* postponed until before the recitation of *ashrei* or even later, care being taken that the blessing not be recited earlier than 35 minutes prior to sunrise. If this is not feasible, the *talit* and *tefillin* should be removed without reciting the respective blessings and the *tefillin* donned once again later in the day for a few moments at which time the appropriate blessings should be pronounced. Rabbi Feinstein agrees that under such circumstances learned individuals should be advised to don the *tefillin* a second time later in the day but indicates that "ordinary people" may be advised to rely upon the authorities who permit recitation of the blessing at an earlier hour. Rabbi Feinstein fears that, if counseled not to recite the blessing, untutored individuals may become lax in their fulfillment of the *mizvah* of *tefillin.* If, on account of the earliness of the hour, the *talit* is removed without recitation of the blessing, the *zizit* of the *talit katan* should be fingered sometime later than 35 minutes before sunrise and the blessing recited at that time over the *zizit* of the *talit katan.*

Individuals who have ample time to recite *shemoneh esreh* after sunrise, but are confronted with the choice of either praying together with a *minyan* which is constrained to recite *shemoneh esreh* at an earlier hour or praying after sunrise without benefit of a *minyan,* should consult a competent rabbinic authority and be guided by his advice.

It is, of course, preferable to arrange one's schedule, if at all feasible, in such a manner that it is possible to pray with a *minyan* at the optimal time. Some will find that they are able to do so; others may, at times, find it necessary to take advantage of the various leniencies which have been outlined. Our Sages long ago observed that not all are able to pray at the same hour: "When Israel prays, you do not find that they all pray at once. Rather, assemblage by assemblage they pray each one. . . After all the assemblages have completed their prayers, the angel who is appointed over prayer takes all the prayers which have been prayed in all the assemblages and fashions them into crowns, which he places upon the head of the Holy One, blessed be He . . . for the Holy One, blessed be He, crowns Himself with the prayers of Israel" (*Shemot Rabbah* XXI, 4).

CHAPTER XII

Reinstitution of the Sacrificial Order

> *All the conversations of mankind center around the land. . . . All the prayers of Israel center around the Temple. . . . Mari matai yitbeni Bet ha-Mikdash—Lord, when will the Temple be rebuilt?*
>
> BERESHIT RABBAH, XII, 2

A chain forged of the prayers and yearnings of centuries rivets the Jew to Jerusalem with a binding force and tenacity greater than that of an iron bond. Despite the length and vicissitudes of the dispersion, at no time were the links of this chain severed, in no place were they corroded. The Temple ruins, standing desolate in far-off Jerusalem, were always, to the Jew, the focal point of his dreams and aspirations. His heart in the East, his thoughts attuned to Zion, wherever his physical abode, he stood "before thy gates, O Jerusalem!"

The dramatic events of June 1967 have made the concern of ages even more vivid. During the ensuing months and years, to a greater degree than ever before, the hearts and minds of world Jewry have been filled with solicitude and care for the Land of Israel. The newly recovered Holy Places command the attention and dominate the conversation of Jews everywhere. Overnight, Halakhah has been called upon to grapple with a whole new set of problems—problems, which, although intrinsically old, are new in the imminence of their applicability. Questions regarding the sanctity of the Temple site, entry onto the Temple Mount, and even the possibility of resuming the sacrificial service have now been transformed into halakhic issues begging for clear-cut and definitive answers.

To Torah students, the examination of these topics was never a mere academic exercise upon which scholars, seeking to develop intellectual acumen and halakhic prowess, honed their minds. Even though its laws are temporarily in abeyance, *Seder Kodshim,* an integral part of Divine Revelation, was always approached with reverence and zeal in the true spirit of *Torah le-shmah.* Such study may often have been denigrated and relegated to the realm of the irrelevant and the inconsequential; cynics may have scoffed, and do indeed continue to quip, that this involvement with charting "the pathways to the Kingdom of Heaven" is misplaced. Yet it is precisely this concern that is so eloquent a testimony to the abiding *emunah* of the Jew, to his recognition of the intrinsic worth of every facet of Torah study and to his vivid and eager anticipation—*"meherah yibaneh ha-Mikdash!"*

Needless to say, in the normal course of communal life, questions of immediate relevance had primary claim on the time and attention of Torah authorities and their investigation quite naturally superseded that of areas divorced from practical application. Moreover, the student of *Kodshim* was at an added disadvantage in that this discipline was surrounded by a labyrinth of abstract technicalities and he was accordingly forced to conceptualize with regard to matters which did not fall within the pale of his experience. The result was the relative neglect of *Seder Kodshim,* a development already decried by so early a figure as Rambam (*Commentary on the Mishnah,* introd. to *Seder Kodshim*), and a consequent paucity of halakhic literature pertaining to this field of inquiry.

While the specific question of the reinstitution of the sacrificial rites has been discussed from time to time in rabbinic writings, for the most part these discussions are recondite analyses of an already obscure subject. Nevertheless, despite the intricate nature of the subject matter, its current relevance demands that we strive for an understanding and appreciation of the grave halakhic issues involved. This review has been undertaken as an attempt at least partially to acquaint the reader with the nature of these issues and to delineate the maze of halakhic difficulties with which they are fraught. As such, the scope of this presentation is far from exhaustive. Hopefully, the reader will find his appetite whetted and will be prompted to peruse the original sources.[1]

---

1. Relevant material may be found in the following works published in recent years: R. Zevi Pesach Frank, *Mikdash Melekh* (Jerusalem, 5728); R. Mordecai Ilan, *Torat ha-Kodesh* (Bnei Brak, 5730); R. Moshe Shlomoh Klires, *Ha-Mikdash ve-Kodashav* (Jerusalem, 5730); R. Moshe Nachum Schapiro, *Har ha-Kodesh* (Jerusalem, 5731); Rabbi H. Zarkowski, *Kedushat Har* (New York, 5732). See also R. Eliezer Waldenberg, *Ẓiẓ Eli'ezer,* X, nos. 7 and 13;

The rebuilding of the *Bet ha–Mikdash* itself is precluded until the coming of the Messiah.[2] Rashi, in his commentary on *Sukkah* 41a and *Rosh ha-Shanah* 30a, states that the third Temple will not be a human artifact but shall miraculously appear as a fully built edifice. According to Rashi's opinion, the verse "The sanctuary, O Lord, which *Thy* hands have established" (Exod. 15:17) refers to the future *Bet ha-Mikdash.*[3] Rambam, on the other hand, enumerates the building of the *Bet ha-Mikdash* as one of the 613 commandments.[4] Since the very nature of a commandment implies a deed to be performed by man rather than an act emanating from God, Rambam obviously maintains that the *Bet ha-Mikdash* will be the product of human endeavor. However, he states explicitly that this *Bet ha-Mikdash* will be rebuilt only with the advent of the Messiah himself. Not only will the Temple be built by the Messiah, but this construction will serve as substantiation of the messianic claim. "If he builds the *Bet ha-Mikdash* on its site and gathers in the dispersed of Israel, he is, in certainty, the Messiah" (*Hilkhot Melakhim* 11:4).

R. Shlomoh Yosef Zevin, *Torah She-be-'al Peh,* V (5723); R. Mordecai ha-Kohen, *Torah She-be-'al Peh,* V (5723); R. Shiloh Rafael, *Torah She-be-'al Peh,* X (5728); R. Ovadiah Yosef, *Torah She-be-'al Peh,* X (5728); R. Bezalel Zolti, *Torah She-be-'al Peh,* X (5728); R. Shlomoh Goren, *Maḥanaim,* no. 119 (5725); R. Shlomoh Yosef Zevin, *Maḥanayim,* no. 119 (5725); R. David Bleich, *Ha-Ma'ayan,* Nisan 5729 and Tishri 5730; R. Chaim Shraga Frank, *Ha-Ma'ayan,* Tishri 5730; Avigdor Nebenzahl, *Ha-Ma'ayan,* Nisan 5730; and R. Moshe Sternbuch, *Mo'adim u-Zemanim,* V, no. 351.

2. Cf. R. Abraham Isaac Kook, *Mishpat Kohen* (Jerusalem, 5697), no. 94. The conclusions expressed in this responsum, dated London, 21 Cheshvan, 5678, were evidently reconsidered in view of the contradictory view expressed subsequently by R. Kook in a letter of approbation to *Yaskil Avdi* by R. Ovadiah Hadaya (Jerusalem, 5691), vol. I. See also R. Eliezer Waldenberg, *Ha-Pardes,* Tishri 5728, and R. Mordecai Ha-Kohen, *Panim el Panim,* 6 Tammuz, 5727 and 21 Cheshvan, 5728. See also below, note 24.

3. Rashi's view is implicit in the *naḥem* prayer of the *minḥah* service for the Ninth of Ab: "For Thou, O Lord, didst consume it [the Temple] with fire and through fire wilt Thou in future rebuild it." The text of this prayer is based upon the Jerusalem Talmud, *Berakhot* 4:3. Regarding the apparent contradiction between Rashi as here cited and Rashi's comments on Ezekiel 43:11, see R. Shlomoh Yosef Zevin, "Mikdash he-Atid le-Or ha-Halakhah," *Maḥanayim,* no. 119, p. 14, for an ingenious resolution based upon *Teshuvot Divrei Ta'am* (Warsaw, 5664). Rambam, despite his view that the *Bet ha-Mikdash* will be constructed by man, cites the text of the *naḥem* prayer in his *Seder Tefilot* appended to *Sefer Ahavah* of the *Mishneh Torah;* cf. Rashi, *Ketubot* 8a.

4. *Sefer ha-Miẓvot, 'aseh,* no. 20. Sa'adia Ga'on, too, includes the building of the *Bet ha-Mikdash* in his list of communal obligations; see *Sefer ha-Miẓvot le-Rabbenu Sa'adya Ga'on, Minyan ha-Parshiyot,* no. 51.

The proposal to reestablish the sacrificial rites despite the absence of a *Bet ha-Mikdash* is based upon the statement of R. Joshua (*Eduyot* 8:6 cited *Shevu'ot* 16a and *Megillah* 10a), "I have heard that [it is permitted] to sacrifice although there is no Temple." This dictum is accepted by Rambam as authoritative (*Bet ha-Beḥirah* 6:15).[5] Further confirmation that the offering of sacrifices in our own day is at least a theoretical possibility is to be found in Rambam's statement, *Ma'aseh ha–Korbanot,* 19:15, that the penalty for *sheḥutei ḥuẓ*—the slaughtering of sacrificial animals other than at the temple site—applies also in our time. Since the penalty is applicable only in those instances in which the animal is *ra'uy le-fenim*—where there are no halakhic impediments to its being offered as a sacrifice at the proper site—the apparent conclusion is that Maimonides accepted, at least in theory, the possibility of reinstitution of the sacrificial service.[6]

There is also some historical evidence that sacrifices—particularly the paschal sacrifice—were offered sporadically during the period immediately following the destruction of the Temple. R. Jacob Emden, *She'elat Ya'aveẓ,* I, no. 89, identifies the Rabban Gamliel quoted in *Pesaḥim* 74a as commanding his servant, Tabi, "Go and roast the Pesach sacrifice," with the Rabban Gamliel who served as head of the Academy in Yavneh after the destruction of the Temple. R. Shimon ben Zemach Duran, in his

---

5. It should, however, be noted that *Ri mi-Gash,* in his commentary to *Shevu'ot* 16a, limits the application of R. Joshua's dictum to cases of temporary demolition or absence of the Temple walls, such as occurred during the period of construction following the return of Ezra or the reconstruction of the Temple by Herod, inferring that it is inapplicable during periods of desolation. Despite the quotation by the Mishnah of the halakhah in the name of R. Judah, Rabad terms Rambam's incorporation of this provision in the *Mishneh Torah* "his [Rambam's] own theory." R. David Alexander of Lissa, *Migdal David* (Warsaw, 5635), p. 27, explains that this characterization of Rambam's position is rooted in Rabad's interpretation of the Mishnah in the manner of *Ri mi-Gash*—an interpretation which effectively negates any inference regarding permissibility of sacrifice after the destruction. In addition, citing numerous parallel uses of the phrase "I have heard," the author of *Migdal David* endeavors to demonstrate that this terminology indicates the transmitter's disagreement with the halakhah he has "heard."

6. It is, however, possible that the intended meaning is that the penalty is actually incurred for the *haktarah*—burning of the various parts of the animal —rather than for the slaughtering. *Haktarah* other than on the Temple site is culpable even though the sacrificial animal is not *ra'uy le-fenim.* See *Mishneh le-Melekh, Klei ha-Mikdash* 5: 16 and R. Zevi Hirsch Chajes, *Kuntres Aḥaron Avodat ha-Kodesh,* chap. 1.

commentary on the Hagaddah, *Yavin Shemu'ah* (Livorno, 5504), makes essentially the same point in his discussion of the section *Rabban Gamliel omer*. Further evidence that sacrifices were actually brought after the destruction is adduced by R. Zevi Hirsch Chajes in his responsa, nos. 2 and 76 and chapter 2 of his *Darkei Hora'ah*.[7] These historical contentions are rebutted by R. Chaim Nathanson in his *Avodah Tamah* (Altona, 5632).

Whatever may have been the case in the period immediately following the destruction of the Temple, the centuries which ensued witnessed the total abrogation of the sacrificial rites.[8] For generations, the resumption of sacrifice was at best a theoretical possibility; its translation into practice could have been no more than an ephemeral fantasy. Nevertheless, the report of a concrete proposal for the reinstitution of sacrifices occurs in an early-fourteenth-century work entitled *Kaftor va-Feraḥ*, written by R. Ishturi ha-Parchi, a victim of the French expulsion. The author recounts having brought his manuscript to a certain R. Barukh in Jerusalem in order that the latter might examine and correct the work prior to publication. R. Barukh is reported to have informed the author of *Kaftor va-Feraḥ* of the surprising fact that in the year 5017, Rabbenu Yechiel (or Rabbenu Ḥananel or Rabbenu Chaim, depending upon the variant textual readings)[9] of Paris wished to emigrate to Israel and there to offer sacrifices. The author raises certain objections but states that due to the pressure of reviewing the manuscript he did not pursue the matter by discussing the questions involved with his mentor. Quite evidently nothing came of these plans; R. Chaim Nathanson in his *Avodah Tamah* concludes that undoubtedly the French scholar was dissuaded from doing so by the sages of his generation.

---

7. Chajes claims to have seen *sifrei ha-'amin* which report that the paschal sacrifice was offered as late as during the reign of Justinian, at which time it was finally abrogated. See Procopius, *Anecdota*, chap. 28.

8. Regarding the declared intention of the Emperor Julian (361–363) to rebuild the Temple so that the Jews might resume the offering of sacrifices and regarding Jewish reactions to this abortive proposal, see Salo W. Baron, *A Social and Religious History of the Jews* (Philadelphia, 1952), II, 160 and 392, n. 41. Cf. Ya'akov Levinger, *De'ot*, Summer 5727, p. 227, n. 10, and R. Kalman Kahana, *She'arim*, 14 Nisan 5728.

9. See *Kaftor va-Feraḥ*, ed. Joseph Blumenfeld (New York, 5718), p. 214, n. 17; and H. J. Zimmels, "Erez Israel in der Responsenliteratur des späteren Mittelalters," *Monatsschrift für Geschichte und Wissenschaft des Judentums*, LXXIV (1930), p. 50, n. 6.

Once more the issue recedes into the background. Nothing more is heard of the proposal and the entire question is permitted to lie fallow until the middle of the nineteenth century when we find a new protagonist actively espousing resettlement of the Holy Land and reintroduction of sacrificial worship. In a letter addressed to Baron Asher Anshel Rothschild, dated 12 Elul, 5596, R. Zevi Hirsch Kalisher solicits the latter's support for plans to colonize the Land of Israel and outlines his views regarding the sacrificial rites. When these opinions regarding the resumption of the sacrificial service were incorporated in a work entitled *Derishat Ẓion* and published a little over one hundred years ago, in 5622, the question for the first time became a live issue.[10] Considerable controversy was aroused and resulted in a meticulous examination by the foremost authorities of the time of the halakhic issues surrounding the proposed innovation. Opposition to Kalisher's views was of a dual nature. Apart from the controversial halakhic ramifications of his proposal, Kalisher's novel eschatological views caused many of his contemporaries to take sharp issue with him. Kalisher argues not only that reinstitution of the sacrificial rites is both permissible and halakhically feasible but that it constitutes a positive *miẓvah* and is, in addition, a *sine qua non* for the advent of the Messiah. The redemption, he maintains, will take place in the following manner: first, a partial ingathering of the exiles, to be followed by the reinstitution of *korbanot;* after this will occur the war between Gog and Magog and the complete ingathering of the exiles, culminating in the advent of the Messiah. As evidence for his position, Kalisher cites the statement of the Palestinian Talmud, as quoted by *Tosafot Yom Tov, Ma'aser Sheni,* 5:2: "The Temple [will] be rebuilt before the reign of the House of David."[11] Referring to the *Sifri* cited

10. In fact, R. Shlomoh Drimer of Skole, in an undated responsum, quotes an unnamed interlocutor who reported that "the sages of the Sephardim and of Lithuania wished to sacrifice [the paschal offering] this past *erev Pesaḥ.*" See *Teshuvot Bet Shlomoh* (Lemberg, 5637–51), *Yoreh De'ah,* II, no. 125.

11. In further support of this view, Kalisher cites the wording of the *Mussaf* service of *Rosh Ḥodesh:* "A new altar shalt Thou establish in Zion and the burnt offering of the New Moon shall we offer upon it" which is subsequently followed by the phrase "and in the service of Thy Temple shall we all rejoice." Kalisher argues that reference to rejoicing in the Temple service—which is general in nature—should logically precede the more specific mention of the burnt offering of *Rosh Ḥodesh.* From this he concludes that the prior reference, which is to a new *altar* (not a *Bet ha-Mikdash*), refers to the reinstitution of communal sacrifices and hence is not dependent upon the rebuilding of the *Bet ha-Mikdash,* whereas the subsequent mention of the Temple service refers

by Nachmanides in his commentary on Deuteronomy 12:5, Kalisher maintains that the offering of sacrifices is causally connected with the reappearance of prophecy and has as its effect the manifestation of the Divine Presence, just as the *Shekhinah* appeared in the Tabernacle in the wilderness only following the sacrificial offerings of the *milu'im*. Therefore, he concludes, the reinstitution of the sacrificial rites is not dependent upon a prophetic injunction; rather, prophecy cannot become manifest without prior sacrificial offerings.[12]

In a letter to Kalisher the famed R. Nathan Adler cites Rashi in his commentary on *Sukkah* 41a and *Tosafot Shevu'ot* 15b to the effect that not only the Temple itself but also the altar and all utensils and appurtenances of the third Temple will be built miraculously by God by means of a heavenly fire. Since miraculous occurrences are to be anticipated only after the coming of the Messiah, the opinion of these authorities obviously contradicts the view of the Palestinian Talmud as cited by Kalisher. R. David Friedman, in a short treatise entitled *Kuntres Derishat Ẓion ve-Yerushalayim* and published as the opening section of his *She'elat David,* maintains that the reading cited by Kalisher and *Tosafot Yom Tov* is erroneous and that the correct textual reading is "*Jerusalem* will be rebuilt," not "the *Temple* will be rebuilt." Furthermore, he argues, from the context of the statement in the Palestinian Talmud it is not at all evident that this is an assertion of a *necessary* order of events leading to the redemption (as Kalisher opines) but, on the contrary, merely of a *possible* order. Thus, even accepting Kalisher's reading, the Jerusalem Talmud falls short of stating that the Temple *must* be rebuilt as a prerequisite to the advent of the Messiah. In the *'amidah* as ordained by the Men of the Great Assembly, the blessing pertaining to the reinstitution of sacrifices follows the blessings alluding to the ingathering of the exiles, the rebuilding of Jerusalem and the restitution of the House of David. This order is seen by Friedman as corresponding to the optimum chronological sequence, whereas according to Kalisher the order is sequentially impossible and hence without apparent rhyme or reason.

---

to private sacrifices which are contingent upon the rebuilding of the Temple (for reasons that will be examined later in this review) and will, therefore, be reinstituted at a latter date.

12. It is a bit puzzling that in endeavoring to establish this point Kalisher does not cite the more explicit and more *a propos* discussion of Ramban contained in his commentary on Leviticus 1:9 in which he analyzes the rationale underlying the sacrificial precepts.

R. Ya'akov Ettlinger, in the first responsum of the *Binyan Ẓion,* states that the authoritative order of the redemption is that given by the Gemara, *Megillah* 17b. There we find the following sequence: the rebuilding of Jerusalem, the reestablishment of the kingdom of the House of David, the rebuilding of the Temple, which shall become a place of prayer for all peoples, and finally the reinstitution of the sacrificial rites. This order is reflected in the blessings of the *'amidah* which were sequentially ordained by the Men of the Great Assembly in a manner paralleling the chronological unfolding of the events leading to the redemption. We may accordingly infer that sacrifices cannot be reinstituted until after the reestablishment of the House of David and the rebuilding of the Temple.[13] To this argument Kalisher replies that indeed the reinstitution of sacrificial offerings, including private sacrifices, is impossible without the coming of the Messiah—and it is to such individual sacrifices that the Gemara and the liturgy refer. Nevertheless, communal sacrifices can be reinstituted, according to his view, even though there is no *Bet ha-Mikdash.*

In addition, it is of interest to note that contemporary scholarship has uncovered manuscript evidence in contradiction to Kalisher's thesis. Rabbi Menachem Kasher, in an appendix to vol. 12 of *Torah Shelemah* (New York, 5708), p. 165, cites a reading of the previously unknown *Midrash Tannai'im:* "Just as you are unable to offer the *Pesaḥ* other than in the Temple, so also with regard to leap years—you shall not ordain leap years other than [when] the Temple [stands]." The obvious inference is that sacrifice of the *korban Pesaḥ* is not sanctioned until such time as the Temple shall be rebuilt.

Kalisher's vigorous advocacy of the reinstitution of sacrifices met with determined opposition on the grounds of halakhic technicalities as well. In his own day, rabbinical authorities of world repute such as R. Akiva Eger, R. Moses Sofer and R. Ya'akov Ettlinger[13a] contended that there exist halakhic impediments which completely nullify the proposal. Despite Kalisher's assertions to the contrary, there is no evidence that

13. R. David Alexander of Lissa, *Migdal David* (Warsaw, 5635), finds this sequence also reflected in the blessing included in the repetition of the *'amidah* prior to the priestly benediction, " . . . cause My *shekhinah* to return to Zion and the sacrificial order to Jerusalem." The prior reference to the return of the Divine Presence is a quite apparent allusion to the rebuilding of the Temple and in this context precedes reinstitution of the sacrificial order.

13a. Kalisher's proposal was also rejected in harsh terms in a letter addressed to him by R. Ya'akov of Lissa. This hitherto unpublished letter appears in R. Yosef Sheinberger's *Amud Esh* (Jerusalem, 5714), pp. 105–109.

any of these three halakhic personalities became reconciled with Kalisher's views.[14] Of the three, R. Ya'akov Ettlinger published his opposition to Kalisher's proposal as the very first responsum in *Binyan Ẓion,* R. Moses Sofer limits the proposal to the *korban pesaḥ* alone and R. Akiva Eger, despite a protracted correspondence with Kalisher, never reversed his views on the subject. Kalisher's work led to the composition of *Avodah Tamah* by R. Chaim Nathanson and *Migdal David* by R. David Alexander of Lissa, both of which are polemical in nature and devoted to the express purpose of refuting Kalisher's contentions. The controversy gave rise to much heated debate, which has continued unabated into recent times.[15] Alluring as it may have been, Kalisher's proposal was deemed unfeasible in practice. Seen as constituting potential barriers to the implementation of the sacrificial services were the concrete questions of ritual impurity, the sanctity of the Temple site, the genealogical purity of the *kohanim,* ascertaining the precise location of the *mizbeaḥ* (altar) and its construction, the unavailability of the materials required for weaving the priestly garments, the problems involved in the appointment of a High Priest, collection of *shekalim,* inauguration of the *kohanim* and dedication of the altar.

Tum'ah

Admitting the contention that the building of the *Bet ha-Mikdash* itself is manifestly impossible without prophetic direction—in the words of Scripture, "All this in writing, as the Lord has made me wise by His hand upon me" (I Chron. 28:19)[16]—Kalisher points out that only the

14. Cf. Jacob Katz, "Demuto ha-Historit shel ha-Rav Zvi Hirsch Kalisher," *Shivat Ẓion,* II-III (5711–5712), 29, n. 11.

15. For some further references, see R. Chaim Chizkiyahu Medini, *Sedei Ḥemed* (Warsaw, 5656–62), III, 1303, *Kuntres ha-Kelalim, Ma'arekhet ha-Kaf,* no. 77, sec. 13.

16. R. Chaim Soloveitchik of Brisk, in his novellae to Rambam, *Hilkhot Bet ha-Beḥirah* 1:10, develops the thesis that deviation from the divine instructions to which reference is made in this verse invalidates the sacrificial offering. R. Mordecai Ilan, *Torat ha-Kodesh,* II, no. 13, explains that, according to this view, while sacrifices may be offered "even though there is no Temple," this is so only if no edifice whatsoever has been constructed on the Temple site. If, however, any structure is erected upon that site, it must conform to these specifications or else the sacrifices offered are invalid. On the basis of this thesis, R. Ilan offers a novel reason precluding sacrifices at present: The Temple Mount is not unoccupied at the present time; mosques and other structures have been erected on the site. Since the architecture of these build-

mizbeaḥ is necessary in order to offer sacrifices and indeed Ezra reinstituted *korbanot* long before the Temple was completely rebuilt. He then himself voices three possible objections to his proposal and endeavors to obviate each in turn. The first problem is that one may not enter the Temple site or offer sacrifies in a state of ritual impurity. At present, however, we have all been defiled through contact with the dead and lack the ashes of the red heifer to effect the requisite purification. The general principle that communal sacrifices may be offered in a state of ritual impurity, if there is no alternative,[17] applies not only to the actual sacrificial acts but also to preliminary entry onto the Temple Mount in order to carry out the necessary preparations.[18] Accordingly, Kalisher limits his

---

ings quite obviously does not conform to the specifications "in writing, as the Lord has made me wise by His hand upon me" any sacrifices offered on the site, argues R. Ilan, would be invalid.

17. *Migdal David* advances a tenuous argument to the effect that the abrogation of the law of *tum'ah* with regard to communal sacrifices applies only to incidental occurrences which necessitate suspension of this prohibition in order not to cause a disruption in the chain of communal sacrifice. However, once the sacrificial service has lapsed because of other factors it cannot be resumed other than in a state of ritual purity.

18. R. Shmuel David Levine, in his *Taharat ha-Kodesh* (Pietrokow, 5690), addressing himelf solely to the question of entering the Temple Mount, argues that though there may be halakhic impediments in our day with regard to offering other sacrifices, nevertheless preparation of the *parah adumah* (the red heifer) is feasible in order to purify those defiled by *tum'at met.* His proposal provides for conditional sanctification and conditional sacrifice of the *parah adumah.* The stipulations to be made are: if the *kohen* is truly a member of the priestly family, and if the original sanctification of the *Bet ha-Mikdash* remains in effect, then the sanctification of the sacrifice be effective and its slaughter and the sprinkling of the blood be effective for sacrificial purposes. If, on the other hand, the *kohen* is not of pure descent, or if the original sanctification of the *Bet ha-Mikdash* is now abrogated, then the sanctification be ineffective and the slaughter and subsequent sprinkling of blood be secular rather than sacrificial in nature. Despite the fact that the slaughter of unsanctified animals is not permitted within the confines of the Temple conditional sacrifice is possible with regard to the red heifer because that sacrifice takes place on the *Har ha-Mishḥah*—the Mount of Olives—rather than on the Temple site. Those purified by this *parah adumah* would then be permitted to enter the Temple Mount through the application of a *sfek sfekah:* Perhaps the original sanctification has been abrogated, in which case entry is permissible without further ado. In the event that the original sanctification has not lapsed, perhaps this is an efficacious *parah adumah* and accordingly capable of effecting the cleansing of defilement. It should, however, be noted that R. Levine's proposal concerning the red heifer is fraught with many of the difficulties surrounding *korbanot be-zman ha-zeh* cited in this review.

proposal to communal offerings and to the paschal sacrifice, to which the principle *tum'ah dehuyah bezibur* is applicable.[19]

Priestly Yihus

Less readily resolved is the problem of authenticating the claims of present-day *kohanim* to be recognized as descendants of the priestly family. Ezra demanded written pedigrees: "These sought their register, that is, the genealogy, but it was not found; therefore they were deemed polluted and put from the priesthood" (Ezra 2:62). Applying himself to this issue—one already raised by the author of *Kaftor va-Ferah*—Kalisher argues that documentary evidence was necessary only in the time of Ezra since many scions of the priestly family had intermarried with gentiles during the course of the Babylonian exile. Once the claims of these aspirants to the priesthood were examined and verified, they and their descendants remained *behezkat kashrut* and required no further credentials. In support of this view Kalisher cites the Mishnah, *Eduyot* 8:7, "Elijah will come neither to defile nor to purify, neither to draw nigh nor to put aside," which he understands as referring not merely to questions of legitimacy of birth but to claims of priestly descent as well.[20]

19. Cf., however, R. Yosef Rosen, *Zofnat Pa'aneah, Tinyanah,* p. 118, and R. Shlomoh Yosef Zevin, *Ha-Mo'adim be-Halakhah,* pp. 156 and 179 f.

20. Both Kalisher and R. Zevi Hirsch Chajes, *Kuntres Aharon, Avodat ha-Kodesh,* chap. 1, cite R. Yechezkel Landau, *Noda bi-Yehudah, I, Orah Hayyim,* no. 35, to the effect that even in our day we may rely upon the genealogical claims of at least some *kohanim.* The case in question is tangential to our topic but relevant nonetheless. An individual who had committed adultery with the same woman on numerous occasions inquired of R. Landau what form of penance was required in expiation of his sins and added that on many of these occasions the woman was a *niddah.* R. Landau tentatively advances the opinion that if the woman in question was a *niddah* on the occasion of their first adulterous act, he requires expiation for the *issur niddah* as well.

The general rule "one prohibition cannot become effective upon another" does not apply in this instance because, although the woman in question is already forbidden to the adulterer as a married woman, the prohibition of *niddah* is an *issur mosif*—a more encompassing prohibition, prohibiting the menstruant to her husband as well. The additional prohibition of *niddah* consequently becomes effective and applies to acts of cohabitation both with her husband and others. However, in the case of an adulteress who was not a *niddah* on the occasion of her first infraction, the very act of adultery renders her forbidden to her husband. Since she is already forbidden to all other men on account of her marital status, any subsequent state of *niddah* cannot add

In his *Binyan Ẓion* R. Ya'akov Ettlinger disagrees with Kalisher's interpretation of this Mishnah. *Tosafot* (*Sanhedrin* 51b and *Zevaḥim* 45a) questions why this statement of the Mishnah does not constitute a *hilkhata le-meshiḥa*—a decision applicable only in the days of the Messiah. As such, this statement seemingly contradicts the procedural principle that such decisions will be left for the Messiah himself to render and consequently are not included among talmudic dicta. Since *Tosafot* fails to answer that such a statement is necessary in order to sanction the services of *kohanim* prior to the advent of the Messiah, R. Ya'akov Ettlinger concludes that the Mishnah in question refers only to questions of legitimacy and bastardy and does not encompass the question of priestly genealogy.

R. Akiva Eger takes issue with Kalisher regarding the requirement for supportive evidence for priestly *yiḥus*. He maintains that the genealogical claims of present-day *kohanim* are uncorroborated and therefore remain in doubt. Chafetz Chaim (*Zevaḥ Todah*[12] *Zevaḥim,* chap. 13) also shares this view. This position is further elucidated by R. David Friedman, who quotes the exposition by the *Sifri, Parshat Shoftim,* of the verse, "One witness shall not rise up against a man for any iniquity, or for any sin,

to the severity of her prohibition (*ein issur ḥal al issur*). Reconsidering, R. Landau argues that subsequent *niddah* (after the adulterous act) is indeed an *issur mosif* since, in becoming effective, it carries with it a prohibition against entering the Temple. If not for the *issur niddah* it would be permissible for the adulteress to enter the Temple courtyard for the purpose of offering the paschal sacrifice. She would be permitted to do so despite the fact that at present we are all *teme'ei metim* because the *korban pesaḥ* may be offered in a state of *tum'ah* if a majority of the community has become defiled through contact with the dead. However, the principle of *tum'ah hutrah be-ẓibur* does not apply to the *tum'ah* of *niddah* or *zivah*. From this entire discussion, Kalisher and Chajes conclude that *Noda bi-Yehudah* considered the offering of the *korban pesaḥ* a distinct possibility. However, a careful examination of the responsum in question shows the opposite to be the case. *Noda bi-Yehuda* cites *Kaftor va-Feraḥ* as objecting to the reinstitution of the paschal sacrifice because we lack priests of verified genealogy. To this he adds that "somewhere in the world there does exist a genealogically pure priest." It would seem that the *Noda bi-Yehudah* accepts the fact that we cannot determine which of the priests are of pure descent. But since the sacrifice of the *pesaḥ* is theoretically possible, and our inability to discover the identity of the true *kohanim* is merely a technical failure, the prohibition of *niddah* does indeed become superimposed upon the prohibition of adultery.

21. *Zevaḥ Todah* is the title of a series of expository notes included by Chafetz Chaim in his *Likutei Halakhot* (Pietrokow, 5670). The entire work is known by the latter name.

in any sin that he hath sinned" (Deut. 19:15). The words *le-khol avon u-lekhol chat'at* are understood by the *Sifri* as teaching that two witnesses are necessary for both admission to the priesthood and exclusion from performance of the priestly functions.[22]

Historically, despite the scrupulous manner in which the courts guarded the priestly genealogy, we know of many uncertainties which arose as early as the talmudic period. For example, those priests who claimed descent from the Hasmoneans were accepted as legitimate for an extended period of time until Rabbi Judah publicized their illegitimacy (*Kiddushin* 70b). Another incident recounted by the Gemara involves four thousand priests who intermarried with the slaves of Pashchur ben Enur, some of whom escaped detection and were mistakenly permitted to perform the priestly functions (*Kiddushin* 70b).

Sanctity of the Har ha-Bayit

The third and perhaps the most weighty problem discussed by Kalisher involves the sanctity of the *Har ha-Bayit* (Temple Mount) following the destruction of the Temple. Kalisher assumes that according to the opinion of Rabad, who maintains that the sanctity of the Temple was abrogated upon its destruction, there ensues no problem regarding sacrifices at the present time. Kalisher maintains that, according to Rabad, even *bamot* or private altars are now permissible as they were prior to the erection of the Temple; hence, an altar erected on the Temple Mount would qualify for the offering of sacrifices no less than a private altar. Rambam declares that the original *kedushah,* or sanctification, of the Temple site continues to be in effect and has not been nullified by the destruction of the Temple. According to this view, an altar built on the Temple site retains the original *kedushah.*

In a responsum addressed to Kalisher and incorporated in the *Derishat Ẓion,* R. Akiva Eger takes strong exception to Kalisher's proposal. R. Akiva Eger's first objection is voiced in a cryptic statement asserting that we cannot effect a decision with regard to the controversy between Ram-

22. R. Levine, *Taharat ha-Kodesh,* cites Rambam, *Hilkhot Parah Adumah* 3:4, who states that a total of nine red heifers was offered from the time of Moses until the destruction of the Second Commonwealth and that a tenth will be brought by the Messiah. He concludes that the reason that the red heifer cannot be prepared in our day is because we have no means of ascertaining the genealogical purity of the *kohanim.* See also R. Shlomoh Kluger, *Ḥokhmat Shlomoh, Even ha-Ezer* 6:8.

bam and Rabad concerning the sanctity of the *Bet ha-Mikdash*. R. Friedman, in the previously cited preface to the *She'elat David,* notes that Rabad expresses no disagreement with Rambam's position (*Bet ha-Beḥirah* 1:3) that, once the Temple was erected, the prohibition against private altars became permanent and, accordingly, continues in effect even after the destruction of the *Bet ha-Mikdash.* Rambam's position in this matter is entirely consistent since he is of the opinion that the original *kedushah,* or sanctification, of the Temple site continues in effect and has not been nullified by the destruction of the Temple. Rabad, who disagrees and maintains that the original sanctification lapsed with the destruction of the Temple, would hence have been expected to append a gloss disagreeing with Rambam's statement regarding the permissibility of private altars in the period following the destruction of the Temple. Since he fails to do so, R. Akiva Eger apparently concludes that Rabad agrees with Rabbenu Chananel as quoted by *Tosafot, Zevaḥim* 61a, and maintains that *bamot* are now forbidden even though *kedushah rishonah lo kidshah le'atid lavo.* Accordingly, since the sanctity of the *Bet ha-Mikdash* has lapsed, an altar on the Temple Mount *bezman ha-zeh* would constitute a *bamah,* according to Rabad, and is therefore forbidden, as are all private altars.

R. Friedman suggests one possible manner in which the inauguration of sacrificial offerings may be considered. The feasibility to be considered hinges upon a conditional sanctification of the sacrificial animal under a formula pronouncing that if the Temple Mount indeed retains its sanctity as a *Bet ha-Mikdash,* as is Rambam's view, then the animal is indeed sanctified as a *korban pesaḥ,* and the slaughter of the animal and the sprinkling of its blood be effective for sacrificial purposes; but if, on the other hand, the sanctity has lapsed, as is Rabad's opinion, then the sanctification of the sacrificial animal be null and void and the subsequent slaughter of the animal and the sprinkling of its blood and burning of its flesh be secular in nature. This suggestion is rejected by Rabbi Zevi Pesach Frank (*Kuntres Har Ẓvi,* appended to *Teshuvot Har Ẓvi, Yoreh De'ah* (Jerusalem, 5724),[23] on the grounds that the priestly garments contain a mixture

23. It is of interest to note that the fourth edition of Kalisher's *Derishat Ẓion* was published in Israel in 5679 and was prefaced by a letter of approbation signed by the *Bet Din* of Jerusalem, of which R. Frank was then the junior member. *Kuntres Har Ẓvi,* authored by R. Frank, in which he emphatically disagrees with Kalisher's conclusions, was first printed as an appendix to that edition of the *Derishat Ẓion.*

of linen and wool and as such cannot be worn other than for the purpose of performing the sacrificial rites. In the event that such an offering does not in reality constitute a sacrifice, as would be the case according to Rabad, the officiating priest would then be violating the prohibition of *shatnez.* Rabbi Frank rejects the argument of R. Zevi Hirsch Chajes and others that the benefit derived is an unintentional one and hence not prohibited. Basing himself upon the treatment of the topic by *Bet ha-Levi,* I, nos. 1–3, he maintains that since no additional garments other than the priestly vestments may be worn while performing the *avodah,* the benefit is inescapable —a *pesik reisha*—which is forbidden even though the benefit is unintentional. Furthermore, Rabbi Frank points out that the *korban pesaḥ* (which, for reasons that will be noted, is the only sacrifice whose inauguration can be seriously considered) could not be offered on a private *bamah* even during the periods when private altars were permissible. This principle is clearly enunciated in *Zevaḥim* 104b.

Moreover, Rabbi Frank expresses astonishment that R. Akiva Eger did not comment on the logical inconsistency inherent in Kalisher's proposal. According to Rabad, a *mizbeaḥ* erected on the Temple site is to be considered a private altar. Hence, according to Rabad communal sacrifices are impossible in our day, since even an altar on the Temple Mount would have the status of a *bamah* and communal sacrifices cannot be offered on a private altar. But, according to Rambam, who maintains that the original sanctity prevails even after the destruction, the question of the reestablishment of the sacrificial rites arises *only* with regard to communal sacrifices, since it follows from his position that only communal sacrifices may be brought in the state of *tum'ah* (impurity). Kalisher's argument is thus dramatically demolished by Rabbi Zevi Pesach Frank.

Rabbi Friedman raises an engaging question based upon the ramifications of Rabad's position. As established by *Sefer ha-Ḥinukh,* the commandment to build a *Bet ha-Mikdash* is not deemed to be incumbent upon us except at such time as a majority of the Jewish people resides in the Land of Israel. (The building of the Second Temple by Ezra, even though this condition was not fulfilled, was the result of a specific prophetic edict.) Nevertheless, the rebuilding of the Temple should be obligatory according to Rabad, not as an intrinsic obligation, but because the attendant sanctification is requisite in order to fulfill the mandatory obligation of offering sacrifices. The offering of sacrifices, if not for technical impediments, would, of course, be mandatory even in contemporary times. Friedman concludes that the prospect of rebuilding the Temple cannot be entertained by us since the Mishnah (*Shevu'ot* 14a) declares that the sanctification of the Temple area requires a king, a prophet, the *urim ve-tumim* and the Sanhedrin. Although there is an opinion in the Gemara that any one of the four requirements enumerated is sufficient, we do not possess any of them at present. In addition, though a prophet, according to this opinion, may not be required for the act of sanctification, the *korban todah* (thanksgiving sacrifice) offered on that occasion requires a prophet in order to direct the manner in which it is to be sacrificed. Moreover, notes R. Friedman, Rabad himself states that Ezra did not promulgate a perpetual *kedushah* because he knew by means of the Holy Spirit that eventually both the Temple site and Jerusalem itself would be expanded, and the enlarged boundaries would be sanctified with enhanced and unprecedented glory; therefore, it does not behoove us to sanctify the Temple Mount other than according to the directions of a prophet.[24]

Mizbeaḥ

As previously indicated, a *Bet ha-Mikdash* is not necessarily required for the offering of sacrifices. Yet any sacrifice must be offered on the precise location of the original altar. In Rambam's phraseology, *"mekom ha-mikdash mekhuvan be-yoter*—the site of the altar [is located] with extreme precision." This spot, hallowed through the ages, is pinpointed by tradition as the exact site of Adam's first sacrifice to the Almighty, of Noah's offering upon emerging from the ark and of the binding of Isaac. The difficulties in the task of locating this site with exactitude are such

---

24. Addressing himself to a different question entirely, R. Moses Sofer (*Teshuvot Ḥatam Sofer, Yoreh De'ah,* no. 236) cites Rashi's interpretation of Exodus 25:9, "According to all that I show you, the pattern of the Tabernacle and the pattern of all the furniture, and so shall you make it." Troubled by the incongruous usage of the word "and" in *ve-khen ta'asu,* Rashi, referring to *Sanhedrin* 16b and *Shevu'ot* 14b, interprets this as an injunction to future generations. Ramban, in his commentary on this passage, raises an obvious objection to Rashi's interpretation; namely, that Solomon did indeed deviate from these specifications. R. Moses Sofer emends Rashi's interpretation and views the phrase "and so shall you make it" as referring back to the very beginning of the passage *"Kekhol asher ani mar'eh otḥa*— according to all that I show you" which he takes to mean that in subsequent generations any rebuilding of the Sanctuary must be in accordance with "all that I show you"—a specific prophetic revelation prior to each construction, as was the case with the building of the Tabernacle. According to this view, it is absolutely impossible to rebuild the Temple other than under clearly enunciated prophetic instructions.

that the Gemara, *Zevaḥim* 62b, relates that at the time of the construction of the Second Temple, the location of the altar was revealed by a prophet who returned from Babylonia for this purpose. Kalisher maintains that this was necessary only because no remnant whatsoever remained of the First Temple, as was foretold: "Raze it, raze it, even to the foundation thereof" (Ps. 137:7). Of the Second Temple, however, there are yet extant sections of the walls; these, Kalisher asserts, may be utilized for purposes of determining the distance between the walls and the altar. In the previously cited responsum, R. Akiva Eger argues that we cannot rely on our measurements in order to determine the exact location of the *mizbeaḥ* since these measurements are based upon the *tefaḥ,* or handbreadth measuring four fingerwidths. These dimensions cannot be determined with exactitude at present since physical proportions have changed over the course of centuries. Although various halakhic standards dependent upon these measurements may vary according to the average physical proportions of mankind in each generation, standards derived in this manner cannot enable us to measure geographical distances and locate spatial points which are unvariable.

Rabbi Friedman expresses the same objection, but with a most interesting twist. Our point of demarcation in any such attempt at determining the location of the *mizbeaḥ* is the Wailing Wall. Our authority for identifying the *kotel ma'aravi* with the western wall of the Temple is the statement found in the *Midrash Tanḥuma* (ed. Salomon Buber), *Shemot* 10, that the western wall will never be destroyed.[25] We are, however, governed by the principle that halakhic applications may not be derived from aggadic sayings. This principle is rooted in the recognition that (1) by virtue of its figurative nature we cannot be certain of the precise meaning of the aggadah and (2) there may well be differences of opinion among the various and varied aggadic sources which are either unknown to us or not properly understood by us. With regard to this particular question, Rabbi Friedman reasons, if we are indeed to take the pertinent aggadic dicta literally, we must also be mindful that the Gemara, *Gittin* 57a, declares the place known as *Har ha-Melekh* to have contained 600,000 cities, each one serving as the dwelling place of no less than 600,000 inhabitants; but today the locale

25. Similar statements are also found in *Midrash Rabbah, Shemot* II, 2; *Midrash Rabbah, Bemidbar* XI, 3; *Shir ha-Shirim Rabbah* II, 22; *Midrash Eikhah* I, 32; *Yalkut Shim'oni, Melakhim* 196; *Midrash Shoḥar Tov,* XI, 5; and *Zohar, Shemot* 5b. Cf. also *Tanna de-bei Eliyahu Rabbah,* chap. 30.

could not encompass 600,000 reeds! If this aggadic statement is to be understood literally, we must conclude that now the area has shrunk in physical size. If so, this phenomenon may very well have taken place in the area of the Temple Mount as well! Then, even accepting the western wall as a landmark on the testimony of the *Tanḥuma,* we may still have no accurate means of measurement, for the location upon which the *mizbeaḥ* stood originally may indeed have shifted. Furthermore, the *kotel ma'aravi* can give us only the western boundary from which to measure the distance to the location of the altar. The wall is not complete in length and therefore we cannot determine the northern and southern extremities. Hence we cannot ascertain where the altar stood *vis-à-vis* the north and south walls. Moreover, a comparison of the pertinent statements in *Yoma* 36a and *Zevaḥim* 53a and in the Mishnah, *Midot* 2:1, discloses a basic contradiction regarding the location of the *mizbeaḥ*. This is reflected in a difference of opinion between *Tosafot, Yoma* 16b, and Rambam, *Bet ha-Beḥirah* 1:6 and 5:16. Since it is not in our power to resolve this dispute we remain in a quandary with regard to the determination of the original location of the the altar. The same hesitation regarding the location of the altar is echoed by the Chafetz Chaim (*Zevaḥ Todah, Zevaḥim,* chap. 13).[26]

The first significant modern investigation of the dimensions of the *Bet ha-Mikdash* site was that undertaken by the Slutzker *Rav*, Rabbi Jacob David Wilovsky. In the *Teshuvot Bet Ridbaz* (Jerusalem, 5665) no. 38, Rabbi Wilovsky questions whether the Wailing Wall is the remnant of the wall surrounding the Temple Mount, as is commonly assumed, or whether it is rather the wall of the Temple courtyard proper. His query is based upon statements found in *Teshuvot Radbaz,* vol. I, nos. 648 and 691. He concludes that, even given the measurements of Tractate *Midot,* we have no single point of demarcation whose location is known with certainty.[27]

---

26. Cf. also *Teshuvot Bet Shlomoh Yoreh De'ah,* II, no. 125; *Yaskil Avdi,* vol. I, letter of approbation bearing the signature of Rabbi A. I. Kook.

27. A further implication of this uncertainty is grounded upon the halakhah that *zavim* and *nidot* are not permitted to enter any section of the Temple Mount. Accordingly, if the Wailing Wall marks the boundary of the Temple courtyard proper (meaning that it is set in a distance from the boundary of the *har ha-bayit*), those possessed of these forms of defilement are forbidden to approach the *kotel ma'aravi.* A further discussion of these questions is contained in *Kuntres Har Ẓvi,* chap. 10; R. Yehudah Leib Graubart, *Ḥavalim be-Ne'imim* (Lodz, 5694), IV, no. 80; and R. Moshe Sternbuch, *Mo'adim u-Zemanim,* II, no. 228.

Astonishingly, Abarbanel, in his commentary on Zechariah 12:6, renders

In addition, the construction of the *mizbeaḥ* entails a technical difficulty involving the stones of which the altar is to be fashioned. These must be absolutely smooth—a niche in which a fingernail may be caught renders the stone unfit for this purpose—and dare not be planed by means of a metal implement. We, of course, are not fortunate enough to possess a *shamir,* the worm employed by King Solomon to perform this task in the building of the original *mizbeaḥ*[28]

Priestly Garments

R. Akiva Eger, in the previously mentioned epistle to Kalisher, raises a further objection based upon the unavailability of one of the materials necessary for the weaving of the priestly garments. One of the four garments donned by the *kohanim* while performing the sacrificial rites was the *avnet* (girdle). This garment contained *tekhelet* (purple-wool), which was dyed the proper color through the use of the blood of the *ḥalazon,* a worm which is now either unavailable or unidentifiable. This argument is also advanced by R. Friedman, *She'elat David,* and the Chafetz Chaim, *Zevaḥ Todah, Zevaḥim,* chap. 13. Answering the contention of the *Tiferet Yisra'el* that the priestly garments do not require the blood of the *ḥalazon* for the making of this dye, R. Bezalel ha-Kohen, *Reshit Bikkurim* (Vilna, 5628), vol. II, no. 2, cites the *Tosefta, Menaḥot,* chap. 9: "Purple wool [dyed] other than through the use of the blood of the *ḥalazon* is unfit." These opinions run counter to Kalisher's view that purple wool dyed in this fashion is not an absolute requirement with regard to the priestly garments. Rabbi Frank, in his *Kuntres Har Ẓvi,* after examining the evidence pro and con, concludes that there is insufficient halakhic evidence to resolve the issue either way.[29]

---

that verse as "And Jerusalem shall be situated again in her place, in Jerusalem." According to this interpretation, the passage indicates that the present city of Jerusalem is not geographically identical with the Jerusalem of the Bible. Hence, for Abarbanel, even the location of the very city of Jerusalem is in doubt. This view is sharply contested by *Me'or Einayim, Imrei Binah,* chap. 12.

28. See *She'elat David* and *Teshuvot Bet Shlomoh, loc. cit.*

29. In *Ha-Levanon,* vol. I, no. 8, p. 63, dated 19 Elul, 5623, the journal wherein R. Friedman's treatise first appeared in serial form, there is a note appended by the editor indicating that R. Samuel Salant, famed rabbi of the Ashkenazic community of Jerusalem, concurred with R. Friedman regarding the question of *tekhelet.* Cf. also R. Yitzchak Schmelkes, *Teshuvot Bet Yiẓḥak* (Lemberg, 5655), *Yoreh De'ah,* II, no. 83.

Another material used in the weaving of the *avnet* was *argaman,* or red wool. R. Akiva Eger points out that, since the nature of *argaman* is the subject of a controversy between Rambam and Rabad, we now simply have no way of determining what ingredients went into the composition of this dye. In the same vein, R. Akiva Eger maintains that a similar objection might be raised with regard to the *tola'at shani,* or scarlet-colored wool, since the *Tosefta, Menaḥot,* chap. 9, states that only the *tola'at* which abounds in mountainous regions may be utilized in the preparation of this dye. Here again the difficulty of proper identification is insurmountable.[30] He further notes that there is a difference of opinion among the *Rishonim* regarding the number of fabrics which went into the weaving of the *avnet,*[31] and that in this instance as well we are not competent to resolve the disagreement. Therefore, concludes R. Akiva Eger, since we cannot provide proper priestly vestments, the *kohanim* cannot possibly perform the *avodah.* This last difficulty is the subject of an appendix "that the paper shall not remain blank" appended to the final page of the *Kuntres le-Kedushat ha-Mikdash,* authored by R. Samuel David Levine and published together with his *Leshed ha-Shemen* (Vilna, 5689). This discussion examines the possibility of the *kohen* donning two *avnetim* at the same time in order to conform to the specifications of the various authorities. The question hinges upon whether or not the prohibition of *bal tosif* applies to such a contingency. (The question of *ḥaẓiẓah* is dismissed as academic because, due to the fact that the *avnet* is only three fingerwidths wide, the two garments may be placed alongside, rather than over, one another.) A similar discussion occurs in the *Taharat ha-Kodesh* by the same author (Pietrokow, 5690), pp. 40 f.

Appointment of the High Priest

In a letter to his son-in-law, R. Moses Sofer, R. Akiva Eger adds that we are no longer able to identify the precious stones which are necessary for the vestments of the High Priest. The import of this objection is not readily apparent, since sacrifices may be offered even though the office of High Priest is vacant. *She'elat David* explains R. Eger's objection by pointing out that the final halakhic decision is *tum'ah deḥuyah be-ẓibur*

30. Regarding these various dyes, see also *Teshuvot Besamim Rosh,* no. 244.
31. For a detailed discussion of these various opinions, see *Mishneh le-Melekh, Klei ha-Mikdash* 8:2.

rather than *hutrah*—the prohibition against offering sacrifices in a state of ritual defilement is merely abrogated, not nullified, with regard to communal sacrifices.[32] It is therefore required that the *ẓiẓ,* or frontplate, be present on the forehead of the High Priest while the sacrificial ritual is performed in order to expiate the sin of defilement.[33] This necessitates the prior appointment of a High Priest and his donning the eight garments of his office for the performance of his functions. However, since we lack the jewels necessary for the breastplate and ephod, it is impossible for the High Priest to perform his duties. The Chafetz Chaim raises the same question regarding the *ẓiẓ* [34] (*Zevaḥ Todah, Zevaḥim,* chap. 13). R. Zevi Hirsch Chajes adds that we no longer possess the special *shemen ha-mishḥah* with which to anoint the High Priest, and hence he cannot be inaugurated into office.

Shekalim

A number of letters dealing with this subject were exchanged between R. Akiva Eger and R. Zevi Hirsh Kalisher, until the former found it physically difficult to continue the correspondence due to the infirmities of advanced age and consequently forwarded the relevant manuscripts to his son-in-law, R. Moses Sofer. In his reply, published as responsum no. 236 in *Teshuvot Ḥatam Sofer, Yoreh De'ah,* R. Moses Sofer rejects the proposal on the basis of the objection expressed by R. Ya'akov Emden in *She'elat Ya'aveẓ,* I, no. 89, in which the latter demonstrates that all communal sacrifices must be purchased with the half-shekel collected from each Jew once a year for this purpose. The obligation of *maḥaẓit ha-shekel* is not incumbent upon us after the destruction of the Temple. Moreover, in any event it would be exceedingly difficult effectively to collect this tax from all Jews. Hence R. Ya'akov Emden concludes that such communal sacrifices would be impossible and he limits the pertinence of reinstitution of *korbanot* to the *korban pesaḥ,* which is purchased with private funds. A similar view is expressed by R. Moses Sofer in the aforementioned responsum and by R. Chajes in his *Kuntres Aḥaron, Avodat ha-Kodesh.*

---

32. For a discussion of this topic, see *Sedei Ḥemed,* I, 437, *Kuntres ha-Kelalim, Ma'arekhet ha-Tet,* nos. 20–23.

33. Cf. *Teshuvot Bet Yiẓḥak, Yoreh De'ah,* II, no. 83.

34. See also R. Yitzchak Aharon ha-Levi Itinga, *Teshuvot Mahari ha-Levi* (Lemberg, 5653), I, no. 88.

Dedication of the Mizbeaḥ and Inauguration of the Kohanim

In view of the conclusions of these authorities that other sacrifices do not come into question, R. Zevi Pesach Frank poses the problem of *ḥinukh* (dedication) of the altar. The Mishnah, *Menaḥot* 49a, states explicitly that a newly fashioned altar must be inaugurated through the sacrifice of the *tamid shel shaḥar,* and no other sacrifice may precede the morning sacrafice on the new altar. Since this sacrifice cannot be offered due to the lack of *shekalim* with which to purchase the sacrificial animal, any altar constructed by us would remain uninaugurated. Consequently no other sacrifice, including the *pesaḥ,* could be offered on this *mizbeaḥ.*[35]

Yet another objection was raised in a letter addressed to Kalisher by R. Elijah Gutmacher of Graetz. Before any *kohen* proceeds to perform his priestly functions for the first time, it is incumbent upon him to offer a *minḥat ḥavitin.* This meal offering has the status of a private sacrifice and as such cannot be offered when the priest is in a state of defilement. Accordingly, runs the argument, how will the priests perform the sacrificial rites, since they cannot offer the inaugural sacrifice due to their defilement through contact with the dead? To this query Kalisher offers an interesting answer based upon a similar problem surrounding the inauguration of the High Priest. *Mishneh le-Melekh, Kelei ha-Mikdash,* 5:16, questions how it is possible for the "substitute" High Priest to perform the ritual of the Day of Atonement in the event that it becomes impossible for the High Priest to do so. The problem is based on the fact that the High Priest has to offer a similar sacrifice as part of his inauguration into office; since this *korban* has the status of a private offering, it cannot be offered on the Day of Atonement. *Mishneh le-Melekh* concludes that the lack of such prior offering on the part of the High Priest does not invalidate his performance of the sacrificial rites and therefore, in instances where this offering is impossible, he may perform his duties despite its absence. Kalisher concludes that the same regulation is applicable to the meal offering of the *kohen hedyot.*

Unacceptability of Sacrifices

Binyan Ẓion includes another noteworthy objection to Kalisher's proposal. R. Ya'akov Ettlinger's major contention is based upon the verse

35. Cf., however, *Teshuvot Kenaf Renanah,* nos. 77–79; and R. Shlomoh Yosef Zevin, *Ha-Mo'adim be-Halakhah,* pp. 161 f.

"And I will bring your sanctuaries unto destruction, and I will not smell the savor of your sweet odors" (Lev. 26:31). The Gemara prescribes that each sacrifice be offered with six "intentions" (*Zevaḥim* 46a); among these are *le-shem reaḥ* and *le-shem niḥoaḥ*. Ettlinger argues that since God says He will not smell "the savor of your sweet odors" while the Temple lies desolate we cannot offer the sacrifice with such an intention. A similar concept is expressed independently in *Emek Berakhah* (Jerusalem, 5708), p. 66, by R. Aryeh Pomeranchik, a distinguished disciple of the late Brisker *Rav*. Quoting an oral tradition related in the name of R. Naftali Zevi Judah Berlin, *Rosh Yeshivah* of Volozin,[36] Rabbi Pomeranchik asserts that while ordinarily a sacrifice in which these intentions are absent remains valid, nevertheless, in instances when these intentions are *impossible,* the sacrifice is rendered invalid. The sole exception is the paschal sacrifice which the Torah never refers to as being offered for purposes of "a sweet odor." Rabbi Pomeranchik explains the difficult phrase in the Haggadah, "May we partake there of the sacrifices and of the paschal offerings, whose blood shall be sprinkled upon Thine altar *for acceptance,*" in light of this novel interpretation. The term *le-raẓon* expresses our prayer that we shall be able to offer the *pesaḥ* in a rebuilt Temple in a perfect manner, so that it will also be accepted as "a sweet odor," although this is not strictly required in the case of the paschal sacrifice.

Concluding Remarks

Apart from the specific problems discussed, there is one theme which is recurrent throughout the vast halakhic literature dealing with our topic. In this most nebulous area it is almost impossible to arrive at a definitive *psak* with regard to the myriads of practical and concrete questions which inevitably arise. Typical of this attitude is an article which appeared in an early journal of Torah scholarship. Writing in *ha-Levanon,* I, no. 8, p. 54, R. Meir Auerbach, Chief Rabbi of Kalish, notes many peripheral questions involving halakhic disputes which we are incompetent to resolve. A case in

36. This view is, in fact, expressed by R. Berlin in his *Teshuvot Meshiv Davar, Kuntres Dvar ha-Shmittah,* no. 56, and in his *Ha'amek Davar,* Lev. 26:31 and Deut. 16:13. See also a hitherto unpublished letter written by R. Berlin, *Ha-Ma'ayan,* Nisan 5734, pp. 9–10, and R. Menachem Gerlitz, *Mara de-Ar'a Yisra'el* (Jerusalem, 5734), II, 16. *Ḥazon Ish, Ohalot* 30:5, expresses a similar but different concept in stating, on the basis of the same verse, that sacrifices are precluded as one of the manifestations of exile. See R. Kalman Kahana, *Ha-Ma'ayan,* Tevet 5731, p. 31, n. 12.

point is the manner of roasting the paschal sacrifice—a matter which is the subject of a disagreement between Rambam and Rabad, *Korban Pesaḥ*. 10:11. Rambam maintains that the animal must be roasted together with its *gid ha-nasheh* (sciatic nerve). To this view Rabad responds, "By my head! There is no greater prohibition. . . . If I will be privileged and will eat the *pesaḥ* and he should bring before me such [an animal] I would hurl it to the ground before his eyes!" Commonplace questions of *kashrut* arising from adhesions on the lung are nowadays rendered *terefah* in instances in which we have no means of reaching a decision. Such questions cannot be disposed of so readily when arising with regard to sacrificial animals. One reason for this is that it is forbidden to dispose of sacrificial animals which are in reality kosher. If the sacrifice is valid, the various portions *must* be consumed, either on the altar or by the *kohanim* or by those offering the sacrifice, as the case may be.

To illustrate the insurmountable difficulties involved in rendering a final decision in this uncharted field, Rabbi Auerbach recounts an anecdote which adds a revealing biographical note to the life of one of the luminaries in the history of Halakhah. Rabbi Auerbach relates that R. Alexander Schorr, the author of the *Tevu'at Shor* (Zolokiew, 5473), a standard and authoritative work dealing in minute detail with the laws pertaining to *sheḥitah* and *terefot,* also composed a similar compendium pertaining to the laws of the sacrificial service. The latter work was patterned upon the format of the widely accepted *Tevu'at Shor*. Before his death R. Alexander Schorr ordered that the unpublished manuscript be placed in his grave. His intention was that the work not be circulated since an ultimate decision regarding these matters cannot be rendered until the advent of the Messiah.

One dare not hastily conclude that such an approach reflects a reticence born of fear or mere lethargy. Expositors of Halakhah always met the social issues of their day forthrightly and did not hesitate to legislate on every facet of personal and communal life. In all generations, Torah scholars have striven to overcome any and all obstacles in order to issue halakhic rulings; consistently the attitude of *Gedolei Yisra'el* has been: *yikov ha-din et ha-har*. However, differing dramatically from all other areas governed by Halakhah, questions pertaining to the construction of the *Bet ha-Mikdash* and the sacrificial order, by their very nature, occupy a unique position unamenable to the usual canons of *psak*. Even a cursory examination of the responsa literature on this topic indicates a dearth of precedents and parallel citations, the very fabric of which legal decisions are woven. One should bear in mind that the monumental works authored by such giants of *hora'ah* as Rif and Rosh do not include a codification of the laws of *Kodshim*. There can be no doubt that in protesting their inability to reach halakhic conclusions—and to adduce sufficient evidence in support of such pronouncements—Torah authorities were not reflecting misplaced humility but were stating the simple truth.

Although there are manifold halakhic impediments which prevent us from fulfilling the many *mizvot* attendant upon the performance of the sacrificial service, our inability to do so is certainly to our detriment: "If not for the *ma'amadot,* heaven and earth would not endure," states the Gemara (*Ta'anit* 27b); the Mishnah, *Avot* 1:2, reckons the sacrificial service as one of the pillars upon which the world stands. But with the lapse of the Temple service we are offered an equally efficacious substitute. The Gemara depicts Abraham as appearing before the Almighty and expressing his fear that the Jewish people might perhaps be destroyed in punishment for their transgressions. To this the Almighty replied, "Take for Me a three-year-old heifer." Whereupon, Abraham countered, "That is well as long as the Temple stands, but when the Temple no longer exists, what shall become of them?" The Almighty answered, "I have ordained for them the order of the sacrifices. Whenever they study it I shall account it as if they had offered a sacrifice before Me, and I will forgive all their sins" (*Megillah* 31b).

Elsewhere the Sages declare that during the period of the exile, worship in the Temple is supplanted by the study of the laws pertaining to the *korbanot* denied us in actuality. "Anyone who engages in [the study of] the law of the sin-offering is accounted as if he had sacrificed a sin-offering" (*Menahot* 111a). The term *ke-'ilu* ("is accounted as") is to be understood quite literally. The study of *Kodshim* effects for us the selfsame benefits which flowed from the sacrificial offerings of our ancestors. If indeed *korbanot,* in addition to their other propitious effects, are also essential for the initiation of prophecy, as Nachmanides asserts, or requisite to effect the advent of the Messiah, as is Kalisher's contention, the use of the term *ke'ilu* indicates that these too are attainable through the study of *Kodshim*. The Chafetz Chaim advocated the establishment of *kollelim* whose students would devote themselves to this field of scholarship. He heralded the appearance of such institutions, citing scriptural references demonstrating that increased proficiency in precisely this area of study will speed the redemption (*Ma'amar Torah Or,* chap. 10).

"Investigate and receive reward!" exhort our Sages (*Zevahim* 45a) in answering a query regarding the purpose of pursuing studies pertinent only during the days of the Messiah. From the words of the Chafetz Chaim it follows that the Sages may be understood to have answered that this reward is, in its ultimate form, the very coming of the Messiah alluded to by the talmudic interlocutor and the hastening of the fulfillment of the prophetic promise, "I shall bring them to my holy mountain. . . . their burnt-offerings and their sacrifices shall be acceptable upon Mine altar, for My house shall be a house of prayer for all the nations" (Is. 55:7).

CHAPTER XIII

The Conversion Crisis

I am the one who drew Yitro nigh and did not repulse him. You, also, when a person comes to you to be converted and comes solely for the sake of heaven, *draw him nigh and do not repulse him.*

YALKUT SHIM'ONI, YITRO 268

The Jew today, no less than in the past, is the heir to an unbroken chain of tradition. The survival of the Jewish people is directly dependent upon the preservation of the divinely sanctified identity of the community of Israel. The sanctity of Israel is a concomitant of Israel's acceptance of the Torah on Mount Sinai, a Torah which is an inseparable whole comprised of both Holy Writ and the Oral Law. Thus, for Judaism itself, the question "Who is a Jew?" can have but one answer: A Jew is one whom Halakhah defines as a Jew.

Jews, jealous of their identity, have always heroically resisted any and all attempts to compromise their ethnic purity. As the Midrash queries, "Why did Jeremiah compare Israel to the olive? All liquids intermingle with one another; oil is immiscible, and remains apart. Similarly, Israel cannot be assimilated among the nations of the world." [1] Our survival as a people may undoubtedly be credited to our tenacity in preserving inviolate the identity of the Jew.

Yet the peoplehood of Israel is not founded upon racist attitudes nor has Judaism suffered from the maladies of xenophobia. Jewish identity has always been a matter of membership in a specific and unique faith-community. As such Judaism has always welcomed all individuals seeking to embrace the tenets of the Torah. Indeed, the *ger ẓedek* (righteous

1. *Shemot Rabbah* XXXVI, 1.

proselyte) is extolled in rabbinic literature and depicted as being the recipient of an extraordinary degree of divine favor. The *ger ẓedek* is regarded with awe and wonder. Whereas the Jews who experienced the giving of the Torah at Mount Sinai were so overwhelmed by the difficulties attendent upon the observance of the commandments that they had to be coerced in order to secure their acceptance of the precepts of the Torah, the proselyte voluntarily accepts this discipline: "Had they not witnessed the sounds and the flames, the thunder and the voice of the *shofrot* they would not have accepted the yoke of the kingdom of heaven. Yet this [convert] did not witness a single one of these and joins himself to the Lord and accepts the yoke of the kingdom of heaven. Can there be anyone more beloved!" [2] The delight which God takes in such converts is reflected in the explicit halakhic obligation making it incumbent upon the rabbinical courts to accept sincere and committed candidates for proselytization.

However, in the demands which it makes upon the proselyte, Judaism is uncompromising. Judaism is not merely a faith-community; its adherents are bound by a rigorous and demanding code of law governing every aspect of life. Commitment must be total. To be accepted as a member of the community of Israel the convert must not only subscribe to the beliefs of Judaism but must willingly agree to observe its precepts. Should the candidate refuse to accept any detail of this code, his conversion is *ipso facto* invalid.

In this Judaism is unyielding. The basic conditions of genuine conversion are clearly enunciated in Halakhah. As the guardians of a divine mandate, Jews must perforce refuse to recognize any conversion not performed in accordance with the norms of Halakhah. This stark reality cannot be altered by the fiat of any civil judicial body. Nor for that matter is any rabbinic court or other ecclesiastic body empowered to overlook the *sina qua non* of Jewish identity.

Present circumstances have added a new dimension to the "Who is a Jew?" problem. The high incidence of intermarriage, both in Israel and the Diaspora, has generated an unprecedented number of applications for conversion. Given the exigencies of the contemporary situation conversion may well be the solution to myriad personal, social and religious problems. On the other hand, improper procedure may not only reduce the conversion ritual to a meaningless charade but may also pose a threat to the very identity of the Jewish people.

---

2. *Tanḥuma, Lekh Lekha* 6.

The responsa literature of the modern period is replete with questions concerning the circumstances under which conversion is permissible and proper. These discussions are clearly germane to any attempt to find a resolution to the current conversion dilemma. The questions posed with regard to problematic contemporary conversions are threefold in nature: (1) Is it permissible for rabbinical courts to accept prospective candidates for conversion when it appears that application is made, not out of religious conviction, but as a matter of convenience, e.g., to facilitate marriage with a Jewish partner? (2) Is a conversion of convenience, i.e., one undertaken for marriage or other ulterior motive, in which the petitioner obviously has no intention of abiding by the precepts of Judaism, a valid one? (3) Granting the validity and propriety of the conversion itself, is it permissible for the convert to enter into marriage with a Jewish spouse with whom the convert has consorted prior to conversion?

I

The Gemara, *Yevamot* 24b, cites the opinion of R. Nechemiah who maintained that any conversion based upon ulterior motivation is null and void. In addition to conversion for purposes of marriage, R. Nechemiah specifically refers to the recorded historical episodes of the conversion of the Samaritans predicated upon fear of lions,[3] conversion by servants of King Solomon in anticipation of being appointed to high office in the royal court and the mass conversions which are recorded in the Book of Esther[4] as instances of invalid conversion. The Gemara rejects the opinion of R. Nechemiah as applied to conversions which are already a *fait accompli*.[5] Once performed, such conversions are valid regardless of motivation. Nevertheless, Jewish law is unequivocal in stating that, before the fact, such candidates are not to be accepted. The *Bet Din* is constrained to reject applicants prompted by motives other than sincere

3. II Kings 17:25–41.
4. Esther 8:17.
5. According to the interpretation of one authority, *Hagahot Mordekhai, Yevamot,* sec. 110, R. Nechemiah's view is not rejected but interpreted as having been expressed with regard to cases in which personal benefit is the sole motivating factor. According to this analysis, R. Nechemiah accepts the validity of conversions which are motivated by a combination of ulterior considerations and "the sake of heaven."

religious conviction. Thus, *Hagahot Mordekhai, Yevamot,* sec. 110, writes that if it is known that the applicants are motivated by desire for personal benefit "they are not to be accepted." Moreover, the Gemara flatly declares that proselytes will not be accepted in the days of the Messiah and, in fact, were not accepted during the reigns of David and Solomon. The reason for blanket rejection of would-be converts during these historical epochs is that in periods during which the Jewish commonwealth is blessed with economic prosperity and prestigious social status there is ample room for suspicion that prospective proselytes are not prompted by reasons of sincere religious conviction.

Rambam,[6] in his codification of these regulations, is even more explicit:

> Let it not enter your mind that Samson, the deliverer of Israel, or Solomon, king of Israel, who was called "beloved of God," married foreign women while they were yet gentiles, but rather the secret of the matter is as follows: The proper performance of the precept is that when a male or female proselyte comes to be converted, he is to be investigated[7] perchance he seeks to enter the [Jewish] religion in order to acquire money or in order to achieve a position of authority or because of fear. In the case of a man, he is to be investigated perchance he has set his eyes upon a Jewish woman; in the case of a woman, [she] is to be investigated perchance she set her eyes upon one of the youths of Israel. If no motive is found in them, the heavy weight of the yoke of the Torah is to be made known to them and the burden which there is for gentiles in its observance. Therefore, the *Bet Din* did not accept proselytes throughout the days of David and Solomon. In the days of David, lest they rejected [idol worship] because of fear, and in the days of Solomon, lest they rejected [idol worship] because of the sovereignty, the prosperity and the greatness which Israel then enjoyed. For whosoever forsakes heathenism for the sake of some worldly vanity is not a righteous proselyte. Nevertheless,

6. *Mishneh Torah, Hilkhot Issurei Bi'ah* 13:14–15.

7. R. Yitzchak Schmelkes, *Teshuvot Bet Yiẓḥak, Yoreh De'ah,* II, no. 100, notes that Rambam carefully chooses the term *bodkin aḥarav,* which connotes a careful investigation of the case, rather than the less inclusive *bodkin oto,* which would indicate merely "examination" or interrogation of the applicant. The implication is that the *Bet Din* must make a full investigation of the facts and not rely upon the declaration of the candidate.

> many proselytes were converted in the days of David and Solomon by ignorant persons and the Great Court accorded them doubtful status, not rejecting them . . . and not drawing them nigh until such time as their subsequent conduct could be observed.

It is quite evident that prospective converts are to be rejected even if proof positive of ulterior motive is lacking. The mere suspicion of impure motive is grounds for rejection of the applicant's candidacy; the burden of proof with regard to sincerity is upon the prospective convert.[8] Apparently, when it is obvious that material benefit or personal gain would accrue to the proselyte, protestations of religious conviction are unacceptable.

There is, however, one exception to this principle. The Gemara records several instances of converts who were accepted despite self-avowed ulterior motivation. In *Shabbat* 31a it is reported that Hillel accepted a proselyte who approached him with the declaration, "Convert me in order that you may appoint me High Priest." Similarly, *Menaḥot* 44a reports that R. Chiya accepted the candidacy of a woman who wished to convert in order to become the wife of one of his students. *Tosafot, Yevamot* 24b, resolves the apparent incongruity by postulating that Hillel and R. Chiya were certain that the respective candidates would ultimately accept Judaism "for the sake of heaven." [9] All authorities agree that an application for conversion may justifiably be entertained only if the *Bet Din* is satisfied that upon conversion the candidate will become a God-fearing Jew and will scrupulously observe the commandments of the Torah. It is clear that, according to Halakhah, certainty of future religious observance is a necessary condition for acceptance of a prospective convert.

In a letter written in response to a question submitted on behalf of the Sephardic community of Buenos Aires, Rabbi Meshullam Roth[10] declares that the candidacy of a prospective proselyte cannot under any

---

8. See R. Chaim Ozer Grodzinski, *Teshuvot Aḥi'ezer,* III, no. 26, secs. 2–3.

9. This interpretation is accepted and cited definitively by R. Joseph Karo in his commentary on the *Tur, Bet Yosef, Yoreh De'ah,* 268, and by *Shakh, Yoreh De'ah* 268:23. See also R. Zevi Pesach Frank, *Har Ẓvi, Yoreh De'ah,* no. 218. This leniency is, however, disputed by R. Ya'akov Ettlinger, *Binyan Ẓion,* no. 149.

10. *Kol Mevaser,* II, no. 8. See also R. Rafael Shapiro, *Or ha-Mizraḥ,* Elul 5717, p. 7.

circumstances be considered unless the candidate assures the *Bet Din* that he will observe the precepts of Judaism, particularly the laws of the Sabbath, family purity and the dietary code. If, in the opinion of the *Bet Din,* it is "virtually certain" that he will fulfill his pledge and the *Bet Din* feels that ultimately the conversion will be "for the sake of heaven," they may then perform the conversion ritual. Rabbi Roth notes, however, that the percentage of converts whose intention is for the "sake of heaven" is so minute that in actuality it "approaches zero." While it must be emphasized that, particularly in recent years, there have been numerous instances of *gerei ẓedek* whose motivation and conduct are to be lauded, Rabbi Roth's description is an accurate characterization of those proselytes who undertake conversion in order to facilitate marriage to a Jewish spouse.[11]

Some authorities grant considerable leeway in determining sincerity of purpose. Rabbi Shlomoh Kluger[12] discusses the propriety of sanctioning the conversion of a young man who threatened to become an apostate if his non-Jewish mistress would not be accepted as a proselyte. Rabbi Kluger rules that under such circumstances the conversion cannot be considered as having been undertaken on account of marriage, since the couple will continue to live together as man and wife in any event. Hence, the conversion may be deemed to be "for the sake of heaven" and not "for the sake of man." A similar view was voiced by Rabbi Eliezer Deutsch and by Rabbi Yechiel Ya'akov Weinberg.[13] This contention is also cited by Rabbi Chaim Ozer Grodzinski[14] and applied by him to the case of

11. Cf. R. Irwin Borvick, "What Has Happened to the Converts?" *Jewish Life,* January 1973.

12. *Tuv Ta'am va-Da'at* I, no. 130. R. Shlomoh Kluger, in a wider-reaching statement, advances the opinion that in the event that the couple have cohabited even once, passion has been reduced and hence the conversion should not be viewed as being "on account of man." With regard to the basic question involving the consideration of apostasy, see R. Moses Feinstein, *Iggrot Mosheh, Even ha-Ezer,* II, no. 4, and R. Ezriel Hildesheimer, *Teshuvot Rabbi Ezri'el, Yoreh De'ah,* no. 234. See also the more general discussion in R. Chaim Chizkiyahu Medini, *Sedei Ḥemed,* II, 276–277, *Kelalim, Ma'areḥet ha-He,* no. 37. The conclusion to be drawn is that, according to these authorities, no otherwise forbidden act may be performed in order to avert threatened apostasy.

13. *Pri ha-Sadeh,* II, no. 3, and *Seridei Esh,* III, no. 50.

14. *Teshuvot Aḥi'ezer,* III, no. 26. *Aḥi'ezer* indicates that possible ulterior motives must be determined by the *Bet Din* on the basis of individual circumstances. Fear of social ostracism or desire to share a common burial plot are

a couple who had undergone a civil ceremony and were living together as man and wife. This opinion is, however, by no means universally accepted. Rabbi Meir Arak[15] rejects this view, arguing that ulterior motivation is indeed present in that the husband may well wish to legitimize his marriage and not continue an illicit relationship. There is evidence that R. Chaim Ozer himself later reversed his position with regard to this matter and adopted a more stringent attitude. In a responsum dealing with a similar problem dated some twenty-two years later and published in vol. III, no. 28, of the same work, *Teshuvot Aḥi'ezer,* R. Chaim Ozer regards conversion under similar circumstances as being undertaken for the sake of marriage and, hence, prohibits it. Even though the couple were not only living together as man and wife but had also sired children without having contracted a valid marriage, R. Chaim Ozer rules that the prospective proselyte was, even in this instance, motivated by reasons of marriage. The dim view expressed by these authorities regarding the permissibility of conversion despite an already existent conjugal relationship merely echoes in greater detail the succinct but unequivocal decision of a much earlier authority, R. Ya'akov Ettlinger.[16]

An argument frequently advanced in favor of the acceptance of converts, regardless of motivation, is that their rejection by an Orthodox *Bet Din* is often followed by acceptance into the Jewish faith by Reform or liberal clergymen. Conversions conducted under such auspices are clearly invalid. As a result, individuals converted in this manner are inadvertently accepted by the Jewish community as *bona fide* Jews and are unlawfully permitted to contract marriages with other Jews. If the alleged convert is a female, children born to her are, of course, not Jewish; if a male, the children, while Jewish, are of tainted lineage. Rabbi Mendel Kirshbaum,[17] who served as *dayan* in Frankfort, argues that, in light of this consideration, such candidates should be accepted for conversion. The Gemara, *Yevamot* 47a, states that a prospective proselyte is to be investigated with regard to his motives for conversion and is to be informed of selected *mizvot* of

---

also factors which, of course, must be weighed. See *Seridei Esh,* III, no. 50. Desire for immigration to Israel as a possible ulterior motive is discussed by R. Isaac ha-Levi Herzog, *Teshuvot Heikhal Yiẓḥak, Even ha-Ezer,* no. 21, sec. 2.

15. *Imrei Yosher,* I, no. 176; R. Yitzchak Ya'akov Weisz, *Minḥat Yiẓḥak,* III, no. 101, concurs with the opinion expressed by *Imrei Yosher.*

16. *Binyan Ẓion,* no. 149.

17. *Menaḥem Meishiv,* no. 42.

both lesser and greater stringency and of the punishments incurred upon their transgression. "For what reason?" queries the Gemara. "So that if he changes his mind, let him change his mind." Rashi, in his commentary on this text, adds, "For if he should change his mind [and decide] not to convert, let him change his mind *and it is of no concern to us.*" Rabbi Kirshbaum contends that one may infer from this comment that if the conversion were to be of concern to Jewry, no attempt at discouragement should be made. In instances in which considerations such as those previously stated are operative, encouragement of conversion is indeed a matter of positive concern to us. Consequently, argues Rabbi Kirshbaum, under these circumstances the convert should be accepted, even if his decision to seek conversion is prompted by impure motives.[18] This contention was rejected by the late Rabbi Ya'akov Mordecai Breish of Zurich in a letter written to Rabbi Kirshbaum upon the publication of the latter's *Menaḥem Meshiv.*[19] Rabbi Breish states that the consideration raised is a specious one and there need be no fear that the candidate will be erroneously accepted as a Jew. In the course of the usual investigation before any prospective marriage it should become clear that the conversion was performed by a Reform rabbi and hence is invalid. Furthermore, adds Rabbi Breish, it is forbidden for the members of the *Bet Din* to participate in a conversion for the sake of marriage and this prohibition devolves directly upon the rabbis involved. Accordingly, they are forbidden to commit this transgression even in order to prevent a more severe transgression on the part of others.[20]

---

18. R. David Hoffmann, *Melamed le-Ho'il, Even ha-Ezer,* no. 8, employs an identical line of reasoning in support of an even more radical contention. It is his opinion that in cases where the conversion is to the advantage of individuals other than the convert himself, the candidate may be accepted despite expressed reservations with regard to the observance of a particular commandment. The case considered by Rabbi Hoffmann concerned a gentile woman who had been living with a Jewish husband for a considerable period of time. Conversion would have obviated the prohibition of consorting with a non-Jewess and would have legitimized the progeny of the Jewish husband. Rabbi Hoffmann, however, offers no suporting evidence for this innovative view. Cf. *Iggrot Mosheh, Even ha-Ezer,* II, no. 4, who rejects Rabbi Hoffmann's position. See also R. Rafael Shapiro, *Or ha-Mizraḥ,* Elul 5717, p. 7.

19. *Ḥelkat Ya'akov,* I, no. 13.

20. Cf. *Aḥi'ezer,* III, no. 26, sec. 7, and below, note 59. *Teshuvot Rabbi Ezri'el, Yoreh De'ah,* no. 234, is not swayed by the concern expressed by his interlocutor lest the conversion be performed by a Reform clergyman.

In addition to the question of the permissibility of conversion for purposes of marriage, there is serious concern because of the fact that such converts almost invariably fail to become observant Jews. Rabbi Abraham I. Kook finds that, because of this lack of observance on the part of the convert, the members of the *Bet Din* who participate in the conversion ceremony commit yet another transgression. As a Jew, the convert is culpable for his misdeeds and will receive divine punishment for his lack of observance. The members of the *Bet Din* transgress, contends Rabbi Kook, in "placing a stumbling block before the blind,"[21] In a reply addressed to the rabbi of the Sephardic community of Buenos Aires, Rabbi Kook fully endorses the policy adopted by the Argentine rabbinate in refusing to accept any proselytes and in insisting that those who are truly serious appear before the Jerusalem *Bet Din* and submit to a comprehensive investigation by that body.[22] In another responsum, addressed to Rabbi Ben-Zion Uziel, Rabbi Kook refuses to countenance conversion undertaken for purposes of marriage.[23]

II

There is strong reason to question the validity of conversion, even as a *fait accompli,* when undertaken for purposes of marriage or, for that matter, in order to obtain benefits accruing to Jews granted Israeli citizenship under the Law of Return. As previously noted, the definitive rule of the Talmud is that conversions, once performed, are valid even if entered into for reasons other than religious conviction. In analyzing the rationale governing the validity of insincere conversions, the most obvious reason which presents itself is the halakhic principle that mental reservations cannot invalidate an overt act—*devarim she-be-lev ainam devarim.* Hence, even if the act were to be mentally nullified, the conversion would be efficacious. Accordingly, the conversion cannot be invalidated by reservations or insincere motives which remain *in pectore.* However, a quite

21. *Da'at Kohen,* no. 164; cf. R. Yehudah Leib Graubart, *Ḥavalim be-Ne'imim,* IV, *Yoreh De'ah,* no. 30.

22. It appears that this policy was formalized and an *issur* issued by the rabbinate. Some twenty years later the ban was violated and a conversion ceremony was performed. Rabbi Frank, *Har Ẓvi, Yoreh De'ah,* no. 116, rules that a conversion performed in violation of the *issur* is null and void.

23. *Ezrat Kohen,* no. 14. Cf. R. Ben-Zion Uziel, *Mishpetei Uziel, Even ha-Ezer,* no. 18, who disagrees. See also the sources cited by R. Meir Amsel, *Ha-Ma'or,* Kislev–Tevet 5735.

different line of reasoning explaining the validity of such conversion is presented by Ritva and *Nemukei Yosef* in their commentaries on *Yevamot* 24b. These authorities state that all conversions stemming from ulterior motivation are not merely lacking in sincerity but, in a sense, are not undertaken in free will and embody an element of coercion. Nevertheless, conversion as a *fait accompli* is valid even under these circumstances because such coercion ultimately engenders a firm decision to accept the obligations attendent upon acceptance of Judaism. The candidate for conversion recognizes that his desired goal can be achieved only by making such a commitment and accordingly accepts the obligations incumbent upon a member of the Jewish faith. Since Ritva and *Nemukei Yosef* are intent upon dispelling the notion that mental reservations exist in instances of insincere conversion we must infer that mental reservations, when and if they *are* present, would, according to these authorities, invalidate the conversion. The ramifications of this crucial issue are discussed by Rabbi Isaac Shmelkes. In his *Bet Yiẓḥak,*[24] he explains that mental reservations do serve to invalidate conversion because, in his opinion, the general principle that mental negations are ineffective applies only with regard to matters affecting interpersonal relationships, such as financial transactions and the like. Matters such as conversion are essentially ritual in nature and "the Lord desires the heart." Hence, it is the ultimate intention which prevails. The Talmud[25] states that a non-Jew who refuses to accept even a single commandment or a single rabbinic ordinance must be rejected, since such non-acceptance invalidates conversion. Accordingly, argues *Bet Yiẓḥak,* converts who have reservations with regard to the acceptance of the dietary laws and laws of family purity cannot be regarded as Jews even if they falsely declare that they are willing to fulfill all the precepts of Judaism. Rabbi Schmelkes declares that such conversions should not be performed, not only because the conversions are themselves farcical in nature, but also because they leave in their wake spurious proselytes who are commonly accepted as Jews. These invalid conversions subsequently lead to unions between Jews and individuals who are gentiles in the eyes of Halakhah.

Rabbi Chaim Ozer Grodzinski[26] agrees that mental reservations with regard to performance of *miẓvot* nullify the efficacy of ritual conversion. He

24. *Yoreh De'ah,* II, no. 100.
25. *Bekhorot* 30b.
26. *Aḥi'ezer,* III, no. 26, secs. 2–3, and II, no. 28.

cites as evidence for this position the terminology of Rambam: "A convert who has not been investigated . . . who has been circumcised and has immersed himself in the presence of three ignorant persons is a proselyte, even if it be known that he has converted on account of some consideration. . . . he is accorded doubtful status until his righteousness becomes clear." [27]

The "doubtful status" of a proselyte prompted by ulterior motivation, explains R. Chaim Ozer, arises from the fact that actual conversion is ultimately a matter of intent. If the candidate does indeed accept Judaism with all its ramifications he is deemed to be a Jew regardless of motivation; but if these considerations do not ultimately lead to a wholehearted acceptance, the conversion is invalid. When no extraneous considerations are present, there is no reason to doubt the validity of the conversion; when such considerations *are* present, the status of the proselyte remains in doubt until such time as his "righteousness is demonstrated," i.e., until such time as his general comportment testifies to ultimate acceptance of the norms of Jewish conduct.[28]

---

27. *Hilkhot Issurei Bi'ah* 13:17.

28. The concluding phrase of *Issurei Bi'ah* 13:15 *"ad sheyeira'eh aḥaritam,"* lit., "until their end is known," is to be understood in the same vein. Accordingly, when quoted earlier it has been rendered, "until such time as their subsequent conduct could be observed."

A similar analysis of Rambam's exposition is advanced by R. Menachem Panet, *Avnei Ẓedek,* no. 27. Quoting Rambam and Ritva in their commentaries on *Kiddushin* 75b, *Avnei Ẓedek* declares that one who converts other than "for the sake of heaven" is deemed to be a convert after the fact only if it is known that he observes the precepts of Judaism even in private. Only when it becomes ascertained that he is scrupulous in his observance is he considered with certainty to be a true proselyte; until such evidence is forthcoming his status is doubtful. The status of one who has no ulterior motive is never in doubt. Since there is no motivation for conversion other than sincere conviction, he is immediately regarded as a true proselyte. *Avnei Ẓedek* employs this line of reasoning in offering a novel explanation of the underlying rationale governing the prohibition against marrying a convert with whom the prospective husband is suspected of having previously cohabited. The prohibition, asserts *Avnei Ẓedek,* is limited to a woman whose status is yet in doubt. A person of good character, having knowledge of her private conduct, may testify to her comportment as a pious Jewess and hence enter into marriage with the convert. One who has consorted with her, or who is suspected of having consorted with her while she was yet a gentile, is not deemed to be a reliable witness and hence may not marry her. He tentatively concludes that the prohibition is not operative if independent evidence of her personal piety

An explication of the concept of mental reservation in this context is formulated by R. Chaim Ozer,[29] who notes a fundamental distinction between *acceptance* of precepts and *observance* of precepts. The stipulation that a prospective convert must accept all commandments of the Torah means simply that he must accept their binding force. Recognition by the candidate that he is lacking in moral stamina or the requisite willpower to withstand temptation does not invalidate a conversion. R. Chaim Ozer adds, however, that when it is evident that the prospective convert intends to desecrate the Sabbath and to partake of forbidden foods as a matter of course, the conversion is invalid. Such an attitude on the part of the candidate is indicative of nonacceptance of these prohibitions in principle and hence nullifies the act of conversion.

R. Chaim Ozer's basic distinction between acceptance and observance of precepts is challenged by the one-time Chief Rabbi of Kovno, Rabbi Abraham Dov Ber Kahane. In his collected responsa, *Dvar Avraham,*[30] Rabbi Kahane contends that acceptance of the "yoke of commandments" coupled with clear intention to transgress is a self-contradiction and cannot be termed "acceptance" at all.[31] While disagreeing with regard to what

---

is forthcoming. Cf. also R. Joseph Rosen, *Ẓofnat Pa'aneaḥ, Issurei Bi'ah* 13:14, and R. Nathan Weidenfeld, *Teshuvot Ḥazon Naḥum,* no. 90. A somewhat different analysis of Rambam's position is presented in *Heikhal Yiẓḥak, Even ha-Ezer,* I, no. 20, sec. 2. Rabbi Herzog, however, agrees that marriage cannot be permitted even though the convert appears to observe the commandments of the Torah "until we come to a recognition of proper inner conviction."

A radically different interpretation is advanced by Rabbi Unterman in *No'am,* XIV (5731), in the course of an essay entitled *"Hilkhot Gerut ve-Derekh Biẓu'an,"* pp. 1–9. Rabbi Unterman argues that conversions such as these are declared to be invalid by Rambam only if the convert subsequently reverts to the worship of foreign gods. In contradistinction to all authorities previously cited, Rabbi Unterman contends that subsequent failure to fulfill other halakhic obligations does not invalidate the conversion.

29. *Aḥi'ezer,* III, no. 26, sec. 4. See also R. Moshe ha-Kohen, *Teshuvot ve-Heshiv Mosheh, Yoreh De'ah,* no. 51.

30. III, no. 28. This responsum also appeared in *Talpiot,* II (Sivan 5705), nos. 1–2.

31. *Aḥi'ezer* draws this distinction in order to resolve a fine point of halakhic reasoning. It may be contended that the candidacy of a woman who is known to have consorted with a Jew should be rejected out of hand if she intends to marry him following conversion. In view of the fact that such marriage is forbidden by rabbinic edict, the prospective convert has, in effect, refused to accept one of the rabbinic prohibitions, thereby disqualifying her candidacy for conversion. *Aḥi'ezer* dismisses this argument by drawing a distinction be-

may constitute mental reservations, both authorities concur that when mental reservations *are* present, the conversion is invalid.

The necessity for the convert's acceptance of the "yoke of *mizvot*" as a *sine qua non* of his conversion raises certain difficulties in our generation. As noted earlier, the rationale advanced by numerous authorities in defense of the *ex post facto* validity of insincere conversions is the consideration that in such instances there is ultimately a determined, albeit reluctant, acceptance of the obligations incurred through the acceptance of Judaism. In the absence of anticipated benefit, a candidate lacking deep religious commitment might not wish to incur such responsibilities. Yet weighing the pros and cons of the situation, determination to accept the tenets of Judaism is reached by the convert upon recognition that only by the acceptance of such obligations will the benefits attendant upon membership in the Jewish faith-community accrue to him. It is, in a sense, a bargain in which the desire for certain benefits forces acceptance of concomitant disadvantages. Rabbi Kahane argues that a changed social and religious climate no longer demands such a decision on the part of a convert. A convert lacking sincerity of motivation is forced to accept the obligations incumbent upon members of the Jewish faith only if he lives in a society which demands that he conform to the normative standards of Jewish life. In such a milieu, the desired benefits can be obtained by the convert only by accepting the tenets of Judaism. Hence, the resolution to embrace Judaism, even if motivated by self-serving considerations, constitutes a valid acceptance. In contemporary society, however, pressure for religious conformity does not exist. Consequently, declares Rabbi Kahane, nowadays, in cases where a deeply rooted commitment of faith is not the moving factor, there is no reason to assume that ulterior motivation mandates even a "coerced" acceptance.

Similar misgivings concerning the status of such conversions in our day are echoed in the relatively recent writings of numerous halakhic authorities. Particularly forceful are the strictures expressed by the late

---

tween categorical rejection of an injunction and recognition that one will sin. *Melamed le-Ho'il, Even ha-Ezer,* no. 8, raises the same question and resolves it on other grounds, as indicated above. Since he recognizes the question as one which constitutes a serious conceptual problem, and fails to advance the distinction formulated by *Ahi'ezer,* it may be deduced that Rabbi Hoffmann's position is in agreement with that of *Dvar Avraham* in opposition to the views of *Ahi'ezer*. Cf. R. Yehudah Leib Kagan, "Hilkhot Gerim," *Ha-Pardes,* XX (Sivan 5706), no. 3, 30–33, and XX (Tammuz 5706), no. 4, 29–31.

Chief Rabbi of Israel, Rabbi Isaac ha-Levi Herzog. In a letter addressed to a Swiss rabbinic body he writes:

> . . . even though the halakhic decision has been formulated that, after the fact, even those converting for ulterior purposes and not for the sake of heaven are converts, I have exceedingly strong reason [to assert] that in these times the law is not so. Since in former times virtually every Jew was forced to observe the commandments, otherwise he would have been disdained and despised as a renegade, this therefore strengthened the supposition that the gentile who comes to convert has, in truth, made a decision to observe the Sabbath, etc. . . . But in our day the situation has changed and it is [now] possible to be a leader in Israel while yet a desecrator of the Sabbath and one who partakes of *nevelah* and *tereifah* in public, etc. Whereby does one arrive at the supposition that the gentile indeed decided, at least at the moment of conversion, to observe Judaism? Moreover, the vast majority and perhaps all converts of this genre do not commence to observe even the fundamentals of [the Jewish] faith . . .[32]

Rabbi Breish[33] voices a similar opinion and states emphatically that if it is evident that the proselyte will not adhere to the tenets of Judaism, the conversion ceremony is in no way efficacious. He further adds that when conversion is preliminary to marriage to a sprouse who is non-observant it may be assumed with virtual certainty that the convert will be no more scrupulous in observing the commandments of the Torah than the marriage partner who is a Jew by birth. Rabbi Meir Arak (*Imrei Yosher,* I, no. 176), Rabbi Menachem Panet (*Avnei Ẓedek,* no. 26), Rabbi Abraham I. Kook (*Da'at Kohen,* no. 154)[34] and Rabbi Yitzchak Ya'akov Weisz (*Minḥat Yiẓḥak,* I, no. 122) concur with the previously discussed views of *Bet Yiẓḥak, Aḥi'ezer, Dvar Avraham,* Rabbi Breish and Rabbi Herzog.

32. This letter was published by Rabbi Breish in the latter's *Ḥelkat Ya'akov,* I, no. 14. Similar sentiments are also expressed by Rabbi Herzog in his *Heikhal Yiẓḥak, Even ha-Ezer,* I, no. 20, sec. 2 and no. 21, sec. 3. Rabbi Herzog adds that if the candidate for conversion is a female the dangers are greater since an invalid conversion may cause grave ramifications with regard to subsequent marriage involving a Jewish partner and affect the genealogical purity of future generations.

33. *Ḥelkat Ya'akov,* no. 13.

34. Cf. *Ezrat Kohen,* no. 14.

This position is also endorsed by Rabbi Bezalel Zolti[35] and Rabbi Moshe Sternbuch[36] as well as by the Sephardic Chief Rabbi of Israel, Rabbi Ovadiah Yosef.[37] All of these many authorities are in agreement that when it is evident that the candidate will be nonobservant the conversion is null and void despite the candidate's oral declaration of acceptance of the yoke of *mizvot.*

It is interesting to note that Rabbi Moses Feinstein, in a responsum dated Luban 5689 (1929), voices an identical opinion and adds:

> I do not understand the reasoning of those rabbis who err with regard to this. Even according to their opinion, what benefit do they bring to the Jewish people in their acceptance of such converts? For it is certain that the Holy One, blessed be He, and the Jewish people are not happy that such converts become intermingled with Israel. According to the Law, it is certain that such [a convert] is not a proselyte at all.[38]

In a later responsum, written in the United States some twenty-one years later,[39] the author, while himself rejecting their position, attempts

35. *Torah She-be-'al Peh,* XIII (5731), pp. 35 and 50.

36. *Dat ve-Halakhah,* no. 3. In addition to the argument already cited, Rabbi Sternbuch suggests that such conversions may be invalid for another reason. Ordination as biblically required has lapsed in our day. The authority vested in a *Bet Din,* enabling it to act without benefit of ordination is rabbinic in nature. The *Bet Din* is empowered to act in accepting converts only because conversion is deemed to be a *zekhut* (benefit). However, if a convert does not intend to observe the commandments, conversion is not a *zekhut* for that convert. Hence, argues Rabbi Sternbuch, the rabbinic license from which the *Bet Din* derives its authority to act despite the absence of biblical ordination, does not extend to such situations. Accordingly, the conversion ritual is of no effect. Cf., however, R. Yehudah Leib Graubart, *Ḥavalim be-Ne'imim,* IV, *Yoreh De'ah,* no. 30.

37. *Yobi'a Omer,* II, *Even ha-Ezer,* no. 3, and *Torah She-be-'al Peh,* XIII (5731), p. 31.

38. *Iggrot Mosheh, Yoreh De'ah,* I, no. 157.

39. *Iggrot Moshes, Yoreh De'ah,* I, no. 160, dated 6 Iyar, 5710. Interestingly, in a responsum written less than four months earlier, on 12 Trevet, 5710, Rabbi Feinstein leans heavily toward his original position. He states, "it is more likely that they are not at all proselytes and that they are still gentiles . . ." (*Iggrot Mosheh, Yoreh De'ah,* I, no. 194). In another responsum, written in 5722, many years later, Rabbi Feinstein again expresses reservations concerning the validity of such conversions. See *Iggrot Mosheh, Even ha-Ezer,*

to find a "slight justification for those rabbis who accept [such converts] in order that they not be considered inferior even to ignoramuses." Rabbi Feinstein cites the argument that mental reservations cannot invalidate a performed act. In contradistinction to previously cited authorities, Rabbi Feinstein accepts this argument in principle, agreeing that this canon (*devarim she-be-lev einam devarim*) encompasses even ritual acts such as conversion. However, he declares that it is inapplicable to the case at hand. Although mental reservations in themselves cannot invalidate the oral acceptance of the yoke of *miẓvot,* nevertheless, in the case of a convert who will definitely not observe the precepts of Judaism, "we are witnesses" to the fact that the oral acceptance is not sincere. We are thus confronted by a phenomenon different in kind from mere mental reservation. Whereas a private mental reservation may not invalidate the conversion, common recognition that such reservations exist elevates such reservations to the status of a public act tantamount to an open declaration annulling the acceptance of commandments. Such a declaration would clearly invalidate the conversion.

Rabbi Feinstein also advances a second consideration in defense of the validity of such conversions. Unfortunately, nowadays nonobservance on the part of many of our coreligionists is so widespread that the candidate for conversion may fail to appreciate what is implied by the acceptance of religious obligations. Thus, the convert may well believe that the normative fulfillment of a religious obligation is an elective act of piety and not required of every Jew. As indicated by the Gemara, *Shabbat* 68b, ignorance of even the most fundamental observance of Judaism does not invalidate conversion if the candidate, on the basis of his or her limited knowledge, has, in fact, accepted the tenets of Judaism.

III

The vast majority of questionable conversions are performed in order to facilitate marriage with a Jewish spouse and quite often occur after a civil marriage has already taken place. However, such unions present

---

II, no. 4. Cf. also *Iggrot Mosheh, Even ha-Ezer* I, no. 27. More recently, in a responsum dated 5728, *Iggrot Mosheh, Even ha-Ezer,* III, no. 4, Rabbi Feinstein reiterates his original position and declares such conversion to be totally invalid. Although another factor is mentioned, Rabbi Feinstein seems prepared to rule that any marriage contracted by such a person subsequent to the conversion ceremony is null and void and hence the Jewish partner may remarry without benefit of a *get* (religious divorce).

a grave halakhic problem. Even when the conversion itself is entered into with the utmost sincerity and conviction, it is questionable whether a converted Jewess may marry a Jew with whom she consorted while still a gentile.

The Mishnah[40] declares that one who is suspected of having cohabited with a gentile woman may not marry the woman in question subsequent to her conversion. The Mishnah adds, however, that if the marriage did take place the couple are not obliged to seek a divorce. Rashi explains that this prohibition was promulgated in order to safeguard the honor and reputation of the husband since marriage under such circumstances is likely to lend credence to rumors of previous immorality. On the basis of the explanation advanced by Rashi, some authorities[41] conclude that this prohibition does not encompass instances in which the couple have been living together publicly, since in such cases previous immoral conduct is an established verity.[42] Other authorities argue that there are more co-

---

40. *Yevamot* 24b.

41. Cf. R. Joseph Colon, *Teshuvot Maharik,* no. 129; R. Yosef Sha'ul Nathanson, *Sho'el u-Meshiv, Mahadura Tinyana,* III, no. 39; and *Binyan Ẓion,* no. 149.

42. Cf. R. Chaim of Zanz, *Teshuvot Divrei Ḥayyim,* II, *Even ha-Ezer,* no. 36; and *Aḥi'ezer,* III, no. 26. Both tentatively make this distinction but later state that cases of non-cohabitation are encompassed by Rashi's explanation. Their argument is that, even according to Rashi, subsequent marriage serves to intensify the scandal. *Aḥi'ezer* demonstrates this on the basis of the *Tosefta,* which declares this prohibition to be binding with regard to an emancipated handmaiden even in cases where previous cohabitation is known with certainty to have occurred. Since, according to Rashi, no other rationale is applicable in the case of an emancipated female servant of whom no act of conversion is required (see below, note 45), Rashi's intention must have been that when previous immorality is public knowledge, subsequent marriage will enhance the scandal. R. Chaim Ozer suggests that in cases where the couple have undergone a civil ceremony, there can be no further intensification of the scandal, but subsequently rejects this line of reasoning since the *Tosefta* indicates that the prohibition remains effective even if the couple have sired children.

Another interpretation of Rashi's opinion, according to which Rashi forbids conversion in cases of definite cohabitation, is offered by *Sho'el u-Meshiv, Mahadurah Tinyana,* III, no. 39. According to this analysis, Rashi accepts the reasoning advanced by Rashba, i.e., that subsequent marriage would give rise to a well-founded suspicion that the conversion was motivated by a desire to facilitate such marriage, but regards this rationale as being limited solely to cases in which prior cohabitation is known to have occurred. Since such conversions are prohibited only before the fact but are efficacious when actually

gent grounds for banning such marriage if prior immoral conduct is a matter of public knowledge. Such arguments are predicated upon an alternate explanation of the considerations upon which the prohibition is based. Rashba[43] explains that the marriage of a converted Jewess to the man with whom she is suspected of having consorted prior to her conversion is forbidden, lest aspersion be cast upon the sincerity of the conversion itself. If the couple are suspected of having lived together previously, their marriage subsequent to conversion will lead to suspicion that the conversion itself was insincerely contrived merely for purposes of marriage. Quite obviously, according to this line of reasoning, the prohibition is more stringent if the relationship prior to conversion was a matter of public knowledge.[44] It is also evident that the *Tosefta* and the

---

performed, Rashi, according to this interpretation, feels that there are no grounds on which to forbid subsequent marriages as long as there is no proof of prior cohabitation. Hence, in the case to which specific reference is made in the Mishnah—i.e., one who is merely suspected of having previously cohabited with them woman in question—Rashi advances another reason, i.e., intensification of the scandal. Only after rumor becomes publicly accepted as a known fact does the fear that the woman will be suspected of having converted solely for the sake of marriage become an operative consideration.

43. No. 1205 of his collected responsa. Rashba's explanation is a bit problematic. Although it is forbidden to accept insincere candidates, nevertheless, such conversions are deemed valid when they become a *fait accompli.* If so, why is it necessary to protect the woman from the charge of insincerity, since in any event her status as a Jewess will not be affected thereby? In resolving this problem, *Aḥi'ezer* cites the words of Rashba in demonstrating that the validity of conversion is contingent upon an acquiescent mental state. Conversions motivated by extraneous considerations are valid after the fact only if accompanied by an act of mental finality. If mental reservations exist the conversion is null and void. The ruling of the Mishnah regarding marriage is designed to eliminate the suspicion that such a mental state did not in fact exist, which in turn would cast doubt upon the status of the convert as a true Jewess.

44. In his previously cited responsum, sec. 4, R. Chaim Ozer speculates that conversion with the intention to marry under forbidden circumstances may in itself invalidate such conversion since such intention constitutes nonacceptance of a rabbinic prohibition. Such reservation, in and of itself, is sufficient to nullify any conversion. (Cf., however, *Heikhal Yiẓḥak, Even ha-Ezer,* I, no. 19, sec. 2., who questions whether nonacceptance of a rabbinic ordinance affects the biblical validity of the conversion. The matter is left unresolved by Rabbi Herzog, who fails to note that *Aḥi'ezer* unequivocally asserts that such reservation nullifies the conversion. *Aḥi'ezer* maintains that such reservation is tantamount to nonacceptance of the biblical injunction to heed the pro-

Palestinian Talmud both regard this prohibition as being operative even in cases of positively known prior cohabitation. Rambam regards transgression of the prohibition to be graver in nature in cases of known immorality than in cases of merely suspected cohabitation. Rambam rules that when it is known with certainty that the couple have cohabited before conversion the husband is obliged to divorce his wife, even though the Mishnah, in discussing cases of merely suspected immorality, rules that when the marriage is a *fait accompli,* divorce is unnecessary. Rabbi Schmelkes and R. Chaim Ozer, in their previously cited responsa, both argue that there is no significant disagreement between Rashi and Rashba. Marriage under the aforementioned circumstances is forbidden for a twofold reason: it will reflect negatively upon the husband's moral reputation and will cast a cloud of suspicion over the validity of the conversion itself. It is the thesis of Rabbi Schmelkes and R. Chaim Ozer that Rashi, in stating the first of these considerations, does not dispute the rationale of Rashba, who, in offering the latter, logically extends the prohibition to instances of known cohabitation. According to this analysis, Rashi presents his own explanation solely for the purpose of explaining a parallel prohibition recorded in the same Mishnah. The Mishnah declares that the same provisions regarding subsequent marriage apply with regard to one suspected of having cohabited with a female slave before her emancipation—an instance in which Rashba's consideration is not applicable since no formal commitment with regard to the acceptance of the precepts of the Torah is necessary on the part of an emancipated slave.[45]

---

nouncements of the Sages.) *Aḥi'ezer* notes, however, that the language of the Mishnah indicates that the prohibition regarding such a union devolves upon the husband rather than the wife. Hence the wife's violation is in the nature of "thou shalt not place a stumbling block before a blind person." Accordingly, R. Chaim Ozer concludes that "perhaps," since the husband is not obligated to divorce her once the marriage is a *fait accompli,* the prohibition before the fact does not constitute a "stumbling block" and thus the woman has not declined to accept any obligation incumbent upon her.

R. Shlomoh Kluger, *Tuv Ta'am va-Da'at,* I, no. 130, asserts that marriage is forbidden even if previous cohabitation is a certainty, arguing that the prohibition would be farcical if it were applicable only to one who had not sinned, but was inapplicable in the case of an actual trangression—the transgressor cannot be permitted to gain by virtue of his transgression.

45. Both authorities note that Rashba is not concerned with providing an explanation for the prohibition with regard to an emancipated handmaiden

Several authorities find reason to draw a sharp distinction between instances of known promiscuity and cases in which conversion has been preceded by a civil marriage. Rabbi Feinstein[46] asserts that even according to Rashba's interpretation, the prohibition against marriage following conversion is not applicable in cases where a civil marriage has already taken place. Since the couple have already established a permanent conjugal relationship, argues Rabbi Feinstein, there can be no grounds for the suspicion that conversion was insincerely sought merely for the sake of marriage. It would seem, however, that the numerous authorities cited in an earlier section, who maintain that the desire to legitimize the relationship and to contract a marriage which is valid in the eyes of Halakhah constitute an ulterior motive disqualifying the candidacy of a prospective proselyte, would also deem marriage subsequent to conversion to be forbidden, according to Rashba, on these self-same grounds. R. Yosef Sha'ul Nathanson expressly forbids the marriage of a Jew and a prospective convert despite the fact that they had been married in a civil ceremony and had sired children.[47] Such marriages are also forbidden by R. Ya'akov Ettlinger[47a] and R. Meir Arak.[47b]

Another argument sanctioning marriage once a civil ceremony has taken place is advanced by R. Meshullam Kutner.[48] Rabbi Kutner cites authorities who maintain that if a civil ceremony has already been per-

---

because he adopts the position of *Tosafot, Yevamot* 48a, to the effect that a slave cannot be forced to accept Judaism upon becoming the chattel of a Jew; hence, if the slave has not previously done so, he must accept the commandment of Judaism upon emancipation. Thus all considerations regarding voluntary acceptance of religious obligations are identical to those of ordinary converts. Rashi, on the other hand, is faced with a difficulty because of his disagreement with *Tosafot* in maintaining that obligation to fulfill precepts on the part of a slave is not contingent upon voluntary acceptance of the obligations of Judaism and hence no final acceptance of the "yoke of commandments" is ever required at the time of emancipation. Questions of sincerity are thus completely obviated.

For a different resolution of this difficulty with regard to Rashba's position, see *Teshuvot R. Akiva Eger,* no. 121. Cf. also R. Yehudah Leib Graubart, *Ḥavalim be-Ne'imim,* III, no. 72; and R. Mordecai Winkler, *Levushei Mordekhai, Even ha-Ezer,* no. 42.

46. *Iggrot Mosheh, Even ha-Ezer,* I, no. 27.

47. *Sho'el u-Meshiv, Mahadurah Tinyana,* III, no. 39.

47a. *Binyan Ẓion,* no. 149.

47b. *Imrei Yosher,* I, no. 176.

48. *U-ke-Torah Ya'asu.*

formed, the applicable halakhah is the ruling of the Mishnah that the husband need not divorce his wife. These authorities declare that this provision is applicable not merely in cases of marriages which are halakhically valid but encompasses all cases where a permanent conjugal relationship has been established. This ruling is also adopted by R. Benjamin Aryeh Weiss[49] and R. David Hoffmann;[50] it is, however, specifically rejected by Rabbi Weinberg.[51] Rabbi Hoffmann qualifies his position by stating that such permission cannot be granted if the rabbi was consulted prior to the civil ceremony and the candidate was rejected as being insincere in motivation. Rabbi Hoffmann further indicates that if, in practice, this lenient decision will lead to a higher incidence of intermarriage, no such candidate should be accepted for conversion. In another responsum,[52] Rabbi Hoffmann further circumscribes his ruling by stating that such candidates cannot be accepted unless they pledge "on their word of honor" to observe all the tenets of Judaism and specifically "the commandments concerning the Sabbath, *niddah* and forbidden foods."

There is yet another argument which may be advanced in favor of countenancing such marriages. In the vast majority of such cases the couple will continue living together as man and wife whether or not conversion and subsequent marriage will receive ecclesiastic sanction. R. Chaim of Zanz[53] raises the question of whether conversion should not be permitted and the marriage tolerated in order to spare the husband from the graver prohibition against consorting publicly with a non-Jewess. The latter transgression is clearly biblical in nature, whereas the prohibition against marriage in this instance is of rabbinic origin. Some authorities argue that in such cases marriage following conversion should be sanctioned as constituting the lesser of two evils. R. Menachem Panet[54] permits such marriages following conversion when it is evident that the couple will, in any event, continue to live together as man and wife.

Employing a similar argument, R. Shlomoh Kluger ruled that the mar-

---

49. *Even Yekarah, Even ha-Ezer,* no. 11.
50. *Melamed le-Ho'il, Even ha-Ezer,* no. 10.
51. *Seridei Esh,* III, no. 50.
52. *Melamed le-Ho'il, Yoreh De'ah,* no. 85.
53. *Teshuvot Divrei Ḥayyim,* II, *Even ha-Ezer,* no. 36.
54. *Avnei Ẓedek,* no. 27. *Heikhal Yiẓḥak, Even ha-Ezer,* I, no. 20, sanctions the conversion of a gentile woman who has already entered into a permanent relationship with a Jewish male on similar grounds, but only when it is known that the convert will observe the commandment of the Torah. A similar position is adopted by *Ḥavalim be-Ne'imim,* III, no. 72.

riage may take place in the previously noted case of a young man who threatened apostasy if not permitted to marry his gentile mistress. *Aḥi'ezer*[55] cites a responsum of Rambam[56] in which the author sanctioned the emancipation of a slave and her subsequent marriage to a young man who was suspected of having had illicit relations with her on the grounds that, although objectively speaking this course of action is not permissible, it constitutes the lesser of two evils. The marriage is an infraction of lesser severity than continued illicit relations with a slave. *Aḥi'ezer* notes, however, that applied to the case at hand this argument is specious if, as is often the case, the couple have no intention of observing the laws of family purity. Apart from violation of the ban against subsequent marriage, valid conversion will cause a biblical prohibition of *niddah* to devolve upon each act of cohabitation—a prohibition which does not extend to cohabitation with a non-Jewess.[57] Consequently, the marriage in such cases does not constitute the lesser of two evils but, on the contrary, leads to transgressions of enhanced severity.

Furthermore, argues *Aḥi'ezer,* the prohibition against accepting insincere converts devolves upon the individual members of the *Bet Din.*[58] Hence, if the conversion is indeed undertaken for ulterior motives, the members of the *Bet Din* are not permitted to commit a lesser infraction in order to spare another individual a graver transgression.[59]

---

55. *Aḥi'ezer,* III, no. 72.

56. *Pe'er ha-Dor,* no. 132.

57. The biblical prohibition of *niddah* applies only to a Jewess. However, the Hasmonean *Bet Din* issued a rabbinic decree extending the *niddah* prohibition to a non-Jewess as well; see *Avodah Zarah,* 36b. According to Rambam, *Issurei Bi'ah* 12:2, this decree applies only in cases of a permanent relationship comparable to a common-law marriage. The biblical prohibition of *niddah* encompasses relations between a Jewess and a gentile male according to all authorities with the (possible) exception of Rabbenu Tam, *Sanhedrin* 74b. Cf. *Heikhal Yiẓḥak, Even ha-Ezer,* I, no. 20, sec. 2.

58. *Ḥelkat Ya'akov,* I, no. 13, assumes an identical position with regard to both points. Rabbi Breish adds that encouragement of conversion and subsequent marriage constitutes a disservice to the gentile consort. As long as the prospective convert remains a non-Jewess she commits no transgression in living with her Jewish consort—the transgression of cohabiting with a non-Jewess applies solely to the Jewish partner. However, after conversion, the *niddah* prohibition applies to both equally.

59. It is evident that R. David Hoffmann, *Melamed le-Ho'il, Even ha-Ezer,* no. 8, adopted a contrary position and permitted this infraction on the part of the *Bet Din* in order to prevent illicit relations with a gentile. See above,

Whatever the final adjudication of the Halakhah with regard to this complex question may be in any particular case, it can be seen that the permissibility of marriage under such circumstances constitutes a matter requiring careful halakhic deliberation.

IV

The conversion problem has recently become a topical issue of major moment and has received a considerable measure of attention in both the general and Jewish press. As the prayerfully awaited Russian immigration turns from a trickle into a steady stream, the question assumes new proportions, since many of these new immigrants are accompanied by gentile spouses. These courageous new arrivals have endured untold hardships and manifested heroic self-sacrifice in effecting their exit from the Soviet Union. It is certainly fitting that every attempt be made to speed and ease their acculturation to life in Israel. When appropriate, and halakhically valid, the Israeli Chief Rabbinate has been most sympathetic in expediting the conversion process. Of late, there has been an added attempt to ease procedural forms without prejudicing fundamental principles. In weighing the merits of such cases, proper cognizance must be taken of all ramifications of the issue, of the practical problems it poses and of the unique predicament of the Russian immigrants. However, in the last analysis, the question is purely one of halakhic determination and certainly is not an area in which political pressure may be brought to bear.

---

note 20. *Iggrot Mosheh, Even ha-Ezer,* II, no. 4, states that there is no "clear prohibition" insofar as the *Bet Din* is concerned. Cf. also *Ḥelkat Ya'akov,* I, no. 13, who, while not quoting *Melamed le-Ho'il,* advances arguments contradicting this view. Rabbi Hoffmann, it should be noted, issued his permissive ruling only on condition that the couple scrupulously observe the laws of niddah; otherwise the prohibitions attendant upon such a union are more severe following conversion. The case brought to his attention concerned a *kohen* who had already married a gentile in a civil ceremony and had fathered a son by his non-Jewish wife. *Melamed le-Ho'il* counseled conversion to be followed by the statutory ninety-day waiting period to determine prior pregnancy. However, since a *kohen* is not permitted to marry a proselyte, he advises that in order to mitigate the severity of their infraction, the couple content themselves with a civil ceremony rather than nuptial rites in accordance with Jewish practice. According to many authorities, a biblical violation of the priestly code occurs only if the marriage is solemnized in accodance with Jewish law. *Melamed le-Ho'il*'s permissive ruling is rejected by *Heikhal Yiẓḥak,* I, no. 19, sec. 3, *Iggrot Mosheh, Even ha-Ezer,* II, no. 4, and *Ḥelkat Ya'akov,* I, no. 13.

Precisely such pressure raised the atmosphere in Israel to a fever pitch in the unfolding of events surrounding the celebrated Seidman case. At the time, controversy raged with regard to the actions of Rabbi Shlomoh Goren, then chief chaplain of the Israeli armed forces. A feature article appearing in the weekend supplement of *Ha-Ẓofeh,* 15 Sivan, 5730, purports to give the rationale governing Rabbi Goren's actions in this case. It is reported that Rabbi Goren is of the belief that in Israel prospective proselytes are to be viewed differently from the way in which they are regarded in the Diaspora. "Beloved is the Land of Israel, for it is receptive to converts," declares *Mesekhta Gerim* 4:3, in a tone remarkably different from that of the oft-quoted dictum of R. Chelbo, "Proselytes are as difficult for Israel as leprosy." [60] Noting that R. Chelbo's aphorism is not incorporated in the Palestinian Talmud, Rabbi Goren asserts that proselytization was frowned upon by the Sages in the Diaspora but welcomed in Israel. It is reported that Rabbi Goren, going a step further, asserts that in Israel sincerity of motivation may be dispensed with as a prior requirement for conversion. In the Diaspora converts motivated by reasons other than religious conviction cannot be accepted since doubts remain with regard to their future comportment; in Israel, where conversion entails not merely religious affiliation but national identification as well, such fears do not exist, contends Rabbi Goren. Hence, in his opinion, even converts prompted by self-serving motives may be accepted in Israel. This, Rabbi Goren argues, is the meaning of the declaration asserting that the Land of Israel is conducive to converts. Such converts, he maintains, automatically fall into the category of those of whom it may be confidently assumed, despite the absence of proper intent at the time of conversion, that nevertheless "their end will be for the sake of heaven."

Rabbi Goren's action in the Seidman case evoked disapprobation on the part of numerous rabbinic authorities, who argued that his conclusions go far beyond what may be rigorously demonstrated on the basis of his sources. In fairness, no detailed analysis of his argument can be undertaken until a published responsum penned by his own hand is available; journalistic accounts are most assuredly not a reliable basis for halakhic evaluations.

One further point is worthy of note. One of the arguments militating against the conversion of Helen Seidman was the fact that Mrs. Seidman was a resident of an irreligious kibbutz in which dietary laws were flagrantly

60. *Yevamot* 47b.

violated. Accordingly, there appeared to be reason to doubt the sincerity of her acceptance of *mizvot.* The report in *Ha-Zofeh* states explicitly that her candidacy was accepted by Rabbi Goren only on the basis of the fact that she was a vegetarian.[61] It would thus appear that there is nothing in Rabbi Goren's line of reasoning which condones acceptance of a proselyte who, we have reason to believe, does not intend to observe the precepts of Judaism.

In an article which appears in *No'am,* XIV (5731), a similarly permissive stance is adopted by Rabbi I. Y. Unterman with regard to the spouses of Russian emigrés. Rabbi Unterman strongly emphasizes that throughout the period of his rabbinate in England he remained adamantly opposed to the acceptance of converts motivated by the desire for marriage to Jewish partners. While not altering his general position in this regard,

---

61. However, this defense contains a specious element. Although he does not make specific reference to the Seidman case, Rabbi Unterman, *No'am,* XIV, 5, and *Torah She-be'al Peh,* XIII, 16, notes that even a vegetarian resident of an irreligious kibbutz must perforce violate the dietary laws by utilizing non-kosher utensils.

A second question with regard to Helen Seidman's acceptance of the "yoke of the commandments" is posed by the fact that her husband is a *kohen.* Marriage between a kohen and a convert is forbidden by Jewish law. This article alleges that Rabbi Goren sanctioned the marriage on the basis of "positions among the latter-day authorities" permitting such unions. Since it is universally recognized that Jewish law bans such marriages, this statement, as recorded, is obviously incorrect. It should be emphasized that even *Melamed le-Ho'il,* cited above, n. 59, does not contend that marriage between a *kohen* and a proselyte is permissible; he merely indicates that this infraction is less severe than transgression involving cohabitation with a non-Jewess and hence constitutes the lesser of two evils. An additional factor noted in Rabbi Hoffmann's ruling was the consideration that the circumstances surrounding the case brought to his attention were such that rejection of the applicant would have evoked manifestations of anti-Semitism among the non-Jewish populace. In a similar case, R. Yehudah Leib Zirelson, *Ma'arkhei Lev,* no. 72, sanctioned the conversion and subsequent marriage of a convert to a *kohen* because of fear that denial of the request would have led to a pogrom. (Despite the gravity of that situation, *Ma'arkhei Lev*'s ruling was severely censured by R. Hillel Posek in a booklet entitled *Go'alei ha-Kehunah.)* The statement attributed to Rabbi Goren conveys the distinct impression that the anonymous authorities cited rule that such marriages are normatively permissible and not merely countenanced in certain circumstances as constituting the lesser of two evils. This statement must be presumed to have been a journalistic error since the Halakhah is clear: marriage between a *kohen* and a proselyte is forbidden.

Rabbi Unterman contends that the specific situation with regard to Russian immigrants to Israel is different on several counts. In the first place, the change in social and cultural climate in the wake of immigration to Israel engenders a commitment to Judaism which is absent in insincere converts in the Diaspora. Presumably, Rabbi Unterman means that although conversions of this genre lack sincerity of motivation, such converts will ultimately accept the tenets of Judaism wholeheartedly and hence fall under the category of those whose conversion may be deemed to have been undertaken "for the sake of heaven." The counterargument which has been advanced against this position is that nationalistic identification should not be confused with religious commitment; willingness to share the destiny of Israel is not necessarily the same as an ultimate leap of faith in the God of Israel and commitment to His Torah. Secondly, argues Rabbi Unterman, rejection of such applicants may cause "a spiritual danger to hover over the entire family." The danger that the Jewish members of such families may be lost to Judaism, in Rabbi Unterman's opinion, creates a situation in which the regulations against accepting insincere converts may be suspended.[62]

V

While it is an axiomatic principle of Halakhah that each case in which a question arises must be decided in light of its own particular ramifications, certain general principles emerge with striking clarity from the preceding discussion. It must be emphasized that a positive obligation exists with regard to candidates for conversion whose motivation is sincere. The number of such converts has, for a variety of reasons, risen in recent years. *Gerei ẓedek* such as these have always met with warm acceptance and have been heralded as welcome members of the Jewish community. However, conversions of convenience are not sanctioned by Halakhah and cannot be countenanced as a panacea designed to minimize the exacerbating problems posed by intermarriage. The situation with regard to converts who have no intention of observing the precepts of Judaism is even graver. The preponderance of halakhic opinion, ranging from Rabbi Chaim Ozer Grodzinski to the late Chief Rabbis Kook and Herzog, is that such conversions are null and void. It follows, of course, that the

62. This line of reasoning appears to be similar to the previously cited view of R. Shlomoh Kluger, who permitted conversion for the sake of marriage in the face of threatened apostasy on the part of the Jewish partner.

children of spurious female converts can also not be recognized as Jews in the eyes of Halakhah. The serious questions arising from such conversions should prompt a cautious attitude on the part of those whose duty it is to deal with these problems on a day-to-day basis, for it is they who are charged with safeguarding and preserving the identity of the Jewish people.

The halakhic strictures surrounding the acceptance of converts are but a reflection of the awesome burden and responsibility which accompanies membership in the community of Israel. One who lightheartedly seeks to join this community has no place in its ranks. "Israel," says the Almighty, "in you shall I glorify Myself." Such election is to be borne seriously and wholeheartedly or not at all. Only he who comes for no motive other than "the sake of heaven" may be permitted to become part of the Jewish people, affirming his solidarity not only with their past history and present fate but also with the totality of their faith, their traditions and their practices.

CHAPTER XIV

Black Jews: A Halakhic Perspective

I call upon heaven and earth to bear witness that whether Jew or gentile, whether man or woman . . . the Divine Spirit rests upon him in accordance with the deed which he performs.

TANNA DE-BEI ELIYAHU RABBAH, 9

There is an apocryphal story which relates that when Ben-Gurion was a young man he met a gentleman from France who pointedly described himself as being a Socialist, a Frenchman and a Jew—in that order. Ben-Gurion responded by indicating that he fully acceded to this descriptive order and explained himself by saying, "Because, you see, we Jews read from right to left." Political affiliation, national citizenship—and color—are all extraneous to the essence of Jewish identity.

Judaism is colorblind; skin pigmentation is unknown as a halakhic concept. The problem of determining the status of the various communities of black Jews is totally unrelated to color. The sole issue is that of Jewish identity. The question of recognition of black Jews as members of the Jewish community must be seen within that context; as such it is simply one instance of the much broader question: "Who is a Jew?"

The problem of Jewish identity is a crucial one. It is not to be dismissed as being merely a theoretical question in the realm of speculative anthropology; it is an issue closely associated with Jewish survival. Jews have managed to preserve their identity over a period of millennia without becoming assimilated into the dominant culture of their lands of habitation whereas other ethnic groups have disappeared within relatively short periods of time. Despite their wide geographical dispersion, frequent (and sometime forced) migration and lack of an autonomous homeland, Jews have neverthless somehow succeeded in preserving their ethnic identity.

The problem of Jewish identity is by no means a new one; it is as old as Judaism itself. *Yalkut Shim'oni*[1] reports that at the time of the giving of the Torah on Mt. Sinai the gentile nations became exceedingly jealous. They, too, wished to be the recipients of the revealed word of God and to share in the prophetic experience at Sinai. The Midrash depicts God as brusquely rejecting their claim with the retort, "Bring me the record of your pedigree as My children are bringing." This, declare the Sages, is the meaning of the verse "and they declared their pedigrees after their families . . ." (Num. 1:18). In order to be counted among the members of the community of Israel and to be granted recognition as a Jew it was necessary for each of the wanderers in the wilderness to present documentary proof or to adduce witnesses prepared to testify with regard to the genealogical purity of the petitioner's lineage. Apparently, even at that early date, there were individuals who sought to identify themselves as Jews but whose claims to lineal descent from Abraham, Isaac and Jacob were spurious. An authentic claim with regard to genealogical identity, then as now, was the *sine qua non* for recognition as a member of the Jewish faith-community by virtue of birth. The sole—but crucial—condition which must be met by a claim to Jewish identity by virtue of birth is that it be predicated upon authentic Jewish parentage, i.e., birth into a family whose claim to Jewish identity is recognized as having already been confirmed, perhaps as far back in the family history as on the occasion of the original census taken by Moses when all families were required to "declare their pedigrees."

The only question with regard to the status of black Jews which is germane is whether or not they have established a valid claim to Jewish identity by virtue of either birth or conversion. There are, however, numerous distinct communities of black Jews and the claim advanced by each group must be examined on its own particular merits.

I

Historically, the question first arose with regard to the Falashas, the black Jews of Ethiopia. The earliest reference to the Falasha community is contained in the diary of Eldad ha-Dani, a ninth-century merchant and traveler who professed to have been a citizen of an autonomous Jewish state in eastern Africa inhabited by the tribes of Dan, Naphtali, Gad and Asher. The reports of Eldad ha-Dani were given credence as a result

1. *Bemidbar,* 684.

of the endorsement of the then Ga'on of Sura, Zemach ben Chaim, who vouched for Eldad's reliability and trustworthiness. Although such scholars as Abraham ibn Ezra[2] and Meir of Rothenberg[3] expressed reservations with regard to the veracity of Eldad's narrative, other rabbinic luminaries, such as Rashi, Rabad, and Abraham ben Maimon, cite Eldad as an unquestioned authority. Eldad ha-Dani speaks of the Falashas as Jews and describes the religious practices followed by the Falasha community. Since at that time, and for generations thereafter, there was little or no traffic between Abyssinia and the Jewish centers of Europe and Asia, the question of the Jewish identity of the Falasha community was entirely a matter of speculative curiosity.

The matter did, however, become the subject of halakhic adjudication in the responsa of R. David ibn Zimra (1479–1589). By that time, a fairly extensive slave trade preying upon inhabitants of North Africa seems to have developed. R. David ibn Zimra, or Radbaz, as he is known in rabbinic literature, was presented with a halakhic question which not only called for a clarification of the religious status of the Falashas but also describes the adversities which they suffered.[4] A Falasha town or settlement was attacked, the males slaughtered and the women and children taken captive. One woman, whose husband was presumably among the slaughtered, was purchased as a slave by a Jew who subsequently entered into a sexual liaison with her which resulted in the birth of a son. Later, the son sought to marry a young lady of Jewish parentage and Radbaz was asked for a ruling with regard to the permissibility of the forthcoming marriage.

For Radbaz, the question of the captive's identity as a Jewess was not at all in doubt. "It is clear that she is of the seed of Israel, of the tribe of Dan," declares Radbaz. Describing the prevailing circumstances, he writes: "There is constantly war between the kings of Abyssinia, for in Abyssinia there are three kingdoms; part of the land is inhabited by Moslems, part by Christians steadfast in their religion, and part by Jews of the tribe of Dan . . . and daily they take captives one from the other." Radbaz was concerned solely with the question of bastardy which, in turn, is predicated upon the possibility that the husband, unknown to his wife, may have been spared or may have escaped. If the captive's husband was yet living

2. *Commentary on the Bible,* Exod. 2:20.

3. *Teshuvot Maharam Rothenberg,* no. 193.

4. *Teshuvot Radbaz,* IV, no. 219 (1290). The identical responsum appears in VII, no. 9.

when she consorted with her master, the child born to them would, of course, be a bastard and forbidden to marry a Jewess of legitimate birth. If, however, her husband had indeed been killed, the captive's status would have been that of an unmarried widow. According to Jewish law, a child born out of wedlock to an unmarried mother does not bear the stigma of bastardy. Radbaz was called upon to decide whether, in the given instance, the child should be considered to be of legitimate birth, whether he should be declared a bastard or whether, in light of the mother's uncorroborated testimony with regard to the prior death of her husband, the status of the child must remain clouded by unresolvable doubt.

Presented in this manner, the question is simply the classic *agunah* problem in one of its many guises. As such, the question as raised was individual in nature and represented a matter of concern primarily to the persons involved.[5] However, the ramifications of this responsum go far beyond the question at hand. The question reflects a matter of far broader concern, since it is one which could not conceivably arise unless the Jewish identity of the Falasha community is antecedently accepted. Since bastardy is a matter of concern only with regard to Jewish issue, no problem is posed unless it is assumed that the child is of Jewish parentage.

Radbaz was concerned with yet another factor which might serve as a barrier to marital alliances with any member of the Falasha community. This latter consideration, also, is germane only because Radbaz regarded the Falashas as Jews. The religion professed and practiced by the Falasha community is a form of Mosaism;[6] the Falashas are totally ignorant of

5. A statement apparently referring to this young man and the ultimate solution to his problem appears in a responsum authored by a disciple of Radbaz. R. Ya'akov Castro, *Ohalei Ya'akov,* no. 11, writes: "It is a commonplace occurrence for a bastard to marry a female slave who has immersed [herself] for purposes of slavery [in order] to purify his progeny that they may enter into the congregation. Such a case occurred in Egypt in [the case of] a Jewish Falasha who had been married in her country and gave birth to a son in Egypt [fathered] by a Jew who cohabited with her in ignorance. [The son] married a female slave and purified his progeny in the time of the scholars of the preceding generation, of blessed memory."

6. It should be noted that many other Ethiopians also practice circumcision, observe the Sabbath and perform ritual ablutions. The Christianity practiced by many Ethiopians is highly syncretistic and retains many Judaic elements. Edward Ullendorf, *The Ethiopians: An Introduction to Country and People* (London, 1960), is of the opinion that the Falashas are descended from elements of the Aksumite Kingdom who resisted conversion to Christianity. Thus their practices mirror the religious syncretism of the pre-Christian Aksumites.

the Oral Law. "They appear to be of the sect of Zadok[7] and Boethus known as Karaites," declares Radbaz. Since they are indeed Jews, marriages contracted by them are entirely valid, but, point out Radbaz, their divorces are defective because they are not performed in accordance with the usages of Jewish law. Furthermore, by virtue of their adherence to Karaite heresies, the Falashas are disqualified from serving as witnesses. Hence, any *get* (bill of divorce) signed and delivered in the presence of Falasha witnesses is invalid.[8] The absence of a valid divorce, of course, precludes the wife from validly contracting a new marriage. The issue of any subsequent (invalid) marriage entered into by the wife would be halakhically categorized as bastards. Radbaz was one of many authorities who were concerned with the permissibility of marriage between Jews and Karaites. In view of the long period of time which had elapsed since the Karaite schism in the ninth century, it was inevitable that numerous Karaite women had, in the course of centuries, been divorced according to Karaite usage. Many undoubtedly remarried and gave birth to children halakhically forbidden to marry Jews of legitimate parentage. Thus, the suspicion arose that any given prospective Karaite bride or groom might bear the stigma of bastardy.

Radbaz, however, does find grounds for permitting Karaites—and Falashas—to marry within the Jewish fold without restriction. He argues that although their divorces are defective by virtue of the use of unqualified witnesses, it may be assumed that members of the Karaite community are also married in the presence of Karaite witnesses. Since Karaites are disqualified from serving as witnesses, marriages contracted in the presence of Karaite witnesses have no halakhic validity. Since a valid marriage does not exist, it follows that a bill of divorce for its dissolution is superfluous.

7. Rabbinic writers frequently refer to Karaites as Sadduces, not as a result of misidentification, but because the Karaites, in common with the Sadducces, rejected the Oral Law. Cf. J. D. Eisenstein, *Oẓar Yisra'el* (New York, 1951), IX, 211.

8. In point of fact, modern scholars report that the bill of divorce is unknown among the Falashas. There is no distinctive Falasha custom in connection with divorce. The formalities are executed in the presence of the local chief. See Wolf Leslau, *The Falasha Anthology* (New Haven, 1951), p. xviii. Since in dissolving a Falasha marriage a bill of divorce is not written and presented to the wife, as is required by Jewish law, there is no question that from the halakhic perspective, the matrimonial relationship has not been terminated. Either Radbaz was unaware of Falasha practices with regard to divorce or the bill of divorce fell into disuse among the Falashas sometime after the sixteenth century.

In light of these considerations, Radbaz rules that there is no suspicion of bastardy with regard to members of the Karaite or Falasha communities. Accordingly, declares Radbaz, marriage to a Falasha is permissible provided that the marriage partner is willing to accept the practices of rabbinic Judaism.

In a subsequent (and presumably later) responsum,[9] Radbaz expresses grave reservations with regard to Falasha eligibility for marriage within the Jewish community, but is explicit and even more emphatic in his opinion that they are unquestionably of Jewish lineage. The responsum in question was written in reply to a query regarding how one should comport oneself *vis-à-vis* a Falasha who had been acquired as a slave. Radbaz declares unequivocally: "Therefore, . . . with regard to the Falasha slave, since it has become clear that he is a Jew, this purchase is nought but the ransom of captives, not the purchase of a slave, and the obligation was encumbent upon all of Israel to redeem him." Although the "slave" must be granted freedom, Radbaz stipulates that the ransomed captive may be obliged to serve as a laborer or as an indentured servant for a fixed period of time in order to compensate the purchaser for the sum of money which had been expended in the "ransom" of the captive.

Radbaz felt constrained to add that Falashas taken captive must be ransomed even though they conduct themselves as Karaites. The halakhic obligation regarding the ransoming of captives does not encompass sectarians, and, accordingly, Radbaz affirms that there is no obligation to ransom a Karaite who is taken captive. Yet, despite Radbaz' belief that the Mosaism of the Falashas is the result of Karaite influences, Radbaz rules that the Falashas have not placed themselves outside the pale of the Jewish community and are not to be looked upon as sectarians. With regard to the absence of an obligation to ransom Karaite captives Radbaz writes, ". . . it seems to me that this is so only with regard to those who dwell among the Rabbanites. . . ."

The Falashas, in particular, are not to be branded as sectarians, Radbaz holds, since "these who come from the land of Kush are without doubt of the tribe of Dan and because there are not among them scholars, masters of tradition, they seize unto themselves the literal meaning of Scripture . . . they are as a child who has been held captive among idolaters." Consistent with this newly formulated position but in contradiction to his earlier stated view, Radbaz concludes: "But with regard to

9. *Teshuvot Radbaz,* VII, no. 5.

genealogy, I fear lest their marriages be valid but that their divorces are not as has been ordained by the Sages, of blessed memory, for they are not at all acquainted with the form of divorces and marriages."[10]

A disciple of Radbaz, R. Ya'akov Castro, in a gloss to *Yoreh De'ah* 158:2, cites the opinion of his teacher and similarly declares the Falashas to be descendants of the tribe of Dan. But, curiously, the same author, in a gloss to *Yoreh De'ah* 267:14, reports that it was customary to execute a writ of manumission (*get shiḥrur*) in emancipating ransomed Falasha captives. Apparently, the established Jewish communities came into contact only with Falashas who had been captured and sold into slavery. It appears that the purchase or ransom of Falasha slaves by a Jew was not an infrequent occurrence. When a Falasha slave was acquired by a Jew, the question of the religious status of the Falashas became a matter of great significance in determining the master-slave relationship. Radbaz, as noted, ruled that since the Falashas were to be regarded as Jews, they could not be held as slaves. Were they to be regarded as non-Jews their status would have been that of a "Canaanite slave" who upon emancipation by means of a bill of manumission acquires the status of a Jew. Since no bill of manumission is required for the release of a Jew from bondage, the fact that such writs were actually executed tends to indicate that the status of Falashas was beclouded and was at least a matter of doubt. Rabbi Castro, however, points out that were a Falasha belonging to a Jewish master indeed to be regarded as a Canaanite slave, in addition to a bill of manumission, immersion in a ritualarium would also be required upon emancipation in order for him to acquire status as a full-fledged member of the community of Israel. Rabbi Castro reports that while delivery of a writ of manumission seems to have been the accepted practice, paradoxically, it was not customary for immersion in a ritualarium to be carried out. Rabbi Castro accordingly concludes that "possibly" the writ was of no religious import, but was drawn up simply to provide documentary evidence of the Falasha's status as a free man.

Despite the unequivocal declaration of Radbaz with regard to the origins of the Falasha community, Radbaz' halakhic decision, handed down in the sixteenth century, may not be valid in the twentieth. In the course of the intervening four centuries it is entirely possible that there has been extensive intermarriage between the Falashas and the indigenous Abyssinian

10. This is also the definitive ruling of *Bet Yosef, Even ha-Ezer* 4, and Rema, *Even ha-Ezer* 4:37.

population. It is reported that R. Chaim Soloveitchik of Brisk adopted a similar position with regard to the Karaite community. R. Chaim contended that while in earlier periods of Jewish history there was room for significant disagreement regarding the permissibility of marriage between Jews and Karaites, there is no question that in our day such marriages are forbidden according to all authorities. R. Chaim pointed out that over the centuries the Karaites accepted gentile converts but did not do so according to the prescribed ritual. Indeed, since Karaites are disqualified from serving as members of a *Bet Din,* conversions performed by them would be inefficacious even if the Karaite *Bet Din* were to adhere scrupulously to all details of the conversion ritual. As a result, declared R. Chaim, every Karaite now has the status of a *safek akum* and his identity as a Jew is in doubt.[11] The same considerations may well be applicable to the Falasha community. However, the Falashas may differ significantly from Karaite communities with regard to the incidence of conversion. The Falashas are known to be shunned as pariahs by the dominant Ethiopian tribes with the result that social intercourse between the communities is severely limited. On the basis of available published information it is impossible to determine whether acceptance of converts over the generations was a common or rare occurrence among the Falashas.

Despite any qualms which might be voiced, the authenticity of the claims to Jewish identity advanced by the Falashas was affirmed not only in the Middle Ages but in modern times as well. The Falasha community was rediscovered over a century ago and their plight brought to the attention of western Jewry. In 1864, R. Ezriel Hildesheimer, a prominent rabbinic spokesman, issued a call for action in order to counteract missionary activity among the Falashas.[12] This was followed by a fact-finding mission undertaken in 1867 by the noted orientalist and Semitic scholar, Joseph Halévy. However, it was not until the beginning of the twentieth century that meaningful endeavors were undertaken on behalf of the Falashas. A relationship with the Falasha community was established largely through the efforts of a single individual, Dr. Jacob Noah Feitlovitch, whose efforts on behalf of the Falasha community were endorsed in the

11. Quoted by R. Ovadiah Yosef, *Torah She-be-'al Peh,* XIII (5731), 28; see also R. Eliezer Yehudah Waldenberg, *Ẓiẓ Eli'ezer,* X, no. 25, chap. 3, sec. 10, who independently makes a similar point with regard to the B'nai Israel of India.

12. *Jeschurun,* XI, no. 2 (November, 1864).

strongest terms in a public manifesto issued in 1921 by the then Chief Rabbi of *Ereẓ Yisra'el,* Rabbi A. I. Kook.[13]

Although neither Rabbi Hildesheimer nor Rabbi Kook addresses himself to the thorny question of the permissibility of marriage between Jews and members of the Falasha community or to the question of the possible requirement of a conversion ceremony because of intermarriage over the course of centuries, both epistles speak of the Falashas in the warmest of terms and proclaim the responsibility of world Jewry both for their material support and for their religious education. Reflected in both statements is deep concen lest the Falashas forsake the Jewish faith.

More recently, the Sephardic Chief Rabbi, Rabbi Ovadiah Yosef, reiterated the commonly accepted halakhic view in stating that the Falashas are "descendants of the tribes of Israel . . . and without doubt the aforementioned authorities who determined that they are of the tribe of Dan investigated and reached this conclusion on the basis of the most reliable testimony and evidence." [14] Therefore, declared Rabbi Yosef, it is obligatory upon the Jewish community to rescue them from assimilation and to "hasten their immigration to Israel, to educate them in the spirit of the holy Torah, and to coopt them in the rebuilding of our holy land." [15] Rabbi Yosef specifically calls upon the government of Israel and the Jewish Agency to facilitate the immigration of the Falashas. It has been reported that Rabbi Yosef has, on other occasions, counseled that Falashas should undergo a conversion ceremony in order to eliminate any possible question with regard to their status as Jews. Curiously, until very recently, a completely antithetical policy was adopted by secular officials of the State of Israel. For many years it was the stated policy of the Israeli government that "Israel does not regard the Law of Return as being applicable to the Falashas" and "is not enthusiastic about the prospect of Falasha immigration." [16] This posture was seemingly motivated by considerations of international diplomacy. Following the fall of Emperor

---

13. Unpublished letter dated 3 Kislev 5682. See also R. Abraham I. Kook, *Iggrot ha-Re'iyah* (Jerusalem, 5722), II, 83, 89f and 318.

14. Unpublished communication dated 7 Adar I, 5733. Rabbi Yosef indicates this was also the opinion of Rabbi Isaac ha-Levi Herzog. Radbaz' position with regard to the descent of the Falasha community from the tribe of Dan is also accepted by *Ẓiẓ Eli'ezer,* X, no. 25, chap. 3, sec. 19.

15. *Loc. cit.*

16. David Zohar, First Secretary, Embassy of Israel, Washington, D.C., in a letter published in *Sh'ma,* 3/47 (February 2, 1973), pp. 54–55.

Haile Selassie, an interministerial committee was appointed to review the status of the Falashas. As a result of the deliberations of the committee, the Falashas have been recognized as eligible for Israeli citizenship and other rights under the Law of Return.[17]

II

The Falashas were accepted as Jews by Radbaz and by others on the basis of the report of Eldad ha-Dani who testified to their long history of Jewish identification. The same cannot be said of other groups seeking to identify themselves as Jews.

Rashi, in his commentary to Numbers 1:18, indicates that in the wilderness either of two modes of proof of genealogical identity was acceptable: a written document certifying the family pedigree or witnesses testifying to *ḥezkat leidatam,* i.e., witnesses presenting presumptive evidence with regard to birth. In Great Britain, prior to the reign of Queen Victoria, it was the practice for both the Archbishop of Canterbury and the Lord President of the Council to be in attendance at every royal birth in order to certify the identity of the newly-born princeling. Jewish law makes no such requirement. Witnesses are not required to be present at the moment of parturition in order to testify to the identity of the infant. A Jew is known and accepted as a Jew on the basis of *ḥazakah,* presumptive evidence based upon deportment and interpersonal behavior. Such presumptive evidence is, in the absence of contradictory evidence, accepted with absolute credibility.

A similar *ḥazakah* serves to establish the existence of familial relationships which in turn may, in certain eventualities, lead to the imposition of capital punishment. Wounding a parent is a capital offense. But how can the existence of a filial relationship be established? It is sufficient declares the Gemara, *Kiddushin* 80a, for evidence to be adduced demonstrating that the person, as a child, was customarily in the mother's tow. The general conduct and deportment of an individual engenders presumptive evidence with regard to the determination of matters of personal status. Exhibition of maternal concern and filial dependence, when continued over a period of time, suffices in and of itself to establish the existence of a parent-child relationship. No further corroboration is required. This *ḥazakah* establishes not only the individual's identity as a member of a

17. JTA Daily News Bulletin, April 15, 1975.

family unit but also as a member of a larger family, the community of Israel. Since Jewish identity depends upon maternal Jewishness, the selfsame mode of conduct which serves as the basis for the establishment of filial obligations and restrictions *ipso facto* establishes identity as a Jew. Subsequent to the establishment of a distinctive faith community, a *prima facie* claim to Jewish identity may be established by means of a simple declaration, provided there is no information or presumptive evidence pointing to non-Jewish parentage.[18] However, apart from documentary evidence, testimony establishing this *ḥazakah* was apparently the sole manner in which such identity could be established at the inception of the community of Israel.

Halakhah, of course, provides for yet another mode of acquiring status as a Jew. A person may be a Jew by virtue of birth or he may enter the community of Israel by means of conversion. Acceptable evidence of conversion may be adduced in one of two ways: either by means of witnesses who are able to identify the proselyte and to testify that they were present during the course of the conversion ritual; or on the basis of a *ḥazakah,* presumptive evidence derived from the individual's comportment and life style. Rambam's codification of the relevant laws with regard to this point is very instructive: ". . . a proselyte who conducts himself according to the ways of Israel . . . and performs *all* [italics added] the commandments is assumed to be (*beḥezkat*) a righteous convert even if there are no witnesses who testify before whom they were converted. . . . Nevertheless if they come to marry in Israel, they are not to be married until they bring witnesses or until they immerse in our presence since they were known (*huḥzaku*) as gentiles."[19]

Rambam clearly indicates that a person claiming to be a convert may substantiate that claim on the basis of conduct and behavior alone. It is the *ḥazakah* which establishes presumptive evidence with regard to the authenticity of this claim despite the individual's antecedent identification as a gentile. R. Abraham Isaiah Karelitz, popularly known as *Ḥazon Ish,* rules[20] that the person seeking recognition as a convert must have conducted himself as a Jew for a period of thirty days and have been unquestionably accepted as a Jew by all observers during that time in order for his claim to be deemed valid.[21] *Ḥazon Ish* adds that such presumptive

18. *Tosafot, Yevamot* 47*b; Shakh, Yoreh, De'ah* 268:2.
19. *Mishneh Torah, Hilkhot Isurei Bi'ah* 13:9.
20. *Ḥazon Ish, Yoreh De'ah* 158:6.
21. See also *Teshuvot R. Akiva Eger,* no. 121; and R. A. I. Kook, *Ezrat*

evidence is acceptable, even though it is generated by self-serving actions on the part of the applicant for recognition as a convert, because it may be assumed that the *Bet Din* of the city would not have allowed such conduct to go unheeded. If, during the period in which the applicant conducted himself as a member of the Jewish community, the local ecclesiastical authorities make no attempt to challenge the *prima facie* status created by his conduct, it may be assumed that the *Bet Din* had sufficient reason to conclude that a valid conversion had, in fact, been performed.

With the exception of the Falashas, whose claim to Jewish identity was, according to rabbinic sources, predicated upon a claim to descent from the tribe of Dan and who, in any event, are not known to have been of definite gentile genealogical origin, all contemporary black Jews are acknowledged to have been *beḥezket akum,* i.e., to have been descended from progenitors known to have conducted and identified themselves as non-Jews. The Jewishness of all such groups is of fairly recent vintage and the *ḥezkat akum* is easily traceable. In view of their earlier known identification with Christianity, any claims advanced by, or on behalf of, these groups to descent from the ten lost tribes of Israel or to being the only authentic descendants of the original ethnic Jewish community must be dismissed as sheer fabrication. From the halakhic perspective, such claims are clearly negated by the earlier *ḥezhat akum* growing out of their own prior conduct and deportment. Any claim to recognition as Jews can be based only upon a contention that they, or their forebears, were at some point converted to Judaism. When no claim to prior conversion is made—and indeed many find the very suggestion insulting since they contend that they, and they alone, are descendants of the original Jewish people—any claim to Jewish identity on their part must be rejected as spurious.

Hypothetically, if an individual, or group of individuals, were to claim Jewish identity by virtue of conversion, or by virtue of descent from ancestors who were converted to Judaism, such a claim, to be given credence, must be supported by conduct indicative of membership in the communty of Israel, *viz.,* observance of all commandments as indicated by Rambam. Furthermore, this *ḥazakah,* or presumptive evidence, in the opinion of *Ḥazon Ish,* is given credence only when the status of the individual manifesting such conduct is recognized by the entire community without question or reservation.

Kohen, no. 13. Cf., however, R. Shlomoh Goren, *Pesak Din be-Inyan he-Aḥ ve-ha-Aḥot* (Jerusalem, 5733), pp. 95–105, and above, p. 171.

With the exception of a small number of individuals who have been formally converted to Judaism in recent years and who have been recognized without reservation as righteous converts, those claiming to be black Jews fail to meet one or more of these tests. None of these groups observes all of the precepts of Judaism. If the opposite were the case, such observance might serve to substantiate the validity of a claim to having undergone conversion at some time in the past. The members of these communities were never unreservedly accepted as authentic converts by the general Jewish community as required by *Ḥazon Ish*. Quite to the contrary, responsible religious spokesmen have repeatedly cautioned that the claims of those purporting to be black Jews require careful investigation before they may be accepted as authentic. Such cautionary exhortation clearly served to thwart the establishment of a *ḥazakah*. Moreover, virtually all of those whose conversion cannot be authenticated openly concede that neither they, nor their progenitors, ever sought to acquire Jewish identity by means of formal conversion.

Claims or, more accurately, speculation that present-day black Jews may be descendants of converted slaves who belonged to Jewish slaveowners are entirely without factual foundation. It has been established that, for sociological as well as religious reasons, Jewish slaveholders made no attempt to convert their slaves to Judaism.[22]

It is indeed true that Halakhah requires that a gentile slave acquired by a Jew undergo immersion in a ritualarium and, in the case of a male, calls for circumcision as well. In the absence of voluntary compliance on the part of the slave, the Jewish master is forbidden to retain ownership of the slave but may dispose of him by sale to a non-Jew.[23] The slave, having undergone this ritual, is required to observe all negative commandments and those positive commandments whose fulfillment is not restricted to stated times. The slave, however, upon manumission, acquires full status as a Jew. A slave may, however, validly stipulate against circumcision and immersion prior to his sale to a Jewish master.[24] The Jew is then permitted to retain the slave and the slave incurs no further religious obligations other than the duty to abide by the Seven Commandments of the Sons of Noah which are incumbent upon all non-Jews. In practice, it appears that for many centuries Jewish slaveholders made no attempt to cir-

22. See Charles Reznikoff with Uriah Engelman, *The Jews of Charleston* (Philadelphia, 1950), pp. 77–78.

23. *Yoreh De'ah* 267:4.

24. Rema, *Yoreh De'ah* 267:4.

cumcise their slaves or to have them undergo immersion in a ritualarium. Rema indicates that this practice lapsed because conversion of any non-Jew to Judaism was illegal in many countries. Halakhic authorities ruled that since a Jew might quite correctly agree at the time of purchase not to convert the slave, such an agreement should universally be assumed to be part of the contract of sale. Thus, every acquisition of a slave contained an implied agreement against conversion.[25] It is indeed the case that there exists no halakhic impediment which would preclude a slave who has not previously undergone immersion for the purpose of acquiring the status of a Canaanite slave from voluntarily converting to Judaism subsequent to his acquisition by a Jew. In fact such an act of conversion carries with it automatic manumission.[26] There is, however, no evidence that this actually occurred in the United States during the antebellum period.

III

There is only one reference to a Jewish black to be found in historical records of the pre–Civil War period. In 1857, Maurice Meyer, who served at the time as rabbi of the Jewish community of Charleston, published an article in a German periodical[27] in which he described a black Jew, a freeman who was a retired newspaper carrier. This person was apparently converted outside of the United States and was described as the "most observant of those who go to the synagogue."[28] From Meyer's account it is obvious that the phenomenon of a black Jew was a rarity. There is no evidence whatsoever to support the claim that some present-day black Jews are descendants of slaves converted by Jewish slaveowners.[29]

The existence of groups in this country describing themselves as black Jews can be traced to the latter part of the nineteenth century. One group, known as the Church of the Living God the Pillar Ground of Truth for All Nations, was founded in Chattanooga, Tennessee, in 1886 and later relocated in Philadelphia. Ten years later, a group known as the Church of God and Saints in Christ was organized in Lawrence, Kansas. This group

25. *Loc cit.*
26. *Ibid.*, 267:18.
27. *Allgemeine Zeitung des Judenthums,* XXI, 339.
28. Translated by Reznikoff, *ibid.*, p. 279.
29. See Bertram Korn, "Jews and Negro Slavery in the Old South, 1789–1865: Address of the President," *Publication of the American Jewish Historical Society,* L (1960–61), 176.

is very active in the Washington, D.C. area, and for many years its headquarters have been in Belleville, Virginia.

These groups, whose origin and development parallel the rapid development of black Christian sects whose devotions and liturgy focus heavily on the Old Testament, claim Jewish identity based upon genealogical descent from the Jews of the Bible. The rise of these sects, both Christian and "Jewish," is not difficult to understand. Old Testament accounts of the persecution and election of the people of Israel had a ready appeal to an enslaved people. Recently emancipated Negroes saw a commonality of experience and anticipation between themselves and the Israelites of the Bible. The parallel between their own situation and that of the ancient Hebrews, who had been rescued from bondage and led to freedom is readily perceived. It is for this reason that typical Negro spirituals show a predilection for biblical motifs. These early group of black "Jews" showed little interest in the white Jewish community.

The Church of the Living God was established by S. J. Cherry, a black seaman and railroad worker. Cherry claimed that God had appointed him as His prophet and that it had been revealed to him that all Jews of the Bible were black. He further claimed that only blacks are real Jews but conceded that not all blacks, either now or in the biblical period, were Jews. Esau was the first red (or white) man and was hated by God. Jacob was black. It follows that white Jews are not born of the stock of Jacob. It is only because the true Israelites were unknown for such a long period of time that "so-called white Jews" succeeded in fraudently identifying themselves as Jews. Cherry, apparently rejecting the efficacy of conversion as a means of acquiring identity as a Jew, taught that one may be a Jew only if born a Jew. Hence, although white Jews may be "Jewish" in their religious observances they are not really Jews. Only black Jews may validly claim to be Jews by virtue of descent from the patriarchs.[30] This church is presently headed by the "Prophet's" son and successor, "Prince" Benjamin F. Cherry. Members of this group observe the Sabbath on Saturday, celebrate Passover and refrain from eating pork and fish lacking fins or scales. Gambling, smoking, swearing, television and movies are banned. The Christian origin of this group is manifest in the continued veneration of Jesus.[31]

30. See Deanne Ruth Shapiro, "Double Damnation, Double Salvation: The Sources and Varieties of Black Judaism in the United States," unpublished Master's Essay, Columbia University, 1970, pp. 121–22.

31. *Ibid.*, pp. 125 ff.

The second such sect to emerge, the Church of God and Saints of Christ, was founded in 1896 by William S. Crowdy, a Negro cook on the Sante Fe Railroad. Crowdy believed he was a prophet charged by God with leading His people, the black race, to Judaism. Crowdy claimed to be the recipient of a series of revelations in which, among other things, he was told that blacks were descendants of the ten lost tribes of Israel. Crowdy maintained that all blacks are Jews and originally all Jews were black. White Jews lost their black pigmentation as a result of intermarriage with whites. Crowdy's followers adopted such distinctive Jewish practices as circumcision, the Jewish calendar, observance of Saturday as the Sabbath, Passover and the wearing of skull caps. At the same time, as indicated by its very title, the sect retained the central beliefs of Christianity, practiced baptism, celebrated a form of the Eucharist and engaged in other Christian practices as well. The present leader of this sect, Bishop A. Z. Plummer, was appointed to his post by "Prophet" Crowdy. Plummer is viewed as a direct descendant of Abraham and is called "Grandfather Abraham" by his followers.[32] Various estimates of the church's membership made between the 1930s and 1960s suggest that the church has between 34,000 and 38,000 adherents among its 112–200 branches. In Belleville, the site of the church's central authority, the group forms a cohesive and isolated enclave. The life-style of the Belleville group is that of a commune.[33]

In 1899 there appeared yet another group which founded a congregation in New York City known as the Moorish Zionist Temple whose spiritual leader, a certain "Rabbi" Richlieu, claimed to have been born in Ethiopia. In the early or mid-1920s, one Arnold Ford became associated with the Temple leadership, either at the time of the reorganization of the Temple in 1921[34] or in 1925, shortly after it became defunct.[35] Ford declared himself to be a rabbi and, after breaking with his colleagues in 1925, founded a group known as Beth B'nai Abraham. Raised in Barbados, Ford was the son of a leader of a Christian evangelical sect and himself served as choirmaster of the United Negro Improvement Association whose leader was Marcus Garvey, one of the earliest advocates of an extreme form of

32. Ibid., pp. 112–16.

33. *Ibid.*, pp. 116–18.

34. Ruth Landes, "Negro Jews in Harlem," *Jewish Journal of Sociology,* IX (December, 1967), 181.

35. Arthur Dobrin, "A History of the Negro Jews in America" (unpublished paper, New York Public Library, Schomburg Collection, 1965), p. 40; cf. Shapiro, p. 90.

black nationalism and founder of a movement which came to be known as Garveyism. Ford adopted the anti-white sentiments of Garveyism and taught that "only true Jews were black; and white Jews were only European offshots of the original black African Hebrews." [36]

Ford rejected the term "Jew" and insisted upon calling his followers "Hebrews." The term "Jew" he felt to be appropriate only as an appellation for European whites who had been converted to Judaism by blacks. He believed that Africans were the true Hebrews, but that knowledge of their heritage had been virtually eradicated through centuries of persecution. The Beth B'nai Abraham became torn by a schism between Hebraic African sympathizers and those who wished to be identified simply as Jews. The Beth B'nai Abraham developed serious financial troubles and collapsed in 1930. Some writers maintain that Arnold Ford relocated in Detroit, changed his name and went on to become the leader of the Nation of Islam. They maintain that the recently deceased W. Fard, the founder of this Islamic cult and Arnold Ford were one and the same person.[37]

At least eight different black cultist groups flourished in Harlem at various times between 1919 and 1931.[38] Probably the best known group of black Jews is the Commandment Keepers Congregation of the Royal Order of Ethiopian Hebrews which made its appearance sometime in the 1920s. The origin and practices of this group have been analyzed in detail by a sociologist, Howard Brotz.[39] The members of this group claim to be descendants of Falasha Jews and have always sought recognition and acceptance as Jews by the white Jewish community. The Commandment Keepers Congregation, headquarters of the Royal Order of Ethiopian Hebrews, was established by the late Wentworth A. Matthew, formerly of the West Indies. Matthew claimed to have been born in a Falasha community in the Gold Coast of Africa. However, in his early life he was clearly a practicing Christian. In his own words: "I got tired of Christianity, of going from church to church. Got the spirit it wasn't right. Just found this by myself because I wanted Hebrew. Like I was reaching out and discovered this." [40]

---

36. Landes, p. 180.

37. See C. Eric Lincoln, *The Black Muslims in America* (Boston, 1961), p. 11.

38. Howard Brotz, *The Black Jews of Harlem* (New York; 1964), p. 10.

39. "Negro 'Jews' in the United States" *Phylon,* XIII (1952), 324–37; "The Negro-Jewish Community and the Contemporary Race Crisis," *Jewish Social Studies,* XXVII (1965), 10–17.

40. Quoted in Brotz, *Black Jews,* p. 96.

Until May 1962 Matthew's congregation was officially listed in the records of the City of New York as the Church of the Living God, Pillar and Ground of Truth and Faith of Jesus Christ.[41] To this day the Passover *seder* celebrated by this group contains elements commemorating the Last Supper."[42]

Brotz reports that Matthew came to Harlem from the West Indies in 1913. After coming into contact with Arnold Ford, Matthew organized his own congregation which originally consisted of only eight men. Hiring an immigrant Jew as a tutor, Matthew studied Hebrew and Jewish practices and acquired some knowledge of Yiddish.[43] Quite apart from his own unsubstantiated claim of Falasha birth, it is clear that his followers are not of Falasha descent. Despite Matthew's characterization of his followers as "Ethiopians," in light of the virtually total absence of Ethiopian immigration to the United States, it is inconceivable that any significant number of Matthew's congregants are of Ethiopian, much less of Falasha, origin.

It is clear that the practices of the Royal Order of Ethiopian Hebrews do not derive from those of the Falashas but originated from contact with white Jews in Harlem. Matthew's claim to Falasha descent may well have been prompted by a well-meaning Jew. Brotz reports that Feitlovitch, the moving figure of the Pro-Falasha Committee, which was then actively trying to awaken world Jewry to the plight of the Jews of Ethiopia, approached the black Jews of Harlem in conjunction with his endeavors. Feitlovitch made these contacts in the belief that members of these sects were descendants of Falasha Jews.[44] In the process, he provided impetus for later affirmation of Falasha origin by the Ethiopian Hebrews. Feitlovitch's own investigations demonstrate that there is no connection between the Ethiopian Hebrews and Falasha Jews.[45]

IV

The problem which currently besets the Jewish community is the manner in which it should respond to the various groups of black Jews seeking recognition and legitimization.

---

41. Robert Coleman, "A Black Jew Speaks," *Jewish Observer,* November 1970, p. 12; *idem, American Examiner–Jewish Week.* November 16, 1974, p. 25.

42. Brotz, *Black Jews,* pp. 40 and 50–51.

43. Brotz, *Phylon,* XIII, 325–28.

44. Brotz, *Black Jews,* p. 49.

45. See Jacques Feitlovitch, "The Falashas," *American Jewish Yearbook* (Philadelphia, 1920), pp. 80–100.

The various black Jewish communities may be seen as separable into three distinct categories. There are some groups whose members maintain that they are the original Jews and that white Jews of European descent are "Edomites," usurpers whose claims to Judaism are spurious. Since these black Jews view themselves as the only true Jews, they see no need, and have no desire, to convert to Judaism. From our perspective, and our view of Jewish history and identity, there is very little that need be said in response to such a claim. Their use of the appellation "Jew" is, from our point of view, a misnomer. Black "Jews" subscribing to this belief and the Jewish community agree on one most significant point: the two communities differ both ethnically and religiously. It would be best for all concerned to recognize that we must agree to disagree and go our separate ways.

There are other black Jews who, regardless of their personal feelings and convictions, recognize that in order to gain acceptance as members of the community of Israel it is necessary for them to undergo the process of conversion. There are indeed a number of instances in which not only individuals but entire groups have become proselytes and have become observant members of the community of Israel. This group poses no halakhic problem whatsoever. They have been recognized and welcomed as righteous proselytes.

The area of most concern is with regard to a third category of black "Jews," comprised primarily of individuals rather than of organized groups. There are significant members of black "Jews" who, for whatever reason, feel a very close affinity to Judaism. These individuals refuse to undergo conversion either because of an erroneous belief that they are Jews by virtue of birth or because of a feeling that since they have conducted themselves as observant Jews for an extended period of time, conversion is superfluous. Resistance to acceptance of the necessity for conversion is based at least in part upon the identity crisis such a process would precipitate. These individuals are understandably reluctant to reorder their thinking with regard to themselves and their religious identity. Some individuals included in this category would certainly be eligible candidates for conversion were they to seek the status of proselytes; others are ineligible for conversion because while they seek to identify themselves as Jews and observe many of the commandments and precepts of Judaism, there remain many precepts which they decline to accept. In any event, unless and until such individuals undergo conversion, their status as non-Jews remains unchanged.

Although it is not possible to recognize such individuals as Jews, they may nevertheless be urged to accept the precepts of the Noachide Code as a minimum level of observance and may conceivably be encouraged to accept other *mizvot* as well, subject, of course, to the limitations which Jewish law places on the observance of the commandments by non-Jews.

Judaism teaches that observance of the Seven Commandments of the Sons of Noah is an obligation which devolves upon all gentiles. In earlier periods of Jewish history, formal acceptance of the obligations of the Noachide Code carried with it recognition and status as a *ger toshav*. Although the institution of *ger toshav* lapsed following the destruction of the Temple and the exile of the Jews from the Land of Israel, Judaism teaches that the binding nature of the Noachide Code is in no way diminished. The black "Jews" under discussion undoubtedly seek closer identification with Judaism than they are likely to feel through observances restricted to fulfillment of the seven Noachide commandments. The Noachide laws are essentially negative in nature and serve primarily to restrict conduct in certain areas. They do not provide for positive forms of religious expression or identification. Moreover, a religion stripped to the bare essentials of the Noachide Code lacks the richness of beauty of the rituals and ceremonies so closely associated with Judaism and Jewish worship. In some situations it may be appropriate to encourage non-Jews to accept many of the 613 *mizvot* incumbent upon Jews in order to satisfy their need for religious expression. Of course, such persons would have the option of selecting as many, or as few, of these commandments as they wish. Indeed, since it will be clearly recognized by them and by the Jewish community that they are in fact neither Jews nor candidates for conversion, there is no reason why their commitment to acceptance of the yoke of the commandments should be total and all-embracing.

V

Judaism does indeed teach that non-Jews are forbidden to study the Oral Law[46] and may not observe Sabbath restrictions in their totality. A non-Jew desiring to observe *Shabbat* would of necessity require rabbinic guidance with regard to the proper mode of observance. Suffice it to say that a non-Jew would find it possible to observe the Sabbath in a manner

46. Me'iri, *Sanhedrin* 59a, permits gentiles to study the laws pertaining to those *mizvot* which they seek to fulfill. See also the comments of Abraham Sofer in his notes on the commentary of Me'iri, p. 229, n.1. Rambam, *Teshuvot ha-Rambam,* ed. Alfred Freimann (Jerusalem, 1934), no. 324, exempts Christians from this prohibition.

that would satisfy both the strictures of Halakhah and his own need for the Sabbath as a day of rest and spiritual renewal.

Many authorities follow the position of Radbaz[47] in permitting non-Jews to perform *mizvot* provided that they clearly recognize that observance of the commandments is not a binding obligation insofar as gentiles are concerned. It would appear that the status of a non-Jew in performing the *mizvot* is that of an *eino mezuveh ve-'oseh*—one who is under no express obligation to perform the *mizvah* but who nevertheless may, at his option, do so. According to this view, the non-Jew fulfilling *mizvot* in this manner will be the recipient of heavenly reward for the deeds which he performs. Radbaz, however, adds a caveat with regard to permitting non-Jews to perform certain specific *mizvot* and states, "Nevertheless, regarding commandments requiring sanctity and purity, such as *tefillin, sefer Torah,* and *mezuzah,* I incline toward stringency, not to allow them to perform such *mizvot.*"

This view is also recorded in the works of several early authorities who expressly affirm that the category of "one who is not commanded but observes" extends to non-Jews who perform *mizvot.* Me'iri, in his commentary to *Sanhedrin* 59a, explicitly states that a non-Jew who performs the *mizvot* "is to be honored even as a High Priest."

Of even greater relevance to a definitive determination of this question are the words of Rambam, *Hilkhot Melakhim* 10:10. After enumerating the specific *mizvot* which a gentile may not perform, Rambam states: "A Noachide who wishes to perform a *mizvah* from among the other *mizvot* of the Torah in order to receive reward is not to be prevented from performing it in the proper manner . . ." Noteworthy is the fact that Rambam explicitly refers to the motivation of the non-Jew in performing the *mizvah* as being "in order to receive reward." Nowhere in halakhic sources is there a suggestion that God has in any sense demanded the performance of *mizvot* by non-Jews. Hence, in observing *mizvot,* gentiles cannot be depicted as being among those who fulfill God's desires and "serve the Master not for the sake of reward" (*Avot* 1:3). Logically the sole remaining motivating factor is the desire to receive compensation. Thus, Rambam incorporates the phrase "in order to receive reward" in his codification of this Halakhah in order to indicate that there is nothing at all ignominious with regard to a gentile performing *mizvot* for the pur-

47. Commentary on the *Mishneh Torah, Hilkhot Melakhim* 10:10; see also *Encyclopedia Talmudit,* III, 359.

pose of receiving reward. He does indeed "serve the Master for the sake of receiving reward" and, since no higher obligation has been placed upon him, he is to be lauded for doing so.[48] The clear implication is that the gentile who performs a *mizvah* is rewarded for doing so. Radbaz, in his commentary on this passage, states clearly that the status of one who conducts himself in this manner is that of an *eino mezuveh ve-'oseh.*

In addition to this statement in *Hilkhot Melakhim,* Rambam, in one of his responsa,[49] states unequivocally, "for a gentile who fulfills a *mizvah* is accorded reward for [the] *mizvah,* but not as one who is commanded." Accordingly, Rambam rules that a non-Jew seeking circumcision in fulfillment of the *mizvah* may be circumcised by a Jew.[50]

One contemporary authority, Rabbi Moses Feinstein, adopts a contradictory view and states that a non-Jew who performs a *mizvah* receives no compensation whatsoever.[51] Rabbi Feinstein carefully distinguishes

---

48. Cf., however, Radbaz in his commentary *ad locum,* who advances a different explanation for Rambam's incorporation of this phrase in his codification of the Halakhah. According to Radbaz, Rambam, by the inclusion of this phrase, intends to indicate that a non-Jew who contends that the fulfillment of a precept is incumbent upon him is to be prevented from performing the *mizvah.*

49. *Teshuvot ha-Rambam,* ed. Alfred Freimann (Jerusalem, 1934), no. 124.

50. The source of Rambam's ruling is *Avodah Zarah* 26b: "A Jew may circumcise a gentile for purposes of conversion but not for purposes of *murana* (excision of a parasite worm)." Rambam, in his responsum indicates that the Gemara forbids only therapeutic circumcision when performed upon a gentile by a Jew, but does not intend to limit permission solely to circumcision for purposes of conversion. Circumcision for purposes of conversion, explains Rambam, is simply an example of circumcision for the sake of a *mizvah.* Rambam's statement, *Hilkhot Milah* 3:7, "Therefore, if the intention of the gentile was for purposes of circumcision, a Jew is permitted to circumcise him" must be understood in the same vein, i.e., as permitting circumcision for the purpose of fulfilling the *mizvah* of circumcision. Cf., however, *Kesef Mishneh, ad locum.*

51. Indeed, some support for the thesis that the concept of *eino mezuveh ve-'oseh* is limited in nature and that gentiles are excluded from sharing in the reward for the performance of *mizvot* may be adduced from a comment of R. Sa'adia Ga'on in his *Emunot ve-De'ot,* Fourth Treatise, chap. 5. (English translation by Samuel Rosenblatt, *The Book of Beliefs and Opinions* [New Haven, 1948], p. 192.) In his discussion of divine omniscience and freedom of will, Saadia raises an obvious question. Since God knows which actions a person will perform and which he will not perform, what purpose is there to

between a non-Jew and a Jewish minor. The latter, opines Rabbi Feinstein, is at the very minimum, in the category of "one who is not commanded but fulfills,"[52] whereas the former is completely excluded from the pale of *mizvot*. Rabbi Feinstein further rules that non-Jews are forbidden to engage in the performance of any ritual *mizvah* on a regular basis.[53] This position is predicated upon a statement by Rambam, *Hilkhot Melakhim* 10:9. Rambam, basing himself upon *Sanhedrin* 58b, declares that a non-Jew may not be permitted to "create" a new *mizvah* or ritual

---

the issuance of formal commandments? In resolving this problem Sa'adia enumerates a number of reasons pointing to the necessity for a revealed system of laws and includes as one of his reasons: ". . . so that man may be rewarded, for if a man serve Him and he not be commanded to do so there would be no reward." The clear meaning of this passage is that if a *mizvah* has not been commanded there can be no reward for its fulfillment. The Gemara, however, does recognize the status of "one who is not commanded, yet fulfills." According to this principle, as enunciated by the Sages, a person who fulfills a *mizvah* even when not subject thereto, receives some form of compensation, albeit a diminished one. Sa'adia apparently reasons that reward for an *eino mezuveh ve-'oseh* is possible only subsequent to revelation but, in the absence of a *revealed mizvah*, the concept of *eino mezuveh ve-'oseh* does not apply. Fulfillment of a *mizvah* is vacuous unless the *mizvah* has been revealed by God.

Rosenblatt's citation of the talmudic dictum "He who is commanded, and does stands higher than he who is not commanded and does" [*Kiddushin* 31a] in this context is misleading. It would appear that he understands Sa'adia as saying that the person performing the *mizvah* enjoys the status of an *eino mezuveh ve-'oseh* and hence receives a lesser reward than one who is commanded. Yet an examination of the passage in question clearly indicates that Saadia is not addressing himself to the *degree* of compensation but says, rather, that *no* compensation would be awarded.

For R. Feinstein, not only is fulfillment of a *mizvah* vacuous unless the *mizvah* is revealed by God but, moreover, the fulfillment of the *mizvah* is a sacramental act only if performed by one who is, at the very minimum, a party to the Sinaitic covenant. For such a person, performance of a *mizvah*, even if not specifically incumbent upon the performer, is a sacramental act and hence merits reward; for others it is meaningless and hence remains unrewarded.

52. *Iggrot Mosheh, Yoreh De'ah,* I, nos. 3 and 6; *Iggrot Mosheh Yoreh De'ah,* II, no. 8.

53. *Iggrot Mosheh, Yoreh De'ah,* I, no. 3 and at greater length in *Yoreh De'ah,* II, no. 7. Rabbi Feinstein recognizes that non-Jews are rewarded for prayer even though prayer is not included among the seven Noachide commandments. See *Iggrot Mosheh, Oraḥ Ḥayyim,* II, no. 25; see also below, n. 56.

observance. Regular performance of a *mizvah* by which he is not bound, argues Rabbi Feinstein, in tantamount to the creation of a new *mizvah* and cannot be sanctioned since non-Jews are enjoined from devising novel observances. However, according to Radbaz' interpretation of Rambam, the voluntary performance of one of the divinely commanded 613 precepts cannot be accounted as the creation of a "new" *mizvah* on the part of a non-Jew. For Radbaz, such a view is contradicted by the previously cited comments on Rambam, *Hilkhot Melakhim* 10:10.[54]

The opposing view of Me'iri is dismissed by Rabbi Feinstein because it is contained in a manuscript which was unknown until very recently. Rabbi Feinstein claims that the authenticity of the newly discovered talmudic commentaries attributed to Me'iri is suspect. Radbaz' statements are dismissed by Rabbi Feinstein for the same reason that he does not give credence to the opinion voiced by Me'iri. Although the commentary of Radbaz is incorporated in all standard texts of Rambam's *Mishneh Torah,* it is based upon a manuscript whose authenticity Rabbi Feinstein does not accept as having been established beyond doubt.[55] However, it would seem to this writer that Radbaz' comments, insofar as the crucial passage is concerned, are simply an explication of the plain meaning of the text. If so, it is the authentic and authoriative view of Rambam himself which may be cited in support of the thesis that non-Jews are rewarded for the performance of *mizvot.*[56]

---

54. See above, n. 48.

55. *Teshuvot ha-Rambam,* no. 124, is not cited by Rabbi Feinstein. Rabbi Feinstein, presumably, would negate this source for identical reasons. It is of interest to note that Ramban questions the authenticity of a responsum attributed to Rif and cited by *Ba'al ha-Ma'or* because there existed no tradition with regard to the responsum in question. See *Milhamot ha-Shem, Sukkah* 26a; cf. also Rabad's comments regarding this responsum in his *Temim De'im* (Lemberg, 5572), p. 46 a. However, with regard to the question at hand, the various manuscripts reinforce a common position. In the light of these several diverse sources, it is difficult to entertain Rabbi Feinstein's thesis.

With regard to the reliability of newly discovered manuscripts, see also the comments of *Hazon Ish, Kovez Iggrot,* I, no. 32 and *Iggrot Mosheh, Even ha-Ezer,* I, no. 63, sec. 6, as well as R. Yechiel Michal Tucatzinsky, *Sefer Erez Yisra'el,* p. 40, and R. Ben-Zion Uziel, *Mishpetei Uziel, Hoshen Mishpat,* no. 6.

56. See also Rambam, *Commentary on the Mishnah, Terumot* 3:9, "Although they are not obligated with regard to *mizvot* if they perform any aspect of them they receive some reward . . . and since they join with us in reward their deeds with regard to *mizvot* are valid." These comments are advanced by Rambam as an explanation of the statement contained in the Mishnah to

There is yet another source which, although in itself not halakhically authoritative, nevertheless lends support to the view that non-Jews are rewarded for the performance of *mizvot*. Scripture records that following Abraham's circumcision ". . . the Lord appeared unto him in the terebinth of Mamre" (Gen. 18:1). Apparently troubled by the necessity for a refer-

---

the effect that *terumah, ma'aser,* etc., become sanctified through the actions of a gentile. *Iggrot Mosheh* is of the opinion that Rambam's comments are limited to certain non-ritual observances.

However, the same question may be raised with regard to the discussion in *Menahot* 42a. One *beraita* rules that a gentile may perform a valid circumcision. This position is negated only by citation of a specific verse which is understood as excluding non-Jews from performance of this rite. Otherwise, circumcision performed by a non-Jew would be significantly different from, for example, circumcision performed at night. The latter does not constitute a fulfillment of a *mizvah* in any sense and hence must be followed by "letting of blood of the covenant." It would appear that circumcision performed by a non-Jew could not be thought to be efficacious unless it constitutes a fulfillment of a *mizvah.*

Similarly, *Yevamot* 62a records a dispute between R. Yochanan and Resh Lakish concerning a convert who had sired children while yet a gentile. Virtually all authorities are in agreement that non-Jews are not bound by the obligation to "be fruitful and multiply." Yet R. Yochanan maintains that the convert is not obligated to engage in procreation and gives as his reason *"kevar kiyyaim piryah ve-rivyah"*—indicating that while yet a gentile, he had *fulfilled* the commandment with regard to procreation. Cf., however, R. Moshe Sternbuch, *Olam ha-Torah,* Tevet-Shevat 5736, p. 17.

A literal reading of *Bereshit Rabbah* LXXVI, 2 indicates that this midrashic comment seems to be predicated upon the premise that non-Jews are rewarded for performance of *mizvot.* The Midrash explains that Jacob's fear of the approaching encounter with his brother Esau was based upon the fact that during the years of Jacob's sojourn in the house of Laban Esau remained in the Land of Israel. Thus Jacob feared that Esau might vanquish him because Esau had accumulated merit during that period of time by virtue of dwelling in the Land of Israel. See R. Ovadiah Yosef, *Torah She-be-'al Peh,* XI (5729), 37. It is, however, doubtful that fulfillment of this commandment was at all a possibility prior to the sanctification of the Land of Israel in the time of Joshua. Thus *Tosafot, Gittin* 2a, maintains that areas not resettled by those who ascended from Babylonia are endowed with no sanctity whatsoever and hence one who dwells in such territories does not thereby fulfill a *mizvah.* The Midrash may perhaps best be understood in light of the comments of *Teshuvot Maharit,* I, no. 47. *Maharit* is in agreement with *Tosafot* but points out that the patriarchs sought burial places in Israel even before the land became sanctified. Merit, then, may perhaps be acquired even if the meritorious act does not constitute the fullfillment of a specific *mizvah.* Cf. above, p. 11, n. 2a.

ence to Mamre and by the identification of this historical personage with the geographical site of God's revelation, Rashi makes the following comment: "It was he [Mamre] who gave [Abraham] counsel with regard to circumcision; therefore [God] revealed [Himself] to him in [Mamre's] portion." Rashi's comment is perplexing to say the least. Abraham is the recipient of an explicit divine commandment. He has been ordered to circumcise himself. Can there be any question that Abraham will obey? If so, why does Abraham seek the counsel of Mamre? What advice need he solicit? *Siftei Ḥakhamim,* in one of the explanations which he advances, indicates that this advice was sought not after Abraham received the divine command regarding circumcision, but prior to the commandment.[57] Abraham, declare the Sages, fulfilled all the precepts of the Torah even though no *mizvah* had as yet been ordained. In keeping with his regimen of observance, Abraham desired to fulfill the *mizvah* of circumcision as well and desired to do so without delay. This *mizvah,* however, presented a unique problem. By virtue of its nature, circumcision is a nonrecurring *mizvah;* it can be performed only once in a lifetime. Hence, Abraham found himself in a quandry: a *mizvah* performed as a result of divine command is greater than one performed in the absence of such directive. On the other hand, performance of a *mizvah* should not be delayed. Abraham's dilemma was whether he should perform the *mizvah* without delay, even though he had as yet not been commanded to do so, and hence its performance would be in the category of *eino mezuveh ve-'oseh,* or whether he should wait until God would command him to do so, in order that he might fulfill the *mizvah* in the optimum manner as a *mezuveh ve-'oseh.* It is with regards to this question, according to *Siftei Ḥakhamim,* that Abraham consulted Mamre. Mamre's advice was to delay the circumcision until the commandment was issued. This advice coincided with the divine design and Mamre was suitably rewarded. God visited Abraham "on the plains of Mamre" during his convalescence and this statement was recorded for posterity as part of the eternal Torah.

The very question posed by Abraham indicates that prior to receiving this commandment he enjoyed the status of *eino mezuveh ve-'oseh* although he was yet a Noachide. It might appear that this contention may be refuted if the thesis of numerous commentators who are of the opinion that the patriarchs enjoyed the status of Jews, albeit "uncommanded"

---

57. Cf., however, *Midrash Tanḥuma, Va-Yeira,* 3. For an interesting explanation in conformity with *Tanḥuma,* see *Ha-Ma'ayan,* Nisan 5734, p. 34.

Jews, is accepted. If so, Abraham would have enjoyed the status of *eino mezuveh ve-'oseh* prior to the divine command, even though a Noachide does not. This is, however, not the case. R. Yehudah Rosanes makes it very clear that the patriarchs may be deemed to have acquired the status of Jews only *after* Abraham's circumcision.[58] All commentators are in agreement that prior to that event Abraham's status was indistinguishable from that of other Noachides. In fact, according to Rabbi Rosanes, Abraham's circumcision at the divine behest was tantamount to an act of conversion and conferred status as a Jew upon him.[59] Had Abraham not enjoyed the status of an *eino mezuveh ve-'oseh* prior to the divine command, there would have been no purpose whatsoever to Abraham's performance of the circumcision rite. There would have been no basis for Abraham's perplexity, and hence no reason to consult Mamre.

Furthermore, the assumption that a Noachide does not enjoy the status of an *eino mezuveh ve-'oseh* leads to a difficulty in understanding the various midrashic references to the fulfillment of *mizvot* by Abraham. According to this opinion, such action would have been pointless were Abraham to be deemed a Noachide. It is rather difficult to posit that these Midrashim are all of the opinion that Abraham, in fact, enjoyed the status of a Jew since the status of the Patriarchs is a matter which is the subject of considerable dispute among latter-day commentators, none of whom cite these sources as evidence. Moreover, all midrashic references to Abraham's performance of *mizvot* would have to be understood as referring to actions performed by Abraham subsequent to his circumcision. No such chronological distinction is made in any of the Midrashim.

In accordance with the view of the many authorities who maintain that non-Jews are rewarded for the performance of *mizvot,* black "Jews" may be supported, in some circumstances, in the selective observance of *mizvot.* However, it cannot be overemphasized that, for one who is not a Jew by birth, membership in the community of Israel is contingent upon formal conversion. No matter how many *mizvot* a non-Jew may perform, his status remains that of an *eino mezuveh ve-'oseh,* i.e., a non-Jew who voluntarily assumes the burden of *mizvot.* Encouragement and support of non-Jews seeking such observance should never be of a nature which would permit this distinction to become blurred.

---

58. *Parashat Derakhim* (New York, 5707), *Derush Rishon,* pp. 4a and 7b. This view is cited in the name of Maharash Yafo, *Commentary on the Bible, Parshat Va-Yigash* 93:5.

59. *Loc. cit.*

VI

The Jewish community has frequently been remiss in its treatment of righteous proselytes. Indeed, one of the interpretations of the talmudic dictum that "proselytes are as burdensome unto Israel as leprosy," advanced by *Tosafot, Yevamot* 47b, is based upon *Tosafot*'s recognition that oftimes we do wrongs to the convert. Such practices are a violation of the admonition "And a proselyte you shall not wrong, neither shall you oppress him . . ." (Exod. 22:20). Since our conduct in this regard is not exemplary, explains *Tosafot,* the greater the incidence of conversion, the greater the instances of transgression and the graver the punishment.

In assessing and analyzing our position with regard to black Jews, it is necessary to take clear cognizance of two opposing imperatives: (1) The Jewish community must be extremely careful not to extend recognition to those claiming to be Jews whose claim to Jewish identity is spurious. (2) We must be exceedingly careful to accord true proselytes—regardless of color—the welcome affection properly due all righteous converts.

The Lord Himself is described as evidencing concern for the welfare of the proselyte, as loving him "in giving him bread and clothing" (Deut. 10:18). The Torah specifically commands us to mirror this divine love in our actions and emotions: "And you shall love the proselyte, for you were proselytes in the land of Egypt" (Deut. 10:19).

The obligations of Jews, individually and collectively, with regard to converts are not limited to concern for their spiritual welfare and essential temporal needs. Mahari Perla, in his commentary to Sa'adia Ga'on's *Sefer ha-Mizvot* (*Aseh,* no. 82), writes that Sa'adia viewed the passage "And if there would dwell among you a proselyte in your land . . . as the home-born among you shall the proselyte who dwells among you be unto you, and you shall love him as yourself . . ." (Lev. 19:33–34) as constituting a positive precept. In commanding that the treatment accorded a proselyte be identical with that accorded the native-born Jew, the Torah expressly forbids any type of discrimination whatsoever. Any form of prejudice, whether expressed in word or deed, constitutes a violation of this precept. The Torah does not countenance discrimination against converts; nor does it tolerate discrimination among righteous proselytes on the basis of color.

CHAPTER XV

Abortion in Halakhic Literature

There are three [persons] who drive away the Shekhinah from the world, making it impossible for the Holy One, blessed be He, to fix His abode in the universe and causing prayer to be unanswered. . . . [The third is] he who causes the fetus to be destroyed in the womb, for he destroys the artifice of the Holy One, blessed be He, and His workmanship. . . . For these abominations the Spirit of Holiness weeps . . .

ZOHAR, SHEMOT 3b

Throughout the history of civilization, abortions have been performed on a surprisingly wide scale among even the most primitive of peoples; feticide is singled out as one of the "abominations of Egypt" which the Torah sought to suppress. Despite the clause in the Hippocratic oath in which the physician declares, "nor will I give to a woman a pessary to procure abortion," artificial interruption of pregnancy, both legal and illegal, remains a widespread practice. While Judaism has always sanctioned therapeutic abortion in at least limited circumstances, the pertinent halakhic discussions are permeated with a spirit of humility reflecting an attitude of awe and reverence before the profound mystery of existence and a deeply rooted reluctance to condone interference with the sanctity of individual human life.

In recent years many attempts were made in the legislative bodies of various states to implement changes in the laws governing the performance of induced abortions. Such proposals were designed to liberalize existing statutes both by enlarging the criteria under which legal sanction would be granted for the interruption of pregnancy and by treating abortion, at least in the early stages of pregnancy, as a private matter between a woman and her physician. These efforts culminated in the now historic Supreme Court decision in *Roe* v. *Wade,* issued in January 1973, which had the effect of rendering most existing abortion statutes unconstitutional. The ensuing discussion led to numerous requests for clarification of religious teachings with regard to these pressing problems. The inevitable demands made upon individual rabbis and communal spokesmen for an explication of the position of normative Judaism regarding this question has made it imperative that we examine this issue and acquaint ourselves with the teachings of our tradition regarding this area of serious concern.

There can be no doubt that a pregnancy contraindicated by considerations of social desiderata and personal welfare poses grave and tragic problems. We are, indeed, keenly aware of the anguishing emotional ramifications of such problems and are acutely sensitive to their moral implications. Yet when we are confronted by these and similar dilemmas, our response cannot simply echo humanistic principles and values, but must emerge from the wellspring of Halakhah. An authentically Jewish response must, by definition, be found in and predicated upon halakhic prescriptions. To us, in the words of one of the foremost rabbinic authorities of the last generation, Rabbi Abraham Isaiah Karelitz, popularly known as the *Ḥazon Ish,* "Ethical imperatives are . . . at one with the directives of Halakhah; it is Halakhah which determines that which is permitted and that which is forbidden in the realm of ethics." [1]

Judaism regards all forms of human life as sacred, from the formation of germ plasm in the cell of the sperm until the decomposition of the body after death. While applicable *halakhot* vary in an appropriate manner from stage to stage along this continuum, fetal life is regarded as precious and may not be destroyed wantonly. This analysis of the halakhic literature concerning abortion has been undertaken as an attempt to refer the reader to the basic sources and relevant responsa and to direct attention to the halakhic intricacies upon which the issues revolve.

Basis of the Prohibition

The basic halakhic principle governing abortion practices is recorded in the Mishnah, *Oholot* 7:6, in the declaration that when "hard travail" of labor endangers the life of the mother an embryotomy may be performed

---

1. *Emunah, Bitaḥon ve-Od* (Jerusalem, 5714), p. 21.

and the embryo extracted member by member. This ruling is cited as definitive by Rambam, *Hilkhot Rotzeaḥ* 1:9, and *Shulḥan Arukh, Ḥoshen Mishpat* 425:2. The halakhic reasoning underlying this provision is incorporated in the text of the Mishnah and succinctly couched in the explanatory phrase "for her [the mother's] life has priority over its [the fetus'] life." In the concluding clause of the Mishnah, a distinction is sharply drawn between the status of the fetus and that of a newly born infant. The Mishnah stipulates that from the moment at which birth, as halakhically definied,[2] is considered to have occurred, no interference with natural processes is permitted, since "one life is not to be set aside for the sake of another life."

It may readily be inferred from this statement that destruction of the fetus is prohibited in situations not involving a threat to the life of the pregnant mother. Incorporation of the justificatory statement "for her life takes precedence over its life" within the text of the Mishnah indicates that in the absence of this consideration abortion is not sanctioned.[3]

---

2. See below, n. 46.

3. This inference is not formulated explicitly by the *Tosafot* cited but is mentioned in passing by R. Ya'ir Chaim Bachrach in his *Teshuvot Ḥavot Ya'ir,* (Frankfort a. M., 5459), no. 31. The omission of this inference is perhaps intentional on the part of *Tosafot* since such omission is consistent with a distinction drawn by *Tosafot, Niddah,* 44a, to the effect that an embryo which has "torn itself loose" from its normal uterine position before the death of the mother enjoys inheritance rights with respect to the mother's property and passes on such rights to its heirs. This provision is based on the premise that the fetus' death is deemed to occur after that of the mother. One might therefore argue that "tearing itself loose" marks the stage at which the fetus is sufficiently viable to be accorded human status. Since the Mishnah refers to a woman who is in "hard travail," there is no evidence therefrom that an embryo in earlier stages of development, i.e., prior to having commenced the process of parturition, is accounted sufficiently human to render its destruction an offense.

Ḥavot Ya'ir endeavors to demonstrate that prenatal life is inviolate even at earlier stages of fetal development on the basis of the talmudic discussion concerning the execution of an expectant mother who has incurred the death penalty. The Mishnah *(Erukhin* 7a) rules that the execution must be deferred until after the child's birth only if the convicted mother has already "sat on the birth stool," which the Gemara defines as being synonymous with the fetus' "tearing itself loose." Prior to this, execution is not delayed in order to preserve the unborn child. With regard to this inference the Gemara queries, *"Peshita! gufah he*—Of course! It [the fetus] is an organic part of her [the mother's] body." *Ḥavot Ya'ir* reasons that since the Gemara adds the phrase

Tosafot (*Sanhedrin* 59a; *Ḥullin* 33a) states explicitly that feticide, although entailing no statutory punishment, is nevertheless forbidden.[4] Else-

---

gufah he in formulating its question, one must conclude that the reason that the child is consigned to the same fate as the mother is that it is an organic part of her body. The logical inference is that were this rationale to be lacking, it would be forbidden to cause the death of the unborn fetus. For a conflicting inference which ignores this point, see R. Joseph Trani, *Teshuvot Maharit* (Fürth, 5528), I, no. 99.

For further discussion of the nature of the prohibition against feticide, see the sources cited by R. Chaim Chizkeyahu Medini in his *Sedei Ḥemed* (New York, 5722), I, 175 ff, *Kelalim, Ma'arekhet ha-Alef,* no. 52, and I, 304 f, *Sheyurei ha-Pe'ah, Ma'arekhet ha-Alef,* no. 19. See also the sources cited by R. Shlomoh Abraham Rezechte, *Bikkurei Shlomoh* (Pietrokow, 5665), *Yoreh De'ah, Hashmatot,* no. 9.

4. Despite these two unequivocal statements, the language employed by *Tosafot, Niddah* 44b, led R. Zevi Hirsch Chajes to note in a gloss, *ad locum,* that *Tosafot* in *Niddah* expresses a contradictory opinion. Writing much earlier both *Ḥavot Ya'ir* in the above cited responsum and R. Jacob Emden in a gloss (*Niddah* 44b) state without elaboration that *Tosafot* does not intend to express a permissive ruling but simply employs misleading phraseology. R. Jacob Emden adds in wonder, "Who is it that permits the killing of a fetus without *reason?"* See also the gloss of R. Shlomoh Eger *ad locum.* A close examination of the line of reasoning employed by *Tosafot* shows that the conclusion reached by *Mahariẓ Ḥajes* cannot be suported. *Tosafot* contends that the absence of statutory punishment with regard to the crime of feticide applies only to cases where the mother is alive at the time of destruction of the fetus; when, however, the mother's death precedes that of the fetus, *Tosafot* advances a tentative assertion to the effect that the fetus is independently viable and hence the killing of the fetus in such instances carries the full penalty for murder. If this is not the case and "it is permitted to kill the fetus," queries *Tosafot,* why is it then permissible to violate the *Shabbat* by carrying a knife through a public thoroughfare for the purpose of removing the fetus from the womb of its deceased mother? A literal reading indicates that, according to *Tosafot,* dispensation for the desecration of the Sabbath can be rightfully invoked only in order to preserve such lives which it is forbidden to destroy. For if the life in question may be destroyed deliberately, why then should the Sabbath be desecrated in order to save that which otherwise may be destroyed with impunity? Interpreted in this manner, there is no continuity whatsoever between this query and the previous assertion pertaining to the *penalty* for taking the life of an unborn child. Feticide might well *not* entail the punishment of homicide yet nevertheless constitute a moral offense, albeit an unpunishable one. Furthermore, *Tosafot*'s refutation of this assumption is unclear if understood in the context of *Mahariẓ Ḥajes*' analysis. *Tosafot* negates the prior assumption by asserting that for the purpose of saving a life the Sabbath may be violated even if the life saved be that of one "whom it is permissible to kill."

where we find that according to rabbinic exegesis (*Mekhilta,* Exod. 21:12;

As evidence for this conclusion *Tosafot* cites the rule with regard to a *goses be-yedei adam* (one who has suffered a mortal wound, humanly inflicted), for the prolongation of whose life the Sabbath may be violated although "one who murders him is not culpable." According to *Mahariz Ḥajes'* understanding of the earlier remarks of *Tosafot,* the latter statement provides no substantiating evidence whatsoever. The status of a murderer of a *goses be-yedei adam* is clear: The killing is forbidden but carries no statutory punishment. Since it is forbidden to take his life, there is no question regarding the permissibility (according to *Tosafot,* but cf. *Teshuvot Shevut Ya'akov,* no. 13) of violating the Sabbath on his behalf; the absence of statutory punishment is deemed irrelevant. The issue in question, according to *Mahariz Ḥajes,* is solely that of the desecration of the Sabbath on behalf of a life (viz., that of a fetus) which might be destroyed with impunity. *Tosafot* endeavors to disprove the contention that it is somehow incongruous to sanction the desecration of the Sabbath in order to preserve that which there is not only no obligation to preserve but which may even be summarily destroyed. Indeed, the logic of this entailment is so strong that it is difficult to fathom its refutation. However, R. Shlomoh Drimer, *Teshuvot Bet Shlomoh* (Lemberg, 1891), *Ḥoshen Mishpat,* no. 120, adopt a contrary view, reasoning that despite the prohibition against feticide, and despite a positive injunction to preserve the embryo, the Sabbath may be violated on behalf of an unborn child by application of the principle "Better to violate one Sabbath in order to observe many Sabbaths." If, on the other hand, we understand *Tosafot*'s position in *Niddah* to be identical with that espoused by *Tosafot* in *Sanhedrin* and *Ḥullin,* the line of reasoning is most clear. In support of the assertion that the destruction of a fetus which has been preceded by the death of the mother incurs the full penalty of murder, *Tosafot* endeavors to show that the desecration of the Sabbath is sanctioned only in order to save a life which it is not only forbidden to destroy but which, if unlawfully destroyed, is juridically punishable as a capital crime. This hypothesis is subsequently rejected by *Tosafot* with the argument that the killing of a *goses be-yedei adam* carries no such penalty, yet the Sabbath may be violated on his behalf. The conclusion, then, is that there is no evidence that the destruction of a fetus whose mother had preceded it in death carries a statutory punishment. That the taking of the life of a fetus is forbidden does not at all come into question according to this understanding of *Tosafot.*

According to any interpretation, the comparison by *Tosafot* of a fetus to a *goses be-yedei adam* defies comprehension. The absence of a statutory death penalty with regard to killing of a fetus is due to consideration of the embryo as not possessing independent animation in the degree requisite for consideration as a "life." The killing of a *goses* is not punishable because in the majority of instances the *goses* would die in any event. The Sabbath may be violated on his behalf because consideration of circumstances surrounding the "majority" of cases are irrelevant when a human life is at stake. Halakhah prescribes such measures even when chances that these measures may be

Sanhedrin 84a) the killing of an unborn child is not considered to be a capital crime—an implication derived from the verse "He that smiteth a *man* so that he dieth, shall surely be put to death" (Exod. 21:12). *Tosafot,* on the basis of the Mishnah, apparently reasons that although feticide does not occasion capital punishment, the fetus is nevertheless sufficiently human to render its destruction a moral offense.

An offense not entailing statutory punishment is certainly not an anomaly. Many such prohibitions are known to be biblical in nature. Others are recognized as having been promulgated by the Sages in order to create a "fence" around the Torah or in order formally to prohibit conduct which could not be countenanced on ethical grounds. Under which category is the prohibition against feticide to be subsumed? Is this offense biblical or rabbinic in nature? At least three diverse lines of reasoning have been employed in establishing the biblical nature of the offense. Rabbi Chaim Ozer Grodzinski demonstrates that the remarks of *Tosafot,* taken in context, clearly indicate a biblical proscription rather than a rabbinic edict.[5] Feticide, as *Tosafot* notes, is expressly forbidden under the statutes of the Noachide Code. The Noachide prohibition is derived by R. Ishmael (*Sanhedrin* 57b) from the wording of Genesis 9:6. Rendering this verse as "Whoso sheddeth the blood of man, *within man* shall his blood be shed" rather than "Whoso sheddeth the blood of man, *by man* [i.e., through a

---

efficacious are dim. The life of a *goses* is intrinsically human and hence the Sabbath is violated on his behalf even though chances of recovery are remote; at the same time his murderer cannot be put to death due to lack of definite assurance that the victim was viable. This does not provide demonstrative evidence contradictory to the hypothesis that provision for the rescue of a fetus through violation of the Sabbath *ipso facto* establishes that it is therefore a human life whose destruction is punishable. Cf. R. Yechiel Ya'akov Weinberg, *Seridei Esh,* (Jerusalem, 5726), III, 350, n. 7. The approach offered in the name of Rabbi Sternbuch does not appear to resolve this perplexity.

5. *Teshuvot Aḥi'ezer* (Wilno, 5699) III, 65, sec. 14. Although not adduced by *Aḥi'ezer,* there is ample evidence that the principle "Is there anything which is forbidden to a Noachide yet permitted to a Jew?" establishes a biblical prohibition. *Tosafot, Ḥullin* 33a, states explicitly with regard to *ḥazi shi'ur* (which is forbidden to Noachides) that the principle "Is there anything which is forbidden to a Noachide yet permitted to a Jew?" is consistent only with the opinion of R. Yochanan, who deems *ḥazi shi'ur* to be biblically forbidden and in contradiction to the opinion of Resh Lakish, who deems *ḥazi shi'ur* to be rabbinically proscribed. Cf. R. Samuel Engel, *Teshuvot Maharash* (Varnov, 5696), V, no. 89, and R. Isaac Schorr, *Teshuvot Koaḥ Shor* (Kolomea 5648), no. 20, page 33b; see also *Sedei Ḥemed,* I, 175.

human court] shall his blood be shed." R. Ishmael queries, "Who is a man *within* a man? . . . A fetus within the womb of the mother." *Tosafot* deduces that this practice is prohibited to Jews as well by virtue of the talmudic principle, "Is there anything which is forbidden to a Noachide yet permitted to a Jew?" Application of this principle clearly establishes a biblical prohibition.

R. Meir Simchah of Dvinsk, in his biblical novellae, *Meshekh Ḥokhmah,* Exod. 35:2, offers an interesting scriptural foundation for this prohibition, demonstrating that, while not a penal crime, the killing of a fetus is punishable by "death at the hands of heaven." [6] He observes that Scripture invariably refers to capital punishment by employing the formula *"mot yumat*—he shall surely be put to death." The use of the single expression *"yumat*—he shall be put to death" as, for example, in Exodus 21:29, is understood in rabbinic exegesis as having reference to death at the hands of heaven. Thus, R. Meir Simchah argues, the verse "and he that smiteth a man shall be put to death—*yumat*" (Lev. 24:21) is not simply a reiteration of the penalty for homicide but refers to such destruction of life which is punishable only at the hands of heaven, i.e., the killing of a fetus. Reference to the fetus as "a man" poses no difficulty since the fetus is indeed described as "a man" in the above cited verse (Gen. 9:6) prescribing death for feticide under the Noachide Code.

Most interesting is the sharply contested view advanced by R. Elijah Mizrachi, in his commentary on Exodus 21:12, that in principle feticide and murder are indistinguishable. The biblical ban on murder extends equally to all human life, including, he claims, any fetal life which, unmolested, would develop into a viable human being. In theory, continues Mizrachi, feticide should be punishable by death since the majority of all fetuses will indeed develop into viable human beings.[7] In practice it is technically impossible to impose the death penalty because punishment may be inflicted by the *Bet Din* only if the crime is preceded by a formal admonition. Since some fetuses will never develop fully, a definite admonition cannot be administered because it cannot be established with certainty that any particular fetus would develop in this manner. Noachides, on the other hand, require no such admonition. Therefore, since the major num-

---

6. However, cf. R. Samuel Strashun, *Mekorei ha-Rambam le-Rashash* (Jerusalem, 1957), p. 45, who writes that although feticide is biblically forbidden "perhaps there is no punishment even 'at the hands of heaven.'"

7. Cf. below, n. 62.

ber of fetuses are viable, feticide is to be punished by death under the Noachide dispensation.

Differing from these various views are the opinions of the many scholars who have espoused the diametrically opposite position that the prohibition against feticide is rabbinic in origin. There is evidence that as early an authority as Rabbenu Nissim is to be numbered among the latter group. R. Chaim Ozer cites Rabbenu Nissim's explanation of the reason for the ruling of the Mishnah (*Erukhin* 7a) that the execution of an expectant mother must not be delayed in order to allow the delivery of her child. Rabbenu Nissim (commentary on *Ḥullin* 58a) fails to offer the explanation adopted by other commentators; namely, that the fetus is regarded as but an organic limb of the mother having no inherent claim of its own to inviolability and hence considerations of its welfare cannot interfere with the statutory provision for immediate execution of the condemned in order to avoid subjecting the convicted criminal to agonizing suspense between announcement of the verdict and execution of the sentence. Rabbenu Nissim offers a simple explanation to the effect that the fetus has not yet emerged into the world and therefore we need not reckon with its well-being. Since Rabbenu Nissim's remarks certainly cannot be construed as sanctioning wanton destruction of a fetus, R. Chaim Ozer infers that it is Rabbenu Nissim's opinion that the prohibition against taking fetal life is of rabbinic origin.[8] If considered as a rabbinic edict, it is understandable that the Sages suspended their ban in order to mitigate the agony of the condemned woman, giving considerations of her welfare priority over the well-being of the unborn child.

There are a number of latter-day authorities who are explicit in their opinion that feticide is a rabbinic rather than a biblical offense. Perhaps the most prominent of these is the renowned seventeenth-century scholar, R. Aaron Samuel Kaidanower, author of the famed commentary on *Seder Kodshim, Birkhat ha-Zevaḥ*. His views regarding this matter are recorded in his collection of responsa, *Emunat Shmu'el* (Frankfort-am-Main, 5443), no. 14. This position is also espoused by R. Chaim Plaggi, *Teshuvot Ḥayyim ve-Shalom* (Smyrna, 5632), I, no. 40, and forms the basis for a number of decisions issued by the contemporary halakhic authority, R. Eliezer Yehudah Waldenberg. The rulings issued by R. Waldenberg,

8. This does not preclude recognition by Rabbenu Nissim of other considerations which would ban feticide under different circumstances on biblical grounds. See below, n. 18 and n. 24. For a divergent interpretation of Rabbenu Nissim, see R. Moshe Sternbuch, *Mo'adim u-Zemanim ha-Shalem,* I, no. 52.

who serves as head of the Jerusalem *Bet Din,* are recorded in his voluminous work, *Ẓiẓ Eli'ezer.*[9]

A tentative distinction between the stringency of the prohibition against abortion involving direct physical removal of the fetus and abortion induced by chemical means is found in a responsum bearing the signature of R. Jacob Schorr and included in the *Teshuvot Ge'onim Batra'i* (Prague, 5576), a compendium edited by *Sha'agat Aryeh.* While the author of this responsum makes no pertinent halakhic distinction between these two methods, he does draw attention to the fact that Maimonides found it necessary to state definitively that in cases of danger "it is permitted to dismember the fetus in her [the mother] womb, whether by chemical means or by hand." The implication is that, if not explicitly obviated, a theoretical distinction might have been drawn between physical dismemberment of the fetus and abortion by indirect means (*gerama*),[10] such as imbibing abortifacient drugs in order to induce the expulsion of the fetus. Such a distinction is in fact made by R. Judah Eiyush, *Teshuvot Bet Yehudah* (Livorno, 5518), *Even ha-Ezer,* no. 14, who maintains that abortion induced by chemical potions is of rabbinic proscription, whereas direct removal of the fetus is forbidden on biblical grounds.[11] On this basis, R. Eiyush grants permission to induce an abortion in a woman who became pregnant while still nursing a previous child in order that the life of the nursing infant not be endangered.[12]

---

9. Vol. VII, (Jerusalem, 5723), no. 48, p. 190; vol. VIII, (Jerusalem, 5725), no. 36, pp. 218–19 and vol. IX, (Jerusalem, 5727), no. 51, pp. 233–40; *Bikkurei Shlomoh, Yoreh De'ah,* no. 10, sec. 2, and *Oraḥ Ḥayyim,* no. 33, sec. 5, also states that the prohibition is rabbinic in nature.

10. *Bet Yehudah* (*loc. cit.*) demonstrates that even indirect destruction of fetal life is forbidden on the basis of the talmudic declaration (*Mo'ed Katan* 18a) that one who casts away his nail pairings is an evildoer since there is the danger that a pregnant woman may pass by and abort her unborn child. This is clearly an indirect cause and yet the perpetrator is deemed an evildoer.

11. This is contrary to the opinion of R. Waldenberg in his *Ẓiẓ Eli'ezer,* VIII, 219, who does not recognize any such distinction. R. Waldenberg, incidentally, does not note this distinction as drawn by *Teshuvot Ge'onim Batra'i.* Elsewhere, however, R. Waldenberg indicates that when termination of pregnancy is permissible, it is preferable to induce abortion by use of drugs if possible. See *Ẓiẓ Eli'ezer,* IX, 240. Cf. also R. Ovadiah Yosef, *Yabi'a Omer* (Jerusalem, 5724), IV, *Even ha-Ezer,* no. 1, sec. 5. See also *Leḥem ha-Panim, Kuntres Aḥaron,* no. 19, who forbids drinking a "cup of roots" in order to kill the fetus.

12. Cf. *Ẓiẓ Eli'ezer*, VIII, 219, and IX, 239.

Preservation of human life is commonly seen as the rationale underlying the ban against induced abortion. Each of the diverse authorities heretofore cited considers the essence of the prohibition to be closely akin to that of homicide. There are, however, other authorities who deem the destruction of a fetus to be unrelated to the taking of human life but nevertheless forbidden on extraneous grounds. Chief among these are the opinions of those who maintain that feticide is precluded as constituting a form of destruction of the male seed or that it is forbidden as a form of unlawful flagellation. R. Shlomoh Drimer (*Teshuvot Bet Shlomoh, Ḥoshen Mishpat,* no. 132) contends that the destruction of a fetus cannot be a form of homicide since the fetus cannot be viewed as "a life" in its prenatal state.[13] He does not, however, spell out the nature of the crime committed in causing the death of a fetus. The origin of this view can be traced to the *Teshuvot ha-Radbaz,* II, no. 695, in which the author states explicitly that destruction of a fetus is not a form of homicide. R. Ya'ir Chaim Bachrach (*Ḥavot Ya'ir,* no. 31), argues that feticide is included in the interdiction against onanism[14] and reasons that destroying the fetus is within the scope of the verse "slaying the children in the valley under the clefts of the rocks" (Isa. 57:5), which is interpreted by the Gemara, *Niddah* 13a, as having reference to the destruction of the male seed.[15] The author of *Zekhuta de-Avraham* offers an identical opinion, adding that feticide and onanism incur the self-same penalty—"death at the hands of heaven." [16] In his responsum *Ḥavot Ya'ir* accepts the ruling of *Tosafot* (*Yevamot* 12b) that women are also bound by the prohibition against destroying the male seed. He notes that, even according to the view of

---

13. R. Drimer similarly argues that the *a priori* principle "How do you know that your blood is sweeter than the blood of your fellow?" cannot be applied in assessing the value of fetal life. Cf. below n. 65.

14. This determination is based upon *Tosafot, Sanhedrin* 59b, and others who maintain that such practices are biblically prohibited. For a comprehensive list of sources, see *Oẓar ha-Poskim* (Jerusalem, 5725), IX, 163–64, and R. Moses D. Tendler, *Tradition,* IX (1967), nos. 1–2, pp. 211–12. Regarding the question of whether Noachides are bound by the prohibition against onanism, see *Tosafot, Sanhedrin* 59b; *Mishneh le-Melekh, Hilkhot Melakhim* 10:7; R. Naphtali Zevi Yehudah Berlin, *He'emek She'elah* 165:2; and R. Joseph Rosen, *Teshuvot Ẓofnat Pa'aneaḥ* (New York, 5714), no. 30.

15. R. Jacob Emden, *She'elot Ya'aveẓ,* (New York, 5721), no. 43, also makes brief mention of this consideration. See also *Zekhuta de-Avraham,* cited by R. Meir Dan Plocki, *Ḥemdat Yisra'el* (Pietrokow, 5687), p. 175.

16. Cited by *Ḥemdat Yisra'el,* p. 175.

Rabbenu Tam that women are not included in this specific prohibition,[17] these practices are nevertheless forbidden to them, for women, too (*Tosafot, Gittin* 41b), are bound to bring to fulfillment the divine design of a populated world as stated in the words of Isaiah 45:18, "He created it [the earth] not a waste, He formed it to be inhabited."[18]

A number of objections to *Ḥavot Ya'ir*'s position are raised in later works. R. Meir Dan Plocki[19] expresses the view that with the promulgation of the Sinaitic covenant, Noachides were absolved from the obligation of procreation and also from the prohibition against wanton emission of semen.[20] Granting this point, it follows that according to *Ḥavot Ya'ir*'s reasoning there would be no apparent grounds for denying Noachides the right to commit feticide. Such a conclusion would be contrary to the clear-cut recognition that destruction of a fetus continues to constitute a capital crime under the Noachide code. *Ḥavot Ya'ir* further states that feticide cannot be punishable by "death at the hands of heaven." Such punishment, he avers, would be incompatible with the exaction of monetary compensation for loss of the fetus, as prescribed by Exodus 21:12, in light of the general rule that a single act cannot result in the infliction of both capital punishment and punitive financial compensation —a principle which R. Nechuniyah b. Hakanah (*Ketubot* 30a) extends not only to the forms of capital punishment imposed by the *Bet Din* but to "death at the hands of heaven" as well. *Ḥavot Ya'ir* arrives at the conclusion that the ban against onanism is operative only with regard to the wasting of one's own seed, since such an act contravenes the obligation "be fruitful and multiply," but is inapplicable with regard to the destruction of fetal progeny other than of one's own parentage.

A somewhat similar objection is voiced by the late Rabbi Yechiel Ya'akov Weinberg.[21] *Ḥavot Ya'ir* maintains that women, although not bound by

---

17. It is on the basis of *Ḥavot Ya'ir*'s declaration that feticide is forbidden as a form of "destruction of the seed" and of the diminished severity of such an act when performed by a woman (according to Rabbenu Tam) that R. Waldenberg counsels that it is preferable to seek a female (Jewish) doctor to perform even those abortions which are halakhically permissible. See *Ẓiẓ Eli'ezer,* IX, 235.

18. Following this line of reasoning, feticide would be biblically forbidden even according to Rabbenu Nissim, who does not consider destruction of a fetus to be a form of homicide.

19. *Ḥemdat Yisra'el,* pp. 175f.

20. See above, n. 14.

21. *Seridei Esh* (Jerusalem, 5726), III, no. 127, pp. 344f. This responsum

the commandment "be fruitful and multiply," are nevertheless obligated to fulfill the intent expressed in the verse, "He formed it [the earth] to be inhabited." This consideration, *Ḥavot Ya'ir* maintains, precludes feticide even on the part of women. Rabbi Weinberg rebuts this contention, asserting that the obligation set forth in Isaiah 45:18 is understood by the authorities as paralleling the injunction "be fruitful and multiply" in that such considerations apply only to one's own progeny. Accordingly argues Rabbi Weinberg, assimilation of the prohibition against feticide to the ban against onanism would lead to the bizarre conclusion that a woman might be permitted to perform an abortion upon any woman other than herself—a conclusion not to be found in any halakhic source.

The early seventeenth-century scholar, R. Joseph Trani of Constantinople, author of *Teshuvot Maharit,* also endeavors to show that the taking of fetal life, while forbidden, nevertheless cannot be considered as constituting a form of homicide.[22] The Mishnah, *Erukhin* 7a, indicates that an expectant mother who has been sentenced to death, as long as she has not already "sat on the birth stool," must be executed without delay in order to spare her the agony of suspense. Whereupon the Gemara in its comments on this Mishnah exclaims *"Peshita!*—Of course!" R. Joseph Trani argues that if destruction of the fetus is tantamount to the taking of human life the amazement registered by the Gemara is out of place. The Gemara provides that the mother be struck on the abdomen against the womb in order to cause the prior death of the fetus. This is done in order to avoid the indignity which would be inflicted upon her body as a result of an attempt on the part of the fetus to emerge after the death of its mother. An act of murder certainly would not be condoned simply in order to spare the condemned undue agony or to prevent dishonor to a corpse.[23] R. Joseph Trani then advances an alternative basis for this stricture. In his opinion, the destruction of an embryo is within the category of un-

---

was originally published as an article in *No'am,* IX (1966), pp. 193–215, and was reprinted subsequently in the third volume of *Seridei Esh* with a number of added notes.

22. *Teshuvot Maharit,* I, no. 97 and no. 99.

23. Other authorities refute this evidence on the grounds that the fetus is an organic part of the mother and hence under identical sentence as the mother. Since it will die in any event, there is no reason why it cannot be put to death earlier in order to spare the mother dishonor. Cf. *Ḥavot Ya'ir,* no. 31; *She'elat Ya'aveẓ,* no. 43; *Maharit,* I, no. 97; and R. Ben-Zion Uziel, *Mishpetei Uziel* (Jerusalem, 5657), III, *Ḥoshen Mishpat,* no. 46.

lawful "wounding," which is banned on the basis of Deuteronomy 25:3.[24] This consideration is, of course, irrelevant in the case of one lawfully sentenced to death, and hence the Gemara raises an objection to the need for specific authorization for the execution of a pregnant woman sentenced to death. A more recent authority, Rabbi Joseph Rosen expresses a similar view.[25]

The dispute concerning the classification of the nature of the stricture against feticide is of more than mere speculative interest. It will be shown that various halakhic determinations regarding the permissibility of therapeutic abortion in certain situations hinge directly upon proper categorization of this prohibition. This issue is also the focal point of an intriguing problem discussed by Rabbi Isser Yehudah Unterman, the former Ashkenazic Chief Rabbi of Israel. Writing in *No'am,* VI, 52, Rabbi Unterman refers to an actual question which arose in the course of the German occupation of Poland and Lithuania during World War I. A German officer became intimate with a Jewish girl and caused her to become pregnant. Becoming aware of her condition, the officer sought to force the young woman in question to submit to an abortion. The German

24. See n. 18. Cf. *Seridei Esh,* p. 249; and R. Moshe Yonah Zweig, *No'am,* VIII (Jerusalem, 5725), 44 ff. Cf. however, *Koaḥ Shor,* no. 20, p. 34a, who argues that the prohibition of Deuteronomy 25:3 does not apply to the striking of a minor, much less to the injury of an embryo. The verse in question expressly refers to the punishment of forty stripes imposed by the *Bet Din* and admonishes the court not to administer more than the prescribed number of lashes. Other forms of physical assault are banned by implication: "If the Torah objects to the striking of a wicked man that he be not lashed more than in accordance with his wickedness, how much more so [does it object] to the striking of a righteous person" (Rambam, *Hilkhot Sanhedrin* 16:2). R. Schorr differs with *Maharit* and argues that only those who have reached their religious majority are included in this scriptural reference since only they are subject to the flagellation imposed by the *Bet Din*. However, R. Aryeh Lifshutz, *Aryeh de-Bei Ila'i* (Przemysl, 5634), *Yoreh De'ah,* no. 6, advances this argument as conclusively demonstrating that *Maharit* is concerned with "wounding" of the mother rather than with injury of the fetus.

25. *Teshuvot Ẓofnat Pa'aneaḥ,* no. 59. R. Ben-Zion Uziel, *Mishpetei Uziel,* p. 213, explains *Tosafot*'s mention of a ban against feticide as referring simply to the general obligation to be fruitful and multiply. One who does not engage in the fulfillment of this precept is accounted "as if he commits bloodshed" (*Yevamot* 63b). Although the context of the quotation deals with passive non-fullfillment of the *miẓvah,* this stricture is applicable all the more to an individual overtly seeking to prevent the development of an already existing life.

officer ordered a Jewish physician to perform the abortion. Upon the doctor's refusal to do so, the officer drew his revolver and warned the physician that continued refusal would result in the latter's own death. If the prohibition against taking the life of a fetus is not subsumed under the category of murder, thereby constituting one of the *avizraiya,* or "appurtenances," of murder, there arises no question of an obligation on the part of the physician to forfeit his own life; on the contrary, he is halakhicly bound to preserve his own life since preservation of life takes precedence over all other considerations. If, however, feticide is considered to be among the *avizraiya* of murder and akin to homicide, which is one of the three grave offenses which dare not be committed even upon threat of death, then the principle "Be killed but do not transgress" is germane.

Rabbi Unterman, however, argues that even if, halakhically, feticide be deemed a lesser form of murder it may be committed in face of a compelling *force majeure.* His reasoning is based upon the ruling of R. Moses Isserles, *Yoreh De'ah* 157:1, that while sacrifice of one's life is required in face of coerced infractions of even *avizraiya,* or "appurtenances," of the three cardinal sins even though the appurtenances themselves do not involve capital culpability, nevertheless, this is demanded only with regard to violation of those *avizraiya* which are themselves explicit negative commandments pertaining to the three cardinal sins. Since feticide is not numbered among the 365 negative precepts recorded in the Bible it does not fall within this category.[26]

Another argument in support of the contention that the admonition "Be killed but do not transgress" does not apply to an act of feticide was advanced at a much earlier date by R. Joseph Babad in his *magnum opus, Minḥat Ḥinukh.*[27] He reasons that this principle, as enunciated with regard to homicide, is based upon an *a priori* principle propounded in the Gemara's rhetorical question, "How do you know that your blood is sweeter than the blood of your fellow man?" The import of this dictum is to emphasize the intrinsic value of every human life and graphically to underscore the fact that no man dare consider his existence to be of higher value than that of his fellow. For in the sight of God all individuals are equally "sweet" and all alike are of inestimable value. Since, however, a fetus is not accounted as being a full-fledged *nefesh,* or "life," and since, as an

26. Further grounds for this ruling are given by R. Unterman in his work *Shevet me-Yehudah* (Jerusalem, 5715), I, 29. See below, n. 53.

27. *Minḥat Ḥinukh* (Wilno, 5672), no. 296, Part II, p. 218.

outgrowth of the unborn child's inferior status, Jewish law exempts its killer from the death penalty, the fetus' "blood" is quite obviously assessed as being "less sweet." [28] Therefore, reasons the author of *Minḥat Ḥinukh,* when confronted by the impending loss of either one's own life or of the life of the fetus, the killing of the unborn child is to be preferred as constituting the lesser of two evils. This conclusion is inescapable, argues *Minḥat Ḥinukh,* since the Mishnah specifically authorizes the sacrifice of a fetal life in order to save its mother. The mother's life is of no greater intrinsic value than that of any other individual. If destruction of the fetus is sanctioned in order to preserve the mother, then it must be permitted in order to save the life of any other person.

Abortion within the First Forty Days of Gestation

We find a declaration of Rav Chisda (*Yevamot* 69b) to the effect that the daughter of a *kohen* widowed shortly after marriage to an Israelite may partake of *terumah* during the first forty days following consummation of her marriage despite the fact that she has become a widow in the interim. Permission to eat *terumah* is a privilege accorded an unmarried daughter of a *kohen* or a widowed daughter who has no children. The concern in the case presented to Rav Chisda is that the widow, unknown to herself, may be pregnant with child, in which case *terumah* would be forbidden to her. Rav Chisda argues, if the widow is not pregnant there is no impediment to her partaking of *terumah*; if she is pregnant the embryo is considered to be "mere water" until after the fortieth day of pregnancy. Therefore she may continue to eat *terumah* for a full forty days after her marriage. The ruling of Rav Chisda indicates that fetal development within the initial forty days of gestation is insufficient to warrant independent standing in the eyes of Halakhah. Another source for this distinction is the Mishnah (*Niddah* 30a), which declares that a fetus aborted less than forty days following cohabitation does not engender the impurity of childbirth ordained by Leviticus 12:2–5.[29] Similarly, according

---

28. See, however, below, n. 65.

29. It is perhaps of interest to note that Aristotle (*De Historia Animalium,* VII, 3) declares that the male fetus is endowed with a rational soul on the fortieth day of gestation and the female on the eightieth. This distinction corresponds not only to the respective periods of impurity prescribed by Leviticus but to the opinion of R. Yishmael in the Mishnah, *Niddah* 30a, who is of the opinion that the prescribed periods of impurity correspond to the number of days

to *Mishneh le-Melekh, Hilkhot Tumat Met* 2:1, the defilement associated with a dead body is not attendant upon an embryo expelled during the first forty days of gestation. Furthermore, in the opinion of many authorities, a fetus cannot acquire property prior to the fortieth day of development.[30]

The result is that the status of an embryo's claim to life during the first forty days following conception is not entirely clear. Is the prohibition against feticide operative during this early stage of fetal development during which the embryo is depicted as "mere water"? It would appear that according to the grounds advanced by *Ḥavot Ya'ir* no distinction can be made between the various stages of fetal development since, according to this opinion, feticide is prohibited, not because it is tantamount to the the taking of a human life, but because it is a form of "destroying the seed." The fact that no specific reference is made in *Ḥavot Ya'ir* to the status of the embryo during this period in no way vitiates this conclusion. In the absence of a distinction there is no reason for such reference.[31]

---

required for the animation of the respective sexes and therefore declares that no impurity results from the miscarriage of a female embryo of less than eighty days. Aristotle's representation of animation as occurring on the fortieth or eightieth day, depending upon the sex of the fetus, was later incorporated in both Canon and Justinian law. See Rabbi Immanuel Jakobovits, *Jewish Medical Ethics* (New York, 1959), p. 175.

30. *Shakh, Ḥoshen Mishpat* 210:2; *Ẓofnat Pa'aneaḥ,* no. 59.

31. Reference by the late Rabbi Zweig of Antwerp (*No'am,* VII, 53) to an opinion by *Ḥavot Ya'ir* to the effect that there is no prohibition during this period is erroneous. *Ḥavot Ya'ir,* in his introductory comments, calls attention to the fact that various stages of fetal development are recognized in different contexts, viz., forty days, three months, and independent movement of the fetal limbs, but quickly adds that it is not his desire to render judgment on the basis of "inclination of the mind or reasoning of the stomach." On the contrary, *Ḥavot Ya'ir*'s failure to note such distinctions in the course of developing his own thesis portends his rejection of such a distinction.

It may be of interest to note that this misconstruction of *Ḥavot Ya'ir* is legend. *Sedei Ḥemed* cites with perplexity conflicting positions attributed to *Ḥavot Ya'ir* by other sources with regard to this question and notes in resignation that he does not have access to the responsa of *Ḥavot Ya'ir,* and hence cannot determine which quotation is correct. Upon reading these comments, R. Solomon Abraham Rezechte wrote to the author of *Sedei Ḥemed* that he has indeed seen the words of *Ḥavot Ya'ir* in the original and reports that the latter views the prohibition against feticide as binding during the early periods of pregnancy as well. See *Bikurei Shlomoh* (Pietrokow, 5665), no. 10, sec. 35. See also, below, p. 346, n. 41.

R. Weinberg's summary declaration (p. 350) that such a prohibition does not exist according to the *Ba'al Halakhot Gedolot,* who permits desecration

Yet the considerations advanced by *Ḥavot Ya'ir* can explain only the nature of the ban against feticide under the Sinaitic covenant. Feticide, a capital offense in Noachide law, may well be viewed as a form of homicide under that code, leaving the possibility of such a distinction with regard to the conduct of Noachides an open question.

Whether or not there is a halakhic distinction with regard to this prohibition during the first forty days of gestation according to the authorities who advance other considerations as the grounds for the banning of feticide remains to be considered. Rabbi Weinberg states flatly (*op. cit.,* p. 249) that R. Joseph Trani's (Maharit) thesis, according to which feticide is a case of unlawful wounding, precludes extension of this prohibition to an embryo of less than forty days since it is deemed as "mere water" throughout this period. Rabbi Weinberg interprets Maharit's reference to "wounding" as depicting the harm inflicted upon the fetus. Despite the cogency of Rabbi Weinberg's reasoning regarding "wounding" of the fetus, his reasoning is inapplicable in cases of abortion by means of dilation and curretage which certainly involves "wounding" of the mother as well, irrespective of the stage of pregnancy at which this procedure is initiated. Following this line of thought, it should be forbidden other than for therapeutic considerations which constitute licit grounds for "wounding." Moreover, R. Aryeh Lifschutz, a nineteenth-century scholar, in his *Aryeh de-Bei-Ila'i* (*Yoreh De'ah,* no. 14, p. 58a), interprets Maharit's view that feticide is forbidden as a form of "wounding" as being predicated upon consideration of the wounding of the mother rather than of the unborn child. R. Lifschutz contends that it would be somewhat incongruous to prohibit the wounding of a being which one is not specifically forbidden to kill. Approached in this manner, there is no room for differentiating between the various stages of pregnancy.

There is further evidence pointing to a prohibition against destroying the life of a fetus during this early period. Nachmanides notes that ac-

---

of the Sabbath in order to save an embryo even within this forty-day period, is contradictory to the reasoning of *Ḥavot Ya'ir,* as indicated by R. Weinberg himself (p. 339). R. Weinberg argues that *Ḥavot Ya'ir* fails to give consideration to the opinion of Nachmanides who maintains that, despite the law against feticide, the Sabbath may not be violated on behalf of an unborn child. This allegation is readily refutable since *Ḥavot Ya'ir* argues merely that permission to violate the Sabbath in order to save a fetus logically entails a prohibition against destroying such a life, but not vice versa. It cannot be inferred from *Ḥavot Ya'ir* that the absence of such permission necessarily entails license to destroy the fetus.

cording to the opinion of *Ba'al Halakhot Gedolot* the Sabbath may be violated even during this forty-day period in order to preserve the life of a fetus.[32] The author of *Ḥavot Ya'ir,* citing *Tosafot, Niddah* 44b, shows that the right to violate the Sabbath for the sake of saving a prenatal life is incompatible with permission to kill it deliberately.[33] It follows that, according to *Ba'al Halakhot Gedolot,* induced abortion during this period is forbidden. Responding to a specific inquiry, R. Plocki grants permission for termination of pregnancy within this forty-day period only when the life of the mother is threatened.[34]

Drawing a parallel from the commandment against the kidnapping and subsequent sale of a person into involuntary servitude, Rabbi Unterman[35] cites the opinion of Rashi, *Sanhedrin* 85b, who maintains that this prohibition encompasses the sale of an unborn child as well. Although the fetus may not be considered a fully developed person, his kidnapper is culpable because he has stolen an animate creature whose status is conditioned by its potential development into a viable human being. Rabbi Unterman further notes that the unborn fetus lacks human status. Consequently, it is excluded from the injunction, "And he [man] shall live by them" (Lev. 18:5), which justifies violation of other precepts in order to preserve human life. Numerous authorities nevertheless permit violation of the Sabbath in order to preserve fetal life. Rabbi Unterman views such permission as being predicated upon a similar rationale. Anticipation of potential development and subsequent attainment of human status creates certain privileges and obligations with regard to the undeveloped fetus. Consideration of future potential is clearly evidenced in the talmudic declaration: "Better to violate a single Sabbath in order to observe many Sabbaths" (*Shabbat* 151b). Rabbi Unterman concludes that reasoning in these terms precludes any distinction which might otherwise be drawn with regard to the various stages of fetal development.

Surprisingly, there is one source which appears to rule that destruction of the fetus by Noachides, at least under some circumstances, does not constitute a moral offense. Maharit[36] writes: "I remember having seen in

32. *Torat ha-Adam, Sha'ar ha-Sakanah,* ed. R. Bernard Chavel, *Kitvei Ramban* (Jerusalem, 5724), II, 29; also cited by Rosh and Ran in their respective commentaries on *Yoma* 82*a;* see also *Korban Netanel, Yoma, Perek Yom ha-Kippurim,* no. 10.

33. See above, n. 31.

34. *Ḥemdat Yisra'el,* "Indexes and Addenda," p. 17.

35. *No'am,* VI, 4 f; *Shevet me-Yehudah,* I, 9 f.

36. *Teshuvot Maharit,* I, no. 99.

a responsum of the Rashba that he bears witness that Ramban rendered medical aid to a gentile woman in return for compensation in order that she might conceive and aided her in aborting the fruit of her womb." [37] It is of course inconceivable that an individual of Nachmanides' piety and erudition would have violated the injunction "Thou shalt not place a stumbling block before a blind person" (Lev. 19:4) or that he would have actively assisted transgressors. Applying the line of reasoning adduced above, Rabbi Unterman draws the conclusion that there is a fundamental distinction between Jewish law and Noachide law with regard to the assessment of potential life. According to many authorities, Noachides are under no obligation to preserve the lives of their fellows, to "be fruitful and multiply" or to refrain from wasting the male seed.[38] They are forbidden to commit homicide and to take the life of "a man within a man" but bear no responsibility for the safeguarding and preservation of seminal life. It would appear, then, that Halakhah holds them accountable only for *actual,* in contradistinction to *potential,* life.[39] Accordingly, there is no objection to Noachides aborting, or to a Jew giving advice and rendering indirect assistance to Noachides in aborting, a fetus within the first forty days of gestation. Since Halakhah considers that during this initial period the embryo has not as yet developed distinctly recog-

---

37. The authenticity of this quotation is highly questionable. R. Unterman (p. 8) notes that he searched *Teshuvot ha-Rashba* in an unsuccessful attempt to locate this responsum. It seems probable that Maharit's quotation is culled from responsum no. 120 of vol. I in the published text (B'nei Brak, 5718). This responsum deals with the permissibility of rendering medical assistance to Noachide women so that they may be enabled to conceive. In language similar to that quoted by Maharit, mention is made of Ramban's actually having done so in return for financial compensation. However, no mention whatsoever is made of Ramban's having assisted in medical abortion. Maharit apparently had a variant textual version. Cf., also, R. Samuel Hubner, *Ha-Darom,* Tishri 5729, p. 33, who attempts to resolve the issue by suggesting an alternate punctuation of this quotation.

38. See above, n. 14.

39. R. Unterman fails, however, to note the comments of R. Jacob Zevi Jalish in his *Melo ha-Ro'im, Sanhedrin* 57b, who expresses a contrary view. Examination of the phraseology of *Ḥemdat Yisra'el,* Part I, p. 108, indicates that R. Plocki also had such a distinction in mind. In cases of danger to the mother he permits abortion of embryos of less than forty days without further qualification and adds that there are grounds for permitting abortion at subsequent stages of development provided this procedure is performed by a Jewish physician.

nizable organs or an independent circulatory system it cannot be considered "a man within a man" and hence its destruction does not constitute murder under the Noachide dispensation. Nachmanides, Rabbi Unterman avers, sanctioned the performance of abortions by Noachides only within this forty-day period.[40]

40. The absence, in the Noachide Code, of a ban on feticide during the first forty days of gestation would, in the opinion of this writer, provide insight into what is otherwise considered an erroneous translation by the Septuagint of Exodus 21:22–23: "And if two men strive together and hurt a woman with a child so that her children depart and yet no harm (*ason*) follow, he shall surely be fined. . . . But if any harm follows, then thou shalt give life for life." Rabbinic exegesis regards the term "harm" as having reference to the death of the mother. Compensation is payable to the husband for the loss of his offspring only if the mother survives. Should the mother die as a result of this assault, the attacker is absolved from the payment of this fine. From these provisions the Gemara derives the principle that the commission of a capital crime, even if unintentional and hence not leading to the invocation of the statutory penalty, absolves the offender from the payment of any other compensation. The Septuagint, however, renders these verses as follows:

> *Ἐὰν δὲ μάχωνται δύο ἄνδρες καὶ πατάξωσι γυναῖκα ἐν γαστρὶ ἔχουσαν, καὶ ἐξέλθῃ τὸ παιδίον αὐτῆς μὴ ἐξεικονισμένον*... And if two men strive and smite a woman with child, *and her child be born imperfectly formed,* he shall be forced to pay a penalty...*Ἐὰν δὲ ἐξεικονισμένον ᾖ*... But if it be perfectly formed, he shall give life for life.

This reading understands the death penalty to which reference is made as being incurred for the killing of the fetus in cases where the fetus is *formed,* i.e., has already reached the fortieth day of gestation. It is clearly on the basis of this passage in the Septuagint that such a distinction is drawn by Philo *(De Spec. Legibus,* III, 108–10) and it was this reading of the Septuagint which influenced the attitude of the Church. Cf. Jakobovits, *op. cit.,* pp. 174, 179, 328, n. 43, and 333, n. 152. Samuel Poznanski, "Jakob ben Ephraim ein Antikaraischer Polemiker des X Jahrhunderts," *Gedenkbuch zur Erinnerung an David Kaufmann,* ed. M. Brann and F. Rosenthal (Breslau, 1900), p. 186, suggests that the mistranslation is based on reading *ẓurah* for *ason.* On the basis of R. Unterman's thesis, the entire matter is quite readily resolved, particularly in light of the rabbinic tradition which states that modifications were intentionally introduced by the Jewish translators (see *Megillah* 9a). Addressed to gentiles, the translation may have been intended to incorporate ramifications of Noachide law. Since a Noachide incurs capital punishment for the destruction of a fetus, provided it is formed, he would be absolved from further punishment even in cases where the mother survives. An exhaustive interpretation of *ason,* then, signifies death of the mother if the attacker is a Jew, and either death of the mother or of a formed fetus if the attacker is a Noachide. The word *ason* as applied to a Noachide thus includes

Rabbi Unterman's distinction between Jews and Noachides with regard to termination of pregnancy within the first forty days following conception was anticipated by an earlier authority. Rabbi Plocki, in his *Ḥemdat Yisra'el* (p. 176), marshals evidence that an embryo may be destroyed with impunity during the first forty days of its development based upon Rabbenu Tam's interpretation of the talmudic dispute (*Yevamot* 12a) concerning the "three [categories of] women" who may resort to contraceptive devices in order to prevent conception. Rabbenu Tam explains that the dispute concerns the insertion of a tampon *after* cohabitation. The *Tanna,* R. Meir, rules that use of contraceptive devices by these women is mandatory since pregnancy would place their lives in jeopardy; the Sages assert that such action is not incumbent upon these women stating that the verse "The Lord preserves the simple" (Ps. 116:6) permits reliance upon divine providence to avert tragic consequences. However, according to Rabbenu Tam, the Sages *permit* the use of contraceptives after cohabitation reasoning that women are not commanded to refrain from "destroying the seed." R. Plocki points out that fertilization most frequently takes place immediately following cohabitation. Contraception following cohabitation is then, in effect, not destruction of the seed but abortion of a fertilized ovum. If abortion is forbidden even in the earliest stages of gestation, how then can Rabbenu Tam permit the use of contraceptive devices following cohabitation? R. Plocki concludes that destruction of the embryo during the first forty days following conception does not constitute an act of feticide but rather falls under the category of "destroying the seed." Since we accept the opinion of those authorities who rule that women are also bound by the prohibition against "destroying the seed," R. Plocki's reasoning (as evidenced by his own remarks) finds practical application only with regard to Noachides. According to those authorities who maintain that the ban against destroying the seed does not apply

---

the death of a formed fetus and is rendered accordingly by the Septuagint. This interpretation is, of course, founded on the premise that the principle of absolution from the lesser of two simultaneously incurred punishments extends to Noachide law as well —a matter which bears further investigation. R. Joseph Babad is of the opinion that the principle *"kim leh be-de-rabbah mineh"* (imposition of the greater of two punishments to the exclusion of the lesser) does not apply to Noachides. See *Minḥat Ḥinukh,* no. 34. However, there is basis for assuming that the question is the subject of controversy between Rashi and *Tosafot, Eruvin* 62*a*. Cf. *Encyclopedia Talmudit* (Tel Aviv, 5711), III, 354.

to Noachides, the latter may be permitted to interrupt pregnancy during the first forty days of gestation.

Distinctions pertaining to the early period of gestation are echoed by numerous other authorities. R. Chaim Ozer (*Teshuvot Aḥi'ezer,* III, no. 65, sec. 14) writes, "It appears that a Noachide is not put to death for this and perhaps even with regard to an Israelite there is no biblical prohibition." *Torat Ḥesed, Even ha-Ezer,* no. 42, sec. 33, states explicitly that the prohibition against destroying an embryo within the first forty days following conception is rabbinic in nature. R. Joseph Rosen, *Ẓofnat Pa'aneaḥ,* no. 59, comments, "Before the fortieth day there is not such a stringent prohibition according to many authorities." In an earlier collection of responsa, *Teshuvot Bet Shlomoh, Ḥoshen Mishpat,* no. 162, R. Shlomoh Drimer of Skole concludes that there is no prohibition against destroying an embryo less than forty days old and notes that in punishment for performing such a deed "even a Noachide is not put to death." An even more permissive view is cited by Rabbi Waldenberg. He quotes a responsum included in *Teshuvot Pri ha-Sadeh* (vol. IV, no. 50) which extends this distinction to the entire first three months of pregnancy.[41] Relying upon this opinion, Rabbi Waldenberg *Ẓiẓ Eli'ezer,* IX, 236, permits the performance of an abortion within the first three months when there are definite grounds to fear that the child will be born deformed or abnormal.[42] Rabbi Waldenberg, however, denies such permission even within this period once fetal movement is perceived. Rabbi Weinberg, in his original responsum (*No'am* IX, 213 f), also concluded that it is permissible to induce abortion prior to the fortieth day of preg-

41. *Pri ha-Sadeh,* in turn, attributes this distinction to *Ḥavot Ya'ir.* In point of fact, this distinction, together with several others, was made by *Ḥavot Ya'ir* only by way of introduction. He concludes his prefatory remarks with the statement that it is not his goal to adjudicate such matters on the basis of *sevarat ha-keres* (an unfounded theory), but rather on the basis the "law of the Torah." At no point in his subsequent analysis does *Ḥavot Ya'ir* again refer to such a distinction. In fact, on the basis of *Ḥavot Ya'ir's* thesis that feticide is a form of *hashḥatat zera* such a distinction would be quite illogical. See above, p. 340, n. 31.

42. R. Shaul Israeli, *Amud ha-Yemini,* no. 32, expresses a permissive view with regard to abortion of a deformed fetus during subsequent periods of pregnancy. His reasoning has, however, not been accepted by any recognized authority. The comments of R. Ayeh Leib Grossnass *Lev Aryeh,* II, 205, do not serve to establish halakhic permissibility; see R. Moses Feinstein, *Iggrot Mosheh, Even ha-Ezer,* I, no. 62. For a recent, more permissive view expressed by Rabbi Waldenberg see above, "Tay-Sachs Reexamined," pp. 112-115. Cf. also R. Shmuel Chaim Katz, *Ha-Pardes,* Tammuz 5735.

nancy, but later added in a note (*Seridei Esh,* III, 350, note 7) that having seen a contrary opinion expressed by Rabbi Unterman in *No'am* (VI, 8f),[43] he reserves decision pending consultation with other halakhic authorities. The late Rabbi Moshe Yonah Zweig of Antwerp, writing in *No'am* (VII, 48), concurs in the view which forbids abortions even during the first forty days of pregnancy other than on medical grounds.[44]

Therapeutic Abortion of Pregnancy Involving Danger to Life

Authority for performance of an embryotomy in order to preserve the life of the mother is derived from the previously cited Mishnah, *Oholot* 7:6. Virtually all authorities agree that the Mishnah does not merely sanction but deems mandatory[45] that the life of the fetus be made subordinate to that of the mother. At the same time the Mishnah expressly forbids interference with natural processes after the moment of birth, which is defined as the emergence from the womb of the forehead or the greater part thereof.[46] In the ensuing talmudic discussion (*Sanhedrin* 72b), the child is described as being in effect an aggressor "pursuing" the life of its mother. As such, its life is forfeit if necessary to save the innocent victim so pursued.[47] At this point the question is raised, why should an embryotomy not be performed in such circumstances even in the final stages of parturition? It is answered by pointing out that the law of pur-

---

43. R. Unterman's opinion was actually expressed much earier in his *Shevet me-Yehudah,* I, 50.

44. See also R. Samuel Engel, *Teshuvot Maharash Engel,* VII, no. 85, who, after drawing a distinction between the first forty days and the subsequent periods of pregnancy, concludes with the statement, "but it is difficult to rely upon this."

45. See, however, R. Shlomoh ha-Kohen of Vilna, who is of the opinion that such rescue of the mother, although permitted, is by no means obligatory. This scholar apparently maintains that the obligation to preserve a life is suspended when such life can be preserved only at the cost of another's life, even though such action involves no overt transgression. These views are recorded in a responsum addressed to R. Moshe Horwitz and incorporated by the latter in his *Yedei Mosheh* (Pietrokow, 5658), no. 4, sec. 8.

46. *Yoreh De'ah* 194:10; *Siftei Kohen, loc. cit.,* no. 26; *Sidrei Taharah, loc. cit.* See also R. David Hoffmann, *Melamed le-Ho'il* (Frankfort a. M., 5696), no. 69, and R. Meir Eisenstadt, *Teshuvot Panim Me'irot* (New York, 5722), III, no. 8.

47. The law of pursuit requires the bystander to disable the aggressor, by a fatal blow if necessary, in order to thwart the pursuer's intent to kill. See Rambam, *Hilkhot Rozeah* 1:6.

suit does not apply when the mother is "pursued by Heaven," i.e., her danger is the result of natural occurrences rather than malevolent human activity. The apparent inference to be drawn from this discussion is that there is no need for resort to the law of pursuit in order to justify destruction of the fetus prior to birth. On the contrary, were there need for such justification, the law of pursuit would be of no avail since it cannot be validly applied in cases where such "pursuit" arises as a result of the processes of nature. Rashi (*ad loc.*) explains that the fetus is sacrificed in order to spare the life of the mother because even though the fetus has a claim to life and is sufficiently human to render its destruction a moral offense, neither this claim nor its status as a human life is equal to that of the mother: "As long as it [the fetus] has not emerged into the light of the world, it is not a human life."

Maimonides codifies the law emerging from this discussion in the following manner: "This also is a negative precept: not to have compassion on the life of a pursuer. Therefore the Sages ruled [regarding] a pregnant woman in hard travail that it is permitted to dismember the fetus in her womb, whether by chemical means or by hand, for it [the fetus] is as one pursuing her in order to kill her; but if it has already put forth its head it may not be touched, for [one] life may not be put aside for the sake of [another] life. This is the natural course of the world" (*Hilkhot Roẓeah* 1:9). This formulation is problematic in that Maimonides invokes the law of pursuit as justification for the performance of an embryotomy in the early stages of labor, whereas the Gemara implies that the deliberate sacrifice of the unborn child is permitted simply because its life is subservient to that of the mother. Furthermore, the explanation offered seems to be contradictory in nature since Maimonides, in his concluding remarks, follows the Gemara in dismissing the applicability of the law of pursuit on the grounds that nature, not the child, pursues the mother. The question of proper interpretation of Maimonides is of the utmost halakhic relevance because in this instance his phraseology is adopted *verbatim* by the *Shulḥan Arukh, Ḥoshen Mishpat* 452:2.

In an attempt to resolve these difficulties, R. Yechezkel Landau[48] points out that the killing of a fetus, while not constituting an act of homicide, is nevertheless an odious offense. Just as there is no justification for the sacrifice of a person suffering from a fatal injury—the killing of whom

48. *Noda bi-Yehudah, Mahadurah Tinyana* (Wilno, 5659), *Ḥoshen Mishpat,* no. 59.

does not technically constitute murder—for the purpose of preserving the life of a normal person, so also destruction of the embryo in order to safeguard the life of the mother would not be condoned if not for its being, at least in measure, an aggressor. R. Ya'ir Bachrach[49] and Rabbi Chaim Soloveitchik[50] employ similar reasoning in explaining Maimonides' position.[51] A somewhat different explanation is offered by R. Isser Zalman Melzer in the name of R. Chaim Soloveitchik. Rabbi Unterman, in his work *Shevet me-Yehudah,*[52] attempts a further clarification of Maimonides' position by explaining that the ban against destroying the life of a fetus stems not from an actual prohibition against the act of feticide *per se,* but from an obligation to preserve the life of the fetus.[53] Since the killing of a fetus is antithetical to its preservation, embryotomy is permissible only when the fetus is, in point of fact, an aggressor. Once the child is born, the prohibition against homicide becomes actual and since, technically, it is nature which is the pursuer, the law of pursuit is not operative.

Resolution of the difficulties surrounding Maimonides' ruling and the reasoning upon which it is based is of great significance in terms of practical Halakhah. According to the explanations offered by R. Yechezkel Landau, R. Chaim Soloveitchik and others following in the same general mode, therapeutic abortion would be permissible only in instances where the "pursuer" argument may be applied, i.e., where the threat to the life of the mother is the direct result of the condition of pregnancy. R. Chaim Ozer[54] and Rabbi Weinberg[55] both contend that a pregnancy which merely

49. *Ḥavot Ya'ir,* no. 31.

50. *Ḥiddushei R. Ḥayyim ha-Levi, Ḥilkhot Roẓeaḥ* 1:9.

51. *Even he-Azel* (Jerusalem, 5696), I, *Hilkhot Roẓeaḥ,* 1:9.

52. P. 26ff. A similar explanation is offered by R. Nachum Rabinovitch, *Ha-Darom* (5729), no. 28, pp. 19f. For yet another interpretation of Rambam (albeit one which does not affect our discussion), see R. Isaac Judah Shmelkes, *Teshuvot Bet Yiẓḥak* (New York, 5720), *Yoreh De'ah,* II, no. 162. See also R. Zweig, *No'am,* VII, 52.

53. The principle "Be killed but do not transgress" applies only to actual homicide but imposes no obligation in face of coercion to prevent fulfillment of the obligation to rescue the life of one's fellowman. Since, according to R. Unterman, killing a fetus does not fall within the category of murder but is inherently contraindicated by the obligation to preserve fetal life, it follows that there is no obligation to refrain from destroying a fetus at the cost of one's own life.

54. *Teshuvot Aḥi'ezer,* II, no. 72.

55. *Seridei Esh,* III, 342; cf. also R. Meir Dan Plocki, *Ḥemdat Yisra'el, Mafteḥot ve-Hosafot,* p. 32, who makes much the same point.

complicates an already present medical condition, thereby endangering the life of the mother, does not provide grounds for termination of pregnancy according to such analyses of Maimonides' position. In these cases the fetus cannot be deemed an aggressor since the mother's life is placed in jeopardy by the disease afflicting her. It is this malady, rather than her pregnant condition, which is the proximate cause of impending tragedy. An identical conclusion was reached much earlier by R. Isaac Schorr (*Koaḥ Shor,* no. 20) who points out that the law of pursuit encompasses only cases where the pursuer seeks to perform an overt act of homicide. If the act only leads indirectly to the death of the pursued, e.g., when the pursuer merely seeks to incarcerate the victim so that he die of starvation or seeks to cut off the intended victim's supply of oxygen in order to cause asphyxiation, the law of pursuit is not applicable, for "we have not heard that the pursued may be saved by taking the life of one who is desirous of preventing a benefit necessary for the life of his fellowman." A fetus, which itself is not the cause of danger but whose presence thwarts the efficacy of medical remedies, clearly falls within this category. At least one other authority, R. Isaac Lampronti, the author of *Paḥad Yiẓḥak* (*Erekh Nefalim,* 79b) states unequivocally that danger caused by an extraneous disease does not warrant performance of an abortion in order to save the mother. Rabbi Schorr emphasizes that (according to Maimonides) it must be known with certainty that the pregnancy *per se* constitutes this danger. This rules out abortion in instances where there is doubt as to whether the pregnancy is the actual case of danger or whether the pregnancy merely complicates a previously existing condition.

The aforementioned discussions concern themselves only with cases in which failure to terminate pregnancy will indubitably result in the loss of life to the mother. The question of termination of a pregnancy which, while jeopardizing the life of the pregnant mother, will not *necessarily* result in imminent loss of life again centers around Maimonides' invocation of the law of pursuit. Citing Rashi, *Sanhedrin* 72b and *Pesaḥim* 2b, Rabbi Schorr demonstrates that the law of pursuit cannot be invoked in cases of doubt. Hence abortion may be permitted only when there exists incontravertible medical evidence that the pregnancy *per se* will result in the loss of the life of the pregnant mother. R. Shlomoh Drimer (*Bet Shlomoh, Ḥoshen Mishpat,* no. 120), however, reaches the opposite conclusion, at least in theory. Following the authorities who maintain that a fetus is "not a life" and hence its destruction does not constitute an "appurtenance" of homicide, Rabbi Drimer concludes that feticide is no different from other transgressions which may be violated even in cases of possible or suspected danger.[56] Nevertheless, in practice, Rabbi Drimer, on the basis of other considerations, withholds permission in cases of merely possible danger to the life of the mother. The Gemara (*Yoma* 82a) specifies that a pregnant woman who becomes agitated at the smell of food on the Day of Atonement may, if necessary, partake of the food which causes this excitement lest she suffer a miscarriage and her fetus be spontaneously aborted. Maimonides, Rabbenu Asher and Rabbenu Nissim interpret this provision as being based, not on a concern for the preservation of the unborn child, but on a concern for the life of the mother. According to their view, expulsion of the fetus *ipso facto* constitutes a threat to the life of the mother. Accordingly, reasons Rabbi Drimer, even if continuation of pregnancy jeopardizes the life of the mother, this consideration is counterbalanced by the fact that termination of pregnancy in itself constitutes a parallel jeopardy. Therefore, a course of "sit and do not act" is preferable. Even if physicians advise that there is no danger involved in the performance of the abortion, their advice is to be disregarded, just as medical opinion is ignored when it fails to recognize cases of "danger" which are delineated by Halakhah as constituting a threat to human life. Halakhah specifies that a woman's life is in jeopardy for a minimum period of three days following childbirth and hence during this time she is permitted to partake of food on the Day of Atonement, the Sabbath is violated on her behalf, etc. Since Halakhah defines childbirth as a "danger," medical opinions to the contrary or protestations of well-being on the part of the patient are disregarded. Rabbi Drimer reasons that the same considerations should apply to the conditions surrounding abortion.

A very different conclusion is reached by R. Mordecai Leib Winkler [57] (*Levushei Mordekhai*), who finds reason to distinguish between miscarriages and abortions performed by medical practitioners. Since there is no explicit reference to the latter, those authorities who state that abortion *per se* constitutes a threat to the life of the mother may not have intended their remarks to encompass therapeutic abortion surrounded by medical safeguards. *Levushei Mordekhai* also introduces the notion of comparative danger and seems to indicate that, while abortion may

---

56. The same opinion is recorded by R. David Dov Meisels, *Binyan David* (Ouhel, 5692), no. 47, in the name of *Avnei Ẓedek, Ḥoshen Mishpat,* no. 19.

57. *Levushei Mordekhai, Mahadurah Tinyana* (Budapest, 5684), *Yoreh De'ah,* no. 87.

itself constitute a danger in the opinion of these authorities, this danger may not be acute since dispensation for violation of *Shabbat* and *Yom Kippur* is granted for even the slightest threat to life. Abortion should therefore be sanctioned in order to obviate a more acute danger. Furthermore, the remarks of these authorities fail to demonstrate that miscarriage *per se* jeopardizes the life of the mother. Their pronouncements are consistent with the conclusion that danger will result only if the woman fails to receive proper care pursuant to the expulsion of the fetus. Since such care would involve desecration of *Yom Kippur* in any event, the woman may break her fast in order to prevent the necessity for such later violations. *Levushei Mordekhai* concludes that there is, then, no evidence that a therapeutic abortion performed under proper medical conditions and with provision for proper convalescence constitutes a jeopardy to the life of the mother.

Relevant to this issue is the tragic case of a pregnant woman suffering from a terminal case of cancer which is pondered by R. Waldenberg (*Ẓiẓ Eli'ezer,* IX, 239). Medical authorities predict that continuation of pregnancy to term will foreshorten her life, but the expectant mother is steadfast in her desire to be survived by a child. Normally her desire would be irrelevant to a halakhic determination that preservation of maternal life is sufficient reason to abort the fetus. With regard to this specific question, Rabbi Waldenberg concludes that since *Bet Shlomoh* and other authorities withhold permission to abort the fetus on grounds that the abortion itself also constitutes a danger to the life of the mother, in this case one is justified in acceding to the wishes of the mother and adopting a stance of passive noninterference.

Returning to our central problem, many authorities take a different view with regard to embryotomy in cases where pregnancy endangers the life of the mother by complicating an already present medical condition. Rabbi Weinberg (*No'am* IX, 204; *Seridei Esh,* III, 343 f.) offers a radically different approach to the resolution of the complex difficulties surrounding the previously cited statements of Maimonides, *Hilkhot Roẓeaḥ* 1:9, in light of the latter's remarks in *Hilkhot Ḥoveil u-Mazik* 8:4. Maimonides rules that although property belonging to others may be appropriated in order to preserve one's own life, compensation must nevertheless subsequently be paid to the lawful owner. Rabbi Weinberg notes that the provision is modified in the event that the property itself is the source of danger (*Nizkei Mamon* 8:15). The paradigm case is that of the threat to the lives of the passengers sailing on an overly laden ship which is in danger of sinking. One who lightens the load by throwing cargo overboard is absolved from payment of property damages since the cargo itself is deemed to be "a pursuer." Rabbi Weinberg opines that Maimonides invokes this provision in his exposition of the law surrounding danger arising from pregnancy. Maimonides does not resort to the law of pursuit, argues Rabbi Weinberg, in order to justify sacrifice of the life of the fetus; this is warranted on the basis of Rashi's explanation that it is not fully "a human life." Rather, continues Rabbi Weinberg, Maimonides invokes the pursuer argument in order to provide a basis for exemption from satisfaction of the husband's claim for monetary damages normally incurred as a result of destruction of a fetus as provided by Exodus 21:22.

R. Chaim Ozer, in another responsum (*Aḥi'ezer,* III, no. 72), points out that Maimonides' phraseology refers specifically to a woman in "hard travail." As previously noted, the Talmud regards a fetus which has "torn itself loose" from the normal uterine position as a separate body. According to R. Chaim Ozer, Maimonides deems it necessary to rely upon the law of pursuit only because he refers to a fetus which, although yet unborn, is already a separate body. The Gemara speaks of earlier stages of pregnancy and hence has no need for recourse to this line of reasoning. According to this interpretation, Maimonides recognizes that prior to the mother's "sitting on the birth stool" the fetus is but an organic limb of her body. It is of course not merely permissible, but mandatory, to amputate a limb in order to save a life. Therefore, concludes R. Chaim Ozer, even according to Maimonides, it is permissible to perform an abortion in cases involving danger to the life of the mother, irrespective of the source of such danger, provided this procedure is performed before the fetus has "torn itself loose." [58] R. Chaim Ozer adds the stipulation that the physicians advising this medical procedure be highly expert and certain in their opinion that the operation itself does not constitute a danger.

Rabbi Weinberg (*No'am,* IX, 205; *Seridei Esh,* III, 344) objects to this line of reasoning because it is predicated upon the consideration that the fetus is to be accounted as "a limb of the mother." His objection is based upon the remarks of *Tosafot* (*Sanhedrin* 80b) that the principle "a fetus is a limb of the mother" applies in all instances save with regard to the laws of *tereifah,* of an animal mortally wounded or afflicted with a terminal disease. The prohibition of a *tereifah* is based upon the animal's lack of

58. A similar interpretation of Rambam is offered by *Mishpetei Uziel,* III, 211.

"animation." Since a fetus possesses "independent animation" and may survive even though the mother is doomed, consideration of the fetus as a limb of the mother does not render it a *tereifah* simply because the mother has become a *tereifah*. Similarly, argues Rabbi Weinberg, since the fetus is possessed of "independent animation," it does not follow that its abortion is comparable to the removal of a limb in order to save the body. Accordingly, Rabbi Weinberg concludes that abortion is not permitted, according to Maimonides, in cases where extraneous illness would lead to the mother's death if pregnancy were allowed to continue.

Therapeutic Abortion of Pregnancy Involving Danger to Maternal Health

A further ramification of these diverse analyses of Maimonides' views relates to the permissibility of therapeutic abortion in situations deleterious to the health of the mother, but not endangering her life. The most permissive ruling with regard to therapeutic abortion, one to which later authorities take strong exception, is that of R. Jacob Emden,[59] who permits performance of an abortion not only when the mother's health is compromised but also in cases of "grave necessity," such as when continuation of the pregnancy would subject the mother to great pain.[60] Such abortions are sanctioned by R. Emden when performed before the onset of labor at which time the fetus has "torn itself loose" from the uterine wall. Citing *Ḥavot Ya'ir*'s explanation that the basis of the law against feticide is the prohibition against destroying the seed, R. Emden maintains that destroying the seed is forbidden only when such emission or destruction is with-

59. *She'elat Ya'aveẓ,* no. 43. This opinion was apparently accepted by R. Shlomoh Kluger, whose views are recorded in *Ẓeḥuta de-Avraham,* no. 60, and by *Ẓiẓ Eli'ezer,* VII, 190; VIII, 219; IX, 237. R. Waldenberg stipulates (IX, 240) that consent of the husband must be obtained in such instances since he is deemed to possess proprietory rights with regard to the unborn child. R. Waldenberg further stipulates (VII, 190) that determination of medical necessity must be made by an Orthodox physician or at the very minimum by a "concerned physician who relates to the laws of the Torah with honor and concern." *Binyan David,* no. 60, requires the concurring opinions of two medical practitioners, neither of whom is aware of the diagnosis of his colleague. R. Ovadiah Yosef, *Yabi'a Omer,* IV, *Even ha-Ezer,* no. 1, sec. 10, rules that an abortion for the purpose of preserving maternal health may be performed only within the first three months of pregnancy.

60. See also *Torat Ḥesed, Even ha-Ezer,* no. 42, sec. 32; *Yabi'a Omer,* IV, no. 1, sec. 8.

out purpose, but may be permitted when it serves a medical function. It should, however, be noted that *Ḥavot Ya'ir* himself quotes Rashi's commentary, *Sanhedrin* 72b, "a woman who is in hard labor *and whose life is in danger,*" from which *Ḥavot Ya'ir* deduces that other than in cases of actual danger to maternal life abortion cannot be sanctioned.

A view similar to that of R. Jacob Emden is voiced by R. Ben-Zion Uziel, the late Sephardic Chief Rabbi of Israel, in his *Mishpetei Uziel, Ḥoshen Mishpat,* III, no. 46. The case brought to his attention concerned a woman threatened with approaching deafness if her pregnancy were permitted to run its normal course. Rabbi Uziel, following the line of reasoning advanced by R. Jacob Emden, rules that abortion is permissible when indicated by any consideration of merit, provided it is performed before the onset of labor, at which time the fetus is considered to have "torn itself loose."

This determination leads Rabbi Uziel to the discussion of an interesting question. A pregnant woman is forbidden to contract a levirate marriage since her deceased husband will no longer remain childless if the pregnancy culminates in the birth of a viable infant. If, however, the widow entered into the marriage with her brother-in-law and later discovered that at the time of consummation she was already bearing the child of her previous husband, the marriage is annulled and a sin-offering brought in expiation of this inadvertent transgression. Why, R. Uziel was asked, is she not advised simply to abort the fetus thereby eradicating her transgression *ab initio?* Obviation of sin certainly constitutes a "grave need" and fulfills the criterion established by R. Jacob Emden. Rabbi Uziel answers that since the husband enjoys rights of proprietorship with regard to the fetus and is indeed entitled to monetary compensation for its loss (Exod. 21:22), the woman has no right to destroy her dead husband's property in order to absolve herself retroactively from the prohibition against cohabitation with a brother-in-law.

On a later occasion Rabbi Uziel seems to have reversed his opinion with regard to the salient point of the responsum. In a responsum dated the following month (*op. cit.,* no. 47), Rabbi Uziel specifically cites the opinion of R. Jacob Emden but reserves decision in cases not involving a threat to the very life of the mother.

R. Joseph Trani, in a somewhat more restricted ruling (*Teshuvot Maharit,* I, no. 99), sanctions abortions when performed in the interests of maternal health. This decision follows logically from his thesis that feticide is not a form of homicide but is forbidden because removal of the fetus constitutes an act of "wounding." [61] It, of course, follows that any wound inflicted for purposes of healing is not encompassed by this prohibition.

Rabbi Weinberg (*No'am* IX, 215; *Seridei Esh* III, 350) observes that according to the previously cited explanations of *Hilkhot Roẓeaḥ* 1:9 by R. Yechezkel Landau and R. Chaim Soloveitchik, abortion would not be sanctioned by Maimonides except when there exists an imminent threat to the life of the mother. Rabbi Weinberg adds, however, that in view of the fact that many authorities dispute Maimonides' position, "perhaps" the lenient ruling of R. Jacob Emden may be relied upon if continuation of pregnancy until term would be detrimental to the health of the mother.

In a similar vein, Rabbi Waldenberg notes (*Ẓiẓ Eli'ezer,* IX, 239) that "there is room for leniency" if the state of maternal health is very precarious or if necessary in order to secure relief from severe pain. As noted earlier, Rabbi Moshe Yonah Zweig (*No'am,* VII, 48) rules that abortion on these grounds is permissible within the first forty days of gestation.

Among the authorities not previously cited who forbid destruction of the fetus other than in face of a definite threat to the life of the mother are: *Koaḥ Shor,* no. 21; *Levushei Mordekhai, Ḥoshen Mishpat,* no. 36; *Bet Shlomoh, Ḥoshen Mishpat,* no. 132; *Pri ha-Sadeh,* IV, no. 50; *Binyan David,* no. 47; *Avnei Ẓedek, Ḥoshen Mishpat,* no. 19; *Afarkasta de-Anya,* no. 169; and *Ẓur Ya'akov,* no. 141.

Preservation of Maternal Life During Parturition

The Mishnah, *Oholot* 7:6, is emphatic in its ruling against embryotomy once the major portion of the child has been delivered. The inferred pre-

61. *Teshuvot Maharit,* I, no. 97. This will serve in a measure to resolve the apparent discrepancy between responsa nos. 97 and 99 which is pointed out by *Sedei Ḥemed,* p. 175. In no. 99 R. Trani states that there is no ban based upon the prohibition against destruction of human life; not mentioned is the prohibition against flagellation to which reference is made in no. 97. The latter prohibition is, of course, inoperative when indicated for therapeutic purposes. The author of *Teshuvot Binyan David* (no. 60), however, regards Maharit as permitting abortions only when the mother's life is in danger. It seems that *Paḥad Yiẓḥak* must also have understood this to be the intention of R. Trani since he records the decision of Maharit yet, in the same paragraph as previously noted, denies the propriety of an abortion in case of danger to the mother resulting from causes other than the pregnancy *per se.* Cf. also, *Yabi'a Omer,* IV, *Even ha-Ezer,* no. 1, sec. 6–8. For other attempts to resolve the problems surrounding these two responsa of Maharit see *Teshuvot Aryeh de-Bei Ila'i, Yoreh De'ah,* no. 19, and *Ẓiẓ Eli'ezer* IX, 234, and *Yabi'a Omer* IV, no. 1, sec. 7.

sumption is that the abandonment of one life will assuredly save the other. There is, however, no specific statement of halakhic determination dealing with cases where non-interference would lead to the loss of both mother and child. The halakhic grounds which justify an embryotomy under such conditions, even subsequent to the commencement of parturition, are delineated by R. Israel Lipschutz, the author of *Tiferet Yisra'el,* in his commentary on this Mishnah. The issue hinges upon the applicability of a law recorded by Maimonides, *Hilkhot Yesodei ha-Torah* 5:5: ". . . if the heathen said to them, 'Give us one of your company and we shall kill him; if not we will kill all of you,' let them all be killed but let them not deliver to them [the heathens] a single Jewish soul. But if they specified [the victim] to them and said, 'Give us so and so or we shall kill all of you,' if he had incurred the death penalty as Sheba the son of Bichri, they may deliver him to them . . . but if he had not incurred the death penalty let them all be killed, but let them not deliver a single Jewish soul."

Maimonides' ruling is based upon the explication of the narrative of II Samuel 20:4–22 found in the Palestinian Talmud, *Terumot* 8:12. Joab, commander of King David's troops, had pursued Sheba the son of Bichri and beseiged him in the town of Abel and demanded that he be delivered to the king's forces. Otherwise Joab threatened to destroy the entire city. From the verse "Sheba the son of Bichri hath lifted up his hand against the king, against David" (20:21), Resh Lakish infers that acquiescence with this demand can be sanctioned only in instances where the victim's life is lawfully forfeit, as was the case with regard to Sheba the son of Bichri, who is described as being guilty of *lèse majesté;* in instances where the victim is innocent, all must suffer death rather than become accomplices to murder. R. Yochanan maintains that the question of guilt is irrelevant, but that the crucial element is rather the singling out of a specific individual. Members of a group have no right to select one of their number arbitrarily and deliver him to death in order to save themselves since the life of each individual is of inestimable value. However, once a specific person has been marked for death in any event, either alone if surrendered by his companions or together with the entire group if they refuse to comply, those who deliver him are not accounted as accessories. Maimonides' ruling is in accordance with the opinion of Resh Lakish.[62]

---

62. Rosh and Ran, however, both rule in accordance with the opinion of R. Yochanan; R. Moses Isserles, *Yoreh De'ah* 157:1, cites both views without offering a definitive ruling.

In a medical context, when confronted by the imminent loss of both mother and child, dismemberment of a partially delivered child having no possibility of survival in order to save the mother would be advocated by those authorities who require merely that the victim be "specified," since they do not require that he necessarily be guilty of a capital offense. However, according to Maimonides, the intended victim must be culpable as well and a newly born child is certainly guilty of no crime. Furthermore, this line of reasoning does not apply to the many cases where either the mother or child may be saved through the sacrifice of the other; in such situations the crucial element of "specification" is totally absent.

Yet another crucial discrepancy between our case and the paradigm instance of "specification" is stressed by R. Chaim Sofer.[63] The provision regarding specification is a direct outgrowth of the law of pursuit. Sheba ben Bichri's refusal to surrender himself was the direct source of danger to his townspeople. This made him, in effect, a pursuer since it was within his power to remove the danger. Justification for turning him over to Joab was simply the application of the law of pursuit to this novel situation. The situation surrounding childbirth, argues R. Sofer, is not at all comparable. Since the birth process is not at all within the control of the child, he cannot be deemed a "pursuer" in permitting the genesis of a threat to the life of the mother. Since we are dealing with a natural process totally independent of human volition, the mother must be deemed as "pursued by Heaven." Even if the element of "specification" were present (i.e., the life of the mother could be saved by sacrificing the child but not vice versa), such "specification" would not render the partially born child a "pursuer" inasmuch as he cannot in this instance "surrender," even if he were capable of such choice.

R. Chaim Sofer further asserts, on the basis of a contrary-to-fact hypothetical argument, that even if Halakhah were to sanction the taking of another's life in order to save one's own, this provision would be based solely on the consideration that an act of murder is inevitable in any event. However, death in childbirth, barring human interference, occurs through natural causes without any mortal becoming sullied by the crime of bloodshed. If so, "better two deaths than one murder." Accordingly, R. Chaim Sofer refuses to grant permission to destroy the child in order to save the mother, even though its life is doomed in any event.

---

63. *Teshuvot Maḥaneh Ḥayyim* (Munkotch, 5635), *Ḥoshen Mishpat,* no. 50.

Presenting a second argument which would render this practice permissible, R. Israel Lipschutz reasons that Halakhah suspects that each newly born child may be premature and possibly incapable of survival and provides that the child's status remain in doubt until it demonstrates viability through survival for a minimum period of thirty days.[64] Therefore, argues R. Lipschutz, since there is an objective criterion for granting priority to the life of the mother, the usual principle "on what account is his blood sweeter than yours" does not apply and hence the child may be sacrificed in order to spare the life of the mother.[65]

This problem is discussed in the writings of several other authorities

---

64. A similar reservation concerning the status of an unborn child was voiced by R. Isaiah Pik (as evidenced by the responsum addressed to him by R. Yechezkel Landau, *Noda bi-Yehudah,* II, *Ḥoshen Mishpat,* no. 59), who apparently was of the opinion that the general ruling that all infants are considered to be viable does not apply to embryos, since the generalization is based upon observation that such is the case in the preponderant number of instances. The establishment of such a "majority" is especially limited to experience associated with born children. No such observation is permissible with regard to unborn children. Hence this principle, argues R. Pik, must be limited and considered as encompassing only born infants, i.e., stating only that the majority of fully delivered infants are viable. Cf. also the previously cited commentary of R. Elijah Mizrachi on Exodus 21:12.

65. An identical distinction is made by R. Isaiah Pik in a communication addressed to R. Landau and quoted by the latter in his *Noda bi-Yehudah,* II, *Ḥoshen Mishpat,* no. 59, and by R. Judah Rosanes, *Parashat Derakhim, Derush* 17. A similar distinction with regard to *tereifah* is made by *Minḥat Ḥinukh,* no. 296. See also *Ẓiẓ Eli'ezer,* X, no. 25, chap. 5, sec. 4.

The view expressed by R. Lipschutz concerning the inapplicability of this principle is somewhat problematic in light of *Kesef Mishneh*'s analysis of *Yesodei ha-Torah* 5:5. The Gemara, *Pesaḥim* 25b, states that the principle "Be killed but do not transgress" as applied to an act of homicide is an *a priori* principle based upon reason alone. If so, questions *Kesef Mishneh,* what is the basis for the extension of the ruling "Be killed but do not transgress" to a situation in which the victim is singled out and the entire group warned that, if the specified individual is not delivered, all will perish. In such cases the dictates of reason would indicate that it is preferable by far to sacrifice a single life rather than to suffer the loss of the entire group. *Kesef Mishneh* concludes that the Sages possessed a tradition extending this principle even to cases in which the *a priori* reason advanced does not apply. See also *Aḥi'ezer,* II, no. 16, sec. 5. The distinction both with regard to fetal life and *tereifah* as drawn by the above cited authorities is rejected by *Nodai bi-Yehudah, loc. cit.*

as well. In his commentary on the Mishnah, R. Akiba Eger[66] poses the question regarding the permissibility of killing a child in order to save the mother where failure to do so would result in the death of both. Quoting *Panim Me'irot,*[67] he concludes that the ultimate decision in this instance requires further deliberation. R. Moses Schick,[68] without citing R. Lipschutz's *Tiferet Yisra'el,* agrees with these conclusions in substance. However, noting a previously expressed opinion of *Ḥatam Sofer,*[69] he adds that facts ascertained solely through the testimony of medical practitioners can be accepted as establishing only a *safek,* i.e., as possibly being the case, but cannot be regarded as having been established with conclusive certainty. Since there remains an element of doubt, a decision on our part to terminate the life of the child is unwarranted. However, if the physician himself is confident of the certainty of his diagnosis and of his assessment of the medical prognosis, he may rely upon his own certainty and govern his own actions accordingly. R. Schick's responsum concludes with the statement that the matter requires further deliberation and that these views are not to be regarded as definitive decisions. In response to a similar query, R. David Hoffman, citing the relevant sources, expresses his agreement with the opinion of *Tiferet Yisra'el.*[70] R. Isaac Judah Schmelkes (*Teshuvot Bet Yiẓḥak,* II, *Yoreh De'ah,* no. 162) expresses some reservation but agrees that R. Schick's ruling may be relied upon, provided that the pertinent medical facts are established on the basis of the concurring opinions of two physicians of the Jewish faith who will appreciate the gravity of the potential transgression.

---

66. *Tosafot R. Akiva Eger, Oholot* 6:17, no. 17.

67. R. Meir Eisenstadt, *Teshuvot Panim Me'irot* (New York, 5722), III, no. 8.

68. *Teshuvot Maharam Schick* (New York, 5721), *Yoreh De'ah,* no. 155.

69. This principle is established by R. Moses Sofer, *Teshuvot Ḥatam Sofer* (New York, 5718), *Yoreh De'ah,* no. 158. The credence given to even a single witness in matters of halakhic proscription extends only to testimony of observed events. Diagnosis and treatment of medical conditions necessarily contain an element of subjective judgment; hence the judgment of a medical practitioner constitutes a *safek* rather than a certainty. As such, it cannot provide sufficient basis for sanctioning that which is forbidden in cases of "doubt." Elsewhere *(Yoreh De'ah,* nos. 173 and 175) *Ḥatam Sofer* states that medical testimony is indeed sufficient to demonstrate that certain physiological processes do occur. Nevertheless such testimony cannot establish that a specific physiological process is actually taking place in a given patient since such diagnosis involves a subjective judgment.

70. *Melamed le-Ho'il, Yoreh De'ah,* no. 69.

The position adopted by R. Joseph Saul Nathanson[71] is most engaging. Citing the decision recorded in *Baba Meẓi'a* 62a,[72] "Your life takes precedence over the life of your fellow," this authority contends that the Mishnah's discussion of the treatment of a woman in "hard travail" and the restrictions placed upon efforts to preserve her life refer only to third parties.[73] An individual lacking personal involvement may not make one life subordinate to another, but as far as one's own life is concerned it takes precedence over the life of one's fellow. R. Joseph Saul Nathanson's view is actually an expression of an identical position cited by *Me'iri, Sanhedrin* (ed. Abraham Sofer, Franfurt-am-Main, n.d.), p. 271, in the name of the "Sages of the Generations," who permit the mother herself to destroy the child even after final parturition has begun while forbidding others to do so. Rabbi Zweig dismisses this view as "the opinion of an individual" and hence having no standing in determination of Halakhah (*No'am* VII, 55).[74]

Maiming vs. Destruction of Fetus

The law of pursuit provides that the life of the pursuer is forfeit only if his malevolent intention cannot be thwarted by otherwise disabling the pursuer. Thus, if it is possible to disable the aggressor by maiming or crippling him, his life may not be taken under the law of pursuit. R. Moses Samuel Horowitz[75] and R. Isaac Schorr (*Koaḥ Shor,* no. 20) both rule that this consideration applies to a fetus as well. Accordingly, when intrauterine amputation of a limb would suffice to save the mother without recourse to an embryotomy, destruction of the fetus cannot be sanctioned. R. Shlomoh ha-Kohen of Vilna, author of the well-known *Ḥeshek Shlo-*

71. *Teshuvot Sho'el u-Meshiv* (New York, 5714), I, no. 22, p. 13.

72. Due to a printer's omission, the text appears to read *Baba Meẓi'a* 71 rather than 62a.

73. See *Teshuvot Tiferet Ẓvi, Oraḥ Ḥayyim,* no. 14.

74. R. Moshe Yonah Zweig, *No'am,* VII, 48, errs in ascribing an identical view to the *Maḥaneh Ḥayyim.* In point of fact, R. Sofer employs the phraseology of a contrary-to-fact conditional, viz., if feticide were at all permissible it would be permissible only if performed by the mother herself. R. Zweig judiciously notes that *Maḥaneh Ḥayyim* was not available to him. Apparently he was forced to rely upon secondary sources, a fact which explains the reason for his inaccuracy.

75. *Yedei Mosheh* (Pietrokow, 5658), no. 4, sec. 8. *Yedei Mosheh* was originally published as an appendix to *Sefer ha-Parnes* (Wilno, 5651), authored by R. Moses Parnes.

moh, deems this conclusion incontravertible and concurs in this ruling.[76]

Indeed, this interesting ramification serves as the basis for a novel reinterpretation of Maimonides' position. Rabbi Horowitz and Rabbi Schorr, apparently without either having seen the other's work, both note the expression "for it is *as* one pursuing her." They infer that Maimonides does not really intend to invoke the law of pursuit. Instead, he relies on the implicit rationale that the fetus is not "a life." Yet one restrictive aspect of the law of pursuit is applicable; namely, that the fetus, even though it is not deemed to be "a life," cannot be destroyed if it is possible to save the mother by merely crippling her unborn child. This then, they declare, is the intention of the phrase "limb by limb" as used by the Mishnah—first one limb, then another is removed in an attempt to deliver the child. While preservation of maternal life is of paramount concern, care must be taken that no unnecessary harm be inflicted upon the fetus.

Interpreted in a similar manner, the further provision of the Mishnah, "but once the major portion has emerged one may not touch it" (the fetus), implies that even the maiming of a partially born child or amputation of a limb is forbidden in order to save the mother. R. Chaim Sofer (*Maḥaneh Ḥayyim, Ḥoshen Mishpat,* no. 50) draws such an inference and indicates that the rationale motivating the decision is the fact that the physician "cannot guarantee with certainty" that the child will survive the surgical procedure. However, if noninterference will result in the loss of both mother and child, R. Sofer permits maiming of the child in an attempt to save the life of the mother.

Abortion of Pregnancy on Psychiatric Grounds

The entire area of psychiatric problems and severe emotional disturbances and their bearing upon halakhic questions has as yet not been adequately explored. Guidelines are to be found in isolated references to various forms of mental illness scattered throughout responsa literature. The earliest references to mental disease sufficiently grave to imperil the life of the afflicted occurs in the *Issur ve-Heter he-Arukh,*[77] attributed to Rabbeneu Yonah of Gerondi. *Issur ve-Heter he-Arukh* cites a specific query addressed to an earlier authority, Maharam, concerning an epileptic who sought advice concerning the permissibility of partaking

76. This responsum is included in *Yedei Mosheh.* The reference is to no. 5, sec. 8, of that work.

77. *Issur ve-Heter he-Arukh* (Wilno, 5651), no. 59, sec. 35. Cf. also *Hagahot Maymaniyot, Hilkhot Ma'akhalot Assurot* 14:15.

of a forbidden food reported to possess medicinal properties capable of curing his disease. The decision, in which Nachmanides acquiesces, is in the affirmative, provided that the efficacy of the remedy has been established. This decision is predicated upon a determination that epilepsy constitutes a danger to life, since at times an epileptic may endanger himself by "falling into fire or water." R. Israel Meir Mizrachi[78] relies upon the decision of Nachmanides in ruling that insanity constitutes a danger to life and accordingly permits an abortion when it is feared that the mother may otherwise become mentally deranged. This position is also adopted by *Levushei Mordekhai, Ḥoshen Mishpat,* no. 39, who is cited by R. Waldenberg, *Ẓiẓ Eli'ezer,* IX, 327,[79] Similarly, R. Yitzchak Ya'akov Weisz, *Minḥat Yiẓḥak,* I, no. 115, and R. Moses Feinstein, *Iggrot Mosheh, Even ha-Ezer,* I, no. 65, declare that mental derangement constitutes a danger to life.

Other authorities, however, apparently do not regard insanity (at least in all forms) as constituting a hazard to life. Thus when R. Moses Sofer[80] was asked whether it was permissible to have a mentally ill child admitted to an institution where he would be served forbidden foods, he discusses all aspects of the case without at all raising the question of *pikuaḥ nefesh* (danger to life). Rabbi Unterman, in an article contributed to *Ha-Torah ve-ha-Medinah* (IV, 27), argues that the instinct for self-preservation is so deeply ingrained, and suicidal tendencies are so rare, that one cannot consider mental illnesses as falling under the category of diseases which imperil life.[81]

---

78. *Pri ha-Areẓ,* III, *Yoreh De'ah* (Jerusalem, 5665), no. 21. Cf. *Piskei Teshuvah,* ed. R. Abraham Pieterkovsky (Pietrokow, 5693), II, no. 261.

79. See also *Ẓiẓ Eli'ezer,* IV, no. 13, sec. 3 Cf. *Teshuvot ha-Rashba ha-Meyuḥasot le-ha-Ramban,* no. 281; *Magen Avraham, Oraḥ Ḥayyim* 554:8 and *Pri Megadim, ad loc.; Teshuvot Admat Kodesh,* I, *Yoreh De'ah,* no. 6; *Pri ha-Areẓ,* III, *Yoreh Deah,* no. 2; *Birkei Yosef, Shiyurei Berakhah, Yoreh De'ah* 155; and *Teshuvot Neẓer Mata'ai,* I, no. 8.

80. *Teshuvot Ḥatam Sofer, Oraḥ Ḥayyim,* no. 83. A careful reading of this responsum indicates that, contrary to R. Unterman's assumption, *Ḥatam Sofer* may be discussing a case of mental retardation rather than a form of mental illness. Cf. *Iggrot Mosheh, Oraḥ Ḥayyim,* II, no. 88.

81. At the same time R. Unterman, *Ha-Torah ve-ha-Medinah,* IV, 29, and *Shevet me-Yehudah,* I, 49 and I, 64, sanctions desecration of the Sabbath in order to effect a cure in cases of insanity. R. Unterman maintains that the principle "Better to violate a single Sabbath in order that many Sabbaths be observed" is applicable in such instances. Cf., however, R. Eliezer Waldenberg, *Ramat Raḥel,* no. 28.

Abortion of a Bastard Fetus

R. Ya'ir Bachrach was asked whether a dose of ecbolics could be administered to a Jewess who had become pregnant as the result of an adulterous relationship in order to induce the abortion of her bastard fetus. Noting that the customary prayer "Preserve this child to its father and to its mother" is omitted at the circumcision of the issue of an adulterous or incestuous union because "the proliferation of bastards in Israel" is not desirable, he concludes that while proliferation of such children may not be a social desideratum, and hence there is no obligation to offer prayer on their behalf, nevertheless there is no legal distinction between a bastard and a legitimate embryo which would sanction any overt action which might threaten its life (*Ḥavot Ya'ir,* no. 31). An identical query addressed to R. Jacob Emden (*She'elat Ya'avez̧,* no. 43) elicited a different response. Taking note of the earlier responsum in *Ḥavot Ya'ir,* R. Jacob Emden finds grounds to differentiate between the seduction of an unmarried maiden and an adulterous relationship with a married woman.[82] The latter, having committed a capital offense, is liable to the death penalty. Were we able to execute judgment in capital cases, the pregnant condition of the condemned would not warrant a delay in administering punishment. This is clearly established by the Mishnah (*Erukhin* 7a) even with regard to cases in which pregnancy occurs after commission of the crime. Since, in this case, the child was conceived in sin, there is all the more reason for immediate execution of the mother. R. Jacob Emden adds the rather astonishing opinion that, although we no longer administer capital punishment, nevertheless, one who has committed a crime punishable by death may commit suicide without fear of sin. R. Jacob Emden even deems self-immolation to be meritorious in such circumstances. R. Jacob Emden reasons that if the mother may destroy herself completely she may certainly destroy a part of her body. Hence he concludes there can be no prohibition against the destruction of a bastard fetus since its life is legally forfeit. From an observation added in the course of his discussion, it appears that R. Jacob Emden intended his remarks to

---

82. Abortion of a pregnancy resulting from rape, even in the case of a married woman, would not be sanctioned by R. Emden according to this line of reasoning. R. Waldenberg, *Ẓiẓ Eli'ezer,* IX, 237, cities a responsum of *Rav Pe'alim,* I, *Even ha-Ezer,* no. 4, who argues that the psychological and sociological difficulties involved in the rearing of such a child constitute "great pain" and "grave need" which R. Emden recognizes as sufficient grounds for termination of a pregnancy.

apply only where formal warning of the nature of the transgression and its punishment was administered prior to the adulterous act, since capital punishment is not inflicted by the *Bet Din* in the absence of such warning.

Rabbi Unterman[83] voices an obvious objection against the above decision. The Mishnah in *Erukhin* which provides for the execution of a pregnant woman is understood by the commentaries as having reference to situations where pregnancy was not detected until the verdict was announced; when pregnancy was known beforehand, the trial was delayed until after confinement in order to spare the life of the child. The status of an adulterous woman in our times is always that of a woman prior to trial. Accordingly, there is no justification for the destruction of a fetus illicitly conceived.

Rabbi Ben-Zion Uziel, in his *Mishpetei Uziel, Ḥoshen Mishpat,* III, no. 46, advances an original line of reasoning in substantiation of R. Jacob Emden's decision regarding the abortion of a bastard fetus. The Gemara (*Sotah* 37b) declares: "The whole section refers to none other than an adulterer and an adulteress—'Cursed is the man who makes a graven or molten image (Deut. 27:15). Is it sufficient merely to pronounce such a person cursed? [His transgression is punishable not merely by a curse but by death.] Rather it refers to one who has engaged in immoral intercourse and begets a son who goes to live among the heathen and worships idols. Cursed be the father and mother of this person, for this is what they caused him to do." Rashi explains that since such a person is debarred from the assembly and cannot marry a Jewish woman of legitimate birth, his embarrassment causes him to mingle with heathens and his heathen associations lead him to idolatry. From this discussion one may deduce that while the act of adultery carries with it a statutory punishment irrespective of future developments, there is yet another "curse" incurred if the union leads to the birth of bastard progeny. Therefore, rules Rabbi Uziel, it is permissible to destroy the embryo in order not to incur this curse. It is of course self-understood that reference is only to cases of bastards falling under the "curse" and not to the progeny of an unmarried woman, for the Torah regards as a bastard only the issue of an adulterous or incestuous union. Rabbi Uziel further declares that only the parents themselves may abort the fetus. His reasoning is

83. *No'am,* VI, 3. He further cites the opinion of *Yeshu'ot Malko* to the effect that the Sabbath may be violated in order to save the life of a fetus even if the mother belongs to the class of those liable to death on whose behalf the Sabbath may not be violated. Cf. *Mishpetei Uziel, Ḥoshen Mishpat,* III, 57.

that only they incur the curse, hence only they may obviate the curse by destroying the fetus. An outsider who incurs no penalty does not experience the "grave need" deemed essential by R. Jacob Emden and has, therefore, no right to interfere with the development of the unborn child.

R. Moses Yekutiel Kaufman, author of *Leḥem ha-Panim* (Fürth, 5526), states unequivocally (*Kuntres Aḥaron,* no. 19, p. 58b) that it is forbidden to give a woman a drug for the purpose of aborting a bastard fetus.[84]

Abortion of an Abnormal Fetus

The status of abnormal and malformed human beings is well defined in Halakhah. Physical or mental abnormalities do not affect the human status of the individual. R. Yehudah ha-Chassid[85] refers to the question of terminating the life of a monsterlike child born with the teeth and tail of an animal. Indeed, the interlocutor raises the question only on basis of the fear aroused by reports that the creature would later "eat people." R. Eliezer Fleckeles of Prague[86] rules explicitly that the killing of even a grotesquely malformed child possessing animal features constitutes an act of murder. Challenging the questioner's view that the Talmud's suspension of the usual ritual impurity following the emission of similarly malformed or animal-like embryos indicates that upon birth a child so formed should not be classified as a human being. R. Fleckeles counters that this exclusion is limited to the laws of impurity applicable to miscarriages. The issue of a human mother, no matter how gravely deformed, enjoys human status and may not be destroyed either by overt act or by passively allowing it to die of starvation.

Rabbi Unterman,[87] in dealing with the question of abortion in cases where an expectant mother contracted German measles early in pregnancy, and Rabbi Moshe Yonah Zweig,[88] in discussing the deformities caused

84. Although termination of a pregnancy resulting from rape is not sanctioned by most authorities, postcoital contraception prior to fertilization of the ovum presents a different halakhic question. Immediate removal of the semen by means of a suction device operated by a female would be warranted according to some authorities, particularly if the rapist is a non-Jew. Cf. R. Eliezer Chaim Deutsch, *Pri ha-Sadeh,* IV, no. 50; and R. Yeruchem Yehudah Perilman (known as the *Minsker Gadol*), *Or Gadol,* no. 31.

85. *Sefer Ḥassidim* (Jerusalem, 5720), no. 186.

86. *Teshuvah me-Ahavah* (Prague, 5669), I, no. 53. Halakhic literature on this topic was reviewed by R. Immanuel Jakobovits, *Tradition,* V (Spring 1963), 268 ff., and *Tradition,* VI (Spring–Summer 1964), 114 ff.

87. *No'am,* VI, 1–11.

88. *Ibid.,* VII, 36–56.

by thalidomide, both conclude that there is no distinction in the eyes of the law between normal and abnormal persons either with regard to the statutes governing homicide or with regard to those governing feticide. Rabbi Waldenberg (*Ẓiẓ Eli'ezer,* IX, 237) is the only authority who deems abnormality of the fetus to be justification for interruption of pregnancy and even he stipulates that the abortion must be performed in the early stages of pregnancy. Rabbi Waldenberg indicates that the difficulties engendered by the birth of an abnormal child may render abortion a "grave necessity" and therefore permissible according to the previously cited view of R. Jacob Emden. Rabbi Waldenberg permits such termination of pregnancy within the first three months following conception provided there is as yet no fetal movement.[89]

Abortions Under Noachide Law

Jewish law recognizes two distinct, divinely revealed codes of law. One of these codes is binding upon Jews as a result of the Sinaitic covenant; the second code, which is more limited in scope, encompassing the basic principles of moral behavior, is known as the Seven Commandments of the Sons of Noah. This latter code is viewed by Judaism as binding upon all non-Jews.

Noachides are specifically enjoined from destroying fetal life upon penalty of death (*Sanhedrin* 57b) on the basis of Genesis 9:6. This prohibition is recorded by Maimonides in his *Mishneh Torah, Hilkhot Melakhim* 9:4. Consequently, any aid extended to a gentile in the performance of an abortion is a violation of the precept "Thou shalt not place a stumbling block before the blind" (Lev. 19:14). This prohibition is clearly enunciated with regard to abortion of a fetus by R. Joseph Trani (*Teshuvot Maharit,* I, no. 97) and confirmed by his pupil, Rabbi Chaim Benevisti (*Sheyarei Kenesset ha-Gedolah, Tur, Ḥoshen Mishpat,* 425, no. 6). Maharit, however, notes that the Gemara (*Avodah Zarah* 6b) states that aid rendered to one transgressing a commandment is proscribed only if the sinner could not otherwise have fulfilled his desire. It is, for example, forbidden to bring a cup of wine to a Nazarite who is on the opposite side of the river and could not otherwise reach the wine; but if both the wine and the Nazarite are on the same side of the river and the Nazarite is capable of reaching the wine without assistance, any help extended does not fall under this prohibition. Such an act, while biblically permitted, is banned by rabbinic edict legislating against "aiding transgres-

89. See above, notes 41 and 42; cf. "Tay-Sachs Reexamined," above, pp. 112–115.

sors." Maharit denies the applicability of the edict to aid rendered non-Jewish transgressors. Accordingly, Maharit rules that assistance in the performance of an abortion under these circumstances is forbidden only if no other physician is available; if others are available it is to be considered analagous to the case of both the Nazarite and the wine standing "on the same side of the river." There are nevertheless many authorities who agree that the rabbinic prohibition against "aiding transgressors" which applies even when both are "on the same side of the river" extends to aiding Noachide transgressors as well.[90] Furthermore, the author of *Mishneh le-Melekh* (*Hilkhot Malveh ve-Loveh* 4:2) argues that the availability and readiness of another individual to transport the wine over the river does not relieve the one who actually does so from culpability. The prohibition is deemed inoperative only if the transgression could be committed without "the placing of a stumbling block" by anyone else; when the transgression requires aid, the one who renders it is liable, according to this view, no matter how many others would have been willing to render similar aid.[91]

But may a Noachide destroy the life of an embryo in order to preserve the life of the mother? *Tosafot* (*Sanhedrin* 59a) poses the question but expresses doubt with regard to its resolution. The question seems to hinge upon the nature of the Noachide prohibition:[92] If, in extending the death penalty to the killing of a fetus under the Noachide Code, the Torah intends to indicate that with regard to Noachides fetal life is to be considered on a par with other human life, then, of course, the mother's life

---

90. Cf. *Sedei Ḥemed,* II, 298.

91. Cf. *Sedei Ḥemed,* II, 303–304.

92. See below, n. 96. *Koaḥ Shor* explains the *safek* of *Tosafot* in yet another manner. Since a Noachide is not commanded to "sanctify the Name," he may commit idolatry for the sake of preserving his life. R. Schorr argues that this dispensation extends to murder as well and infers that it is the extension of this provision to encompass murder which was the subject of *Tosafot*'s "doubt." However, *Mishneh le-Melekh, Hilkhot Melakhim* 10:2, states explicitly that the taking of another's life in order to save one's own is forbidden even to Noachides, since with regard to homicide this injunction is not derived from the commandment to "sanctify the Name" but upon the *a priori* principle "Why is your blood sweeter than that of your fellow?" The author's grandson raises this point in a note (p. 35a) appended to this responsum of *Koaḥ Shor* but fails to cite *Mishneh le-Melekh.* See, however, *Pitḥei Teshuvah, Yoreh De'ah,* 155:4, who discusses the question of whether or not the principle "and you shall live by them" applies to Noachides. See also *Perashat Drakhim, Drush* 2.

cannot be saved by a Noachide at the expense of the fetus. The law of pursuit cannot be invoked if the fetus is deemed "a life" under the Noachide dispensation, just as the law of pursuit does not apply in Jewish law after the commencement of birth, at which juncture the fetus is deemed "a life" according to the Sinaitic covenant.[93] On the other hand, the Torah may not deem the fetus to be "a life" even with regard to Noachides, but bans feticide under the Noachide code as a transgression totally unrelated to the concept of taking human life. If the Noachide prohibition is extraneous to the exhortation against homicide, it follows that the life of the mother would take precedence over that of the fetus. A virtually identical discussion establishing the prohibition against destruction of the fetus is presented by *Tosafot, Ḥullin* 33a, but without any suggestion whatsoever of the possibility that destruction of the fetus by a Noachide would be permissible under these circumstances. R. Isaac Schorr (*Koaḥ Shor,* no. 20, p. 32) concludes that since, at best, the matter remains in doubt the life of the fetus must remain inviolate.[94] He further advances a rather involved argument demonstrating that, regardless of the position adopted by *Tosafot,* there is no question that Maimonides forbids the destruction of a fetus by Noachides, even when the life of the mother is at stake. *Minḥat Ḥinukh*[95] advances yet another reason which precludes destruction of the fetus by a Noachide even if necessary in order to save the mother. According to this opinion, a Noachide may not transgress any provision of the Noachide Code in order to preserve a human life.[96]

---

93. Furthermore, since the law of pursuit must be invoked if the fetus is deemed to be "a life," performance of an abortion by a Noachide would be precluded by those authorities who maintain that the law of pursuit is not operative in the Noachide Code. Cf. *Teshuvot Ben Yehudah,* no. 21; and *Sedei Ḥemed,* II, 14, no. 44. However, *Minḥat Ḥinukh,* no. 296, and *Koaḥ Shor,* p. 32b, argue that the law of pursuit extends to Noachides, as well as indeed seems to be indicated by the language of Rambam, *Hilkhot Melakhim* 9:4,

94. See R. Aryeh Leib Grossnass, *Ha-Pardes, Shevat* 5732, and *Lev Aryeh,* II, no. 32, who suggests that the "doubt" expressed by *Tosafot* is limited to the destruction of the fetus of a Jewish mother in order to save her life, but does not extend to the abortion of a non-Jewish fetus.

95. *Minḥat Ḥinukh,* no. 296.

96. The Gemara, *Sanhedrin* 74b, states that a Noachide may commit any transgression in private, including idolatry, in order to preserve his own life. The Gemara also discusses the question of whether or not he is permitted to do so in public, since he is not explicitly commanded to "sanctify the Name." There is no explicit reference in the Gemara with regard to violations in order to preserve the life of another. *Koaḥ Shor,* p. 33a, adopts a view diametrically

Nevertheless, R. Isaac Schorr finds a basis upon which a non-Jewish physician might be requested to terminate the pregnancy of a Jewish woman. Requesting such aid should normally be discountenanced as a violation of "Thou shall not place a stumbling block before the blind." However, this commandment is no different from other negative prohibitions (excepting the three cardinal sins) which may be ignored when life is at stake. Since R. Moses Isserles (*Yoreh De'ah* 157:1) rules that this ban may be violated even if the "stumbling block" is the commission of one of the three cardinal sins, there is no barrier to requesting the non-Jewish physician to undertake such a procedure, if he is willing to do so, provided no Jewish physician is available. If a Jewish physician is available, his aid should be sought in order to obviate the necessity of "placing a stumbling block."[97]

A Final Caveat

In light of what may at times appear to be a harsh and forbidding stance, one might be tempted to conclude that Jewish law manifests an indifferent attitude toward the individual and his plight. It is important that we recognize that, quite to the contrary, Halakhah is motivated first and foremost by concern and solicitude for all living creatures. It is this extreme concern for man's inalienable right to life, both actual and potential, which permeates these many halakhic determinations.

A Jew is governed by such reverence for life that he trembles lest he tamper unmindfully with the greatest of all divine gifts, the bestowal or withholding of which is the prerogative of God alone. Although he be master over all within the world, there remain areas where man must fear to tread, acknowledging the limits of his sovereignty and the limitations of his understanding. In the unborn child lies the mystery and enigma of existence. Confronted by the miracle of life itself, man can only draw back in silence before the wonder of the Lord:

---

opposed to that of *Minḥat Ḥinukh* and asserts that a Noachide may transgress any commandment, including the three cardinal sins, in order to save the life of his fellow.

97. When it is necessary to employ a non-Jew for this purpose, *Teshuvot Maharash,* V, no. 89, counsels that it is preferable to transmit the request to the non-Jewish physician through another gentile. This determination is based upon *Avodah Zarah* 14a, which rules that one need not avoid making accessible a "stumbling block" to one who in turn will place it before the blind. This indirect procedure thus circumvents the transgression of "placing a stumbling block."

> Where wast thou when I laid the foundations of the earth?
> Declare, if thou hast the understanding . . .
> Have the gates of death been revealed unto thee?
> Or hast thou seen the gates of the shadow of death? . . .
> Declare, if thou knowest it all.[98]

Indeed,

> As thou knowest not what is the way of the wind,
> Nor how the bones do grow in the womb of her that is with child;
> Even so thou knowest not the work of God
> Who doeth all things.[99]

98. Job 38:4–5, 17–18.
99. Eccles. 11:5.

CHAPTER XVI

Establishing Criteria of Death

I acknowledge before You, my God and the God of my fathers . . . that my cure is in Your hand and my death is in Your hand. . . . And if my appointed time to die has arrived You are righteous in all that befalls me.

CONFESSION OF THE DYING

A man of serious conscience means to say in raising urgent ethical questions that there may be some things that men should never do that, now or in the future, they could do. The good things that men do are made complete only by the things they refuse to do. It would perhaps be better not to raise the ethical issues of medical practice in an age when public policy and research requirements threaten to be overriding than not to raise them in earnest. (Paul Ramsey, *New England Journal of Medicine,* April 1, 1971)

The task of defining death is not a trivial exercise to be relegated to the purview of the lexicographer. It is perhaps the most pressing concern in a newly developing field of inquiry which has come to be known as bioethics. The formulation of such a definition involves an attempt to arrive at an understanding of the very essence of human life and an endeavor to identify the nature of the ephemeral substance which is lost at the time of death.

The loss of that elusive component which transforms the human organism into a living being effects a change in the moral and legal status of the individual. The traditional view is that death occurs upon the separation of the soul from the body. Of course, the occurrence of this phenomenon does not lend itself to direct empirical observation. Accordingly, traditional definitions of death have focused upon cessation of circulatory and respiratory functions as criteria of the ebbing of life. *Black's Law Dictionary* (4th ed., 1951), in recording the accepted legal definition, describes death as ". . . total stoppage of the circulation of the blood and a cessation of the animal and vital functions consequent thereupon, such as respiration, pulsation, etc."

Contemporary medical science has developed highly sophisticated techniques for determining the presence or absence of vital bodily functions. Moreover, improvements in resuscitatory and supportive measures now at times make it possible to restore life as judged by the traditional standards of persistent respiration and continuing heart beat. This can be the case even when there is little likelihood of an individual recovering consciousness following massive brain damage. These new medical realia have led to a reassessment of traditional definitions of death. Some members of the scientific community now advocate that previously accepted criteria of death be set aside and have formulated several proposals for a redefinition of the phenomenon of death.

Chief among these is the now popular concept frequently, though inaccurately, referred to as brain death. According to this view, death is equated with the complete loss of the body's integrating capacities as signified by the activity of the central nervous system and is determined by the absence of brain waves as recorded by an electroencephalogram over a period of time. It is most interesting to note that reports have appeared, both in the popular press and in scholarly publications, of a significant number of instances in which patients have made either partial or complete recoveries despite previous electroencephalogram readings over an extended period of time which registered no brain activity.[1]

1. *Jerusalem Post,* November 14, 1968; *Hirntod* (Stuttgart, 1969), pp. 63, 66, 98, and 106. See Jacob Levy, "Mavet Moḥi," *Ha-Ma'ayan,* Nisan 5732, p. 25; J. B. Brierly, J. H. Adams, D. I. Graham, *et al.,* "Neocortical Death after Cardiac Arrest," *Lancet* 2:560–65, 1971; Hadassah Gillon, "Defining Death Anew," *Science News* 95 (January 11, 1969), p. 50; Harold L. Hirsch, *Case and Comment,* September–October 1974; *Rochester Democrat and Chronicle,* March 19, 1975, p. 19. Cf. also Henry K. Beecher, "Definitions of 'Life' and 'Death' for Medical Science and Practice," *Annals of the New York Academy of Sciences,* vol. 169, art. 2 (January 21, 1971), pp. 471–472; E. Bental and U. Leibowitz, "Flat Electroencephalograms During 28 Days in Case of 'Encephalitis,'" *Electroenceph. Clin. Neurophysiology,* XIII (1961), 457–460; R. G. Bickford, B. Dawson and H. Takeshita, "EEG Evidence of Neurologic

Several years ago the Ad Hoc Committee of the Harvard Medical School to Examine the Definition of Brain Death was established. The published report of this committee[2] states that its primary purpose was to "define irreversible coma as a new criterion of death." In order to arrive at a clinical definition of irreversible coma, the Ad Hoc Committee recommends establishment of operational criteria for the determination of the characteristics of a permanently nonfunctioning brain. The three recommended criteria are: (1) lack of response to external stimuli or to internal need; (2) absence of movement or breathing as observed by physicians over a period of at least one hour; (3) absence of elicitable reflexes ("except in some cases through the spinal cord").[3] A fourth criterion, a flat, or isoelectric, electroencephalogram, is recommended as being "of great confirmatory value" but not of absolute necessity. Subsequently, Dr. Henry K. Beecher, the chairman of the Ad Hoc Committee, noted, "Almost everybody else has required the use of the electroencephalogram. We think it adds helpful confirmatory evidence, but we do not think that it is necessary by itself."[4] The procedure advocated by the Ad Hoc Committee calls for repetition of the relevant tests following a lapse of twenty-four hours. Repeated examinations over a period of twenty-four hours or longer are required in order to obtain evidence of the irreversible nature of the coma.

Most revealing is the quite candid statement of the committee chairman: "Only a very bold man, I think, would attempt to define death. . . . I was chairman of a recent *ad hoc* committee at Harvard composed of members of five faculties in the university who tried to define irreversible coma.

Death," *Electroenceph. Clin. Neurophysiology,* XVIII (1965), 513–514; T. D. Bird and F. Plum, "Recovery from Barbiturate Overdose Coma with Prolonged Isoelectric Electroencephalogram," *Neurology,* XVIII (1968), 456–460; R. L. Tentler *et al.,* "Electroencephalographic Evidence of Cortical 'Death' Followed by Full Recovery: Protective Action of Hypothermia," *Journal of the American Medical Association,* CLXIV (1957), 1667-1670; P. Braunstein, J. Korein *et al.,* "A Simple Bedside Evaluation of Cerebral Blood Flow in the Study of Cerebral Death," *The American Journal of Roentgenology Radium Therapy and Nuclear Medecine,* CXVIII (1973), 758; and P. Braunstein, I. Kricheff, *et al.,* "Cerebral Death: A Rapid and Reliable Diagnostic Adjunct Using Radiosotopes," *Journal of Nuclear Medecine,* XIV (1973), 122.

2. "A Definition of Irreversible Coma," *Journal of the American Medical Association,* vol. 205, no. 6 (August 5, 1968), pp. 337–40.

3. This modification appears in Beecher, *Annals,* p. 471.

4. *Loc. cit.*

We felt we could not define death. I suppose you will say that by implication we have defined it as brain death, but we do not make a point of that." [5]

More recently, the adequacy of even this notion of brain death has been challenged in some quarters. Proponents of a broader definition ask, "Why is it that one must identify the entire brain with death; is it not possible that we are really interested only in man's consciousness: in his ability to think, reason, feel, interact with others and control his body functions consciously?" [6] According to this latter view, death is to be equated with irreversible loss of consciousness. If this definition were to gain acceptance, the effect would be that in cases where the lower brain function is intact while the cortex, which controls consciousness, is destroyed, the patient would be pronounced dead.

Much of the debate concerning the definition of death misses the mark. A definition of death cannot be derived from medical facts or scientific investigation alone. The physician can only describe the physiological state which he observes; whether the patient meeting that description is alive or dead, whether the human organism in that physiological state is to be treated as a living person or as a corpse, is an ethical and legal question. The determination of the time of death, insofar as it is more than a mere exercise in semantics, is essentially a theological and moral problem, not a medical or scientific one.

For Jews, questions of this nature can be answered only within the framework of Halakhah. The great strides made in the life sciences in the past number of years have reopened a host of medico-halakhic problems. With the invention and refinement of life-saving apparatus, the life of a terminally ill patient may, in some instances, be prolonged for a significant period of time. As a result, a precise definition of death becomes of crucial importance because only the presence of the criteria of death which are recognized by Halakhah relieves the physician of his obligation to use all available means in order to preserve the life of the patient. The most breathtaking of recent scientific breakthroughs is no doubt the development of the techniques for successful heart transplantation. While discouraging results have resulted in virtual suspension of such transplants, there is reason to anticipate that with further research

5. *Loc. cit.*

6. Robert M. Veatch, "Brain Death: Welcome Definition or Dangerous Judgment?" *Hastings Center Report,* II, no. 5 (November 1972), p. 11.

the difficulties which have been encountered will be overcome. From the perspective of Jewish law, there are a number of halakhic and ethical questions which must be analyzed before a definite position can be formulated regarding the permissibility of this or similar procedures. Chief among these problems is the halakhic definition of death, since for medical reasons the donor's heart must be removed without delay if the operative procedure is to be successful.

The surgeon is faced with a dilemma. In order to save the life of his patient, he must remove the donor's heart at the earliest possible moment consistent with the latter's claim to life. When may he proceed? Certainly, all to whom human life is sacred would answer: the instant death occurs. But this answer merely begs the crucial question: when *does* death occur? The sanctity of human life is a cardinal principle of Judaism. It is self-evident that every measure must be taken to preserve the life of every human being. By the same token, the slightest action which might hasten the death of another is proscribed. Hence the extreme importance of determining with exactitude the halakhic definition of death.

In view of the far-ranging significance of this problem, a detailed analysis of the sources from which such a definition must be derived is in order. Moreover, as will be shown, there exists a crucial conceptual difficulty which requires careful analysis; namely, do the hallmarks of death as given by Jewish law constitute a definition of death *per se,* i.e., is the physiological state described by such signs synonymous with death in the eyes of Halakhah, or are such signs merely symptomatic of death, the state of death itself, from the point of view of Halakhah, being beyond analytic definition in empirical terms? This problem requires careful elucidation and examination since it is a question which is not explicitly formulated in responsa literature.

I

It is axiomatic, according to Halakhah, that death coincides with cessation of respiration. The primary source of this definition is to be found in *Yoma* 85a in connection with suspension of Sabbath regulations for the sake of the preservation of human life. The case in point concerns an individual trapped under a fallen building. Since desecration of the Sabbath is mandated even on the mere chance that a human life may be preserved, the debris of a collapsed building must be cleared away even if it is doubtful that the person under the rubble is still alive. However, once it has been determined with certainty that the person has expired, no further violation of the Sabbath regulations may be sanctioned. The question which then arises is how much of the body must be uncovered in order to ascertain conclusively that death has in fact occurred? The first opinion cited by the Gemara maintains that the nose must be uncovered and the victim of the accident be pronounced dead only if no sign of respiration is found. A second opinion maintains that death may be determined by examination of the chest for the absence of a heartbeat. It is evident that both opinions regard respiration as the crucial factor indicating the existence of life; the second opinion simply adds that the absence of a heartbeat is also to be deemed sufficient evidence that respiration has ceased and that death has actually occurred. This is evident from the statement quoted by the Gemara in the name of R. Papa in clarification of this controversy. R. Papa states that there is no disagreement in instances in which the body is uncovered "from the top down." In such cases the absence of respiration is regarded by all as being conclusive. The dispute, declares R. Papa, is limited to situations in which the body is uncovered "from the bottom up" and thus the heart is uncovered first. The controversy in such cases is whether the absence of a heartbeat is sufficient evidence to establish death in and of itself, or whether further evidence is required, i.e., uncovering of the nostrils. The necessity for examination of the nostrils is based upon the assumption that it is possible for life to exist even though such life may be undetectable by means of an examination for the presence of a heartbeat—as Rashi succinctly puts it, "For at times life is not evident at the heart but is evident at the nose."[7] In demonstration of the principle that respiration is the determining factor, the Gemara cites the verse ". . . all in whose nostrils is the breath of the spirit of life" (Gen. 7:22). Both Maimonides[8] and *Shulḥan Arukh*[9] cite the first opinion as authoritative. Hence in terms of normative Halakhah, regardless of whether the head or the feet are uncovered first, death can be established only by examination of the nos-

---

7. There is no opinion recorded in the Babylonian Talmud—majority or minority—which *requires* examination of the heart. See, however, Palestinian Talmud, *Yoma* 8:5, where the correct textual reading is the subject of dispute. According to the version of *Korban ha-Edah,* one *Amora* requires examination of the heart. *Pnei Mosheh,* in accepting a variant reading, rejects this contention.

8. *Mishneh Torah, Hilkhot Shabbat* 2:19.

9. *Oraḥ Ḥayyim* 329:4.

trils and determination of the absence of signs of respiratory activity at that site.

However, even according to the accepted view, namely, that determination of death is contingent upon lack of respiration, absence of cardiac activity is a relevant factor. Cessation of respiration constitutes the operative definition of death only because lack of respiration is also indicative of prior cessation of cardiac activity. This may be inferred from Rashi's choice of language. The phrase, "At times life is not evident at the heart but is evident at the nose," would indicate that, hypothetically, if confronted by a situation in which "life" is not evident at the nose for whatever reason, but *is* evident at the heart, cardiac activity would itself be sufficient to negate any other presumptive symptom of death.[10] This view is clearly expressed by R. Zevi Ashkenazi, *Teshuvot Ḥakham Ẓvi,* no. 77. *Ḥakham Ẓvi* notes that in some cases a heartbeat may be imperceptible even though the individual is still alive. A weak beat may not be audible or otherwise perceivable since the ribcage and layers of muscle intervene between the heart itself and the outer skin. Respiration is more readily detectable and hence the insistence upon an examination of the nostrils. However, concludes *Ḥakham Ẓvi,* "It is most clear that there can be no respiration unless there is life in the heart, for respiration is from the heart and for its benefit." Similarly, R. Moses Sofer, *Teshuvot Ḥatam Sofer, Yoreh De'ah,* no. 338, states that absence of respiration is conclusive only if the patient "lies as an inanimate stone and there is no pulse whatsoever." [11]

These sources indicate clearly that death occurs only upon the cessation

---

10. See R. Eliezer Waldenberg, *Ẓiẓ Eli'ezer,* X, no. 25, chap. 4, sec. 7. Cf. also *Ẓiẓ Eli'ezer,* IX, no. 46, sec. 5, who cites medieval writers on physiology—among them *Sha'ar ha-Shamayim,* a work which is attributed to the father of Gersonides—who declare that life is dependent upon nasal respiration because warm air from the heart is expelled through the nose and cold air, which cools the heart, enters through the nose. It was thus clearly recognized that respiration without cardiac activity is an impossibility.

11. However, according to the previously cited reading and interpretation of *Korban ha-Edah,* there is one opinion in the Palestinian Talmud which requires examination for presence of a heartbeat to the exclusion of examination for respiration. The most plausible explanation of this ruling is that it is based upon the empirical belief that the presence of a heartbeat is more readily detectable than respiration and hence absence of a heartbeat is deemed to be a more reliable clinical symptom of respiratory stoppage than absence of perceived respiration.

of both cardiac and respiratory functions. The absence of other vital signs is not, insofar as Halakhah is concerned, a criterion of death.

II

Although, in theory, the cessation of respiration is the determining criterion in establishing that death has occurred, in practice this principle is considerably modified so that the absence of respiratory activity in itself is not sufficient to establish that death has occurred. Halakhah provides that the Sabbath may be violated in order to save the life of an unborn fetus. Therefore *Shulḥan Arukh*[12] states that if a woman dies in childbirth on the Sabbath a knife may be brought through a public domain in order to make an incision into the uterus for the purpose of removing the fetus. However, R. Moses Isserles, commonly known as Rema, in a gloss to this ruling, indicates that this provision, while theoretically valid, is nevertheless inoperative in practice. Rema declares that, quite apart from the question of desecration of the Sabbath, it is forbidden to perform a post-mortem Caesarean in order to save the fetus, on weekdays as well as on the Sabbath, because we are not competent to determine the moment of maternal death with exactitude.

Since it is forbidden to as much as move a limb of a moribund person lest this hasten his death,[13] there can be no question of an incision into the womb until death has been established with absolute certainty. In view of the fact that by the time the death of the mother can be conclusively determined the fetus is no longer viable, this procedure would be purposeless and consequently would constitute an unwarranted violation of the corpse.

The principle enunciated by Rema[14] is that what may appear to be cessation of respiratory activity cannot be accepted as an absolute criterion of death. Our lack of competence is due to an inability to distinguish between death and a fainting spell or swoon. In the latter cases respiratory activity does occur, although respiration may be so minimal that it cannot be perceived.

---

12. *Oraḥ Ḥayyim* 330:5.
13. *Yoreh De'ah* 339:1.
14. *Koret ha-Brit,* no. 330, sec. 15, infers from the phraseology adopted by Rema that the latter does not at all disagree with the *Shulḥan Arukh* but simply endeavors to provide the rationale underlying the prevalent custom. See *Ẓiẓ Eli'ezer,* X, no. 25, chap. 4, sec. 4.

In stating that we are incompetent to determine the moment of death with precision and cannot apply the criterion of respiration with reliability, Rema does not spell out clinical signs which may be accepted as conclusive. Nor does he indicate how much time must elapse following apparent cessation of respiration before the patient may be pronounced dead. There is some discrepancy in the writings of later authors with regard to establishing such a time-period. A contemporary authority, Rabbi Yechiel Michal Tucatzinsky, *Gesher ha-Ḥayyim,* I chap. 3, p. 48, records that the practice in Jerusalem is not to remove the body from the deathbed for a period of twenty minutes following the presumed time of death. Earlier, Rabbi Shalom Gagin, *Teshuvot Yismaḥ Lev, Yoreh De'ah,* no. 9, stated that the custom in Jerusalem is to wait a period of one half-hour. Rabbi Gagin further noted that our incompetence to determine time of death with precision should not necessitate a delay of "more than half an hour or at the most an hour" for final pronouncement of death.[15]

Writing in the Tammuz 5731 issue of *Ha-Ma'ayan,* Dr. Jacob Levy, an Israeli physician and frequent contributor to halakhic journals, argues that, in light of the clinical aids now available to the physician, the considerations which previously necessitated this waiting period are no longer operative. Rema's declaration that the ruling of the *Shulḥan Arukh* is not followed in practice is based upon the fear that a fainting spell or swoon may be misdiagnosed as death. Dr. Levy points out that in many cases the possibility of such errors can be eliminated by use of a sphygmomanometer to determine that no blood pressure can be detected, in conjunction with an electrocardiagram to ascertain that all cardiac activity has ceased. Accordingly, Dr. Levy strongly recommends that rabbinic authorities declare that the original ruling of the *Shulḥan Arukh* now be followed in practice.

Dr. Levy adds that this proposal should not be construed as an abrogation of Rema's ruling, since many authorities recognize that Rema's

15. A waiting period of "at least one full hour" before moving the deceased is also cited by Hyman Goldin, *Ha-Madrikh,* p. 111, in the name of *Derekh ha-Ḥayyim.* Although there are several works bearing this title which discuss laws of mourning and related topics, none of them appears to contain a source for this citation.

It is interesting to note that the previously cited report of the Ad Hoc Committee of the Harvard Medical School requires "observations covering a period of at least one hour by physicians" to satisfy the criteria of no spontaneous muscular movements or spontaneous respiration as one of the characteristics of irreversible coma.

statement is based upon empirical considerations and admits to exceptions. For example, R. Ya'akov Reischer, *Shevut Ya'akov,* I, no. 13, in discussing the bizarre case of a pregnant woman who was decapitated on the Sabbath, states unequivocally that the physician who had the presence of mind to incise the abdomen immediately in order to remove the fetus need have no pangs of conscience, since in this instance the mother's prior death is established beyond cavil.[15a] Similarly, concludes Dr. Levy, Rema's statement should not be viewed as normative under changed circumstances which enable medical science to determine that death has already occurred. This argument is cogent in view of the fact that Rema himself remarks that it had become necessary to disregard the earlier authoritative decision of the *Shulḥan Arukh* solely because of a lack of medical expertise.[15b]

Granted that with the use of clinical aids one can establish conclusively that all cardiac activity has ceased, Dr. Levy's contention that no further waiting period is needed is borne out by *Ḥakham Ẓvi*'s previously cited statement, "There can be no respiration unless there is life in the heart."

Ḥakham Ẓvi's original ruling elicited the sharp disagreement of R. Yonatan Eibeschutz and sparked a controversy which has become classic in the annals of Halakhah. The dispute centered around a chicken which, upon evisceration, proved to have no discernible heart. The chicken was brought to *Ḥakham Ẓvi* for a determination as to whether the fowl was to be considered *tereifah* because of the missing heart. *Ḥakham Ẓvi* ruled that it is empirically impossible for a chicken to lack a heart because there can be no life whatsoever without a heart. The chicken clearly lived and matured; hence it must have had a heart which somehow became separated from the other internal organs upon the opening of the chicken and was inadvertently lost. The impossibility of life without a heart, in the opinion of *Ḥakham Ẓvi,* is so obvious a verity that he declares that even the testimony of witnesses attesting to the absence of the heart and the impossibility of error is to be dismissed as blatant perjury. R. Yonatan Eibeschutz, in a scathing dissenting opinion, argues that such a possibility cannot be dismissed out of hand. In his commentary to *Yoreh De'ah,*

15a. See also R. Ephraim Oshry, *She'elot u-Teshuvot mi-Ma'amakim,* II, no. 10.

15b. Also, the phraseology used by Rema is different from that which is usually employed by Rema in disagreeing with a ruling of *Shulḥan Arukh.* See numerous sources cited by R. Shlomoh Schneider, *Ha-Ma'or,* Kislev-Tevet 5735.

Kereti u-Pleti 40:4, R. Yonatan Eibeschutz contends that the functions of the heart, including the pumping of blood, might well be performed by an organ whose external form is quite unlike that of a normal heart and which may even be located in some other part of the body. This organ might be indistinguishable from other, more usual tissue, and hence the observer might have concluded that the animal or fowl lacked a "heart."

There is nothing in this opinion which contradicts the point made on the basis of *Ḥakham Ẓvi's* responsum with regard to determination of the time of death. R. Yonatan Eibeschutz concedes that life cannot be sustained in the absence of some organ to perform cardiac functions. R. Yonatan Eibeschutz argues only that, in the apparent absence of a recognizable heart, cardiac functions may possibly be performed by some other organ; he does not at all assert that life may continue following cessation of the functions normally performed by the heart.

However, at least one authority indicates that life can continue, at least theoretically, after the heart has been removed. Specifically rejecting the opinion of authorities who have concluded that "it is impossible to exist even for a moment" without a functioning heart, *Mishkanot Ya'akov, Yoreh De'ah,* no. 10, declares that such a contingency is a distinct possibility. According to this opinion it may perhaps be the case that a waiting period of some duration, as demanded by Rema, cannot be waived even when heart stoppage is confirmed by clinical apparatus, since cessation of cardiac activity does not, in and of itself, indicate that death has occurred. Acceptance of Dr. Levy's thesis would quite probably involve rejection of the opinion of *Mishkanot Ya'akov* in favor of the view expressed by *Ḥakham Ẓvi.*

III

There is, as previously noted, one fundamental problem with regard to a clear analysis of the halakhic position which views time of death as being simultaneous with cessation of respiration. Is cessation of respiration to be equated with death itself, or is it merely a physiological symptom enabling us to ascertain the time of death? Couched in different terminology, are respiration and life itself one and the same, so that the absence of respiratory activity, by definition, constitutes the state of death? Or is life some ephemeral and indefinable state or activity which cannot be empirically perceived but of which absence of respiration is a reliable indication?

There is some *prima facie* evidence indicating that lack of respiration and the state of death are, by definition, synonymous. The Sages inform us that the soul departs through the nostrils, thereby causing respiration to cease and death to occur. The *Yalkut Shim'oni, Lekh Lekha,* no. 77, observes that after sneezing one should give thanks for having been privileged to remain alive.[16] The *Yalkut,* noting that the first mention of sickness in Scripture occurs in Genesis 48:1, remarks that prior to the time of Jacob sickness was unknown. It is the view of the Sages that illness became part of man's destiny in answer to Jacob's plea for prior indication of impending death in order that he might make a testament before dying. Before the days of Jacob, according to the *Yalkut,* an individual simply sneezed and expired without any indication whatsoever that death was about to overtake him. The *Yalkut* can readily be understood on the basis of the verse ". . . and He blew into his nostrils the soul of life" (Gen. 2:6). In the narrative concerning the creation of Adam, the soul is described as having entered through the nostrils. According to the *Yalkut,* the soul departs through the same aperture through which it entered; hence terminal sneezing is associated with the soul's departure from the body. Apparently, then, respiration and life both cease with the departure of the soul.

Likewise, we find that the nose is deemed to be the site of the soul's departure from the body with regard to the provisions surrounding the *eglah arufah* (the broken-necked heifer). Biblical law (Deut. 21:1–9) provides that if homicide is committed outside a city and the identity of the murderer is unknown it becomes incumbent upon the elders of the city closest to the site where the corpse is found to perform the ritual of breaking the neck of a calf in expiation of the untraced murder. In the event that the body be found in a spot virtually equidistant between two cities, the Mishnah, *Sotah* 45b, cites the opinion of R. Akiva who states that the distance to the neighboring cities is to be measured from the nose in order to determine which is closest. In explaining R. Akiva's opinion, which in this case is authoritative, the Gemara states that his view is predicated upon the premise that "primary life—*ikar ḥiyuta*—is in the nose." This would seem to indicate that death and cessation of respiration are synonymous.

---

16. Cf. R. Baruch ha-Levi Epstein, *Torah Temimah,* Gen. 7:22.

There is, however, evidence from the Talmud itself that at least in rare instances individuals have lived despite previous cessation of respiration. *Semaḥot,* chap. 8, records that in times when burial was made in cavernous crypts, it was customary to visit the crypt during the first three days following interment in order to examine the burial site for signs of life.[17] It is recorded that on one occasion a person so buried was later found to be alive. Moreover he is reported to have sired a number of children before his ultimate death some twenty-five years later.[18]

In any event, if life may at times continue after respiration has ceased, it would then appear that absence of respiration is at best a sign that death may be presumed to have occurred but is not, in itself, one and the same as death. This is indeed the conclusion drawn by R. Shalom Mordecai Schwadron, the author of *Teshuvot Maharsham.* In vol. VI, no. 124 of his responsa, this authority states that the dictum "primary life is in the nose" indicates that in ordinary situations, where there is no evidence to the contrary, one may rely upon examination of the nostrils, since in virtually all instances life has completely ebbed prior to cessation of respiration. Instances where this is not the case are so extremely rare that such contingencies need not be considered. Yet, maintains Maharsham, if any sign of life is observed in other limbs, examination of the nose may not be accepted as conclusive. In the case presented for his consideration, he indicates that a noise apparently emanating from the body after breathing had ceased would necessitate further delay in order to determine with certainty that death had indeed occurred.

Maimonides, *Guide for the Perplexed,* Book 1, chap 42, describes the occurrence of such a phenomenon in support of his contention that the term *mavet* is a homonym and that in biblical usage this term in certain

---

17. It should be noted that both *Ḥatam Sofer* and Rabbi Gagin in his previously cited responsum, *Yismaḥ Lev, Yoreh De'ah,* no. 9, state that this procedure was by no means obligatory; the practice was merely sanctioned as not constituting *darkei ha-Emori,* a forbidden pagan practice.

18. Indeed, Moses Mendelssohn sought to use this source as a basis for permitting delayed burial in contravention of the halakhic requirement of immediate burial. Mendelssohn contended that such delay is necessary in order to ascertain that death has actually occurred. See *Ha-Me'assef* (1785), pp. 152–55, 169–74, and 178–87. This material was reprinted in *Bikkurei ha-Ittim* (1824), p. 219–24 and 229–38. Mendelssohn's advocacy of delayed burial and the ensuing controversy are discussed in detail by Alexander Altmann, *Moses Mendelssohn: A Biographical Study* (University, Ala., 1973), pp. 288–93. See also *Teshuvot Ḥatam Sofer, Yoreh De'ah,* no. 338.

places means "severe illness" rather than "death." In the narrative concerning Nabal's demise Scripture reports, ". . . and his heart died within him and he became hard as stone" (I Sam. 25:37), and then goes on to state, "And it came to pass after ten days and the Lord smote Nabal and he died" (I Sam. 25:38). Maimonides cites Andalusian authors who interpret the phrase "and his heart died within him" of the earlier passage as meaning "that his breath was suspended, so that no breathing could be perceived at all, as sometimes an invalid is seized with a fainting fit and attacks of asphyxia, and it cannot be discovered whether he is alive or dead, and in this condition the patient may remain one day or two."[19]

It would appear that a divergent view is espoused by *Ḥatam Sofer,* who indicates that death is synonymous with cessation of respiration. *Teshuvot Ḥatam Sofer, Yoreh De'ah,* no. 338, states that the commandment "And if a man have committed a sin worthy of death, and he be put to death . . . his body shall not remain all night upon the tree, but thou shalt surely bury him the same day . . ." (Deut. 21:23) implies a clearly defined definition of death. Halakhah deems cessation of respiratory activity to constitute such a definition. This tradition, according to *Ḥatam Sofer,* was either (1) received from the scientists of antiquity, even though it has been "forgotten" by contemporary physicians, or (2) received by Moses on Mt. Sinai, or (3) derived from the verse "all which has the breath of the spirit of life in his nostrils" (Gen. 2:6). "This necessarily is the *shi'ur*

19. This exposition of Maimonides' position follows the interpretation advanced by Abarbanel in the latter's commentary on the text of the *Guide* and appears to be the most facile analysis of Maimonides' comments. Cf., however, Shem Tov, who sees the Andalusians as denying the miraculous resurrection of the son of the woman of Zarephath (I Kings 17:17) and claims that Maimonides himself accepted the position of the Andalusians. Narboni and Ibn Caspi also ascribe such views to Maimonides. Ibn Caspi attempts to show that Maimonides was herein following the talmudic interpretation of this narrative. According to Ibn Caspi, the talmudic exposition does not consider the described phenomenon to be a case of resurrection. Maimonides was severely (and, according to Abarbanel, erroneously) attacked by others for denying that the son of the woman of Zarephath was resurrected since these authorities view Maimonides' position as being contradictory to the rabbinic interpretation of the relevant passages. Cf. the letter of R. Judah ibn Alfacha to R. David Kimchi in *Kovez Teshuvot ha-Rambam* (Lichtenberg, Leipzig, 1859), p. 29, and *Teshuvot Rivash,* no. 45. Cf. also *Teshuvot Ḥatam Sofer, Yoreh De'ah,* no. 338, who interprets Maimonides as accepting the resurrection of the son of the woman of Zarephath literally but denying Elisha's resurrection of the son of the Shunamite. (II Kings 4:34–35).

[the term *shi'ur* should in this context be understood as meaning "clinical symptom of death"] received by us with regard to all corpses from the time that the congregation of the Lord became a holy nation." *Ḥatam Sofer,* while not spelling out the issue at stake, quite obviously views cessation of respiration as itself constituting death rather than as being merely symptomatic of death. However, in developing this thesis, *Ḥatam Sofer* appears to broaden his definition of death by requiring the presence of yet another necessary condition. *Ḥatam Sofer* cites the previously mentioned phenomenon described by the Andalusians and accounts for the situation described by them by stating that although in the incident described respiration had ceased, nevertheless the pulse was still detectable either at the temples or at the neck. Without making an explicit statement to this effect, *Ḥatam Sofer* here seems nevertheless to amend his definition of death and now appears to state that death occurs only if both pulse beat and respiration have ceased.[20] This definition of death is thus compatible with the previously cited view supported by *Yoma* 85a that death is to be identified with absence of respiration coupled with prior cessation of cardiac activity. Although death occurs only upon the conjunction of both physiological occurrences, cessation of respiration is accepted as the sole operational definition because, in the vast majority of cases, it is indicative of prior cardiac arrest. *Ḥatam Sofer* summarizes his position in the statement, "But in any case, once he lies like an inanimate stone, there being no pulse whatsoever, and if subsequently breathing ceases, we have only the words of our holy Torah that he is dead." Accordingly, concludes *Ḥatam Sofer,* the corpse must be buried without delay and a *kohen* dare not defile himself by touching the corpse after these signs of death are in evidence. Cases such as those described in *Semaḥot* 8 are extremely unusual, to say the least, and are dismissed by *Ḥatam Sofer* as being comparable to the celebrated story of Choni the Circle-Drawer (*Ta'anit* 23a), who slept for seventy years. Oddities such as these occur with such great

---

20. Rabbi Moshe Sternbuch, *Ba'ayot ha-Zeman be-Hashkafat ha-Torah,* I, 10, asserts that according to *Ḥatam Sofer,* absence of respiration is sufficient to establish death unless the peron is in a swoon. However, in a state of swoon it is possible for the person to be alive and yet not to breathe. Hence the possibility of a swoon must be ruled out before lack of respiration may be accepted as conclusive evidence that death has occurred. Rabbi Sternbuch evidently interprets *Ḥatam Sofer* as believing that lack of respiration is merely symptomatic of death rather than constituting death in and of itself.

rarity that Halakhah need not take cognizance of such contingencies.[21] In the same vein, R. Chaim Yosef David Azulai, *Teshuvot Ḥayyim Sha'al,* II, no. 25, declares that when the statutory signs of death are present, it is incumbent upon us to execute burial without delay, "and if in one of many tens of thousands of cases it happens that he is alive, there does not [devolve] upon us the slightest transgression, for so has it been decreed upon us . . . and if we err in these signs [of death], such was His decree, may He be blessed."

IV

Currently, in an age of medical progress, the paramount question is not simply whether burial should be delayed on the chance that life may yet exist, but rather to what extent it is mandatory to engage in attempts at resuscitation. In terms of definitive Halakhah, there is no question whatsoever that the physician is obligated to utilize all means available to him in order to revive the patient. This may be established in several ways. It goes without saying that according to the authorities who deem the cessation of respiration to be merely symptomatic of the absence of life, there obviously exists such an obligation as long as there is any prospect of resuscitation, no matter how remote the chances of success may be. Such an obligation most certainly exists if any other clinical signs of life,

21. Rabbi I. J. Unterman, *"Ba'ayot Hashtalat ha-Lev le-Or ha-Halakhah," Torah She-be-'al Peh* (5729), p. 13 and *No'am,* XIII (5730), p. 3, points out that *Ḥatam Sofer* is speaking specifically of a patient suffering from a lingering illness and whose condition has steadily deteriorated. These symptoms, declares R. Unterman, cannot be regarded as definitive signs of death with regard to one who has experienced a sudden seizure. In such cases, all resources of medical science must be employed to save human life. Although he does not elaborate, R. Unterman presumably means that we may not accept our inability to detect these signs of life as conclusive evidence of their absence. R. Waldenberg, *Ẓiẓ Eli'ezer,* X, no. 25, chap. 4, no. 5, quite obviously disagrees with this view. *Ẓiẓ Eli'ezer* cites the symptoms advanced by *Ḥatam Sofer* as reliable criteria of death in all instances. R. Waldenberg explains the numerous cases in which the patient has been restored to life following cessation of respiration as instances wherein respiration was indeed present but not perceived. The physician may, nevertheless, rely upon his determination that respiration has ceased in pronouncing death. Nevertheless, "if it is possible for him to conduct further tests in the anticipation that he may perhaps find life, certainly it is incumbent upon him to do so; however, as to the primary determining factor, with regard to this we have only the words of our Torah and the tradition of our fathers . . ."

such as brain activity as recorded by an electroencephalogram, are in evidence. Secondly, in light of Rema's ruling that we are incompetent to apply the criterion of respiration, there exists a *safek,* or doubt, as to the presence of death during the twenty, thirty or sixty minutes following what appears to us to be cessation of respiration. There obviously devolves upon the physician a definite obligation to resuscitate the patient within this period even if this involves violation of the Sabbath laws or of other biblical prohibitions. The question, then, requires analysis only with regard to the position of those authorities who maintain that death is to be defined as the cessation of both respiration and cardiac activity. In light of Rema's ruling, the question becomes actual only after the requisite period of time has elapsed following the cessation of respiratory activity so that death may be established with certainty. Despite these considerations, it may be argued that if any clinical signs of life are present the patient may not be presumed to have actually died. A contemporary authority, Rabbi Eliezer Waldenberg, *Ẓiẓ Eli'ezer,* X, no. 25, chap. 4, sec. 5, asserts that inherent in *Ḥatam Sofer*'s position is the assumption that whenever other clinical signs of life are evident, respiration is indeed taking place, albeit unperceived by us. Accordingly, the physician is obligated to use all available means to preserve life, even in the absence of perceivable respiration. In a similar vein, Rabbi Moshe Sternbuch, in a recently published booklet, *Ba'ayot ha-Zeman be-Hashkafat ha-Torah,* I, 9, states that the talmudic source (*Yoma* 85a) advisedly employs the example of a person crushed under a heap of rubble as a paradigm case because in situations where artificial respiration or similar measures are possible the person cannot be considered to be dead simply because breathing has ceased. Nevertheless, adds Rabbi Sternbuch, when such measures are of no avail, the time of death must be retroactively established as coinciding with cessation of respiration.[22]

The question thus becomes purely theoretical. As noted, *Ḥatam Sofer* maintains that death is to be defined as the total absence of respiration and cardiac activity to the exclusion of other clinical signs. It follows from this position that if it could be determined with absolute certainty that these activities had indeed ceased—and it must be borne in mind that the previously cited authorities maintain that such a determination is impossible—subsequent resuscitation, if accomplished, would, in fact,

22. This is also the position of R. Shlomoh Zalman Auerbach. See R. Gavriel Krauss, *Ha-Ma'ayan,* Tishri 5729, p. 20.

constitute a form of "resurrection" of the dead. Is there any obligation upon the physician to restore life to the dead, or are his obligations limited to healing the living? If it could be conclusively determined that the patient has already expired, may Sabbath laws and other halakhic proscriptions be set aside in order to effect resuscitation?

This question in one of its guises is raised by *Tosafot, Baba Meẓi'a* 114b, who questions the permissibility of Elijah's resuscitation of the son of the widow of Zarephath. The talmudic view is that Elijah and Phineas were one and the same person. Since Phineas was a priest, he was forbidden to defile himself by physical contact with the dead. How, then, was he permitted to revive the son of the widow of Zarephath?

Several commentaries, by virtue of their answers to the query presented by *Tosafot,* indicate that, in their opinion, there is no obligation whatsoever to resurrect the dead. The *Shitah Mekubeẓet* parallels the previously cited view of Maimonides in stating that the child was not dead but merely in a swoon. Rosh,[23] Radbaz,[24] and Abarbanel[25] all state that Elijah's act was a form of *hora'at sha'ah*—an action having express divine sanction limited to the specific case at hand—and from which no normative halakhic practice can be deduced.

Tosafot answers that since Elijah was certain of the success of his endeavor, violation of the priestly code was permissible for the sake of preservation of human life. *Ḥemdat Yisra'el,*[26] in quoting *Tosafot*'s line of reasoning, points out that we do not find any source indicating an obligation

23. Quoted by *Shitah Mekubeẓet, Baba Meẓi'a* 114b.

24. Vol. V, no. 2203.

25. Commentary on the *Guide,* I, 42. Puzzling is the parallel cited by Abarbanel concerning the slaying of Zimri and Cozbi by Phineas (Num. 25:6–8), a deed which necessarily involved the latter's defilement. The rabbinic view is that since Phineas was born before the consecration of Eliezer, he was not a priest by virtue of genealogical descent and, accordingly, required personal consecration to achieve priestly status. Rabbinic tradition views the verse "Behold I give him my covenant of peace" (Num. 26:12) as recording that this status was accorded him as a reward for his zeal in the matter of Zimri. Thus, at the time of the slaying, Phineas had not yet attained the status of a priest and was not bound by the priestly prohibition regarding defilement(See *Zevaḥim* 101b).

26. R. Meir Dan Plocki, *Ḥemdat Yisra'el, Mafteḥot ve-Hosafot,* p. 33. This position is also stated emphatically by R. Moses Feinstein, *Iggrot Mosheh, Yoreh De'ah,* II, no. 174. Rabbi Feinstein suggests that the preservation of life referred to by *Tosafot* is either the life of the child's grief-stricken mother or perhaps that of Elijah himself.

to resurrect the dead; the obligation to preserve human life extends only to those yet living, not to those already deceased. Furthermore, if the halakhic category of preservation of life encompasses resurrection of the dead, then the obligation should logically extend even to cases of doubtful success, no matter how remote such chances may be, as is the rule with regard to preservation of the life of those living. Accordingly, all halakhic restrictions should be suspended even in cases of doubt. If so, *Tosafot*'s insertion of the words "since he was certain of being able to resurrect life" is incomprehensible. It has been suggested[27] that there is an obligation to resuscitate or "resurrect" the dead, but that this obligation is not encompassed within the general obligation to preserve life. Rather, according to this interpretation, the obligation to restore life to one who has already died is based upon the rationale adduced by the Gemara, *Yoma* 85b, "Better to desecrate one Sabbath on his behalf in order that he may observe many Sabbaths." The concern then is to enhance the total number of *mizvot* performed. Since this is the sole halakhic consideration mandating resuscitation of one already dead, *Tosafot* reasons that no halakhic prohibition may be violated in the process unless there is absolute certainty with regard to the success of such efforts.[28]

In sharp disagreement with this interpretation of *Tosafot,* R. Yechiel Ya'akov Weinberg asserts that *Tosafot* does not mean to invoke the commandment regarding preservation of human life; rather, asserts R. Weinberg, *Tosafot* regards resuscitation as a form of "honor of the deceased" since there can be no greater honor than resuscitation. Halakhah stipulates

---

27. See R. Yechiel Ya'akov Weinberg, *No'am* IX, (5726), p. 214, reprinted in *Seridei Esh,* III, no. 127, p. 350. Rabbi Weinberg cites this exposition as that of *Ḥemdat Yisra'el* and after disagreeing substitutes his own interpretation. However, an examination of *Ḥemdat Yisra'el, loc. cit.,* shows that R. Plocki offers an interpretation similar to that advanced by R. Weinberg himself.

28. A similar view is expressed by R. Naftali Zevi Yehudah Berlin, *Ha'amek She'elah,* no. 166, sec. 17. R. Berlin asserts that the ruling of *Ba'al Halakhot Gedolot* permitting desecration of the Sabbath on behalf of an embryo even within the first forty days of gestation applies only to cases where the medical efficacy of the therapeutic technique is a known certainty. The argument is that such activity can be sanctioned within the first forty days of gestation only upon application of the principle "Better to desecrate a single Sabbath on his behalf so he may observe many Sabbaths," which is operative only if there exists positive knowledge of the capacity for such future observance, rather than upon the general obligation to preserve human life which would mandate suspension of Sabbath laws even if the outcome is doubtful.

that a priest may defile himself in order to accord the honor of burial to a corpse which would otherwise remain uninterred (a *met mizvah*). According to this interpretation, *Tosafot* reasons that priestly defilement is also permissible under the same conditions in order to accord the deceased the "honor" of resurrection. Since Elijah alone was capable of reviving the dead child, Elijah was permitted to defile himself for this purpose. However, such defilement is permitted only if success is assured since defilement is sanctioned only when resultant honor to the deceased is a certainty. Thus, according to Rabbi Weinberg's analysis of *Tosafot,* other commandments may not be violated even if success could be predicted with certainty, since only the prohibition against priestly defilement may be set aside in order to honor the dead; whereas, according to *Ḥemdat Yisra'el,* all prohibitions, e.g., desecration of the Sabbath, are suspended under such circumstances.

It should be reiterated that the foregoing discussion is purely theoretical. In terms of practical Halakhah, both Rabbi Waldenberg and Rabbi Sternbuch stress that the exact moment of death cannot be determined with precision. Accordingly, when there is a possibility of resuscitation, everything possible must be done to restore the patient to life.

V

It must be emphasized that in all these questions involving the very heart of a physician's obligations with regard to the preservation of human life, halakhic Judaism demands of him that he govern himself by the norms of Jewish law whether or not these determinations coincide with the mores of contemporary society. Brain death and irreversible coma are not acceptable definitions of death insofar as Halakhah is concerned. The sole criterion of death accepted by Halakhah is total cessation of both cardiac and respiratory activity. Even when these indications are present, there is a definite obligation to resuscitate the patient, if at all feasible. Jewish law recognizes the malformed, the crippled, the terminally ill and the mentally retarded as human beings in the full sense of the term. Hence the physician's obligation with regard to medical treatment and resuscitation is in no way diminished by the fact that the resuscitated patient may be a victim of brain damage or other debilitating injury.

Of late, there has been increased discussion of a patient's right to "die with dignity" and a general urging that physicians not overly prolong the lives of comatose patients who are incurably ill. It is exceedingly difficult to argue against an individual's right to "die with dignity." This phrase, so pregnant with approbation, bespeaks a concept which is rapidly joining motherhood, the Fourth of July and apple pie as one of the great American values.

Certainly one has a right to dignity both in life and in death. But is death, properly speaking, a *right?* Suicide is forbidden both by religious and temporal law. It is proscribed because Western culture has long recognized that man's life is not his own to dispose of at will. This fundamental concept is expressed most cogently by Plato in his *Phaedo*. Socrates, in a farewell conversation with his students prior to his execution, speaks of the afterlife with eager anticipation. Thereupon one of his disciples queries, if death is so much preferable to life, why did not Socrates long ago take his own life? In a very apt simile, Socrates responds that an ox does not have the right to take its own life because it thereby deprives its master of the enjoyment of his property.[29] Man is the chattel of the gods, says Socrates. Just as "bovicide" on the part of the ox is a violation of the proprietor-property relationship, so suicide on the part of man constitutes a violation of the Creator-creature relationship.

Man does not possess absolute title to his life or to his body. He is but the steward of the life which he has been privileged to receive. Man is charged with preserving, dignifying, and hallowing that life. He is obliged to seek food and sustenance in order to safeguard the life he has been granted; when falling victim to illness and disease he is obligated to seek a cure in order to sustain life. Never is he called upon to determine whether life is worth living—this is a question over which God remains sole arbiter.

Surely, even on the basis of humanistic assumptions, one must recognize that human life must remain inviolate. As long as life is indeed present, the decision to terminate such life is beyond the competence of man. In pragmatic terms, a decision not to prolong life means precluding the application of some new advance in therapeutics that would secure a re-

29. In halakhic literature this concept is developed by Radbaz in his commentary on Rambam, *Hilkhot Sanhedrin* 18:6. It is a basic halakhic principle that, while a defendant's testimony is accorded absolute credibility with regard to establishing financial liability, a confession of guilt is never accepted as evidence of criminal culpability. Citing the verse "Behold, all souls are Mine" (Ezek. 18:4), Radbaz explains that while material goods belong to man and may be disposed of at will, the human body is the possession of God and may be punished only by Him. See also Rambam, *Hilkhot Roẓeaḥ* 1:4 and *Shulḥan Arukh ha-Rav,* VI, *Hilkhot Nizkei Guf* 4.

mission or cure for that patient should a breakthrough occur. But, more fundamentally, man lacks the right to assess the quality of any human life and to determine that it is beneficial for that life to be terminated; all human life is of inestimable value. If the comatose may be caused to "die with dignity," what of the mentally deranged and the feeble-minded incapable of "meaningful" human activity? Withdrawal of treatment leads directly to overt acts of euthanasia; from there it may be but a short step to selective elimination of those whose life is deemed a burden upon society at large.

Undoubtedly, caring for a patient *in extremis* places a heavy burden upon the family, the medical practitioner and hospital facilities. It is natural for us, both individually and collectively, to harbor feelings of resentment because of the toll exacted from us. But we must recognize that preservation of any value demands sacrifices. Above all, we must be on guard against self-interest cloaked in altruism, against allowing self-serving motives to find expression in the language of idealism.

Attempts have been made in the past to make the right to life subservient to other values. The results have been tragic. Hannah Arendt and others have pointed out that in the scale of values accepted in Germany during the World War II era obedience to law took priority over the sanctity of human life. Yet we have refused to accept this argument as a valid line of defense, because we believe it to be self-evident that the right to life is a right which has been endowed upon all men by their Creator. A person's right to life, as long as it does not conflict with another's right to life, is inviolate. And the right to life precludes the right to hasten death either overtly or covertly. The teachings of Judaism in this regard are nowhere expressed more eloquently than in the *Siddur:*

> My God, the soul which You have placed within me is pure. *You* have created it; *You* have fashioned it; *You* have breathed it into me and *You* preserve it within me; *and You will at some time take it from me* and return it to me in the time to come. As long as the soul is within me I will give thanks unto You . . .

Index

T

Z